Origins of
the English Language

A Social and Linguistic History

Joseph M. Williams

THE FREE PRESS
A Division of Macmillan Publishing Co., Inc.
NEW YORK

Collier Macmillan Publishers
LONDON

1976

The Free Press
A Division of Macmillan Publishing Co., Inc.
866 Third Avenue, New York, N.Y. 10022

Collier Macmillan Canada, Ltd.

Library of Congress Catalog Card Number: 74-12596

Printed in the United States of America

printing number

2   3   4   5   6   7   8   9   10

Library of Congress Cataloging in Publication Data

Williams, Joseph M
    Origins of the English language.

    References, subject and name index, and word index

    1.   English language--History.   2.   Sociolinguistics.
I.   Title.
PE1075.W55   420'.9   74-12596
ISBN 0-02-935280-0

Contents

Part III Grammar and Sound

Preface to the Teacher

Because this is primarily a pedagogical history, there are aspects of the evolution of English which I have slighted, particularly the very powerful insights into phonological change provided by generative phonology. But to develop the background for that would have gone far beyond what is possible or needed in a survey of this kind. I have also adapted a rather conservative version of a transformational grammar to deal with syntactic change. A case grammar of the sort proposed by Charles Fillmore or the model of generative semantics offered by James McCawley or George Lakoff is more interesting than the model used here. But again, the problem of striking a balance between what can be done with a class and with a seminar requires a good deal of compromise.

The problems, I would like to think, are the heart of this text. They can be used in several ways:

1. A single student can teach himself the history of English if he merely reads the text and turns in the problems to be checked by an instructor. The text is relatively independent of a teacher.
2. The instructor can assign some problems and entirely ignore others.
3. The instructor can have certain problems turned in as written exercises and use the data in others for class discussions.

4. He can divide the class into groups and have each group do selected problems.

5. He can assign different problems to different students and/or groups and have them present their solutions to the class for discussion.

The most frequent complaint will be from the student who does not understand what "Comment" at the end of many problems requires. I am aware that students are often unable to break away from the need to believe that there are fixed answers to fixed questions. The vagueness of "Comment" is intended precisely to force the student to pose his own questions, to over-come the intellectual rigidity that comes from high schools and junior high schools which teach that all the questions have been asked and that the student's only task is to remember the answer. He will be relieved of a good deal of his own anxiety if he is informed the first day of class that part of his task in the course is to find shape in vagueness.

Incorrect approaches (or no approach) to solutions to the problems are as useful material for class discussion as interesting solutions. A discussion of why a possible solution is not a good one will get to the heart of what education is about if it centers not merely on **what** the better solution is but **why** it might be better and how one might have arrived at that solution.

The Czech formalist critics believe that one function of literature is to "make strange" that which we know too well. Approaching the history of language in the right way can provide the same experience. English need not be as it is now. It could have been otherwise. If some inflections had not dis-appeared, if more had disappeared, if the Normans hadn't successfully tricked the English at Senlac, if we had never borrowed prefixes, if there were no such phenomenon as metaphor, if the Great Vowel Shift had never occurred, if any of these conditions applied to English and its history, our language would be a very different thing. And if we can bring our students to appreciate these factors, then what is like the air they breathe will become something to be aware of, to be curious about. By awakening their sensi-bilities, they can expand the frontiers of their imagination.

Some of the more speculative questions (e.g., What **would** we be like if we stored memories not in the brain but in those parts of the body that had the experience?) are designed to make language itself strange. These ques-tions, I would like to think, will permit a moment or two of speculative play.

In any event, the point of this text is to get something going in the class-room beyond the instructor telling his class what is in the text and the students dutifully writing it down in their notebooks.

A criticism that will be made of this text is that it is not "tight," that there is a good deal of repetition. At least some of this redundancy is inten-tional. This is not a "programmed" text. But many concepts are introduced in one context with the view that they will be useful later or because they are important enough to re-emphasize (behaviorists, read "reinforce"). I mention umlaut in a number of places because it is a relatively complicated phenomenon. I repeatedly cite sociolinguistic theory and data because I want to emphasize certain concepts about language, social class, and "good grammar." Whether this repetition is finally only redundant deadwood or strategic reinforcement and clarification of important concepts will be determined only at the end of the course when the student ponders how well he knows what he knows.

Finally, there are a good many who have contributed to the creation of this text. Foremost among this group are those found in the bibliography. Without the work already done by linguists such as Otto Jespersen, Albert C. Baugh, Samuel Moore, Albert L. Marckwardt, Thomas Pyles, Fred Cassidy, Henry Cecil Wyld, Randolph Quirk, Fernand Mossé, and a hundred others, texts like this would never exist. More particularly, I would like to thank the students who made many valuable suggestions: Yoshi Morita, Elizabeth Temple, Mitchell Marks, B. J. Jost, and many others. I am grateful to Nancy Hall, and to Eileen Fitzgerald of The Free Press for their invaluable assistance in catching many slips in the original manuscripts. Any that remain are my own responsibility. Professor William Hunter of the University of New Hampshire has my gratitude for very helpful suggestions and for his encouragement when this text was in its formative stages. My gratitude also goes to Professor Donald Green for his help in reading the final proof.

Manset, Maine

PART I

HISTORY AND LANGUAGE

Chapter 1

HISTORY AND LANGUAGE

HISTORY, HISTORIES, AND HISTORIANS

When some people argue that histories should tell the truth, they usually mean by truth the straightforward, unadorned facts of what happened. They believe that historians who select, arrange, and shape their data to make a point about the past or who use the past to prove something about the present are not being objective, and, hence, not telling the "truth." History, they believe, is properly the objective facts the historians can recover from the past arranged just as they occurred to relate what really happened.

Such histories have never existed and never will. The individual mind of the historian, shaped by his times, influenced by his theory of history, and controlled by his unique personal character, must always stand between the leavings of the past and the work that represents his understanding of how those leavings reveal what happened and why. Just choosing what to write about reveals the mind of the historian evaluating and selecting from all the events of the past only those most important to him.

The very material he works with will become one thing for a historian who believes that history turns on the actions of great men and something else for one committed to an economic interpretation of the past. Indeed, the

3

modern study of history is becoming less the narratives of individual men acting in individual situations and more the analyses of broad economic and social forces that can be discovered only by highly specialized researchers, armed with sophisticated statistical and sociological tools. The intellectual focus of our age has shifted from man the individual free agent to man's part in the overall social fabric.

This shift away from the concrete individual to more abstract social forces has been encouraged by the growth of one academic specialty after another: statistics, demography, sociology, economics, psycho-history. Each has created more and more refined analytical techniques until it is now no longer so easy as it once was for a single person to be the broadly based, general researcher who might have understood an entire age. Thus, as the specialist has narrowed and refined his tools, so conversely have the available tools narrowed and refined the specialist. The existence of sophisticated analytical techniques pushes every investigator—historian, physicist, sociologist, literary critic—to follow the methodological paths his discipline opens up to him. All researchers find not only what their age and interests urge them to find, but what their theories and techniques predispose them to find.

Not surprisingly, the reasons men write histories in the first place are as diverse as the theories that guide them and the methods they use. At its simplest and most elemental level, historians create a past because their community wants to know where it came from and how things got to be the way they are. The earliest myths, the stories of the most primitive peoples about their gods, are a kind of history that explains how the universe and the earth came about—why the sun and the moon, why the animals, why man. The voyage of Mariner 10 beyond Jupiter and out of our solar system represents our curiosity about the origins of the universe. The Bible was once unquestioned history for most Christians. For many it still is. So once for some were the legends of the Plains Indians, and the Greek myths and **Beowulf** and the story of Valley Forge, Gettysburg, Lewis and Clark, and the Alamo. We no longer call all of these history because our age has different criteria for accepting some stories rather than others as satisfying ways to organize and explain our past.

But the most common reason most of us would give for writing about the past is that we think we can learn from it. Santayana's belief that those who do not remember the past are condemned to repeat it may be extreme. But it is a traditional belief. Whether or not we can in fact avoid the mistakes of history, knowing something about the past does make us understand our own condition differently than if we knew nothing about its origins. But if history is to teach us about today, the historian must arrange and shape the past to make it relevant to the present. Only then can he convince us that we should know what has happened if we are to understand what is now happening or anticipate what is about to happen.

Because statements about the past so frequently touch on social values, a historian has to take a position, sometimes explicitly but always implicitly, in regard to the values of his community, accepting and interpreting or rejecting them according to both his own personal standards and those of his time. One has only to recognize how our own history is being rewritten to include the contributions of Afro-Americans to realize how even scholarly values are changing. Only a few years ago, the intellectual-social climate did not encourage most historians to regard the Negro as a significant contributor to American history. That historians everywhere are now investigating Black history reflects a new political and social, as well as intellectual, reality.

When we read any history, then, we must understand the historian's sense of what is important about history. We must understand that the data he selects and how he arranges them depend on his reasons for writing history in the first place, that "truth" depends finally on how his theories interpret what the interests and values of an age allow him to recognize as the truth. (112) British historian E. H. Carr perhaps put it most simply:

> ... you cannot fully understand or appreciate the work of the historian unless you have first grasped the standpoint from which he himself approached it; second, that the standpoint is itself rooted in a social and historical background.
>
> E. H. Carr, **What Is History**, Vintage Books, 1967.

HISTORY AND THE STUDY OF LANGUAGE

At first glance, most of these questions may appear irrelevant to a subject seemingly as value-free as a history of the English language. A language is not a series of spectacular events. It was once fashionable to claim that Chaucer, Shakespeare, and Milton strongly influenced the growth and structure of English, but no longer. A language is not the product of great men acting in dramatic situations, but rather something created and shared and recreated every day by an entire people, for the most part something shaped without any forethought or conscious planning.

In fact, a history of a language is significantly different from a history of a series of clearly discrete events. The "events" in a history of the English language are difficult even to define. They are the sequence of changing abstract patterns behind the sum of countless concrete events—of hundreds of thousands of people talking roughly alike on, say, January 1, 450 A.D., in an infinitesimally different way on January 2, and so on up to the present, when hundreds of millions speak billions of words every minute. A historian of English describes not how an individual speaker used language at some moment in the past, but how through time the shared abstract patterns of language have gradually changed since the fifth century A.D., when those first

Germanic tribes from Northern Europe invaded the island of Britain and, by the mere political fact of that invasion, thereupon began speaking a language we no longer call West Germanic or Frisian or Jutish or whatever, but Old English (which we shall henceforth frequently abbreviate as OE).

Traditionally, historians of language have studied three kinds of patterns or structures in language: the sound patterns, or its **phonology**; the syntactic and inflectional patterns, or its **grammar**; and the patterns of meaning, or its **semantics**. We could study these aspects of English without ever referring to a single person or historical event. We would then have an **internal history** of the language, a history of changing structures and patterns with no reference to the **external history** of the language.

The external history of a language is partly defined by a list of events which influenced masses of speakers to change those phonological, grammatical, and semantic patterns which make up its internal history. So in that sense, the internal history of a language determines what we choose to call its external history. The major events in the external history of English are easy enough to list:

c. 450: The Northern Germanic tribes invade and occupy Britain.
c. 850: The Danes invade and occupy the north and east of England.
1066: The Norman French invade and conquer England.
1204: The Normans in England are forced to choose England or Normandy as their homeland.
c. 1348: The plague wipes out one-third of the English population.
1476: Printing is introduced into England.
1607: America is colonized by English speakers.
c. 1945: American political and cultural dominance makes American English a candidate for a world standard.

But, in addition to these major events, are less easily defined pressures exerted by the changing social class structure that began to replace the rigid feudal system of pre-1200 England, social pressures which ever since have shaped and reshaped our speech.

Since all these events have caused our linguistic patterns to change, we would want any history of the English language: (1) to describe English structure at various critical stages of its development, and (2) to explain why one form of the language was replaced by another through the social forces set in motion by those large and small events.

THE AIMS OF LANGUAGE HISTORY

All of this seems to be straightforward, value-free history. But if we conclude that writing a history of a language is divorced from the kinds of problems a historian faces when he writes a social or economic history of, say, the post-WWII period, we would be quite mistaken. The same kinds of problems about theories of history (and language) determining a historian's questions, about his intention determining his selection and arrangement of data, about the values and social uses of linguistic history—all should confront the historian of language no less severely than they do the historian of politics and wars.

For example, almost all histories of English ignore the development of forms such as these:

He gone now, ain't he?   My frien' done left.   He always be late.

Until recently, such sentences were thought by many grammarians (and most teachers) to represent an ignorant, illiterate, lazy, uneducated, probably unintelligent and certainly ungrammatical English. It is the English of the lower classes, stereotypically Southern, often Black, a dialect of English traditionally beneath intellectual contempt.

But for many obvious social and intellectual reasons, linguists have recently begun to explore much more seriously than before the patterns of "nonstandard" English in general and the English of certain Black Americans in particular. Because these researchers have also found new investigative tools in modern linguistic theory, they have decided that such sentences are not un-grammatical in the sense that they have no predictable regular pattern. Quite the contrary. They have a complex, orderly structure that has just never been sought, discovered, and incorporated into grammar books meant for those being taught the prestige dialect of our culture—except as examples of what to avoid. No one really knew what the structure of nonstandard English was because few researchers ever bothered to study it.

But in the last decade, as our attitudes toward minority groups in this country have changed, as more and more "nonstandard" speakers have confronted a "standard"-speaking society that for decades has kept them out of the colleges and the centers of social and political power, as new linguistic theories have become available, the historian of the English language has begun to look for—and find—new "facts" about the history of nonstandard English, facts that exist only as a consequence of a changing intellectual climate and a new body of linguistic theory. This text will deal with these questions because its author, influenced by his time, finds them intellectually challenging and socially important.

Language varies through time, largely because it varies through social space. Lower class, lower-middle class, and upper-middle class speakers interact in a variety of ways. One way that crucially affects the development of language is how the speech patterns among those groups differ and the way each group responds to the other's speech. We choose one pattern of speech rather than another not by some immutable rule of logic or history, but by noting how those who wield social, political, and economic power habitually speak. If we attempt to rationalize why we choose to speak in one way rather than another, we may use the history of English, logic, or dogmatic opinion to justify our usage. But how we speak—whether we say *ain't I* or *aren't I* or *am I not*—finally depends not on rational, logical reasons but on the (usually) unconscious linguistic preferences of those who command our respect and who, by their prestige, silently influence the writing of textbooks and the conduct of education.

In some small way, then, perhaps an understanding of the historical sources of both standard and nonstandard dialects and the social bases by which we decide about standards might qualify some of the historically un-justified responses many of us have toward those who use "ungrammatical, illiterate, uneducated speech."

More significantly influencing the nature of this particular history, how-ever, are its larger pedagogical goals. Most histories of English seek only to summarize the outstanding ways in which the language has changed and some of the causes for those changes, to comment on the rise of dictionaries and changing attitudes towards standards of usage, and to suggest the range of language diversity across geographical space—all presented for the reader's information. If the student succeeds in committing the facts to memory, he has satisfied his responsibility toward the subject and the book.

The intention and design of this history are different. It will try not only to transmit information about the history of English but also to suggest in some modest and very incomplete way what historical linguists do when they study and describe the history of a language. It is not a history to be read passively. It will ask the reader to engage himself with historical data pre-sented as problems. In most cases, a discussion follows each problem, so it will be easy for the student to ignore the problems and read just the discussion. I can only urge the student who wants to do more than memorize facts to wrestle with the problems before he goes on to the discussions. The bibliog-raphy lists several excellent histories of English that summarize and present many facts about the language in an interesting and scholarly way. For the reader interested only in facts, I recommend them. (7, 58, 95, 172, 182, 209, 244) This history will ask the reader to create much of the history of the lan-guage himself. It will force him to become as much of a historical linguist as can practically be managed in a book where all the relevant data has already been culled and the questions at least tacitly formulated.

In addition to acquiring some sense of an intellectual discipline that has its roots in Plato's **Cratylus** and beyond, and of some of the particular fruits of that discipline, the student will, I hope, also come to understand something about language in general. I have already mentioned how important our speech patterns are in our social dealings with one another. We identify ourselves as members of a geographical dialect, a social class, even a partic-ular age group by our speech.

But our language is unique in the animal kingdom. We do not exaggerate when we say that nothing defines man better than the fact that he is only the animal that uses language creatively. He is the only animal that can create out of a finite number of linguistic units a potentially infinite number of sentences that can correspond to the potentially infinite number of situations he faces in the world:

Lake Erie is polluted.

and, even more importantly, to the equally large number of conceptions that do not yet correspond to the real world:

If we continue to pollute the oceans, maybe they will die.

and, indeed, to those that can **never** correspond to reality:

The rectangular ontogeny unfurled its insolent symmetry.

Finally, some of the problems will ask the student to exercise his linguistic imagination to create new words, new meanings, new grammatical patterns, new metaphors, to explore new semantic space which his mind must create. One of the current commonplaces of education is that our language creates our world. It provides us with the categories of our experience, and in so doing closes off from us other ways of structuring our cognitive world. So strongly stated, such a claim is wrong. But by flexing his verbal imagination, by creating new linguistic patterns, the student may become more sensitive to some of the creative possibilities of language. These problems have no right or wrong answers.

Finally, much of the data here has been over-simplified, an unavoidable consequence of trying to present a unified view of what is in reality often diverse and contradictory data. Regional and personal variations, inconsistent historical developments, have now and then been ignored in an effort to make the history of the English language coherent enough for one to grasp at least the broad outlines of 1500 years of change. And yet it is probably that wrestling with inconsistency and variation that most characterizes the historical study of a language. A paradigm of verb endings or a dictionary entry or a neat vowel change is the misleadingly tidy product of combing masses of often doubtfully reliable data for evidence, selecting only what is relevant to the problem, resolving contradictions, and, for the sake of a strong generalization, setting aside as exceptions those data which do not fit the generalization. That activity can only be appreciated after one has dealt with the original texts themselves.

Chapter 2

THE NATURE OF LANGUAGE

THE BEGINNINGS

A story often cited to illustrate an idea which some have held about the origin of language is the one Herodotus relates about King Psammetichos of Egypt. To determine whether the Egyptians or the Phrygians were the older race, he ordered two children to be raised entirely isolated from speech. He believed one would, quite on his own, begin speaking one of the languages as the original Ur-language of man. When one day one uttered the sound *bekos*, which meant bread in a dialect of Phrygian, he concluded that Phrygian was the older language. An early Scottish king who performed the same experiment concluded that the first sounds the isolated children uttered were pure Hebrew.

This idea that our language has descended from some older, probably "purer" and more fundamental source is reflected not only in the Roman belief that Latin was corrupt Greek, but that the babel of languages afflicting the human race results from the confusion visited upon the one original, pure language spoken by the builders of the tower of Babel.

The belief persists even today: At some earlier time, language reached a state of perfection; since then, it has been all decay and corruption. Some have claimed that English is particularly degenerate, for "it has no grammar" to speak of in comparison with the rich inflectional systems of older languages such as Latin and Greek. English inflects nouns for only two cases: genitive— *the boy's hat*, and the general case, distinguished by the lack of any endings— *the boy*. Latin has six inflectional cases: nominative, accusative, dative, genitive, ablative, and vocative. Sanskrit, the oldest fully recorded known language related to English, had eight cases: nominative, accusative, dative, genitive, ablative, vocative, locative, and instrumental.

Obviously, then, English is in the final stages of a decay that began at least 3000 years ago. In a few hundred years perhaps, even the inflected genitive in *boy's* will disappear, along with the third person singular *-s*, the past tense *-ed*, and the comparative *-er* and *-est* endings, leaving us with the rotten hulk of a once richly grammatical language.

If we want an authority to decide a problem of grammar or usage or meaning, then, we should (it is claimed), look to the past, usually to Latin, less often Greek: One does not end sentences with prepositions in English because one does not do so in Latin. Nor does one ask *Who did you see?* because as the object of *see*, *who* should be *whom*, the accusative case. Case agreement, of course, is required in good Latin. (45, 183)

Unfortunately, the real origins of language are as completely unknown as its evolution preceding the last four or five millennia. Assuming we can reject the idea that language was a gift of the gods, we have to ask how it was possible for a hominid that presumably communicated not too much differently from our present primate relatives to evolve into a creature who can do what you and I are now doing.

In the nineteenth century, speculation about the origin of language was so widespread in the scholarly journals that in 1866 the **Société de Linguistique de Paris** finally had to ban the publication of any more articles on the subject. Then for about a century, the question was unfashionable. A few eminent scholars speculated about the origin and evolution of language, but it was not a problem actively pursued. In the last few years, however, the subject has once again become a live issue, particularly among anthropologists.

The problem can be broken down into at least three parts:

1. What are the biological differences between the neurological and peripheral speech mechanisms of man and other primates?
2. What are the important differences in the "design features" of the language of man and other creatures and how can they be related to the biological differences?
3. How could the biological and design features have evolved from those possessed by a creature that was the ancestor of both ape and man?

Man and Ape: The Biological Foundations

The biological question is a very difficult one to answer because so little is known about the neurology of speech in man, much less the neurology of communication in apes, and because what is known sheds very little light on the question or is of debatable reliability. There are some obvious differences between man and ape.

Man has a bigger brain. But this alone is insufficient to explain the capacity for language. There are creatures known as **nanocephalic** or **birdheaded dwarfs**, humans who are normally proportioned but who never grow more than two-and-a-half or three feet tall. Their brains average perhaps .4 kilograms compared to an average adult's 1.35 kilograms. Some female chimpanzee brains weigh as much as .45 kilograms, larger than the brains of many nanocephalic dwarfs. Yet while the dwarf, though often retarded, usually speaks as well as a five- or six-year-old, the chimpanzee never speaks. Nor does the ability to speak lie entirely in brain-to-body ratio. A human adult brain-to-body ratio is about 1:50 or so. The adult chimp ratio is 1:100 or so, but the adult rhesus ratio is 1:40. There is more total surface area in the human cerebral cortex because of its extensive folding. But it seems fairly clear that brain size alone is insufficient to explain language capacity. (130)

It has been claimed (and denied) that the neural anatomy of man's brain is fundamentally different from an ape's in at least three ways.

First, man's brain is **lateralized**: That is, certain cognitive and motor skills have localized in either the left or right hemisphere. For most right-handed people, the left hemisphere of the brain controls manual skills and language (and vice versa for most left-handed people). Although apes often seem to prefer one hand over another, suggesting a potential for lateralization, it does not seem to be as profound a tendency as in man. The fact that manual skill (i.e., the skill associated with tool-making and tool-using) is usually localized in the same hemisphere as speech has led some anthropologists to speculate that tool-making either necessarily preceded or developed concurrently with language. Since the most recent finds in Africa suggest that the earliest tools date from perhaps two-and-a-half million years ago, it may be that man has been talking for about that long. But even if this is the case, it is very difficult to understand why speech should depend on lateralization. Furthermore, there is abundant evidence to show that if the left hemisphere is severely damaged in very young children, the right hemisphere will take over the neurological speech functions. Thus it is not merely lateralization that is responsible for speech in man.

Second, it has been claimed (and denied) that there is an area in the human brain, the **angular gyrus** (see Figure 2.1) that is not found in other primates. In man, no neural pathways directly connect the visual, auditory,

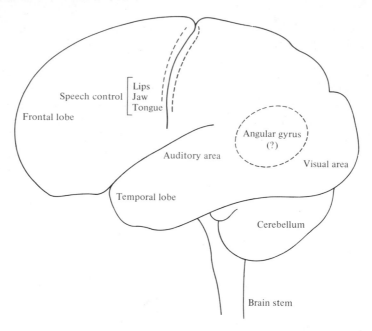

Figure 2.1. The Human Cerebrum

and somesthetic (tactile feedback) areas. Rather, neural pathways from each of these areas are mingled in the angular gyrus, creating a neural switchboard of great complexity, one which perhaps allows us to coordinate the ability to utter (requiring fine motor control) a sound (requiring aural feedback) that becomes the name of something seen (a visual experience). Apes allegedly do not have such an area, a claim somewhat supported by the observation that they do not learn to obey spoken commands very readily, but do respond to visual cues.

Third, it has been alleged (and denied) that man's linguistic system is more independent of his **limbic system** than that of the apes. (The limbic system is that inner part of the brain and brain stem which is in evolutionary terms, much older than the cerebral cortex and which controls basic motivation, emotions, the more primitive mental functions.) What this is claimed to explain is our ability to verbalize independently of our emotional needs. Apes appear to communicate only when their emotional needs are involved: sex, social contact, fear, hunger, and so on, perhaps because their communication system is more directly linked to their limbic system. We need not be sexually aroused to make noises about it, nor need we make noises about it when we are. (123)

Finally, it is clear that our peripheral speech mechanism is substantially different from the ape's. Although the same gross anatomical features can be found in both man and ape: lungs, diaphragm, larynx, glottis, tongue, teeth, lips, and so on, in the ape, they are not integrated into a speech system. Even in man, none of these features was originally intended specifically as part of a communications system. Each feature has its own biological function entirely independent of talking. But in the ape, those organs still serve almost exclusively their original functions: breathing, swallowing, closing off the lungs to prevent the escape of air, chewing, and so forth. The laryngeal structure of apes simply does not allow them to articulate human sounds. In fact, it is for this reason that a number of researchers are now attempting to teach, chimps language through some medium other than verbal: sign language, plastic chips, computer panel displays, for example. (68, 168, 186)

So along with the development of brain anatomy, we have to explain how a set of independently functioning organs came to be integrated into a physiological system connected with a cognitive system. Presumably, it did not happen in one great leap across genetic space. Presumably, environmental pressures selected those creatures who were best able to use even the beginnings of such a system toward an end that enhanced their chances for survival.

Design Features of Human Languages

Keeping these very tentative biological possibilities in mind, we might now ask what the crucial design features of human language are and whether any of them depend on what is biologically unique in man. One set that has been proposed is the following (87, 88):

1. **Vocal-auditory:** Although other channels may be used (sign language or braille, for instance), human languages are fundamentally spoken and heard.
2. **Broadcast transmission:** The signal is ordinarily transmitted in all directions simultaneously rather than through a narrow channel (the difference between a smoke signal and spelling letters in the palm).
3. **Rapid fading:** The signal does not remain in the channel. When a word is uttered, it disappears from our perception virtually instantly, unlike the lingering chemical traces of dogs or ants.
4. **Interchangeability:** Ordinarily, all normal users of human languages can both transmit and receive, unlike many insects whose direction of communication is sex-determined.
5. **Complete feedback:** Normal speakers are aware of their own message.
6. **Specialization:** The energy needed to communicate is less than the results intended by the communication. One need not cut down a tree to communicate the idea.
7. **Semanticity:** The signal has meaning. It regularly correlates in some sense with that which is within the perceptual or cognitive universes of the sender and the receiver.

8. **Arbitrariness:** The signal bears no **iconic** relationship to that which is communicated. The angle of a bee dance relative to the sun directly represents the direction of the food source from the hive. The less intense the dance, the farther the food from the hive. The sentence, *The food is a mile north of here* does not represent distance or direction iconically.

9. **Discreteness:** The message has parts. Each word in this sentence discretely represents a bloc of information that combines into larger structures, and those structures into larger structures (phrases and clauses). The three distinct warning cries of a vervet monkey (one for overhead danger, one for large-creature ground danger, one for snake-creature ground danger) holistically communicate each message. They have no decomposable inner structure that could be represented by discrete bits of information:

$$\left[\begin{array}{l} \text{overhead} \\ \text{ground} \begin{bmatrix} \text{large} \\ \text{snake} \end{bmatrix} \text{danger} \end{array} \right]$$

10. **Displacement:** The message can be communicated at a distance from that which it refers to. Humans can speak of ancient Egyptians, who are displaced in both time and space. The ability of a non-human to "hold" the message associated with a stimulus is distinctly limited.

11. **Openness:** New messages can be constructed about any aspect of experience. Bee dances concern only food and the location of new hives. They do not (cannot) "talk about" the weather, what is happening back at the hive, and so on.

12. **Tradition:** The particular forms of particular human languages are passed on culturally from generation to generation. Bee languages are passed on through the genetic code.

13. **Learnability:** The particular forms of particular languages can be learned. Bees from one species cannot learn to communicate with the bees of another. (Certain birds, however, do acquire the "dialects" of other birds of the same species. When neighboring flocks have slightly different territorial songs, it is possible for them to "learn" the others' dialect.)

14. **Prevarication:** Human speakers can consciously construct messages about that which is counterfactual. Some primates may also have this ability.

15. **Reflexiveness:** Humans can use language to talk about language.

16. **Duality of patterning:** Human communication is materially structured on a phonetic level through the discreteness of a finite number of discernible sound classes, on a grammatical level independently of the phonetic level through part-of-speech, subject-verb structures, and so on, and through an associated semantic level that is partially independent of the grammatical level.

More recently, some linguists have claimed additional universal characteristics of human languages. (31) Among them are the following:

17. **Deep-surface structure:** Sentences are organized on two levels: Their surface level, the observable order of parts of speech, and so on, and a deep level, the underlying grammatical relationships. (This is dealt with more fully later.)
18. **Grammatical categories:** All human languages have grammatical categories which can be generally covered by the terms substantives (or nouns) and verbs. Substantive-verb relationships include actor-action, recipient-action, instrument-action, and a few others.

When we concentrate just on the ability of speakers to **use** language, however, we bring out what may be the most important differences between man and his relatives, making the problem of an evolutionary accounting yet more complex.

19. **Non-instrumental communication:** The message may be freed from any immediate consequences. That is, non-human communications seem always intended to bring about or maintain a state of affairs involving territorial claim, danger, mating, food, or social status. But a human can utter a sentence like *I wonder who's kissing her now* without wanting to bring about a new state of affairs. A further consequence of this is that human messages need have no audience to validate them. Animal signals usually do.
20. **Message isolation:** The message may be communicated independently of the communicator. Even among the most advanced primates, message forms ordinarily consist of not only sound, but a complex of features including facial expression, posture, eye fixation, distance from receiver, and so on. Except for agonistic cries, primates in their natural state usually require a multi-modal transmission of a message. Man can communicate by telegraph, which screens out virtually all paralinguistic signalling.
21. **Cross-modal communication:** The message may be detached from a sign in one channel-type and attached to a sign in another; i.e., we can tap out morse code, read signal flags in reply, and relay the message in braille.
22. **Meaning isolation:** The meaning of a message may be detached from any overt articulation of the message. That is, we can (though we need not) think in language without any obvious enervation of muscles controlling articulation.
23. **Meaningful violation:** Human speakers may consciously violate rules governing the structure of a message, and their audiences can impose an interpretation on them; e.e. cummings' *anyone lived in a pretty how town/*

(*with up so floating many bells down*) does not elicit a blank uncomprehending stare. But if a mutant bee began doing his own dance, the other bees would be unable to impose an appropriate meaning on it.

24. **Sign change:** The form of a word may be separated from its original meaning to take on a new meaning. The word *grasp*, for example, has transferred from the manual to the cognitive sense. Similarly, the meaning of any word may change or the word may disappear entirely: *Meat* once meant any food; *scora*, an Old English word for a garment, has disappeared entirely.

Evolution toward Language

Now the great problem with all of this is to synthesize what we know about the biological foundations of language with which of these features we decide must have been among the first steps toward language. We might reasonably assume that the peripheral physical anatomy evolved as a consequence of selection for greater cognitive language ability. It seems difficult to understand how the diaphragm, larynx, tongue, etc. could integrate into a speech system before the neural groundwork had developed in the brain.

The next question is whether the brain changed in one massive genetic mutation or whether different parts of the brain slowly integrated into a linguistic neural system in perhaps the same way the peripheral speech system must have slowly integrated into what it is now.

The crucial innovations toward a language that we would call rational are **displacement** and **openness**. The others—duality of patterning, semanticity, broadcast transmission, and so on—either necessarily follow these two or obviously precede them. As a category, displacement includes the ability to verbalize or not in the presence of a stimulus that might ordinarily elicit verbal behavior: fear, hunger, sexual attraction. The corollary is the ability to produce the signals associated with those stimuli when they are not present. But uttering a signal of some sort when no gratification is involved is such startlingly innovative behavior that it demands a preceding change in neural organization. If indeed we can use our verbal system independently of our limbic system (as apparently we can), then we must postulate a mutation that has had major consequences: A food cry that could be produced when no food was in the immediate perceptual environment could eventually become a signal cry for an intention to find food, and then the "name" of food. This kind of displacement ultimately allows us to hypothesize, to lie, to wish, to predict, to contradict, to contradict a contradiction, and so on, for all of these are speech acts independent of any immediate physical referent. At the same time, however, the other characteristic, openness, the ability to combine a finite repertoire of signals into novel sequences with novel meanings, also had to develop. Otherwise, we could not now wish for, predict, or lie about that which never was.

It is the combination of these two unique abilities: displacement, which allows us to verbalize about that which is not immediately present either in our environment or in our internal emotional state, and openness, which allows us to create completely new messages never before uttered, that is at the basis of rational language. For if either of these are lacking in a creature, we do not attribute to him the capacity for rational conversation.

Almost certainly, the hominid that was able to use and understand the greatest number of signal cries was best able to hunt, mate, and survive. At some moment, perhaps, one such creature must have uttered two signal cries in succession to create what was, in effect, a new message never before uttered. But now we face the additional problem of explaining how his audience was able to **understand** such a radical communicative innovation. For any advance in communication requires two concurrent abilities: The ability to transmit by means of the innovation, but also the ability to receive and understand it.

Now, what is known about the ecology of our simian ancestors that might have created the selectional pressures leading to openness and displacement? Because their period of existence has repeatedly been pushed back farther and farther into the mists of pre-history, explanations based on changing environmental conditions in any given era must be suspect. For a time, it was believed that our distant ancestors descended from the trees when a climate change caused their forests to disappear, leaving them grasslands as a new habitat, a more differentiated world than their forest. Because more open spaces may have required a greater capacity to deal with new visual experiences, visual sensitivity came to be much more highly valued. Perhaps (a favorite word, along with *possibly* and the phrase *it may have been*, when anthropologists come to the crucial moment in their argument), perhaps those hominids needed a great many more signal cries in the grasslands than they originally needed in the trees. Finally overburdened with too many discrete cries, even while larger brains (i.e., larger cerebral cortexes) were being selected for memory, a creature or creatures "hit" on combining cries as the answer. As the brain grew, its organization changed, allowing the cries to be used in contexts where they were not intended as immediately relevant signals. Perhaps as the cerebral cortex grew, it also assumed a larger share of control over behavior, replacing the limbic system to a greater and greater extent, allowing those creatures to utter a signal independently of limbic involvement.

One possible context in which such signal cries might have been used without their "referents" being present is play. If the young of our hominid ancestor played as the young of all primates play, they "acted out" a good deal of adult behavior. Part of that behavior may (Note the equivocation) have included play hunting, with appropriate signal cries. (No reader should be unaware of the leap through evolutionary space in that sentence.) The brightest of the young were thus able to use language independently of its primary stimuli, perhaps those who played the longest into young adulthood. The fact that the young of humankind is so dependent for so long makes them unusually "plastic" in their development, unusually susceptible to environmental experience as opposed to innately ingrained behavior.

The whole question has such a fascination that one understands why so many scholars want to propose their pet explanations. One should not wax too metaphysical over every puzzling biological phenomenon. But, along with life, sentience, and self-consciousness, human language may have to be included among those features of creation which are built on principles of organization that transcend our ability to understand, much less explain.

In any event, how man progressed from even this primitive potentiality for syntax to the highly inflected languages of Sanskrit, Hebrew, Greek, and Latin is similarly an object of pure speculation. But whatever their origin, to get back to the original point, there is no a priori reason to argue that this evolution inevitably led to extensive inflections as the highest form of linguistic organization. It may well be that languages develop through cycles, at one time relying on inflections, then losing them as they come to rely more on word order and phrasal ways to express ideas, then developing new inflections out of words closely associated with other words, then losing inflections again. But this theory covers such a vast period of linguistic evolution that there is little solid evidence to confirm it as a universal of language history.

Probably the main reason many do believe that the complexity of a grammar depends on its inflections is that the first grammars, the grammars of Sanskrit, Greek, and Latin, were written for highly inflected languages, languages which we now esteem because in them we find much that is at the foundation of Western and Middle Eastern civilization. These languages became so intellectually prestigious that for centuries, they determined how scholars thought about the grammar of all languages. Yet, as we shall see, English, which lacks an elaborate set of inflections, still has a grammar so complex that we shall scarcely be able to give it more than a superficial examination.

DESCRIBING LANGUAGE

The question of where to look for the primary data for a description of linguistic structure, for the derived data of our history, is a crucial question. We have already mentioned the popular idea that only upper-middle class educated speakers have a grammar worth studying. And because the most prestigious representation of that prestigious dialect is usually in its written literature, many believe that writing is where the real grammar of a language can be found, that speech is merely corrupted writing. This encourages still more those who would look to the past for grammatical respectability, because all we have left from our distant linguistic past is writing. And ordinarily, all that is preserved are the most important and hence most self-consciously composed documents: laws, religious writings, and so on.

Written Language

The question of whether to begin with a description of written Latin or Old English or whether to construct first a description of contemporary English against which older forms of English can be contrasted might be put as follows: If we want a theory of language that forces us to ask more rather than less demanding questions, would such a theory emerge if we based it on what we know about the language of texts in a dead language or on what we know about our own, living language?

What is left from dead languages is like a drop of water from an ocean of speech. The only concrete evidence of how language was used in the past is from what those speakers happened to write down and what the viscissitudes of time have spared. But even if a theory of language were based on written material from modern languages, it would still ignore some of the most crucial facts that uniquely characterize the way humans use language.

Writing is a comparatively recent invention, only about 5000 years old. Modern man has been around for at least 200,000 years, perhaps several times that long, and certainly talking the whole time. In fact, when we consider that a minority of just the some four to five thousand languages spoken today have ever had their own written form, we realize that writing is a relatively rare mode of communication, that long before writing existed, thousands of languages must have developed, flourished, and died unrecorded.

More importantly, writings that have survived from the distant past of English (more than 1000 years ago, let us say) do not give us a clear record of the language used in ordinary, everyday communication by the great mass of people. Reading and writing were—and in many cases still are—arcane skills known only to a relative handful of educated men. Yet, while writing inevitably has greater prestige than speech, we know that writing changes because speech changes more often than speech changes in response to writing. We also know that languages change because of the ways prestigious and non-prestigious forms of speech influence one another. Many features of what we would now call "grammatical" writing certainly had their source in what once would have been called "ungrammatical" speech.

Thus if we relied only on evidence from the past to construct a general theory of language, we might seriously underestimate the diversity of dialects spoken within a single language. We might possess documents reflecting different geographical dialects. But we would not have records reflecting the speech of the ordinary speaker, or, for that matter, even the casual speech of the person who did the writing.

Spoken Language

Another aspect of languge that writing preserves at best imperfectly is the way a language sounds. Much has been made of the fact that humans vocalize their language. In fact, one common definition of language among the school of linguists called **descriptivists** it that it is a set of arbitrarily structured uttered sounds. Modern linguistics in the first half of this century strongly emphasized this aspect of language for two reasons.

First, they inherited a rich tradition from nineteenth-century philologists who had achieved great success in establishing through parallel sound patterns the fact that the Germanic languages (English, German, Dutch, and the Scandinavian languages), the Romance languages (Latin, French, Spanish, Italian, Portuguese, Rumanian), Greek, the Slavic languages (Russian, Polish, Czech, and so on), Persian, the ancient language, Sanskrit, and some modern languages spoken in Northern India were all descended from a hypothetical common ancestor, Indo-European. The detailed analysis of sound changes showed, for example, that English *brother*, German *bruder*, Latin *fräter*, Greek *phrater*, and Sanskrit *bhraatr* were **cognates**, or words descended from an earlier word that can only be theoretically reconstructed as **bhräter* (the * indicates that the word has never been found in any recorded text, that it is a **reconstruction**). It was one of the great intellectual achievements in the history of language study. (163, 183)

Second, and more importantly, in the second quarter of this century, a new breed of linguists emerged from an anthropological discipline built around the questions anthropologists faced when they first walked into a village that spoke a language completely unlike any of the Indo-European languages. Before they could begin their research, they had to decode what they heard. Because the first aspect of the language accessible to them was its sound, descriptive linguists from the twenties to the present have labored to devise ways to discover and describe sound patterns. They were also influenced by an attitude among other social scientists that valued most highly that data which was objectively measurable. (235)

As we shall see, because linguists have devised many ways to recover from writing the general outlines of past phonological systems, we are not completely cut off from the sound patterns of a dead language. But the imperfect relationship between spelling and sound in English should make it clear how difficult it is to use writing to discover pronunciation.

One aspect of sound that is almost completely lost, however, is the rising and falling of our voices in questions, statements, etc., the different ways we accent one syllable rather than another as in *PERvert* and *perVERT*, *John ALso found some money* and *John also FOUND some money*. Again, there are ways to approximate what these **suprasegmentals** may have been like—particularly through the meter of poetry—but these ways are imperfect at best. And of course, it is just about impossible to determine what sorts of vocal signals speakers of an extinct language used to express surprise, anger, bewilderment, sadness, and so on. We cannot assume that all speakers of all languages use the same signals to indicate these emotions, for **paralinguistic** features of language vary from culture to culture.

So in addition to excluding much of the variation of language across social, stylistic, and geographical boundaries, writing also partially cuts us off from the patterns of its sounds. Relying on the past to construct a theory of language would severely limit the power of our theory.

PROBLEM 2.1: Man could conceivably have developed a communication system based on any of his senses: sight, smell, feeling, taste, hearing. Assuming that evolution tends to work towards the most efficient biological system possible within the genetic limitations of the organism, how would you justify sound over any of the other sensory systems that might have evolved to an extremely high level of complexity as a basis for communication? That is, assuming that our sense of smell might have evolved to a very high degree, what disadvantages would it still have in comparison to hearing?

PROBLEM 2.2: Review the design features and capabilities of human languages. Then outline a science fiction plot in which humans confront a society that lacks any two of the features. For example, what would happen in a society which communicated by producing balloons with sentences spelled out, as in a comic strip? And suppose those balloons did not have the characteristic of rapid fading but rather dissolved over a period of an hour or so. Where would choral societies have to practice? How would secrets be transmitted? What would **Hamlet** feel like? What would Beethoven's **Ninth** smell like? What would Homer taste like?

PROBLEM 2.3: What features of language can writing communicate which speech cannot?

GRAMMAR AND GRAMMARS

More about a dead language can be found in its written form when we investigate its grammar, or the ways words are made up out of smaller pieces and then put together into larger phrases and clauses, the way *unhappiness* is made up of *un-*, *-happi-*, and *-ness*; the way a sentence like *Unhappiness can be an educational experience* can be structured:

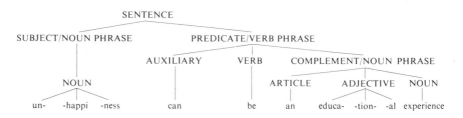

But now a multitude of questions arise when we ask what is involved in formulating the grammar of a language we all speak, much less one we don't.

Traditional Grammars

Traditionally, writing a grammar has meant first identifying parts of speech, usually by means of semantic definitions: A **noun**, like *boy*, is the name of a person, place, or thing; an **adjective** modifies or restricts the idea of boy: *big* boys; a **verb** shows action: big boys *play*. These parts of speech are then placed into **paradigms**, or lists that show the inflectional endings they occur before: *boy–boys–boy's–boys'*; *walk–walked–walked–walking*, for example. Even though English has a very limited paradigmatic inflectional system, traditional grammarians have emphasized these patterns and their meanings (past, future, present, perfect, progressive, and so on, for verbs; singular, plural, possessive for nouns) because grammars of highly prestigious languages like Latin and Greek depend heavily on elaborate inflectional paradigms. Without considering whether a new conception of grammar might be appropriate for English, the least enlightened of the traditionalists simply force English into those molds.

Once the individual words are classified, traditional grammarians list and define, again semantically, the ways in which word classes relate to one another in phrases and clauses: Noun–Verb (*boys play*) is a **subject-verb** construction in which the subject is typically the "actor." Verb-Noun (. . . *play ball*) is often a **verb-object** construction in which the object is the "receiver" of the action. The largest unit of all, the **sentence**, is again semantically defined as a "complete thought." Sentences are then classified, again semantically, according to whether they ask questions, give commands, make statements, or express an optative (*Oh, that he would stop!*)

Traditionalists emphasize semantic definitions so strongly for several reasons, but largely because of a common definition of language on which they base their analysis: Language is a means to communicate ideas, a definition that makes meaning central to the description of a language.

When a traditionalist sets himself to writing the grammar of a dead language, his first concern is to identify parts of speech in older texts according to the principles he has inherited from many centuries of language study. Once he has identified those parts of speech, he sets to arranging them in paradigmatic orders that will show what kinds of endings the parts of speech occurred with. His next concern is to describe how those parts of speech function in sentences in terms that will help him explain what those sentences mean.

An area of major concern to the traditional historical grammarian, for example, would be the tense, mood and aspect system of the verb phrase, both because in languages like Latin and Greek it was communicated through a very highly developed inflectional system, and because the system itself communicated a very complex set of meanings. The traditional historical grammarian of the year 2500 would try to explain the grammatical meaning of Modern English verb phrases like *He could have been found, He will be working, He has been being questioned* in terms of the state of the action, the time relative to the present, past, or future, in terms of whether the action is real or unreal. Another of his tasks would be to explain clausal relationships in terms of their meanings: *Because he left* would be a **causal** relationship; *though he left* would be **concessive**; *after he left* would be **temporal**; *if he left* would be **conditional**. (35, 97, 134, 174)

PROBLEM 2.4: The traditional definition of a noun is a word that names a person, place, or thing: *boy, country, rock, aggression, ambition, mind, force, spirit, meaning, love, peace, honesty, coincidence, luck.* The traditional definition of a verb is that it indicates action: *run, jump, imitate, resemble, reflect, weigh, stand, have.* Comment on the usefulness of these definitions in a sentence like *Coincidence resembles luck* or *Honesty has many aspects.*

PROBLEM 2.5: A **subject** is frequently defined as either the "actor" of the sentence, or that which the sentence is "about." How would these definitions apply to the subjects (in bold face) of the following sentences? (1) **My car** *drives easily.* (2) **The key** *opened the door.* (3) **The table** *has a key on it.* (4) **George** *received a wound.* (5) **Bill** *resembles his father.* (6) **He** *lacks intelligence.* (7) **Somebody** *said the world is going to end tomorrow.* (8) **The wall** *crawled with roaches the size of your fist, like the one on your collar.*

PROBLEM 2.6: Rather than defining language as a way to communicate ideas, suppose we began with the following definition: **Language is a way of performing actions with speech.** (1) How would a grammar be organized if it were based on such an assumption? How would units of speech be defined? (2) Are there any other preliminary definitions of language that would lead to different ways of organizing and writing a grammar?

Descriptive Grammars

The descriptivists, who as we noted came out of an earlier anthropological tradition, rejected the traditionalists and their use of meaning to describe the grammatical structure of a language, first because the temper of the twenties and thirties stressed scientific objectivity, analysis of data without presuppositions, and a materialist, empirical approach in psychology that considered only objectifiable, quantifiable, observable behavior as legitimate data. For behaviorist psychologists and their linguist colleagues, the mind as an observable entity did not empirically exist. Hence theories built around its supposed operations were invalid.

This intellectual atmosphere was reinforced when linguists found that many of the exotic languages they were studying required ways to categorize parts of speech and sentence functions that were quite different from the traditional ways. In some languages, the distinction between nouns and verbs seemed scarcely to exist. Nouns were discovered to be inflected for tense; the traditional categories of prepositions, articles, and adverbs were often impossible to apply consistently. The notion of verbs inflected for past or present was irrelevant for a language whose primary interest in verb inflection was not time but whether the speaker knew from his own experience that an event had occurred, whether it had been reported to him, whether it was an accepted fact. The traditional categories of perfect and progressive were insufficient for a language that inflected its verbs for the physical shape of their objects.

The descriptivists, therefore, adopted the stance of the behaviorist psychologists and tried to devise purely objective, entirely formal ways to discover and describe the structure of any language including English. First, instead of prescribing what English sentences should be like on the basis of their preconceived notions about sentences in Indo-European languages, they collected vast amounts of linguistic data, examples of sentences from letters, newspapers, telephone conversations, and so on. After identifying individual words and parts of words on the basis of how they were pronounced, they grouped the words into parts of speech primarily by what kinds of **inflections** they occurred before or after, and by their typical position in a sentence relative to other parts of speech.

In English, for example, anything that occurs before a possessive or plural marker is (in one grammar) called a Class I word, *noun* being rejected because it is too closely associated with the traditionalists. Any word before a third person -*s* marker, a past tense marker, and an -*ing* ending is a Class II word, *verb* being rejected for the same reason *noun* was. Descriptivists also use **position** as a way to define parts of speech. Thus any word that occurs between *the* and a form of *be* is also a noun or Class I word: *The* _____ *was good.* Anything that occurs after a Class I word and ends the sentence is a verb or Class II word: *The man* _____. This system generates several new categories of words, such as the category including *yes, no, uh-huh*; the category including *hello, goodbye, hi, so long*; the category including *very, somewhat, rather, quite.*

Once individual words are put into these categories, descriptivists try to state their order relative to one another and how they group into phrases and clauses: *very* and *old* form a unit called an **adjective phrase** because the adjective *old* may occur after or without the *very*, but not vice versa: *He was very old* or *He was old*, but not *He was very.* Larger relationships like subject-verb are again defined not semantically as "actor" and "action" but formally: Whatever the verb agrees with (or might agree with) in number is the subject: *The boy leaves* vs. *The boys leave.*

The largest structure, the sentence, is defined in various ways. Those descriptivists most strongly committed to the belief that sounds are the bedrock of language define a sentence as whatever occurs under a single **intonation contour**, a rising and falling of the voice that occurs between points of potential silence. Less rigorously phonological descriptivists define a sentence not as a "complete thought" but as a complete structure composed of a subject and inflected verb plus all grammatical elements dependent on those elements. (59, 66, 84, 219)

Working this way seems perfectly suited to historical linguistics. Instead of collecting data from contemporary speakers, the linguist collects texts from an older period. He pores through the texts, discovering the pieces of words and whole words and how they fit together. He then groups the words into larger classes, into parts of speech, not on the basis of reconstructed meaning but on the basis of their inflections and positions. Then he tabulates how the various classes of words co-occur with one another to form larger units. He then describes the order of the larger elements. The complete descriptive grammar, historical or contemporary, consists of:

1. An inventory of sounds and sound classes and how they occur relative to one another.
2. An inventory of words and pieces of words put into various categories.
3. A description of how the pieces combine with the words or with one another.
4. A description of how categories of words combine into larger units and how those larger units combine with one another to form yet larger units.

PROBLEM 2.7: (1) What kinds of inflectional criteria would define a descriptive category we traditionally call **adjective** and **adverb**? (2) What problems result from using **only** inflectional criteria with these words: *beautiful, additional, representative, adjacent, tennis, ought, chaos, must, chief*?

PROBLEM 2.8: (1) Set up a category based purely on observable descriptive criteria that would unambiguously define the category of these words: *may, will, can, shall*. (2) Do the same for *in, on, at, by, over, through, under, across, of, beside, between, behind, with*.

PROBLEM 2.9: What is the subject of *There are men at the door*?

Generative Grammars

In the late fifties there occurred another revolution in linguistics. Intellectual revolutions begin when paradigms of questions exhaust themselves and someone recognizing that fact can formulate questions directed toward a quite different conception of a subject. This happened when MIT professor Noam Chomsky argued that the questions descriptivists had been asking depended on some serious misapprehensions they held about the nature of language and the goals of language study. Chomsky argued that what we can discover about language strictly from collecting data made up of objectively observable units of speech will give us but a fraction of what we actually know about the mental grammar we have all developed from before the time we began speaking. Chomsky proposed that representing this grammar that we carry about in our heads should be the goal of linguists. This grammar is locked away in the brain, inaccessible to direct observation. But by asking what we know about our ability to produce and understand sentences, we can discover something of its properties and perhaps partially and very indirectly represent that ability in the grammar we write down on paper. (31, 32)

In fact, this question—what indeed do we implicitly "know" about sentences?—is the problem. We may not "know" in the explicit sense that we can technically explain how sentences are put together. But we all implicitly, tacitly "know" a grammar. Otherwise, we could not speak our own language.

GRAMMATICALITY

Usage vs. Structure

Obviously, the nature of the grammar we write down in order to represent the grammar we carry about in our heads is going to depend on what we discover we know about sentences. First, we know that some sentences are correctly structured and others are not. The terms **grammatical** and **ungrammatical** are commonly used here. But they mean something quite different from junior-high-school ideas about "good grammar." We shall use these terms as value-free labels to categorize sentences that do or do not correspond to the possibilities of English sentences that are ordinarily used by any group of English speakers. We do not mean the prescriptions taught in junior high about not ending sentences with prepositions, not using *ain't*, when to use *shall* instead of *will*, and so on. These are problems of **usage**. Many teachers call them grammatical errors. And in a very special and restricted way, perhaps they could on occasion be called that. More accurately, though, they are only grammatical patterns or word choices varying slightly from the patterns that some educated speakers use, often only in their self-conscious moments and usually only when they are writing. Indeed, most educated speakers, quite unselfconsciously, split their infinitives, end sentences with prepositions, use *will* for all persons and numbers.

Unfortunately, except when past rhetoricians specifically commented on usage, it is almost impossible to discover much about the distant history of prestigious and non-prestigious speech patterns. A few comments about the appropriateness of the London dialect as a linguistic standard and the use of certain dialects for comic purposes in Chaucer and elsewhere have come down to us from Middle English. But not until the sixteenth century do we find any specific observations about contemporary attitudes toward usage, and even then, the comments are often contradictory. It is a problem we will (shall?) deal with again. (131)

PROBLEM 2.10: Here are some sentences that deviate from standard English, some because they belong to a non-standard dialect, others because they violate a basic core of English structure. If you can identify those that **would** be used by non-standard speakers, how would your ability to do so serve as evidence that such sentences are in fact regularly structured with their own grammar? (1) *He ain't can't have no money.* (2) *He ain't got no money.* (3) *He he have may gone.* (4) *He gone now.* (5) *She can may go.* (6) *She may can go.* (7) *Him and me done finished now.* (8) *They done may be finished with he and she.* (9) *Can't nobody tell him nothing.* (10) *Isn't somebody tell him anything?*

Structure

A more significant kind of ungrammaticality is that which violates the central core of grammatical structures shared by all speakers of a language. These next sentences, for example, would not be uttered by a native speaker of English. Or, if they were, he would either correct himself, or, on reflection, recognize that they were somehow "odd":

1.   *Street went down man the.*
2.   *The man walked the down street.*

3.   *The man went not down the street.*
4.   *Went the man down the street?*

All of them are wrong for speakers of Modern English. But while the pattern of (1) and (2) would have been wrong at any time, (3) and (4) would have been correct for Shakespeare.

The second part of that conclusion is not difficult to arrive at since we find lines in Shakespeare's plays like

5.   *Know'st thou Fluellen?* **Henry V.** III.1.
6.   *Stands Scotland where it did?* **Macbeth.** IV.iii.
7.   *I know not by what power I am made bold.* **MSND.** I.i.
8.   *Nay, goe not from me . . .* 3 **Henry VI.** I.1.

But the first part or the conclusion has to be entirely inferential because we cannot ask any speaker of ModE what a speaker of OE or ME (Middle English)[1] would think about such sentences as (1) and (2). We can only conclude that such sentences would probably have been ungrammatical because we can find no sentences similar to them.

The problem becomes much more difficult, however, when we wonder whether a sentence like *He should have been working* would have been grammatical for, say, Chaucer. It is perfectly grammatical for a ModE speaker, but nowhere in ME do we find a combination like *should* + *have* + *been* + *V-ing*. Does that mean it was ungrammatical and therefore never used? Or does it mean it just never happened to be written down?

This is not a serious problem for the descriptivist or traditionalist who concerns himself primarily with describing the language found only in extant texts. It **is** a serious problem for a historical linguist if he looks upon evidence from the past as only a very small part of what a speaker **might** have written or said, and his intention is to create a grammar that will account for more than just extant data. He must constantly ask himself whether structures that are possible for him in ModE but not attested to in OE or ME are missing from the texts accidentally or because they were not part of the grammar. "What might have been" is a crucial problem for such a linguist. (231)

Ambiguity and Relatedness

Another ability that a modern transformationalist is concerned with is demonstrated in a sentence like *The chicken is ready to eat* and in the pair of sentences *John is easy to please* and *To please John is easy*. The first sentence is grammatically **ambiguous**. It can mean either that the chicken is about to eat or be eaten. The fact that any native speaker of English can recognize such

1 The dates assigned to OE and ME are arbitrary; most linguists put the end of OE at about A.D. 1100, the end of ME at about A.D. 1500.

an ambiguity illustrates that we are able to recognize how the observable surface order of elements that make up the grammatical structure of what we hear or read can communicate very different underlying relationships among linguistic elements.

This implies that a sentence has two levels of grammatical structure. There is the observable order of words and their observable connections, or the **surface structure** of a sentence. And there is a **deeper structure** that relates elements on a more abstract level. In *The chicken is ready to eat*, nothing in the form of the sentence reveals that *chicken* can be either the subject or object of *eat*. But at some level of structure deeper than the simple order of elements in that sentence, we know that that is the case. Otherwise, we could not detect the ambiguity.

PROBLEM 2.11: All these sentences have two different meanings that depend on different grammatical deep structures. How are they ambiguous?

1. *The man was too old to help.*
2. *Flying planes can be dangerous.*
3. *They called him a butler.*
4. *He didn't marry her because he loved her.*
5. *In conclusion, he said many foolish things.*
6. *George was cooking in the kitchen.*

We come to the same conclusion about grammatical surface structures and grammatical deep structures if we ask how it is we know that the sentences, *John is easy to please* and *To please John is easy* are synonymous. They have very different surface structures, very different word orders, yet at a deeper level, they mean precisely the same thing; they have precisely the same set of abstract relations among their elements. In other words, relatedness is the other side of the coin from ambiguity: Ambiguous sentences have one surface structure and at least two different deep structures. Related sentences have two surface structures and one deep structure. (94, 132)

And here again, if we take as one of the goals of our grammar a description of this fact, we raise some very difficult problems for the historian of language. Because these relationships can become very abstract and very difficult to describe even for a speaker of a modern language, they are even more difficult to describe for languages which no one any longer speaks.

The point of this brief summary of the kinds of concerns linguists have when they ask questions about the grammar of a language is that as new theories of language come to dominate the thinking of those writing grammars of contemporary languages, historians of languages are forced to ask new kinds of questions about the data they are examining, indeed, to "see" data that linguists of other persuasions do not. As their understanding of what a living language is like changes, so do their goals in describing a language no longer spoken.

the most crucial point is that modern linguists no longer
to the past to help them understand the grammar of a lan-
ɔ their own intuitions as native speakers of a human language.
rds, we will understand our linguistic history only when we
our linguistic present.

LANGUAGE AND MEANING

In addition to the sounds and structures of the past, of course, we are concerned with words, their meanings, and the meanings of the sentences they
occur in. But we have only to think how inadequate any dictionary definition
is for words like *love*, *peace*, or *democracy* to realize that most of what we call
meaning cannot be written down. And when those words are combined into
sentences like *Peace with honor is justice in a democracy*, we recognize that even
if we could define individual words, those words in grammatical structures add
up to a total meaning that is not the mere sum of the individual meanings.

Traditional grammarians have always been concerned with meaning, but
meaning of a rather narrow kind: verb tenses, clausal relationships, kinds of
nouns (common and proper, abstract and concrete), and so on. Descriptive
grammarians set aside the problem of meaning in order to concentrate on
observable forms and how they occur with one another. They talk in terms
of grammatical meaning that can be abstracted from lexical meaning, of the
grammatical meaning of *'Twas brillig, and the slithy toves | Did gyre and gimble
in the wabe....* More recently, however, transformational linguists have
turned back to lexical meaning because they have set as their task a description
of how semantic content is "mapped" onto syntactic and phonological forms.

Unfortunately, no area of language study is more obscure, more difficult
to formulate in terms that would let us study it. The meaning of "meaning"
has been debated at least since the pre-Socratic philosphers of ancient
Greece. It is a question that has so preoccupied modern thought that some
philosophers have claimed that philosophical problems are really linguistic
problems and that the proper task of philosophy is to untangle linguistic
confusions in the way we pose our questions.

Because different disciplines have approached the problem of meaning
differently, it is no surprise that there are as many different ways to describe
meaning as there are disciplines. Neurologists define meaning as the selective
activation of neural networks at varying amplitudes and frequencies in
response to linguistic and nonlinguistic stimuli, resulting in chemical changes
in the molecular structure of large molecules. Psychologists have defined
meaning variously as mental images, as conditioned substitutions for word
referents, as dispositions to behave, as the network of associations a word is

part of. Philosophers have defined meaning in a multitude of ways: as how a word or sentence is used, in what is necessary to confirm its truth, in the existence of word-referents, in the "essence" of a referent. . . . (191, 207)

When a question about the meaning of a **particular** word arises, though, we usually think first of the dictionary, where along with a good deal of additional information about spelling, pronunciation, etymology, and so on, we can find its "meaning." A typical entry minus all irrelevancies might look like this:

> Chair: A seat for one person; now usually the four-legged
> seat with a rest for the back.

Typically, the definition puts the word to be defined into a larger or **superordinate** class, in this case *seat*. *Seat* names the larger class of concepts to which the concepts covered by *chair* belong, along with the concepts covered by *stool, bench, hassock, settee, perch*, and so on. Once the superordinate category, *seat*, is named, those features which distinguish the word *chair* from those other words organize the definition into finer and finer subordinate classes:

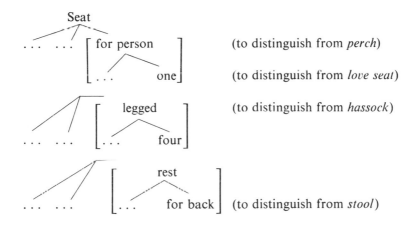

We may choose different kinds of subset differentia to distinguish members of the superordinate set, choosing criteria by what the object is used for, as we would have to with *hammer*; how it is made, for *net*; what it is made of, for *glacier*; what it does, for *heart*, and so on. But if the word is not defined merely by listing synonyms or pointing to a picture, the pattern of definition is invariably the same: The word to be defined is placed in a superordinate set and then distinguished by subordinate differentia.

A problem of theory in regard to dictionary definitions is that every definition depends on words the reader already knows and the words that happen to be in the language. This, of course, finally leads to theoretical circularity since the words used in a definition must themselves be defined by other words, which in turn must be defined, and so on.

PROBLEM 2.12: Pick any fairly general word in the dictionary that would be used in the definition of a more specific word, a word like *shape, substance, man, good*, and look up a key word in its definition. Then look up the key words in its definition. At how many removes do the definitions become circular, referring back to an earlier word?

Recently, linguists have approached the problem of meaning from a different direction. When we examine the meaning of groups of words that belong to the same **semantic space** or **lexical field**, we often find they occur in symmetrical sets. Kinship terms, for example, always occur in sets whose members are distinguished by only a few components of meaning. The only semantic distinction between the members of the pairs *husband–wife, aunt–uncle, sister–brother, son–daughter, father–mother* is whether the referent is male or female; *father–brother–son, mother–sister–daughter, aunt–cousin–niece, uncle–cousin–nephew* differ only in whether the referent is in the ascending, descending, or the same generation. *Sibling–cousin, nephew–son, parent–uncle/aunt* differ in whether the referent is a direct lineal relation or once removed. In fact, we could define all these words more economically than a dictionary would by specifying only which of the pairs of complementary **semantic features** are in the meaning:

1. father: [+male, +1 generation, +lineal]
2. mother: [−male, +1 generation, +lineal]
3. son: [+male, −1 generation, +lineal]
4. daughter: [−male, −1 generation, +lineal]
5. uncle: [+male, +1 generation, −lineal]
6. aunt: [−male, +1 generation, −lineal]
7. brother: [+male, 0 generation, +lineal]
8. sister: [−male, 0 generation, +lineal] (72, 203)

PROBLEM 2.13: (1) What features compose the meanings of *nephew, niece, cousin, parent, relative, father-in-law*? (2) Are there clusters of semantic features for which we have no words? What word means [±male, −1 generation, −lineal]; for [−male, 0 generation, −lineal]?

Originally, these techniques were of interest only to anthropologists interested in describing taxonomic semantic systems such as kinship, disease, and plant names. More recently, generative semanticists have attempted to adapt such a system to describe words in general. The meanings of *idea* and *rock*, for example, contrast in one basic way: abstract vs. concrete, a contrast we can represent as [±concrete]; between *grass* and *snail* is the opposition

[± animate]; between *snail* and *woman*, [± human]; between *woman* and *girl*, [± adult]; between *girl* and *boy*, the familiar contrast of [± male]. (29, 101, 102)

Because this approach to meaning is still in its formative stage, many problems remain to be solved: the kinds of conceptual oppositions, the number of features, whether some features might require a scale of numbers rather than just [+/−]. Most importantly, it is clear that the features must be grouped and structured. The definition of *chair* as a seat with a back for one person to sit on would have to include at least this information:

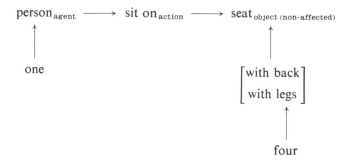

In other words, we are dealing with meaning as if "a meaning" were decomposable into molecules, atoms, and perhaps even atomic particles, all of which are organized into very complex structures.

When this theory of meaning is applied to problems of historical semantics, however, the same problems of describing grammatical structure in dead languages arise, but more severely. For this theory of meaning, like the theory of generative grammar we described, relies on introspection, on asking oneself about meaning and contrasts of meaning. But this is no simple task even when we ask about our own language. It is very difficult to recover this kind of meaning entirely from the contexts in which we find words in those relatively few texts a dead language has left us.

What this also demonstrates is the futility of looking to older forms of a language to tell us about our own. We know infinitely more about the meanings of words in the language we speak than we ever will about words in any dead language. So again, we cannot **begin** with the past in constructing a theory of meaning, much less a theory of language.

To summarize the point of this very superficial outline of some theories about linguistic structure: When we ask questions about the nature of language or about its history, the theory we base our questions on will determine what questions we ask. The assumptions we base our theory on—whether we look to the past for a more perfect form of grammar and consequently have to rely on writing as the source of our information, or whether we rely first on what we can discover about our own linguistic competence, as difficult as it may be to probe and represent in a written grammar—such assumptions will strongly determine the kind of theory we construct.

SOME CAUSES AND EFFECTS OF LANGUAGE CHANGE

Now these theories will provide us with a way to describe what has changed in the internal structure of our language. But a grammar (including phonology and semantics) is only one component in what we might term a theory of **language**. Language is more than its grammar. It is an instrument by which we perform most of the social acts that constitute a society. It reflects, indeed may on occasion **determine**, our social class. Some believe that it even determines how we structure our perceptions of reality. In short, language is part of a larger set of interlocking cultural and social structures that we move in from the moment the doctor announces *It's a* _____, with all the social values the terms *boy* and *girl* entail, to the obligatory final ritual (most stereotypically expressed in westerns and nautical movies, when someone is required to "say a few words" over a body). We can recognize how highly valued language is in our culture when we celebrate the first word a child utters and make collections of the last words of great men. In such a context, language will change when culture and social conditions change. And it is in these external changes that we may be able to find **some** of the causes of internal linguistic change.

We have already touched on one obvious source of linguistic change: external social forces. The invasion of England by the Danes and Normans profoundly affected our language. So did printing. So did the social turmoil of the fourteenth century. So has our science and technology. Another important social source of linguistic change are the differences among geographical and social dialects. Inevitably, given several social/geographical dialects, a prestige dialect will emerge to influence and be influenced by other dialects. In order to explore this aspect of language, we must describe the social conditions in which language is used and the elements that may cause a rigid social structure to become fluid, so that speakers from different classes will come into contact with one another.

But other sources of change may be found in the internal structure of the grammar itself. This will be a very difficult question to discuss because we have to treat the structure of the grammar as if it were a real model of the speaker's mind. Once a native speaker unconsciously formulates in his mind the grammar of his language, that grammar may be very well organized and very well integrated. But at certain points, it may also be unnecessarily complex or redundant. The simplest example of this kind of inefficient complexity in English is found in our verbs. The most economical rule that would account for the past tense of verbs would be something like this: *Verb + past→ verb-ed*. In ModE, though, we have to list well over a hundred exceptions to this rule: *buy–bought, sell–sold, sing–sang*, and so on. But in OE, there were hundreds of exceptions. We seem to be very slowly simplifying a point of unnecessary complexity in the grammar.

The reason speakers simplify their grammars is undoubtedly to be found in some kind of principle of least effort that all humans rely on when they construct schema or models for their behavior and understanding But this principle probably operates most powerfully among children as they learn a language. Children, for example, often go through four stages when they learn irregular verbs. In the first stage, they often are able to use irregular verbs correctly: *He saw.* In the second and third stages, they combine the irregular past or the infinitive with the *-ed* ending: *He sawed* and *He seed.* Finally, they learn to use the verbs as they are used in the dialect they grow up in. If it happens to be standard English, then they will eventually learn to say *He saw* again. But between every generation there is probably a slight grammatical discontinuity. The language is not passed on from parent to child perfectly. The child will make some mistakes. If enough similar mistakes are made by enough children, then those mistakes may become part of the grammar for that generation of children, a grammar that will be passed on to the next generation.

These, then, are the kinds of problems we shall investigate. Because we have to understand the social and cultural contexts in which changes occur, we shall begin by examining those contexts through the sources of our vocabulary, an aspect of language particularly sensitive to cultural change. Then in Chapter Six we shall deal with how we create words out of the basic material of our lexicon, and in Chapter Seven how the meanings associated with those forms evolve. In Chapters Nine through Fourteen, we shall examine how the grammar and sound patterns of our language have changed.

PROBLEM 2.14: (1) What are some occasions in our culture, other than birth and death, where the use of language is essential, where if certain words are not spoken, the moment loses its significance or becomes entirely invalid? (2) Why does the Gospel according to John begin as it does? (3) What would it feel like, do you suppose, to be an adult and literally have no name? Not to have forgotten it or to be unable to find it, but literally to have been given no name ever? (4) Are there any social situations or events where speech is tacitly forbidden?

PROBLEM 2.15: Between the bee and man there is a great linguistic gap. In a series of minimal steps, evolve the language of bees until it approximates the communicative capacity of man. Bees communicate distance by dancing increasingly less intensely as distance from the hive to the source of food increases. Direction is indicated by translating the axis of the sun–hive to a vertical line inside the hive and then by dancing at an angle from vertical corresponding to the angle formed between the sun–hive–food source. Their mode of communication, of course, would have to develop out of the intensity of their buzzing and the movements of their dance.

PROBLEM 2.16: What would be the minimal unequivocal evidence that a primate now being trained to communicate via sign language or plastic counters had the ability to communicate on a level approximating human communication? (It is almost certain that the mode would not be verbal, since the laryngeal structure of primates is not well adapted to the production of finely articulated sounds.)

PROBLEM 2.17: The boldface examples in the following sets are considered "ungrammatical." Construct a logical argument that would support the claim that they are preferable to their grammatical counterparts.

1. *Myself, yourself,* **hisself,** *herself, ourselves,* **theirselves.**
2. **I ain't,** *you aren't, it isn't, we aren't, they aren't.*
3. *I wasn't,* **you wasn't,** *it wasn't, we weren't, you weren't, they weren't.*
4. *I jumped, you danced,* **she runned, we singed, you goed,** *they worked.*

PROBLEM 2.18: Here are several words from the semantic field referring to the use of language. They all seem to imply judgment. (1) What can you conclude from these words about our attitudes toward how people use language? (2) Are attitudes toward the use of language the same in all parts of the English-speaking world? Are there stereotyped ethnic or sex differences in language use? (3) What use of language appears to be most highly valued, reticence or non-reticence?

1. *talk, chatter, gab, prattle, gabble, babble, jabber, clack, gossip, chat, converse.*
2. *talkative, gabby, wordy, gossipy, voluble, loquacious, garrulous, prolix, diffuse, bigmouthed, fatmouthed, glib.*
3. *shrew, nag, gossip, fishwife, chatterbox, windbag, bigmouth, fatmouth, magpie, scold, harpy, termagent.*
4. *taciturn, laconic, reticent, concise, trenchant, brief, terse, pointed, pithy, succinct, crisp, sententious, epigrammatic, elliptical, crabbed, curt.*

PART II
WORDS AND MEANINGS

Chapter 3

WORDS: NATIVE AND BORROWED

Of all the aspects of language that change through time—pronunciation, spelling, usage, grammar, meaning, and vocabulary—meaning and vocabulary are the most sensitive to the external social and historical forces that determine which words a culture preserves from its own heritage and which words it borrows from others. Particular meanings change the most idiosyncratically. We could never have predicted that the meaning once attached to *dwell* would shift from "lead into error" to its current sense. There are some large generalizations we can make about how meanings change, but they are relatively few.

The total lexicon of a language, however, is a very accurate linguistic barometer to the broad social and historical changes in the history of a culture. Given the relevant cultural information, we could have predicted fairly accurately the general makeup of our ModE vocabulary and its sources. We know that some kinds of words are so durable that they will for centuries resist the most violent viscissitudes of time: *hand, foot, mother, father, head, heart, sun, moon, sleep, eat,* and so on. Other words predictably disappear: OE *wergild,* the money a murderer had to pay to the family of his victims;

OE *scora*, a hairy garment; OE *þeox*, a hunting spear. Cultural necessity has forced other words into the language through borrowing, derivation, or creation: *machine, cab, crime, jazz, etiquette, chocolate, albino, ghetto, syrup, candy, shawl, jungle, tycoon, taboo, tote, blender, television, retrorocket.*

The Origin of Words

How and where the first words originated has always puzzled linguists and philosophers. When Socrates and Hermogenes debated the question 2000 years ago, they argued whether words related naturally to the things they named. It is a notion that helps explain much of the magic and folk belief found almost everywhere in the world. The Egyptians, for example, gave everyone two names, a public name and a secret one; they believed if someone knew a person's real name, he would have power over the person. In other cultures, word-magic takes the form of taboos against uttering the name of a god, or the name of certain relatives, or even words that sound like those words. (60)

The relationship between a word and its referent is for the most part arbitrary. The shape or sound of a word has no natural relationship to the thing it names. There may be a narrow range of words that could illustrate phonetic imitation: *boom, clang, hiss, screech,* and so on. And a few others may illustrate principles of conventionalized phonetic symbolism: *Teeny* is smaller than *tiny*, for example. But among the hundreds of thousands of English words, they are a very tiny (even teeny) minority. So if primitive man did create words by imitating sounds around him, the words have changed so greatly that almost all traces of the original association have disappeared. The sound of the word *dog* does not resemble one.

The other speculated sources are equally problematical: the grunts and groans of work, cries of joy and sorrow, sounds made by the tongue imitating the shape of an object. Nor does it help to study the language of the most primitive peoples in the jungles of South America or the Philippines. Such languages are as mature, as complex, as expressive for the needs of their speakers as any modern European, African, or Asian language.

Thus what we must begin with as we seek out the history of any specific language are not speculations about fancied linguistic prehistory, but the "givens," the oldest words that we can trace back to the earliest texts.

The Oldest Words in English

In English, the oldest data are the words we can find in written texts and carved monuments surviving from the Old English period (c. A.D. 450–c. 1100).

PROBLEM 3.1: While it is not easy to explain why every item among the words left to us from OE should have endured, been replaced or lost, we can make some general preliminary observations if we examine this list of words. Those starred have been completely lost from the language. The others are direct ancestors of the Modern English word found in parentheses. Why have we lost some and retained others?

> *corsnæd* (consecrated bread used as a test for truth), *dolgbot* (compensation for wounding), *wif* (wife), *fod* (food), *þoft* (bench for rowers), *scora* (a hairy garment), *stan* (stone), *þeox* (hunting spear), *winter* (winter), *eafor* (tenant obligation to king to convey goods), *god* (good), *flytme* (a blood-letting instrument), *wæter* (water), *feohfang* (the offence of bribe-taking), *broðor* (brother), *eam* (mother's brother), *hræd* (quick), *barda* (beaked ship), *corn* (corn), *blod* (blood), *hand* (hand), *grund* (ground), *land* (land), *faðe* (father's sister), *win* (wine), *heorte* (heart), *heafod* (head), *lufu* (love), *slepan* (sleep), *slæting* (hunting rights), *sittan* (sit), *æwul* (a narrow-necked basket).

A Note on Pronunciation: The letters in OE had roughly the following values. ⟨ð⟩ and ⟨θ⟩ were pronounced like ⟨th⟩ in *thing* when they occur at the beginning or end of a syllable or next to a ⟨p⟩, ⟨t⟩, ⟨c⟩, or ⟨h⟩. Otherwise they are pronounced like ⟨th⟩ in *the*. ⟨f⟩ and ⟨s⟩ were pronounced like ⟨f⟩ and ⟨s⟩ in *fit* and *sit* at the beginning or end of a syllable or next to a ⟨p⟩, ⟨t⟩, ⟨c⟩, or ⟨h⟩. Otherwise they were pronounced like ⟨v⟩ and ⟨z⟩ respectively. ⟨sc⟩ were pronounced like ⟨sh⟩ in *ship* before the letters ⟨i⟩ and ⟨e⟩, like ⟨sk⟩ in *skip* elsewhere. At the end of a word or before a consonant ⟨h⟩ had the German quality of ⟨ch⟩ in *Bach*. Before or after ⟨i⟩ or ⟨e⟩, ⟨g⟩ was like a heavily aspirated ⟨y⟩ in *yield*; before or after back vowels ⟨a⟩, ⟨o⟩, and ⟨u⟩, it was pronounced like the voiced equivalent of German ⟨ch⟩. Otherwise it was like ModE ⟨g⟩ in *grass*. ⟨g⟩ was always pronounced after ⟨n⟩, as in ModE *longer*.

OE vowels were either long or short, but since OE manuscripts did not indicate quantity by diacritical marks or spelling, we have not used length marks here. The vowels have their continental values: ⟨i⟩ as in *see* or *sit*; ⟨e⟩ as in *bate* or *bet*; ⟨æ⟩ as in *bat* or a lengthened pronunciation of *bad*; ⟨a⟩ as in *hot* or a lengthened pronunciation of *hod*; ⟨o⟩ as in *bought* or *boat*; ⟨u⟩ as in *put* or *pool*. In early OE, ⟨y⟩ was like a long or short German ⟨ü⟩, but in later OE it represented the same values as ⟨i⟩.

THE MOST DISTANT ORIGINS: INDO-EUROPEAN

If we can infer a good deal about an older culture from the words it no longer uses, we can also discover a good deal from the words it passes on. From the words in Problem 3.1 and from others, we know that those which have been preserved cover some of the most basic objects, actions, and concepts of daily life, words like *hand, food, wife, sun, house, stone, go, sing, eat, see, sleep, good, wise, cold, sharp, in, on, off, over*. These concepts are so independent of particular cultures, so basic to human life that it is almost certain we would find in all languages that words for these concepts have been passed on from generation to generation for centuries, pronounced and spelled differently, perhaps, but basically the "same" word. (3, 44, 128)

PROBLEM 3.2: Words from several languages that refer to roughly the same concepts are shown in Table 3.1. What do you conclude from the fact that in some cases, among several languages, roughly the same meaning is represented by words that are rather similar to one another, but in other cases are not? That is, *night* is rather close to Sanskrit *naktam* but very different from Japanese *ban*.

PROBLEM 3.3: Here are some words in various languages for aluminum: French: *aluminium*, Spanish: *aluminio*, Italian: *alluminio*, Dutch: *aluminium*, Danish: *aluminium*, Polish: *aluminjum*, Hungarian: *aluminium*, Turkish: *alüminyom*, Indonesian: *aluminium*, Russian: *alyumíni*, Arabic: *alaminyoum*, Japanese: *aruminyuumu*. Why are they alike?

As Problem 3.3 demonstrates, words can resemble one another from language to language because they have been **borrowed** from some common source. But when we consider the likelihood of borrowing the word for aluminum and the likelihood of borrowing words so basic and common as *snow, night, hundred*, and so on, we can also tentatively reject borrowing as an explanation of widespread similarities among **the most common words** in different languages. The more plausible explanation assumes that in each language, the words must have been inherited from some common ancestor language, and that through time, in different descendant languages, the forms of the words gradually changed.

Once we establish the principle that similar words with similar meanings (or meanings which at one time we might speculate were similar) may be descended from some common but now lost ancestor form, it becomes possible to reconstruct in very rough outline some of those earlier ancestral words. If, for example, we compare the word for *mother* in the languages we suspect are related to a single ancestor, we can create a form from which the recorded ancient and modern words for mother can be consistently derived. Compare these words: English *mother*, Dutch *moeder*, Icelandic *moðir*, Danish *moder*, Irish *máthir*, Russian *mate*, Lithuanian *motè*, Latin *māter*, Persian *mādar*, Sanskrit *mātr*. From the features these share, we could postulate as the parent form this hypothetical root: **mater*. Each letter in the root is a symbol from which we can derive by means of a set of phonological rules

TABLE 3.1   COGNATE AND NON-COGNATE WORDS

	night	snow	seven	foot	fish	heart	hundred	ten	tooth
English	night	snow	seven	foot	fish	heart	hundred	ten	tooth
German	nacht	schnee	sieben	fuss	fisch	herz	hundert	zehn	zahn
Dutch	nacht	sneeuw	zeven	voet	vis	hart	honderd	tien	tand
Swedish	natt	snö	sju	fot	fisk	hjärta	hundra	tio	tand
Latin	noctis	nivis	septem	pedis	piscis	cordis	centum	decem	dentis
French	nuit	neige	sept	pied	poisson	cœur	cent	dix	dent
Spanish	noche	nieve	siete	pie	pescado	corazón	ciento	diez	diente
Italian	notte	neve	sette	piede	pesce	cuore	cento	dieci	dente
Rumanian	noapte	zăpadă	şapte	picior	peşte	inimă	sută	zece	dinte
Greek	nuktos	nipha	hepta	podos	psari	kardiā	hekaton	deka	odontos
Polish	noc	śnieg	siedem	stopa	ryba	serce	sto	dziesięč	ząb
Czech	noc	sníh	sedm	noha	ryba	srdce	sto	deset	zub
Russian	noch	snyék	syém	nagá	riba	syértse	sto	dyésit	zup
Sanskrit	nakta	snēhaś	saptá	pāt	matsyah	hṛd-	śatám	daśa	dánt
Hungarian	éjszaka	hó	hét	láb	hal	szív	száz	tíz	fog
Finnish	yö	lumi	seitsemän	jalka	kala	sydän	sata	kymmenen	hammas
Turkish	gece	kar	yedi	ayak	balik	kalb	yüz	on	diş
Arabic	layla	galid	sabaa	qadam	samak	qalb	maah	ashara	sin
Swahili	usiku	theluji	saba	mguu	samaki	moyo	mia	kuma	jino
Japanese	ban	yuki	shichi	ashi	sakana	shin	hyaku	juu	ha
Chinese	wan	hsueh	chi	chiao	yü	hsin	pai	shih	che

the sounds of cognate words found in descendant languages. It does not necessarily represent the way the ancestor word was actually pronounced at any given moment in our linguistic prehistory, though it very likely is reasonably close to it.

Certainly, **Indo-European**, the name of the reconstructed hypothetical common ancestor language, was itself once a dialect or collection of dialects of some even more distant progenitor. Some linguists have attempted—and failed—to group them with the Hamito-Semitic languages (including Arabic, Hebrew, Aramaic, Coptic, Berber, and the North African Cushitic dialects) or the Finno-Ugric (Finnish and Hungarian). But no one has found enough evidence to confidently relate the large and scattered group of modern Indo-European languages with any other language family.

PROBLEM 3.4: We have seen that from OE words and their meanings, we can deduce something about Anglo-Saxon culture, even if we had no firsthand knowledge of England, its location, or its climate. OE words for referents like the ocean, winter, ships, deer, fish, oak trees, chalk, and so on would lead us to a Northern European location somewhere close to the sea. Numerous words for concepts in law suggest an elaborate legal code based on duty and payments. Words for mother's brother and father's brother suggest a kinship system more complex than ours and one that seems to emphasize male kinship structures.

Here are some data (some of it misleading) about words common to Indo-European languages, plus some geographical, botanical, and sociological data that will allow a rough guess about the general area of the original Indo-European homeland. (1) Sanskrit, the oldest of the IE languages with extensive extant documents (c. 1500 B.C.) was spoken in Northern India. (2) *Tobacco*, referring to a plant now found around the eastern end of the Mediterranean, is found in almost all modern IE languages. (3) Cognates for the following words or other words for their referents are found in a wide variety of IE languages: snow, freezing cold, winter, summer, spring; oak, beech, birch, willow; bear, wolf, otter, beaver, weasel, deer, rabbit, mouse, ox, horse, sheep, goat, pig, dog, snake, tortoise, ant, eagle, hawk, owl, herd, salmon, cow, udder; cheese, mead (a fermented drink containing honey); wheel, axle, door, timber, thatch, yoke, wagon, bronze, ore; seed, sow, sew, weave; father, mother, son, daughter, brother, sister, widow, woman's relatives by marriage; the numbers one through ten and the number one hundred. (4) Cognates for the following words or their referents are **not** found in a wide variety of IE languages: monkey, elephant, camel, tiger; olive, palm tree, desert, rice, bamboo, grain, furrow, wheat, mow; gold, iron, steel; ocean, sea, ship; king, man's relations by marriage such as *son-in-law*. (5) The silver birch is found in thick forest north of 45° north latitude and west of the Vistula River. The beech is indigenous east of Poland and the Ukraine and south of 60° north latitude. (6) Bees are not indigenous to most of Asia. (7) The salmon is found in northern European waters and a similar fish is found in the Caspian Sea.

(1) What can be reconstructed of the culture of those IE speakers? (2) How might we estimate the approximate age of IE from cognate words?

Exactly what happened five or six thousand years ago is, of course, impossible to reconstruct. But it is likely that for some reason, groups among the IE tribes began migrating first to the east and south, then in all directions from their original homeland. Not long after, their language, probably already more a collection of dialects than a single uniform tongue, began to change until the dialects became mutually unintelligible languages. With no written standard and with virtually no significant contact over what for their speakers must have been immensely long distances, nothing interfered with the natural tendency of every language to change. (7, 8, 23, 62, 218)

Indo-European > West European

It has been thought that IE first split into Eastern and Western branches because of the widespread correspondences of one particular sound change east and west of a line running roughly north and south at about 20° east latitude.

East of this line, the original *k- sound in IE changed to a **sibilant**, a s or sh sound. The IE root for hundred, *kmtóm, became satam in Sanskrit, šimtas in Lithuanian, suto in Old Slavic. In the Western branch, it remained k, as in Latin centum and Celtic cant, then changed to h in the Germanic languages: hundred, or to s or ch in Romance languages: cent, ciento.

PROBLEM 3.5: Does this confirm or contradict your conclusions about the IE homeland? Why?

The Eastern branch then split into two: (1) the **Balto-Slavic**, which includes Lettish, Lithuanian, and Old Prussian among the Baltic; and Bulgarian, Slovenian, Serbo-Croatian, Polish, Czech, and Russian among the Slavic; and (2) the **Indo-Iranian**, which includes modern Persian, Hindi, Bengali, and Romany—the traditional language of the Gypsies (a word adapted from Egyptian, from whence the Europeans believed them to have come).

The Western branches split into at least four more branches: **Hellenic, Italic, Celtic** and **Germanic**. Most scholars also include a dead language discovered in the early years of this century: **Tocharian**, surprisingly found in Central Asia, far to the east of the Western IE languages, which it resembles in some important ways. It was probably spoken by a group that originally belonged to the Western branch but shortly after the Centum-Satem split (as it has been called), migrated eastward. One other language, **Hittite**, evidence for which has been discovered in Turkey, is also included among the IE languages, though it is unclear exactly how it related to the two main branches.

PROBLEM 3.6: Here are a few cognates in the Western branch that do **not** appear in the Eastern.

> Comment. *corn, grain, furrow, bean, meal, mow, sea, salt, fish, elm, finch, starling, swallow.*

Of the several Hellenic dialects, Attic Greek, spoken in Athens, became the standard, a natural consequence of its being the political and cultural center of the early Western world. From the Italic descended two dead languages, Oscan and Umbrian, and Latin, from which descended French, Spanish, Italian, Portuguese, and Rumanian. Celtic split into the extinct Gallic, Gaelic (the ancestor of Manx, Scots Gaelic, and Irish Gaelic), Britannic (the ancestor of the now dead Cornish and Pictish), the dying Breton, and the mildly robust Welsh.

Indo-European > West European > Germanic > West Germanic

The most important subgrouping for our purposes is Germanic. Its earliest records go back to some fourth-century Scandinavian inscriptions and a translation (by Bishop Ulfilas [c. 311–381]) of parts of the Bible into Gothic, a now extinct East Germanic language. The largest body of early literature appears in OE after A.D. 700, and in Old Icelandic after 1100.

Germanic is conventionally divided into three branches on the basis of certain phonological and grammatical changes that occurred before about A.D. 600: (1) **East Germanic**, which includes the dead Gothic; (2) **North Germanic**, which includes two groups: (a) Icelandic, Norwegian, and Faeroese (from the Faeroesean Islands); and (b) Danish and Swedish; and finally (3) **West Germanic**. This includes Dutch, Flemish, Afrikaans, Low German, modern standard German, Yiddish, Frisian, and English.

PROBLEM 3.7: Cognates of these words are found only in the Germanic languages.

> Comment. *broth, brew, dough, knead, loaf, wheat, gold, silver, lead, tin, buy, ware, worth; borough, king, earl; book, lore, write, leech* (healing); *cliff, island, sea, sound* (as in Puget Sound), *strand* (beach); *whale, seal* (the animal); *ship, steer, sail, north, east, south, west.*

PROBLEM 3.8: (1) What is dangerous about relying on **negative** evidence in attempts to reconstruct cultures or geographical origins from linguistic data? That is, what does it prove when a number of languages known to have descended from the same ancestor language are shown **not** to share cognate words for *fish*? What does it indicate when we discover that cognate words from the root for *hand* are found **only** in Germanic languages? (2) What further problem in cultural reconstruction does the following example introduce? In Great Britain, the word *robin* denotes a red-breasted member of the warbler family. When the colonists arrived in North America, they found a red-breasted member of the thrush family. They called it *robin*.

PROBLEM 3.9: We can show how the Indo-European languages relate to one another by means of a tree, as shown in Figure 3.1. This figure is a model of

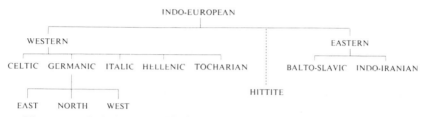

Figure 3.1. Relationship of Indo-European Languages

the historical relationships as well as the linguistic relationships. How does it lead us to think about the way one language splits into two or more languages? What problem does the following diagram and explanation introduce? (14, 171, 204)

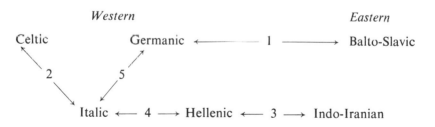

1. Both the Germanic and Balto-Slavic languages have a similar inflectional ending for instrumental plurals. Other languages have endings related to a different sound.
2. The Celtic and Italic groups have a similar passive voice inflection.
3. The Hellenic and Indo-Iranian have similar past tenses.
4. The Hellenic and Italic share a characteristic of feminine nouns with masculine suffixes.
5. The Germanic and Italic use the perfect tense as a general past tense.

From the common vocabulary, archeological remains, and the observations of Roman historians, we can sketch the outlines of pre-historic Germanic society. Because their common vocabulary included for the first time many words referring to advanced agriculture, farming must have become more important than it had been. More significantly, the ocean had also become important. It would be the Viking long-ships that would carry the Germanic warriors across the seas to raid, plunder, and conquer from Britain to France to the Mediterranean. Their social and economic organization must also have begun to develop. *King, earl,* and *borough* indicate a government and an incipient feudal society; *gold, silver, lead, tin, buy, ware,* and *worth* indicate an economic life beyond trading in kind.

They were a diverse lot, though. They included the Franks, the Goths, the Vandals, and the Lombards, all warlike enough to harass France, Spain, Rome, and Africa and give the Teutons their fierce reputation among the Roman historians. They also included the Germans, who did not wander far from Central Germany, and the Northmen (hence *Norseman,* which finally became *Norman*), who both farmed and sailed. They shared a common mythology of Odin and Thor and an epic poetry that celebrated the values of honor, loyalty to chief and kinsman in return for their generosity with gifts, and bravery and glory in battle. (103)

From certain Latin words borrowed into Germanic before the Anglo-Saxons invaded Britain in the fifth century, we know that they must have had some contact with Rome. (7, 194)

PROBLEM 3.10: From these borrowed words, speculate about the kind of contact the Germanic tribes had with Rome. The first word in the list is the original Latin word. The second is the OE adapted from Latin with a modern translation in parentheses if the word has been lost. The third is the descendant ModE word or its closest equivalent. Where the word has been lost in ModE, the symbol $\emptyset$ appears.

campum–camp (field, battle)*–$\emptyset$*
tribūtum–trifet (tribute)*–$\emptyset$*
mango–mangian (to barter with)*–monger* (as in *fishmonger*)
tolōnēum–toll–toll
pondō–pund–pound
mīlia passum (a thousand steps)*–mil–mile*
monēta–mynet (a coin)*–mint*
calcem–cealc–chalk
cuprum–copor–copper
pic- –pic–pitch (the substance)
būtyrum–butere–butter
cāseus–cese–cheese
uīnum–win–wine

mentha–minte–mint (the plant)
pīsum–pisa–pea
piper–pipor–pepper
prūnum–plume–plum
planta–plante–plant
balteus–belt–belt
soccus–socc–sock
puluinus–pyl(w)e–pillow
catillus–citel–∅ (ModE *kettle* is borrowed from Danish, which also borrowed it from Latin)
candēla–candel–candle
pīpa–pipe–pipe
benna–binn–bin
cuppa–cuppe–cup
discus disc–dish
panna–panne–pan
coquīna–cycene–kitchen
pinna–pinn–pin
gemma–gimm (gem)–∅ (ModE *gem* is borrowed from French)
līnea–line–line
uallum–weall–wall
febris–fefer–fever

Pre-Anglo-Saxon Britain

Long before these northern Germanic tribes attacked the native Britons (or Celts), the Romans had long since raided, invaded, colonized, and deserted the island. Julius Caesar (100 B.C.–44 B.C.) invaded Britain twice, failing the first time in 55 B.C.; but the next year with a larger force, he conquered the island. Though he had invaded Britain to shore up his northern flank, he was also looking for slaves and tribute. Finding neither in sufficient quantity or quality to justify his effort, he turned from Britain to his problems in Gaul, giving the island a brief period of freedom from Roman domination.

Then in A.D. 43, Claudius (10 B.C.–A.D. 54) invaded the island, and after putting down an uprising led by the Celtic Queen Boadicea, finally brought Britain into the Empire. But because Rome was unwilling to expend the men and effort to conquer the Picts in the wilds of Scotland while being harassed from the rear by the still unruly Southern Celts, its sway ended at Hadrian's Wall along the northern bank of the Tyne in the Lowlands. Thus, Roman civilization was limited to what is now known as the Midlands and the Southeast, where Romans built their walled towns and villas and connecting roads in an attempt to reproduce a sunny Mediterranean life on (what was to become after a global climatic change) a wet and cloudy distant outpost. (13, 34)

ANGLO-SAXON BRITAIN: THE BEGINNINGS

It was to be shortlived. Before the end of the fourth century A.D., Scandinavian raiders from the north had already begin to harry the British coast. Simultaneously, the Picts and Brigantes, Celtic tribes from northern Britain, were burning and looting exposed Roman villas just when Rome had to withdraw more and more troops to reinforce an uncertain empire on the continent. Finally, unable to assist any further a society now accustomed to relying on professional soldiers to defend it, the Roman legions withdrew at the beginning of the fifth century, leaving the colonists and Romanized natives to face the continental Germanic tribes alone.

The Saxons who occupied the area between the Rhine River and what is today Denmark, probably conquered the island in two stages. In the first, beginning around A.D. 449, they swept through Britain in a succession of plundering and looting raids. Beaching their longboats far up the navigable rivers, they crossed the islands to the Western Sea and back on some of the same roads the Romans had built to defend themselves with, an irony to be repeated six centuries later when the Normans would use some of the same roads in their conquest of the Anglo-Saxons.

In the second stage, beginning a few years later and lasting until late in the century, groups from what is now northern Germany, from the Rhine to Jutland, arrived to colonize, farm, and trade.

These raiders and colonists spoke West Germanic. But because no hard textual evidence remains from pre-Old English dialects, it is difficult to determine whether they spoke one dialect or several. The traditional account of the invasion is in **Historia Ecclesiastica Gentis Anglorum**, written about A.D. 731, almost 300 years after the event, by the Venerable Bede (c. 673–735).

> Then, about 449 years from our Lord's incarnation, Emperor Martianus seized the kingdom and held it for seven years. He was the 46th Emperor after the Emperor Augustus. Then the Angles and Saxons were invited by the aforementioned king [Vortigern], and came to Britain in three great ships. At the king's request, they took up dwelling in the east part of the island, so that they should fight for their own territory. And they soon battled with their enemies that often before battled them from the north and overran them. And the Saxons won the victory by fighting. Then they sent home a messenger and told them to tell of the fertility of this land and of the Britons' cowardice. And they then soon sent a great naval fleet, stronger with warriors than before. It was an invincible host when they were united. And the Britons bestowed on them a dwelling place on condition that they fight

for peace and for the welfare of their native land and strive against their enemies. And they gave them substance and property for their struggle. They came from three peoples, the boldest of Germany, from the Saxons and the Angles and the Jutes. Concerning the Jutes, in the beginning they are in Kent, and the Isle of Wight; that is, the people who dwell in the Wight Island. From the Saxons, that is from the land which people call Old Saxony, come the East Saxons, and the South Saxons and the West Saxons. And from the Anglia come the East Angles and the Middle Angles and the Mercians and all the Northumbrian people. The land between the Jutes and the Saxons is called the Angulus; it is said that from the time when they departed until today, it remains waste.

So, it was at first thought that the Jutes came from what we now call Jutland; the Angles from the Western side of the Jutish peninsula and the east bank of the Elbe; the Saxons from the Elbe to perhaps the mouth of the Rhine. More recent archeological evidence locates the Angles farther southeast and the Jutes on the coast, near the Frisian Islands off the coast of Germany and the Netherlands (see Figure 3.2).

Figure 3.2. Origins of Invaders and Raiders

Figure 3.3. Old English Dialect Areas

But then it is not entirely certain that the Jutes ever existed at all. Two other Old English commentators never even used the word *Jute*. They called all the invaders *Saxons*, or *Angles* and *Frisians*. Bede himself never used *Jute* again nor does it occur in Kent place-names. Archeological evidence, in fact, suggests that Kent was settled by a variety of groups.

Indeed, the traditional idea that whole tribes moved en masse from the Continent to Britain may be wrong. It may be that small groups moved to Britain, fanning out from southeastern England to settle the west and north. The dialect areas that existed in Anglo-Saxon England (see Figure 3.3) may not reflect patterns of settlement from the continent, but rather social changes that occurred before Bede wrote his history. Believing that distinct dialect areas must have resulted from distinct social groups, Bede may have assumed that 300 years earlier, the same social and tribal groupings had moved intact from the Continent. (37)

PROBLEM 3.11: Here is a list of some of the Celtic words borrowed into English at various periods in the history of English. What do you conclude about the overall influence of Celtic culture on the Anglo-Saxon or on later society? (57)

> **Pre-Anglo-Saxon:** *rice* (kingdom), *ambiht* (servant), *dun* (hill)
> **Post-Anglo-Saxon:** *bratt* (cloak), *bannuc* (piece of cake), *gafeluc* (small

spear), *brocc* (badger), *carr* (rock), *luh* (lake), *torr* (rocky peak), *dry* (magician), *clucge* (bell), *ancor* (anchorite), *stær* (story), *æstel* (thin board), *cine* (sheet of folded parchment).

From later periods
Irish: *shamrock, leprechaun, galore, banshee, shillelagh, blarney, colleen, keen* (wail). A few more than 40 borrowed into English.
Scottish: *clan, bog, plaid, slogan, cairn, whiskey.* A few more than 30 borrowed into English.
Welsh: *crag, penguin, gull.* A few more than 10 borrowed into English.

THE RISE OF ANGLO-SAXON ENGLAND

Whatever the sources of the dialect differences in these areas, political divisions developed to create the **Anglo-Saxon Heptarchy**, seven political spheres that often overlapped geographically: Northumbria, Mercia, East Anglia, Essex, Sussex, Wessex, and Kent. (See Figure 3.4.) The major dialect areas distinguished Northumbrian and Kentish, roughly coinciding with their

Figure 3.4. The Anglo-Saxon Heptarchy

political boundaries. But Mercian included both East Anglia and Essex, while West Saxon covered both Wessex and Sussex.

During the reign of Aethelberht (c. 552–616), Kent's political and cultural superiority eclipsed the rest of England. Its close commercial ties with the Frisian traders on the Continent are reflected in the large number of English coins found among the remains of Frisian settlements and the number of Frankish coins found in Kent. In the seventh century, Kent's cultural dominance extended northward to the Humber, perhaps reflecting its prestigious position as a link to the commercial and intellectual life on the Continent, a life which at the time was probably still superior to England's.

In the seventh and eighth centuries, cultural and political supremacy passed from Kent to Northumbria, then to Mercia, and finally to Wessex, where under Alfred (849–899), there flourished a culture that surpassed anything on the European continent since the brightest days of Rome. In fact, were it not for the West Saxon rise to power and its accompanying literary flowering, we would have relatively few texts from before the Norman invasion. Except for some laws and charters, a little verse, and a few translations of the Bible, the other OE kingdoms have left us no great number of documents.

The Christian Conversion and a National Character

The conversion of England to Christianity began during the reign of Aethelberht. In 597, St. Augustine (?–604) became the first in an army of missionaries that would Christianize Kent in just seven years. And after contesting with Celtic Christianity (the Celts having already been converted by the Romans), they would win over Northumbria in 664. By 700 England could be called a moderately Christian nation.

But Christianity did more to England than institute a new religion that encouraged new values. It re-introduced Latin and created monastic environments in which learning and scholarship flourished so richly that Europe was soon sending its students to Canterbury, Jarrow, and York. From the eighth to the eleventh century, southern England was one of the most advanced intellectual communities in the western world.

During this period, England also began to develop a national character. From the eighth through the tenth centuries, Old English poetry flowered. It was during this time that the great poems of mixed Christian and Nordic themes were composed: **Beowulf**, **The Wanderer**, **The Seafarer**, the Caedmonian and Cynewulfian poems. The efficient administration of a large institution, the church, provided a model for the secular kings in their attempts to complement Rome's spiritual dominion of England with their worldly one. The organization of townships was roughly coterminous with parishes, each ruled spiritually by a priest who at first was often the chaplain to the local thegn (chieftain). The marriage of religious laws and secular enforcement created a governing institution of potentially great power and wealth. (2, 206, 223)

PROBLEM 3.12: In Problem 3.10 were listed some words borrowed from Latin during the Germanic continental period, before the invasion of Britain. Had we listed them all and divided them into semantic categories, the proportions would have been very roughly as follows:

Plants and animals: 30%
Food, vessels, household items: 20%
Buildings, settlements: 12%
Dress: 12%
Military, legal: 9% ·
Trade, commerce: 9%
Religious, scholarly: 3%
Miscellaneous: 5%

Altogether, about 170 words were borrowed during this pre-OE period. Below are listed a **weighted** sampling of OE words adopted from Latin during the next two periods: 400–650, and 650 to the end of the OE period.

400–650
prafost (provost), *ceaster* (town), *cugle* (cowl), *mentel* (cloak), *cist* (chest), *pægel* (pail), *pott* (pot), *munuc* (monk), *traht* (text), *catt* (cat), *truht* (trout), *peru* (pear), *glædene* (gladiola), *leahtric* (lettuce), *æbs* (fir tree), *senep* (mustard), *laser* (tare, a kind of weed).

650–1000
milite (soldiers), *centur* (centurion), *yndse* (ounce), *fenester* (window), *cluster* (cloister), *purs* (purse), *cæppe* (cope), *coc* (cook), *scutel* (dish), *rabbian* (to rage), *scrofel* (scrofula), *creda* (creed), *discipul* (disciple), *mæsse* (church mass), *papa* (pope), *ælmesse* (alms), *eretic* (heretic), *martir* (martyr), *organ* (song), *son* (musical sound), *scol* (school), *philosoph* (philosopher), *cometa* (comet), *bises* (leap year day), *biblioðece* (library), *palm* (palm), *balsam* (balsam), *caric* (dried fig), *lilie* (lily), *peonie* (peony), *ysope* (hyssop), *cancer* (cancer), *loppestre* (locust), *tiger* (tiger), *fenix* (phoenix), *camel* (camel).

What can you conclude about the nature of Latin–OE contacts? (7, 194)

PROBLEM 3.13: Just as we can discover something about a culture from the words it has lost, so can we tell something from the words it often uses. Here is a sampling of words that occurred very frequently in OE compounds, words made up out of two parts to express an idea no single word can, words in Old English like *boccræft* (literally book-craft, or literature), *folclagu* (folk-law, or law of the people), *widsæ* (wide-sea, or ocean). What might you very tentatively speculate about a culture that used words like these fairly often?

1. *sumor* (summer), *winter* (winter), *tid* (time), *corn* (corn), *lyft* (air), *niht* (night), *wudu* (wood), *wyrm* (dragon), *blod* (blood).

2. *gold* (gold), *isen* (iron), *burg* (dwelling), *ham* (home), *sele* (hall), *medu* (mead), *hring* (ring), *win* (wine), *lar* (learning), *leod* (song, poem), *word* (word), *boc* (book), *gielp* (boast, fame, pride), *hord* (treasure), *ceap* (price, sale).

3. *wif* (woman), *wer* (man), *þeow* (servant), *þeod* (people, nation), *broðor* (brother), *ceorl* (peasant), *cyning* (king), *hlaford* (lord), *þegn* (retainer).

4. *hell* (hell), *heofan* (heaven), *cirice* (church), *crist* (Christ), *deofol* (devil).

5. *woh* (error, iniquity), *teona* (injury), *tæl* (blame), *syn* (sin), *sar* (sorrow, pain), *nið* (strife, spite), *morðor* (murder), *man* (evil deed), *bealu* (harm), *cwealm* (death), *deað* (death), *dwola* (error, heresy).

6. *eaðe* (easy), *wynn* (joy), *gliw* (pleasure, sport).

7. *æsc* (spear), *beadu* (battle), *bord* (shield), *camp* (battle), *here* (army), *dryht* (army, people), *wæpon* (weapon), *guð* (war).

8. *sæ* (sea), *scip* (ship), *wæter* (water), *yð* (wave).

9. *lof* (praise), *sige* (victory), *wuldor* (glory, honor).

10. *gast* (soul), *hyge* (mind), *mod* (mind).

11. *(un)riht* (right/wrong), *soð* (truth), *eald* (old), *eard* (native place).

PROBLEM 3.14: What might you guess about a culture that has a kinship system with the following terms? Compare it with Modern English. (Review Problem 2.13.)

> *fæder* (father), *modor* (mother), *sunu* (son), *dohtor* (daughter), *broðor* (brother), *sweostor* (sister), *fædera* (paternal uncle), *eam* (maternal uncle), *faðe* (paternal aunt), *modrige* (maternal aunt), *suhterga* (brother's son), *swigra* (sister's son), *fæderencnosl* (father's kin), *modorcynn* (maternal descent), *wæpnedhand* (male line), *wifhand* (female line).

The Danish Invasions

But as the West Saxons in particular were creating their cultural golden age, their kin from Denmark, more comfortable in their dragon ships than the now-landed Saxons, began in the late eighth century to find easy targets among the rich monasteries along the eastern and southern English coast. Finding how defenseless Northumbria and East Anglia were, they escalated their raids to a full scale invasion from 850 to 878. By the time the Danes had overrun, occupied, and begun to colonize large portions of eastern England, only Wessex was able to resist them successfully.

Figure 3.5. The Danelaw

In 878, King Alfred finally defeated the Danes in the Battle of Ethandun. In the subsequent Treaty of Wedmore, the Danes agreed to remain east of a line running roughly from north of Chester to London, an area called **Danelaw** (see Figure 3.5), in which the Danes were free to live as Danes under Danish law. (A second Danelaw, which, if anything, would prove to be even more significant to the future of England, was established in the Frankish Kingdom on the continent directly across from England. It was called, after the Northmen or Normans, *Normandy.*)

Having united at least half of England, Alfred, as noted above, set about creating almost single handedly a prose tradition by his various translations from Latin into Old English, both by his own hand and at his direction by others, by his initiation of the **Anglo-Saxon Chronicles**, and by the importation of European scholars and books. He also founded the first public schools, creating a literate audience for the literature as well as an educated class able to administer the growing bureaucracy of a growing state.

In fact, Alfred organized Anglo-Saxon government so well that the Danes in their Danelaw, who were less well organized than the English, were finally unable to withstand the unified political and military attacks by Alfred's son, Edward the Elder (c. 870–924), and his son, Athelstan (c. 895–940). In 957, Edward's grandson, Edgar (944–975) became ruler over Northumbria and Mercia. And in 959, upon his brother Eadwig's death, he became king of

Wessex as well, ruling an England that extended from the Tyne south and west to the Welsh mountains, roughly the England we know today. Here are two samples of OE literature with literal translations.

The first excerpt is from The Venerable Bede's story of Caedmon, a cowherd at a Yorkshire monastery who in a dream was given the divine gift of creating religious songs. Below are the opening lines of that story. The second is from the "Battle of Brunanburg," a poem included in the **Anglo-Saxon Chronicle** from the year 937. It narrates a victory of the Anglo-Saxons over the Scots and Danes. (The text has been normalized somewhat to make spelling more regular.)

In ðeosse abbudissan mynstre   wæs   sum   broðor syndriglice mid
In this   abbess's   monastery was a (certain) brother especially   with

godcundre gife gemæred ond geweorðad, for þon he gewunade
heavenly   gift famed   and blessed,   for   he accustomed (was)

gerisenlice leoð wyrcan, þa ðe   to æfæstnisse ond to arfæstnisse
appropriate songs (to) make, which to piety   and to virtue

belumpen; swa ðætte swa hwæt swa   he of godcundum stafum þurh
pertained; so that   what(ever) he of heavenly   letters through

boceras geleornode, þæt he æfter medmiclum fæce in scopgereorde
scholars learned   that he after moderate   time in poet's language

mid þa mæstan swetnisse ond inbryrdnisse geglengde, ond in
with the most   sweetness and humility   adorned,   and in

Engliscgereorde wel geworht forþ brohte. Ond for his leoþsongum
English-language well worked   forth brought. And for his poemsongs

monigra monna   mod oft   to worulde forhogdnisse ond to
many   (of) men's minds often to world   contempt   and to

geþeodnisse   þæs heofonlican lifes onbærnde wæron.
association (of) the heavenly   life inspired   were.

Her Æþelstan cyning, / eorla drihten	Here, Athelstan king, earls' lord
beorna beahgifa, / and his broðor eac,	warriors' ringgiver and his brother also,
Eadmund æðeling, / ealdorlangne tir	Edmund nobleman, lifelong glory
geslogon æt sæcce / sweorda ecgum	won at battle (with) swords' edges
ymbe Brunanburh; / bordweall clufon,	around Brunanburg; shieldwall clove,
heowon heaðolinde / hamora lafum,	hewed warlinden (with) hammers' leavings
eaforan Eadweardes; / swa him geæðele wæs	sons Edward's; so (to) him noble was
fram cneomagum, / þæt hi æt campe oft	from ancestors that they at battle often
wið laðra gehwone / land ealgodon,	against foes any land protected
hord and hamas. / Hettend crungon,	treasure and home. Army died,
Scotta leode / and scipflotan,	Scottish people and sailors,
fæge feollon; / feld dennode	doomed fell; field streamed
secga swate, / siþþan sunne upp	(with) warriors' sweat since sun up

on morgentid, / mære tungol,	on morningtime, famous star,
glad ofer grundas, / Godes candel beorht,	glided over grounds, God's candle bright,
eces Drihtnes, / oð sio æðele gesceaft	eternal Lord, until the noble creation
sah to setle. / Þær læg secg monig	sank to seat. There lay warrior many
garum forgrundan, / guma Norðerna	(by) spears killed, men Northerners'
ofer scyld scoten, / swylce Scyttisc eac	over shield shot, so Scot also
werig wiges sæd.	weary (of) battle sated.

Here, King Athelstan, lord of earls, ring-giver of warriors, and also his brother, Edmund the nobleman, won lifelong glory in battle with their swords around Brunanburg. The sons of Edward clove shieldwalls, hewed linden-shields with the leavings of the hammer (swords). It was natural from their noble ancestry that they in battle often protected any land, treasure, and home against any foes. The army fell, Scottish people and sailors fell doomed. The field streamed with the blood of warriors from the time the sun rose up in the morning, that famous star, the bright candle of God, the Eternal Lord, glided over the land, until the noble creation set. There lay many a warrior, killed with spears, Norseman shot over their shields, Scots too, weary and sated with battle.

PROBLEM 3.15: You have already seen two foreign influences on English, Latin and Celtic. Here are some Danish words that were borrowed into English. (Some of them have been subsequently lost.) (1) What kind of contact did the Danes and Anglo-Saxons have?

Before A.D. 1000

barda (beaked ship), *cnearr* (small warship), *liþ* (fleet), *ha* (oarlock), *orrest* (battle), *ran* (rapine), *mal* (action at law), *hold* (freeholder), *wapentake* (an administrative district), *husting* (assembly).

After 1000

Nouns: *band, booth, bull, dirt, down* (feathers), *egg, fellow, freckle, kneel, kid, leg, link, reindeer, reef* (of sail), *scab, scales, scrap, seat, sister, skin, skirt, sky, snare, steak, swain, window; birch, boon, gait, gap, guess, loan, race, rift, score, skill, slaughter, stack, thrift, tidings, trust, want, gift.*

Verbs: *call, crawl, die, get, give, lift, raise, rid, scare, take, cast, clip, crave, droop, flit, gape, kindle, nag, scowl, snub, sprint, thrust.*

Adjectives: *flat, loose, low, odd, tight, weak, awkward, ill, meek, seemly, sly, rotten, tattered, muggy.*

Pronouns and other words: *they, their, them, both, same, though, till.*

(2) In the **Oxford Universal Dictionary**, there are approximately 30 or so words beginning with *sk-/sc-* of Danish origin still in our active vocabulary. In the **English Dialect Dictionary**, there are over a thousand simple words

beginning with *sc-/sk-*. What do you conclude about the durability of borrowings in non-standard dialects? What dialect area would you guess they are from? (3) Is the part of speech significant in the borrowings listed above? Why? (11) (4) Review the borrowings from Latin and Celtic. What difference is there in the tone of words like *droop, scare, nag, muggy,* and *freckle* on the one hand and, on the other, words in Problems 3.10 and 3.12?

When the Danes were forcibly brought into a not very solidly united England, it did more than begin the political unification of the land. While surpassed by few in their military zeal, the Danes were equally skilled in commercial affairs and in honing their legal points to a fine edge in their **Thing**, or meeting of elders. Earlier, in Anglo-Saxon England, a violation of the law was often followed by a blood-feud. The strong sense of Danish legality combined with the increasingly strong English local government made crime less a private question of one individual compensating the kin of an injured party with a fine called *wergild* than something to be dealt with by those who spoke in the name of the local thegn, the king, and God.

Real, immediate, practical political power, though, was still exercised by the local thegn and priest. The thegn supplied land in return for his people's labor and its fruits, protected them, and dispensed justice. In this system lay the seeds which would grow into a social structure powerful enough to shape the English social system for hundreds of years after the Norman invasion. The ploughman ploughed and the thegn governed and fought. And if this meant a more stable and productive society for everyone, it also meant less freedom for those who pushed their ploughs.

Because the power of the throne was not yet strong enough to reach down to the individual thegn and churl, it could not enforce a single standard of justice. Long after the putative unification of the kingdom, the Danelaw continued to exercise a considerable degree of independence in its own affairs. As a consequence, England was still divided in spirit when new Danish raids broke out, particularly during the reign of Ethelred the Redeless (c. 968–1016), a rather incompetent ruler. Since the union between the peoples was not an easy one, the Danes did little to resist the raids against Wessex, an area outside their Danelaw.

After Ethelred's death, Saxon and Danish England engaged in a brief civil war before Cnute (c. 994–1035), a Dane, defeated Wessex in 1015. He and Edmund Ironside (c. 980–1016), Ethelred's son, briefly divided the island between them, and when Edmund died in 1016, Cnute became the king of the entire kingdom. As it turned out, not only did Cnute rule wisely, but his accession to power opened southern England, particularly London, to Danish businessmen and traders, making London an even more powerful and cosmopolitan city than it already was. (223)

PROBLEM 3.16: Words borrowed from the Danes do not begin to occur frequently in English texts until the Middle English period. What might be one explanation for this?

The Rise of London

Because London figures so centrally in the development of a standard English, we have to account for its unique position in English history. Although some sort of settlement undoubtedly existed on the Thames before the Romans arrived, it was during Roman times that London began to develop into the first city of the country. The spot on which London sits was the only piece of hard ground on the northern side of the Thames that afforded a solid bridgehead for roads coming from the Kentish towns and a suitable landing place for ships coming up from the English Channel. Because half the roads built also converged on London Bridge, London was long destined to be the future commercial center of England.

Under the Saxons of Mercia, London declined somewhat in prestige since commerce with the continent was not as great as during the Roman occupation or Kent's ascendancy. But though of little relative importance, London maintained a measure of independence from both Mercia and Kent, and when Alfred settled with the Danes in 878, he managed to exclude London from the Danelaw, thereby preserving its Saxon character. Because it was the main entry to the heartland of England, he fortified it and encouraged its growth in order to defend it from the Danes. Then when Cnute assumed the throne in 1016, Danish merchants became some of the leading tradesmen and citizens.

Before the end of the eleventh century, London had become the most important commercial city in England, populated by a variegated and sophisticated people, many from continental Europe. Always more powerful than her official status would suggest, London finally regained the status it had held in Roman times. By 1066, her population stood at perhaps 14,000— several thousand more than the next largest city, Winchester, and perhaps 6000 more than the estimated 8000 population of York.

After the Norman Conquest in 1066, William the Conqueror was crowned near London in Westminster. But when he built a residence, he moved from inside the walls of the City closer to his new Cathedral at Westminster, two miles away. In this single action, he made the few miles encompassing Westminster and London the political, commercial, and cultural center of the land. At the same time, by living outside the walls of London, he helped preserve its independent political, cultural, and economic spirit.

London's later political and cultural strength eventually resulted in its dialect becoming the prestige dialect of the land. While Alfred and his descendants made their court in the South, West Saxon was the dialect of

English in which the major literature and law was written. When the Norman Conquest ended Wessex's ascendancy and reduced the flow of literature written in English to a trickle, the only **prestige** dialect among the upper class was Norman French. When English began to re-assert itself three centuries later, it would be the dialect of London, of the East Midlands, that would eventually become the national standard.

This raises a difficulty in studying the history of English because West Saxon, the earlier prestige dialect, and Mercian, the OE dialect that would father East Midland, were different in some important ways. When we study OE, we study West Saxon, because that dialect was used in the great preponderance of OE texts. But standard ModE stems not, ultimately, from West Saxon but from East Midland speech.

Chapter 4

FROM MIDDLE ENGLISH TO MODERN ENGLISH

THE NORMAN CONQUEST

After the migration of the Anglo-Saxons in the fifth century from the Continent to Britain, the Norman Conquest was the single most significant event in the external history of the English language. The Danes added many words to the vocabulary and a very few grammatical changes, but because Danish was somewhat like OE to begin with, its impact could not have been as influential as Norman French. The Norman Conquest has led to a language that is qualitatively different from what it was before 1066.

The groundwork for Norman dominion began long before 1066. During Cnute's rule, Edward the Confessor (c. 1002–66), son of Ethelred and Emma, daughter of a former Duke of Normandy, returned from a long exile in Normandy, strongly influenced by the Norman clergy and more interested in being a monk than a king. In fact, when he assumed the throne in 1042 he probably spoke better French than English. Because of his background, he appointed Normans to high positions in the English clergy and government, and by allowing Normans access to London, he introduced them into English commercial life. Moreover, he made no attempt to unify the island, strengthen its defenses, or redress the growing imbalance of power exercised by a few earls jealous of one another's power.

When Edward died in January of 1066, a seriously divided and weakened England faced the additional problems brought about by his fidelity to his monkish vow of chastity. He left no direct heir. There were, however, two possible oblique heirs. One was Edgar Atheling (c. 1050–c. 1125), considered by most to be at 16, too young to assume the throne. The other was Harold II (1022–66), a more distant relation but one with the blood of King Olaf of Sweden. He was finally chosen by the **Witan** (the king's council) to be king.

Then only eight months later, England found herself once again attacked by Scandinavians: by Harold Haardraada, King of Norway, and by William (1027–87), Duke of Normandy, who believed he had the only legitimate claim to the throne. In 1051, Edward had promised him the crown and in 1064, William had made Harold II promise that he would help him, William, gain the throne.

On September 25, 1066, at Stamford Bridge, Harold II defeated a force led by Harold Haardraada of Norway. But four days later William landed at Pevensey. On October 14 at Senlac, about nine miles from Hastings, the English and Normans fought until nightfall. The Normans drew the English from their impregnable position with a pretended flight and defeated them. An arrow through the eye felled Harold. Thus England became a part of the Latin-influenced rather than Scandinavian-influenced life of Europe. In a few years, through persuasion and massacre, William largely erased the old political distinctions between the Danelaw and the South. England was, though brutally oppressed, at last politically united under one sovereign king.

William simultaneously deprived the English earls of their power by breaking up the last vestiges of the traditional mini-kingdoms of Mercia, Wessex, and the others, and replacing them with a system of shires and baronies with his own local officials, all Norman. As might be expected, William also replaced the English nobility with Norman barons and the native church establishment with his own Norman clergy. By 1076, not a single English earl remained. Only three of 21 abbots were English.

Under William, incipient feudalism became a harsh social reality. The half-free Danish freemen in their Danelaw lost much of their freedom to choose which lord to follow or in some cases, even to have no lord at all. For now both freemen and serfs had to serve some lord.

THE LINGUISTIC CONSEQUENCES

In retrospect, the linguistic consequences of this invasion and colonization are easy enough to recognize. Although certain grammatical and phonological changes may be attributed to the Norman Conquest, it is in vocabulary and semantics that the changes have been the greatest. The enormous influx in ME of not only French but also Latin words certainly would never have occurred without the Conquest. But if the effects are easy to discern, the precise social milieu in which they occurred, the specific reasons for their occurrence, are less easy to reconstruct.

PROBLEM 4.1 : This problem will require cooperative effort. (1) Select three or four different kinds of twentieth-century prose texts: scholarly, popular, technical, comic books, etc. Be certain to get a contrast. In a 250-word sample of each kind, tabulate the percentage of native to French/Latin to all other words. Simplify the task by counting as native words all prepositions, articles, pronouns, auxiliaries (*may*, *must*, *be*, *have*, etc.) without looking each one up. Would the percentages change if **just** nouns, verbs (excluding *be*), adjectives and adverbs were counted? How would your conclusions differ? (2) Select three dictionaries: a very short, paperbound one; a larger standard desk-size one; and a larger reference dictionary such as **Webster's Third** or **The Random House Dictionary of the English Language**. Compute the percentages of native English words to French-Latin and all others under 50 randomly chosen words for each of six or seven letters. What is wrong with this method? What variables make the problem more complex than meets the eye? (3) What are the significant differences among the kinds of texts in question 1? What are the significant differences among the kinds of dictionaries? What are the significant differences between these two ways of counting percentages of word sources? How do you account for these differences? What would have happened if you had counted the words under V? The words under A? under K?

PROBLEM 4.2: If we group the vocabulary into the first most frequent thousand words, second most frequent thousand, third most frequent thousand, and so on, then compute the percentage of native versus borrowed words in each of these groups of a thousand, we find figures such as these:

Decile	English	French	Latin	Danish	Other
1	83%	11%	2%	2%	2%
2	34	46	11	2	7
3	29	46	14	1	10
4	27	45	17	1	10
5	27	47	17	1	8
6	27	42	19	2	10
7	23	45	17	2	13
8	26	41	18	2	13
9	25	41	17	2	15
10	25	42	18	1	14

(The "other" group includes mostly mixed or doubtful words, or words that only might be assigned to English, French, or Latin words. Only Dutch among "others" exceeds 1 percent in any of the deciles). When all the words in running text are put into one group, the percentages are as follows: English: 78.1; French: 15.2; Latin: 3.1; Danish: 2.4; other (Greek, Dutch, Italian, Spanish, German, etc.): 1.3. Comment. These data were compiled from several thousand business letters. (181) Comment.

Here, in considerable detail, are sets of demographic statistics, social anecdotes, facts about official documents, and so on that may be relevant to understanding how French and English were used at various levels of English society. Some historians have claimed that French virtually ousted English at all levels, or at least that almost all Englishmen were bi-lingual. Others have claimed that only a thin layer of the nobility habitually used French and that the vast majority of English were effectively monolingual.

As a background, here are some sketchy over-generalizations about Norman society: Ruling all were the king and his court. Below him were his barons, and below them were "enfeoffed" knights who were granted the right to land by the king through his barons in return for service to them. Under the knights were a middle-management layer of officials: reeves, bailiffs, stewards, and so on who ran the estates and local affairs. Below them were the great mass of Englishmen and some Norman peasants: the churls, the villeins, the laborers.

In the towns or boroughs, the great mass of citizens were skilled and unskilled laborers. Above them were the tradesmen and businessmen. A third less statistically significant element of the population was the clergy.

Some axioms:

1. When social order is fluid, upwardly mobile lower classes are more likely to behave in ways they believe upper middle classes behave than when the society is rigid.
2. Social order becomes more fluid during periods of social upheaval.
3. In areas of high population density, contact between social classes is greater than when they are thinly distributed.
4. Contemporary observers of a social scene are more likely to comment on the unusual than the usual.

The initial numbers in the data below refer to century and decade. Following each set are Problems based on the data.

Economic-demographic Estimates

11.7   In 1066, the English population stands between 1.1 and 1.7 million, the great majority south of a line running from Bristol to The Wash, the deep inlet of the North Sea between Norfolk and Lincoln. The Norman invasion force is estimated at between 5000 and 12,000 men. After the Conquest, when land is distributed to Norman knights, there are about 5000 Norman knights enfeoffed (granted land) out of 10,000 smaller landlords. The other 5000 are presumably English.

11.9   On the basis of the Domesday survey in 1086, a kind of census and economic survey ordered by William for tax purposes, the English and Norman population is still estimated at between 1.1 and 1.7 million by modern scholars. They are distributed roughly as follows: Rural, at least 85 percent; vaguely or certainly urban, no more than 15 percent, probably less. Among these is the clergy at about .5 percent. The population of London is about 14,000. The other large towns constituting a large part of the urban population are Winchester, Lincoln, Norwich, Gloucester, York, and Canterbury. The East Midlands, the area north of London, is the most densely settled part of England and the least ravaged by the Invasion and its aftermath. The north is the least populated. The heaviest concentration of Norman population is probably in the commercial towns along the southern and eastern coast, though a great many settle inland.

13.1   In the twelfth and thirteenth centuries, the East Midlands grows rich exporting corn and wool.

13.6   The richest cities in England are London, Lincoln, Winchester, Canterbury, Worcester, Oxford, York, Northampton, and Norwich.

13.10 Before the end of the thirteenth century, the earlier immigration from the south and southeast shires ends. Before 1300, 38 aldermen and 18 sheriffs in London can be identified as coming from southern counties. The East Midlands contributes 10 aldermen and 7 sheriffs.

14.1   In 1300, the London population is still about 14,000.

14.5   In 1348, just before the Black Death, the total population of England is between 3.1 and 3.7 million. Before the century is out, the Black Death will eventually kill 30 to 40 percent of the English population.

14.5   In 1349, 47 monks who die of the Black Death in one monastery are replaced by uneducated Englishmen. Large numbers of uneducated men whose wives have died of the plague turn to holy orders.

14.7   In the first half of the fourteenth century, emigration from the East Midlands and the North into London increases. Between 1300 and 1365, southern immigrants contribute 32 aldermen and 7 sheriffs. The East Midlands contributes 33 aldermen and 10 sheriffs. Northern areas contribute 5 aldermen and 2 sheriffs before 1300. 10 aldermen and 2 sheriffs between 1300 and 1365.

14.8　By 1375, after more plague, the English population stands at about 2,250,000.

15.1　By 1400, the population of England falls to about 2.1 million. The heaviest mortality has been among the very young and the old, particularly in the crowded monasteries.

PROBLEM 4.3: If we had only these data and no linguistic evidence whatsoever, what predictions might we make about the prestige of Norman French, its general influence across the entire island; what area of the country would become socially most prestigious, including its dialect?

Political Events

11.7　In 1066, William invades and conquers England.

11.8　In 1075, 13 of 21 bishops signing the decrees of the Council of London are English. By 1087 only three are.

11.9　In 1086, there are 190 barons, all Normans. No English earls survive the suppression of the English nobility.

11.9　In 1087, William I dies; William II becomes king.

12.1　In 1100, William II dies; Henry I becomes King.

12.4　In 1135, Stephen succeeds Henry I.

12.6　In 1154, Henry II succeeds Stephen.

12.9　In 1189, Richard I succeeds Henry II.

12.10　In 1193, London becomes the first town to have its own mayor.

12.10　In 1199, John succeeds Richard I.

13.1　In 1204–05, Philip of France, whose court is in Paris, seizes the Norman estates of several powerful Anglo-Norman barons plus all the French lands of knights who live in England. Anglo-Normans must now choose whether to become Englishmen or Frenchmen. King John is left with possessions only in the south of France.

13.2　In 1215, King John gives Londoners the right to elect their mayor.

13.2　In 1215, King John assents to the Magna Carta.

13.2　In 1216, Henry III succeeds John.

13.4　In 1233, because of his close connections with the south of France, Henry III dismisses the native officers of his court and replaces them with French from Poitou. Two thousand French knights and soldiers from southern France are placed in charge of castles and lands, oppressing natural English-Norman subjects and noblemen.

13.4　In 1236, when Henry III marries Eleanor of Provence, a new influx of southern French arrive in England to be given more power and lands.

13.5　In c. 1246, a third influx of southern French occurs when Henry III's mother dies. Having married a southern Frenchman on the death of

John and borne him several sons, she leaves Henry with half brothers and their daughters to provide with lands.

13.6   The Barons Wars from 1258–65 sets native English against French usurpers in England; the latter are finally driven from the island.

13.8   In 1272, Edward I succeeds Henry III.

14.1   In 1307, Edward II succeeds Edward I.

14.3   In 1337, Edward III succeeds Edward II.

14.4   In 1337, the Hundred Years' War with France begins.

14.5   In 1346, the English gain a great patriotic victory over French at Crécy.

14.6   In 1356, English patriotism is aroused again with a victory at Poitiers.

14.8   In 1377, Richard II succeeds Edward III.

14.9   In 1381, many peasants refuse to remain tied to their feudal Lords any longer when they can sell their labor at higher prices. The Peasants' Revolt occurs.

14.10   In 1399, Henry IV succeeds Richard II.

15.2   In 1413, Henry V succeeds Henry IV.

15.2   In 1415, English gain another great patriotic victory at Agincourt.

15.3   In 1422, Henry VI succeeds Henry V.

PROBLEM 4.4: (1) Which political events would probably have had an impact on the use of French in England? (2) Are the consequences of any of the political events reinforced by demographic events, or vice versa?

Written English, French, and Latin in Official Texts and Legal Documents

(Note: All "firsts" should be understood to mean "earliest known.")

11.8   In 1070, William issues writs in English, some in Latin, none in Norman French.

11.9   After 1080, writs in English virtually disappear. William has laws written in Latin.

12   Throughout the twelfth century, Old English laws are ordinarily translated into Latin.

12.1   Until 1109, the **Annales Anglo-Saxonici Breves**, compiled at Canterbury, are written in English, thereafter in Latin.

12.5   An Anglo-Norman charter appears, the first known in the language of the Normans.

12.6   First laws written originally in Norman French dated 1150 or a bit earlier.

12.6   In 1154, the **Peterborough Anglo-Saxon Chronicle**, the only native language chronicle that had been maintained, lapses.

12.9   Only a few charters and other documents appear in English until the reign of Richard I (1189). Latin is by far the more common language.

13.2 The earliest extant deed written in Norman French dates from 1215.

13.4 A Royal Charter in 1233 says that English law terms have been translated into French so that "everyone will understand."

13.6 In 1258, the first Letters Patent, official documents, appear in French. Previously, they were in Latin.

13.6 In 1258, a group of barons and upper-class Englishmen win from Henry III the Provisions of Oxford, guaranteeing certain rights to the barons. It is set forth in French and English—the first such public document in English in almost 200 years.

13.8 Before Edward I, most petitions and bills to Parliament are in Latin, after that time in French. First Parliamentary writ in French in 1274–75; first petition to Parliament in French in 1278.

13.8 From 1275, laws are normally drawn up first in French.

13.9 By the close of the century, French is used in most official documents. But petitions to Parliament in French are translated into Latin so that "all may understand."

13.10 In 1299, an order regarding the use of the forest is published in English.

14.1 In the closing years of Edward I's reign, French first appears in Privy Seal documents, official documents of less than major significance.

14.1 Throughout fourteenth century, it is common for deeds, bills of sale, contracts, and so on, to be written in French.

14.5 Before the middle of fourteenth century, most petitions and bills to Parliament are in French. The earliest petition (to the chancellor) in English appears in 1344.

14.5 In 1345, the Pepperers Guild of London uses English in their guild records for the first time, the first guild to do so.

14.6 First wills begin to appear in French.

14.8 Earliest deeds written in Middle English appear near the end of Edward III's reign.

14.8 In 1376, first private legal instrument written in Middle English appears.

14.9 In 1383, first will written in Middle English is filed.

14.9 In 1386, the London Mercers Guild sends Parliament first petition written in Middle English.

14.9 In 1388, in answer to Parliament's request for information, the English guilds respond mostly in Latin, but more responses are in English than in French.

14.9 Between 1369 and 1384, French deeds registered on Close Rolls, official records for private transactions, average about 29 a year.

15.1 During reign of Henry IV, English begins to supplant French in royal documents.

15.1   In 1404, English write to French government in Latin and ask them to reply in same.

15.2   The last official Letters Patent are written in French during reign of Henry V.

15.2   Between 1403 and 1418, French deeds on Close Rolls average four a year.

15.2   In 1413, Henry IV dies, leaving first will of a monarch written in English.

15.3   In 1422, first Privy Seal document in English appears.

15.3   In 1422, London Brewer's Guild, praising the English language, begins to keep records in English.

15.3   Until 1423, most petitions to Parliament are written in French; after this date, they are frequently in English.

15.4   Last will in French registered in Close Rolls appears in 1431.

15.4   Between 1419 and 1434, French deeds registered in Close Rolls average one a year; none after 1434.

15.4   About 1430, several towns and guilds begin translating their official documents from French into English.

15.4   In 1437, French is discontinued for use in Great Seal documents, documents of the greatest national importance.

15.5   Between 1433 and 1443, Parliamentary petitions in French decline markedly, none occurring in French after 1444.

15.6   One of the last legal instruments in French is dated around 1450.

15.6   By about 1450, most records of towns and guilds are in English.

15.6   By the middle of the fifteenth century, Parliament needs a Secretary in the French language.

15.9   In 1485, English occurs with French in Statutes of Parliament.

15.9   By 1489, French disappears entirely from Statutes of Parliament.

15.10   By the end of fifteenth century, French is used only in law cases—English in almost all other kinds of documents (except for Latin scholarship and ecclesiastical records).

18.4   In 1731, records of lawsuits are regularly written down in English.

PROBLEM 4.5: (1) Which of these events reflect political events? (2) Plot the shift from OE to Latin to French to English in official documents. (3) Even from this very sketchy data, can you determine the crucial periods?

Written English, French, and Latin in Social Communication and Literature

12   Early twelfth-century translators say they translate from Latin into French so that "the common man" will understand.

c. 12.5 A Latin vocabulary is produced with words glossed only in French.

12–13   Much literature is written in French for literate Englishmen in the twelfth and thirteenth centuries, relatively little in English.

12.8 Beginning about 1175 and continuing through the middle of the thirteenth century, many passages in works written in French for Englishmen suggest they are written in French so that "all" can understand.

12.10 **The Owl and the Nightingale**, one of the best debate poems in ME, appears.

13.1 Layamon's **Brut** is written, one of the first romances in ME.

13.1 The Chancellor under Richard I is charged with having flattering songs written about himself to be sung in the streets of London by minstrels and singers from France.

13 Phrase books for teaching French to Englishmen for business purposes begin to appear.

13.1 Three young upper-class women are advised to do their reading in either French or English.

13.2 The earliest extant letter in Anglo-French in Middle English period dates from 1215.

13.3 A Latin vocabulary is produced glossed in both French and English.

13.5 Beginning around 1245, many statements appear in Norman French works written in England decrying the decay of the Norman French language.

13.6 In 1250, a short treatise in Latin appears, explaining the French verb.

13.7 After the middle of the thirteenth century, English literature begins to revive. **Havelok the Dane**, one of the earliest romances about an English subject, appears.

13.8 About the end of the thirteenth century, educated writers begin to apologize for their "false French," i.e., incorrect French. Mistakes in grammar and awkwardness in style begins to appear.

13.9 In the last quarter of the thirteenth century, most private letters to and from the nobility are in French, the rest in Latin.

13.10 An admirer congratulates Giraldus Cambrensis on his writings, but regrets that Cambrensis did not write in French instead of Latin, for he then would have been more widely read.

13.10 At the end of the thirteenth century, the opening lines of **The Romance of Richard the Lion-Hearted** include: *Lewede* (unlearned) *men cune* (know) *Ffrensch non | Among an hondryd vnnepis* (scarcely) *on.*

14.1 About 1300, these lines appear in a metrical homily: *Forthi wil I of my povert | Schau sum thing that Ik haf in hert, | On Ingelis tong that alle may | Understand quat I wil say. | . . . Bot al men can noht, I-wis, | Understand Latin and Frankis.*

14 In the fourteenth century, the overwhelming majority of private letters from nobility, religious houses, and so on are in French, the rest in Latin.

14.1   About 1303, in the preface to **Handlyng Synne**, appear the lines: *For lewde* (unlearned) *men y vndyrtokel On englyssh tunge to make þys boke.*

14.1   About 1300, in the **Cursor Mundi**, appear the lines: *Þis ilk bok es translate | Into Inglis tong to rede* (counsel) *| For the love of Inglis lede* (folk), *| Inglis lede of Ingland, | For the commun at* (to) *understand.*

14.3   About 1325, the opening lines of **Arthour and Merlin** include these: *Mani noble ich haue yseiʒe* (seen) *| Þat no Freynsche coupe* (can) *seye.*

14.3   About 1325, these lines occur in William of Nassyngton's **Speculum Vitae**:

> In English tonge I schal ʒow telle,
> ʒif ʒe wyth me so longe wil dwelle.
> No Latyn wil I speke no waste,
> But English þat men vse mast,
> Þat can eche man vnderstande,
> Þat is born in Ingelande;
> For þat langage is most chewyd (shown)
> Os wel among lered (learned) os lewyd (unlearned).
> . . .
> And somme can (know) Frensche and no Latyn,
> Þat vsed han cowrt (court) and dwellen þerein.
> And somme can of Latyn a party,
> Þat can of Frensche but febly;
> And somme vnderstonde wel Englysch,
> Þat can noþer (neither) Latyn nor Frankys.
> Boþe lered and lewed, olde and ʒonge,
> Alle vnderstonden english tonge.

14.5   By the middle of the century, virtually all correspondence is in French. In the last half of the century, writers make more and more grammatical mistakes.

14.7   Between 1360 and 1400 appear the most important Middle English works of literature: **The Pearl**, a dream vision; **Sir Gawain and the Green Knight**, a romance; and **The Vision of William Concerning Piers the Plowman**, a combination of satire, social commentary, religious allegory, and homiletic. All of these were part of the alliterative survival in the late fourteenth century that drew on Old English verse forms. From about 1360, Geoffrey Chaucer (c. 1340–1400) begins creating the greatest English literature of the period and some of the best of all time, including **The Canterbury Tales**. About this time, the **Alliterative Morte Arthure** appears, a romance about King Arthur, written in the native alliterating verse that goes back to the OE tradition.

14.8   About 1370, the author of **Piers Plowman** writes:

> Gramer, the grounde of al, bigyleth now children; / For is none of this newe clerkes, who so nymeth hede, / That can versifye faire ne formalich enditen; / Ne nouȝt on amonge an hundreth that an auctour can construe, / Ne rede a lettre in any langage but in Latyn or in Englissh.
>
> (B-text, XV, 365–369)

14.9   About 1375 to 1425 or so, English writers switch back and forth between English and French in their correspondence, a phenomenon uncommon either before or after.

14.9   John Wycliffe's (c. 1320–84) translation of the English Bible is published posthumously.

14.9   In 1385, Thomas Usk writes:

> Let then clerkys endyten in Latin for they have the propertee of science, and the knowings in that facultee: and let Frenchmen in their Frenche also endyten their queynt terms, for it is kyndely to their mouthes: and let us shewe our fantasyes in such words as we lerneden of our dames tonge.

14.10   The first known private letter in English dates from 1392–93; the next from 1399.

14.10   Until the end of Richard II's reign (1399), manuals for letter writers with model letters in French abound. They do not instruct in the basic grammar of French but in socially correct writing.

15.1   In 1400, a writer to Henry IV apologizes for writing in English rather than French or Latin, but, he says, he understands English better.

15.1   About 1403, Richard Kingston, Dean of Windsor, writing to Henry IV:

> Jeo prie a la Benoit Trinite que vous ottroie bone vie ove tresentier sauntee a treslonge durre, and sende ȝowe sone to ows in helþ and prosperitee; for, in god fey, I hope to Al Mighty God that, ȝef ȝe come ȝoure owne persone, ȝe schulle have the victorie of alle ȝoure encmyes....

15.1   Many upper-class writers write some letters in English, others in French, seemingly indifferently.

15.1   In the early fifteenth century, John Barton in **Donet François** advises that adults should learn French so they can (1) get along in France, (2) understand laws, (3) write polite letters to other upper-class Englishmen.

15.3   In 1424, the earliest letters in English from English nobility to religious houses begin to appear.

15.4   Joan, second wife to Henry IV (from 1403), seems to be the last English queen to use French in her correspondence. (She was French.)

PROBLEM 4.6: (1) When did English begin to replace French in social usage in comparison to French in official usage? (2) Why the difference? (3) Can any of the social patterns be said to be influenced by any of the political or demographic events?

Spoken English, French, and Latin on Official Occasions

12.2 It is reported that in 1116, a defendant in court testifies in English.

12.10 It is reported in 1198 that in court a native English speaker gives evidence through an interpreter, who translates his testimony into French.

14.1 In 1300, a regulation protecting ecclesiastical property is sent to priests, who are ordered to explain it in English to their parishioners.

14.1 In 1301, Edward II has letters in Latin from the Pope translated into French in order to be read to the army.

14.3 In 1327, Edward III's presentation of certain privileges to Londoners is made in English.

14.4 In 1337, Edward III's claim to the throne of France is explained to Parliament in English, though the lawyer doing so was proficient in Latin, French, and English.

14.6 In 1356, the oral proceedings of the sheriff's court in London are ordered to be conducted in English.

14.7 In 1362, oral proceedings in all the courts of England are ordered to be conducted in English, in place of French, which, it is claimed, is little known in the realm.

14.7 In 1363, Parliament is opened in English for the first time.

14.7 In 1363 and 1365, Parliament again is opened in English.

14.8 It has been claimed that French is no longer used in House of Commons debates in the last half of fourteenth century, though the evidence is unclear.

14.9 In 1381, during the Wat Tyler rebellion, Richard II addresses people in English.

14.9 In 1381, Parliament is opened with a sermon in English.

14.9 In 1389, on election day, legal ordinances for the town of Shrewsbury are read to the citizens in French.

14.10 Proclamations to the citizens of London are made in French until the end of the fourteenth century.

14.10 In 1394, a formal apology made in the House of Lords is recorded in English, indicating it was spoken in English rather than French, as would have been customary.

14.10 In 1397, a confession by the Duke of Gloucester is conveyed to Parliament in English.

14.10 In 1399, the deposition of Richard II and the accession of Henry IV is conducted in both English and Latin. Henry claims the throne in a few sentences in English.

15.1   Henry IV makes a short speech in English to his first Parliament.

15.1   Though the record is unclear, debates in the House of Commons in the early fifteenth century seem to be conducted mostly in English, some in French.

15.1   In 1404, ambassadors to Paris from Henry IV claim, for diplomatic reasons, that they cannot negotiate in French.

15.6   Judges are still conducting trials in French.

15.9   It has been claimed that French was probably discontinued in the House of Lords after 1483.

PROBLEM 4.7: (1) How did the use of written Latin, French, and English in official contexts correspond with the use of spoken Latin, French, and English? (2) How were political events relevant to the use of spoken English?

Spoken English, French, and Latin in Social, Educational, and Religious Contexts

11.7   In 1066, William's army is composed of men from every part of France, and of some not from France.

11.8   Odericus Vitalis claims that William tried to learn English, but with no great success.

11.9   In 1085 at the age of 10, Odericus Vitalis, son of an upper-class Norman father and an English mother, is sent from England to Normandy, where, he says, he was like Joseph in Egypt: he heard a language which he did not know.

11.10– During this period there are many citations of abbots, priests, and
12.2   so on, teaching and preaching in English.

12.4   At approximately this time, it is noted that two French canons, ignorant of English, must tell a story to a group of English monks in Latin.

12.4– Henry II is perhaps the first English king since William to understand
12.10 English, though he probably does not speak it.

12.6   John of Salisbury observes that it is fashionable to use French words in English conversation.

12.6   In the reign of Henry II, it is reported that an English knight retains a Norman to teach his son French.

12.8   Late in this century, a poem complains that although 500 years ago Bede taught and preached in English, it is now no longer done.

12.8   About 1175, William of Canterbury relates the following story: At a moment of alleged danger, Helewisia de Morville warns her husband in English, "Huge de Morvile, ware, ware, ware, Lithulf heth his swerd adrage (sword drawn)!"

12.9   At about this time, Abbot Samson, a famous churchman, encourages his monks to preach in French rather than in Latin and better yet in English, as he is able to do. It is also said that he gave his manor of Thorp to "a certain Englishman" because he was a good farmer and could speak no French.

12.10 In 1191, in regard to a legal dispute, it is written that one of four supposed knights involved in a legal case cannot speak French.

12.10 About this time, a young servant is praised "even though" he is country-bred and ignorant of any language except English.

13.1 In a thirteenth-century romance, a young man is described who spends his time teaching French to ladies in attendance to a countess.

13.4 Robert Grosseteste, Bishop of Lincoln, encourages preaching in English and does so himself.

13.5 The rules for monks of St. Peter's Westminster forbid the use of English.

13.6 William of Westminster writes about this time that the common English people despise anyone unable to speak English.

13.6 A thirteenth-century saint's life mentions three French convents where English girls can improve their French.

13.8 In 1277, a bishop suggests that a letter he has written to a group of nuns be explained to them several times a year in French or English.

13.9 Walter of Bibbesworth writes his **Traité** to teach French to children of upper-class families. It introduces French through a description of the everyday objects and actions of common life, the parts of the body, and so on. It is reproduced several times.

13.9 In a late thirteenth-century exemplum there is a story about a steward who is addressed by his lord in French but does not understand.

13.9 In 1284, Bishop Pecham complains that the Fellows at Merton College talk English at table.

13.10 By the end of the thirteenth century, there are few references to upper-class speakers knowing English.

13.10 Rules for the Black monks of York order that Latin or French be spoken and forbid English.

14.1 About 1300, Robert of Gloucester says that Normans could speak only French when they arrived in England, continued to do so and taught their children French. For unless a man knows French, he continues, he is considered of little account. But the lower classes, he adds, hold fast to English.

14.3 In the early 1320's, the colleges Exeter and Oriel allow undergraduates to speak French conversationally if they cannot speak Latin. English is not expressly forbidden.

14.4 About 1327, Ranulph Higden in **Polychronicon** says that the English tongue has become corrupted because unlike other countries where children do their lessons in their own language, English children do their lessons in French and upper-class children learn French from the cradle. He goes on: ". . . and oplondysch men wol lykne hamsylf to gentilmen, and fondeþ wiþ gret bysynes for to speke Freynsch, for to be more y-tolde of."

14.4 In 1332, Parliament decrees that "Lords, barons, knights and worthy men of great towns" should have their children instructed in French so that they would be better able to fight in wars.

14.9 Sometime before 1380, Oxford University orders that grammar masters make their students construe in both French and English lest French be forgotten.

14.9 In 1385, John Trevisa, commenting on Higden's observation about French and English in 1327, says that after the Black Death, instruction in schools switched to English and that French is not so commonly taught to children among the upper classes any more. Consequently children no longer know French.

14.10 Chaucer's Prioress in **The Canterbury Tales** is gently mocked for speaking bad French: *And Frenssh she spak ful faire and fetisly, | After the scole of Stratford atte Bowe, | For Frensh of Parys was to hir unknowe.*

14.10 Though there is some evidence that Richard II is completely bilingual in English and French, Henry IV is generally considered the first monolingual English-speaking monarch.

14.10 In 1396, a new kind of French handbook appears—sets of model conversations designed for commercial travelers, businessmen, and so forth.

15.10 At the end of the fifteenth century, Caxton says "the mooste quantyte of the people vnerstonde not latyn ne frensshe here in this noble royame of englond."

PROBLEM 4.8: (1) Can any of the examples or anecdotes be considered to reflect political or social changes? (2) Is there a particular period when spoken English becomes important? (3) What evidence is there for class distinctions?

Some Additional Data Relevant to the Use of English

11.8 Matthew Paris claims that English-Norman marriages were encouraged by William the Conqueror, and, in fact, many Norman noblemen marry English women.

12.1 In 1100, a Henry I document is addressed to all his faithful people, both French and English in Hertfordshire.

12.5 By the middle of the twelfth century, native Englishmen are giving French names to their children: Humphrey, Stephen, Roger, Robert, Richard, for example.

12.5 During the reign of Stephen particularly, knighthood becomes associated with nobility of birth, chivalry, ceremony, and romance through the many French tales written in this period.

12.8   Around 1177, in **Dialogus de Scaccario** occurs the observation that, after a century of living together and marrying, it is hardly possible to tell who is of English and who is of Norman descent.

12.9   About 1183, William FitzStephen writes that among the cities of the world, London is the most renowned, boasting the finest in manners, raiment, and dining.

13.1   Knighthood is beginning to become a burdensome service in the frequent juries of Grand Assizes, tribunals set up to settle property ownership questions and which can be manned only by knights.

14   Through the fourteenth century, knighthood becomes less important as a social class as the increasing wealth of the East Midlands and London create a growing and more affluent commercial class.

15.8   Because of a labor shortage after the Black Death, villenage begins to disappear. Laborers sell their time for money, pay their landlords with money instead of with their labor.

15.8   In 1476, William Caxton introduces printing presses to England, establishing himself in Westminster, just outside London.

15.10 After Caxton's death in 1491, his successor moves the printing business into London.

PROBLEM 4.9: Which of these events illuminate or reflect any of the preceding data of linguistic history? (7, 10, 48, 61, 127, 187, 196, 216, 223, 229, 241, 242.)

PROBLEM 4.10: Here are several French borrowings from before and during the Middle English period. (1) What would you have concluded about the nature of English-French contact? (2) Do the kinds of words borrowed reflect anything found in the data presented above?

Pre-1066

proud, sot, tower, castle, tomber (dancer), *market, chancellor.*

c. 1066–1250

abbot, canon, cardinal, clerk, countess, empress, duke, court, rent, cell, justice, miracle, baptist, dame, prince, chapel, image, lion, reason, pilgrim, saint, virgin, obedience, religion, sermon, prophet, patriarch, archangel, circumcision, sacrament, fruit, sepulchre, custom, admiral, baron, prelate, crown, astronomy, council, nunnery, abbey, discipline, physician, parishioner, city, crucifix, purgatory, tournament, desert, unicorn, sponge, journey, rob, large, silence, dangerous, jealous, glutton, joy, tempt, witness, chapter, lesson, story, medicine, confessor, constable, heir, chair, galley, butler, canticle, peace, justice, uncle, aunt, cousin, basin, lamp, rose, catch, change, mercy, poor, rich, wait, prove, war, arrive, pay.

c. 1250–1350

action, cost, deceit, dozen, ease, fault, force, grief, labor, number, opinion, pair, piece, season, sound, square, substance, task, use, bucket, calendar, face, gum, metal, mountain, ocean, people, actual, brief, certain, clear, common, contrary, eager, easy, final, honest, real, second, single, solid, strange, sudden, usual, allow, apply, approach, arrange, carry, close, continue, count, cover, defeat, destroy, excuse, force, form, increase, inform, join, move, please, proceed, push, remember, travel.

c. post-1350

adolescence, affability, appellation, cohort, combustion, distribution, harangue, immensity, ingenious, pacification, representation, sumptuous, aggravation, diversity, furtive, prolongation, ravishment, encounter, deraign, sojourn, solace, affray, languor, disparage, conjecture, disdain, explicit, proportion, register, respite. (7, 158, 194)

PROBLEM 4.11: Here is another lists of words, organized by cultural area. Comment.

a. *government, state, royal, authority, parliament, assembly, tax, revenue.*
b. *prince, duke, count, baron, squire, page, sir, madam, peasant, slave.*
c. *religion, sermon, prayer, clergy, cardinal, chaplain, friar, crucifix.*
d. *crime, defendant, judge, attorney, jury, evidence, bail, verdict, fine.*
e. *army, navy, peace, enemy, battle, combat, defense, soldier, captain.*
f. *fashion, gown, robe, lace, button, boot, satin, fur, ruby, pearl, blue.*
g. *dinner, supper, taste, feast, venison, beef, veal, mutton, pork, toast, cream, sugar, salad, lettuce, fruit, cherry, peach, herb, roast, boil, stew, fry, grate, mince, goblet, saucer, plate, platter, table.*
h. *art, painting, sculpture, music, beauty, color, figure, post, prose, romance, story, tragedy, title, volume, paper, pen, study, logic, grammar.*
i. *palace, mansion, ceiling, chimney, tower, porch, curtain, lamp.*
j. *recreation, leisure, dance, melody, chess, characters, conversation.*
k. *medicine, physician, surgeon, apothecary, malady, pain, plague, stomach.*
l. *place, part, use, city, large, line, state, sure, change, close, course, pay, please, face, quit, coat, brown, air, country, flower, hour, manner, noise, number, people, river, able, large, nice, poor, real, safe, second, carry, move, pass, wait.*

(1) Pick two or three of these categories (except l) and add five random words. Are they French borrowings or native? (2) Try specifically to add five native words. (3) Try to replace any set of words above entirely with purely native words. (4) How is category l significant?

PROBLEM 4.12: Albert C. Baugh (7) studied a representative sampling of French words in English to determine the chronology of their entry into English. He compiled the following figures: (1) Before 1100: 2 words, (2) twelfth century: 9 words, (3) thirteenth century: 134 words, (4) 1301–1350: 108 words, (5) 1351–1400: 198 words, (6) fifteenth century: 164 words, (7) sixteenth century: 157 words, (8) seventeenth century: 98 words, (9) eighteenth century: 59 words, (10) nineteenth century: 71 words. (1) How do you explain this distribution? Why was the peak of French imports appearing in print not reached until 300 years after the Invasion? (2) What problem in interpreting these figures is raised by their being derived from written texts?

NORMAN FRENCH VS. ENGLISH (1066–1450)

Most of this data speaks for itself, so only a brief resumé is needed here. Two dates mark the major turning points in the influence of French on English after 1066. The first is 1204, when King Philip of France seized the Norman estates of barons whose primary allegiance was to King John of England and forced them to choose between France and England. The second date is 1348, when the Black Death began to sweep across England, accelerating the social changes that had been underway for some years.

Before 1204, the dialect of Normandy was naturally enough the prestige dialect of those French in England who maintained close contact with their fellow countrymen in Normandy, traveling back and forth, as they did, some living in both countries. Norman French was very likely spoken: (1) by the vast majority of the French invaders and colonists (the Normans), but not by all the French who settled in England; (2) relatively soon after 1100 by most, if not all upper-class native Englishmen; (3) by those middle-class commercial Englishmen who had to deal with Normans; and (4) by most of the middle-management personnel on the large estates who served French lords and supervised English serfs.

Evidence for the use of French among the 90 percent or so lower-class English peasants and laborers is hard to find and evaluate. We can probably dismiss the statements of those who claimed they were writing in Anglo-French, the dialect of Norman French spoken in England, so that both the "lewid" and the learned could understand their romances. "Lewid" or "common" certainly did not mean illiterate, which by far most Englishmen probably were, but rather those unable to read Latin, the most prestigious language of learning. The vast majority of English speakers, the lower class, were undoubtedly monolingual.

After a few generations, it is also almost certain that most Normans were bilingual. Those knights and barons on the larger estates and the royalty in their castles were probably able to maintain a French environment in which they required no English. But the fact that many French knights and nobility married English women who taught or had their children taught English suggests that at least some, perhaps most of the upper-class French knew some English. And it is virtually certain that those below the level of knights who settled on the land and those businessmen who settled in the cities would have learned English rather quickly, surrounded as they were by an English-speaking population.

Of course, the major unsolved problem is exactly how many Normans settled where. The highest estimate, 200,000 settlers, would mean that by about 1250, one in every eight to twelve on the island was a Frenchman or French-descended, a proportion that would have been considerably higher in the major cities. Since the total population in the major urban centers amounted to less than 75,000 or so, and since we might generously estimate that less than half the Normans who settled in England settled on the land, it would mean that perhaps 100,000 urban Normans would have outnumbered the English in the major cities. And there is no evidence that Normans took over the cities to that extent. It is more likely that the French in England originally numbered closer to 20,000 than to 200,000. This would keep the Normans in the minority both on the land and in the cities, a situation that would more logically allow spoken Norman French gradually to disappear after social and commercial ties to the Continent were interrupted in 1204. The example of French in modern Canada is illuminating here. A very high density of speakers is required to keep a language alive over several generations.

For a century after 1066, written English continued to be used for occasional official purposes after spoken French had widely replaced English as the working language of everyday government and law. In the first century and a half after the Conquest, in fact, written Latin, not French, replaced English. Not until the thirteenth century did French begin to replace Latin as the official language for charters, deeds, wills, and so on.

Probably the most important influence of spoken and written Norman French at this time was that it created a linguistic criterion for upper-middle class membership. Without any question, bilingual Normans searching for a word associated with government, culture, entertainment, and so on would use French words in their English speech. And Englishmen striving to function successfully in an upper-middle class milieu would without any question not only learn some French but imitate the Norman-laced English of bilingual French speakers. The comment by John of Salisbury that it was considered stylish to use French words in English conversations could not be more illuminating. Moreover, within half a century after the Conquest, the native population began giving their children first names like John and Hugh, indicating that the Saxons certainly did not universally despise their Norman upper-class. Thus during this period but particularly from the later twelfth century on, Norman French was strongly influencing the character of upper-middle class English speech.

After 1204 and following the second, smaller political invasion of

French speakers during the reigns of Henry III and Edward I, attitudes towards spoken Norman French changed considerably. With the cultural center of France now in Paris, Parisian French, not Norman French, became the new prestige dialect. Since the French habitually spoken in England would have been the Norman dialect, itself different from what it was in 1066 and now considered uncouth, pressure to learn "correct" (i.e., Parisian) French would not be so strongly or so directly felt from immediate conversational contact with upper-middle class Anglo-Norman speakers. Consequently, more and more we find instruction in "good" French a social fact of life.

Furthermore, in the fourteenth century, the character of the upper-middle class was changing. Knighthood was not the romantic profession it had been during the reign of King Stephen. In fact, it was becoming something of a chore. Moreover, the increasing wealth of the Midlands was creating a commercial class that could command its own kind of respect. This growing wealth seeped down to the laboring class until in the later fourteenth century they rebelled against being tied to the land. They could profit more by selling their labor to the highest bidder and then paying their lords in money rather than in labor. Thus an important social institution that tended to fix the geographical location of the lower class began to break down.

Intensifying this tendency in 1348 was the first of a series of catastrophic plagues that swept across England, killing perhaps a third of the population before the century was out. It was most deadly to the very old, the very young, and to those in the close confines of monasteries. Combined with the social forces already at work, the Black Death made an increasingly fluid social order even more so. Before this, French was still a prestige language, as Higden (1327) pointed out. But after the plague, the schools began to use English instead of French as the language of instruction. And it was at least ordered that the law courts should conduct their business in English (1356, 1362). The order was not obeyed, but the fact that it was given is significant enough. Thus during the period following 1204, spoken Norman French began to fade as a major sociolinguistic influence. Parisian French replaced it, but that was a dialect spoken by the most-hated Frenchmen in England, and one not commonly spoken by Anglicized Norman families. (Compare attitudes toward the German language during World Wars I and II.)

But if during the thirteenth century English was beginning to replace spoken French at almost all levels of society and in many official and unofficial social institutions, written French not only continued to be used well into the fifteenth century, but became even more widespread as the medium for social correspondence. It was not until the late fourteenth century and the first quarter of the fifteenth that the final shift toward English as an official and unofficial national written language occurred.

Chaucer wrote **The Canterbury Tales** in English. Letter-writers began to switch back and forth between French and English. Official documents and records began to appear in English rather than French. Richard II and Henry

IV were probably the first English monarchs completely fluent in English. Henry IV, in fact, was probably monolingual. By the middle of the fifteenth century, only the House of Lords and the law courts were still bound to French. The Lords would switch to English in a few decades, but the courts would continue with some of their "law French" until the eighteenth century. (In fact, we can still hear one of the last archaic remnants of law French when the bailiff announces the entry of the judge with *Oyez, oyez . . .* , the imperative plural of *oir*, to hear.)

It is also clear from the data that London English was destined to set the national standard. The most prestigious, the richest, the most culturally influential city in the land, London became a melting pot of dialects as Englishmen from all over England migrated to the city. In the fourteenth century, however, one can detect a shift of immigration from the south to immigration from the Midlands, a fact which made the southern dialects somewhat less important at a time when the national standard was being set. London English as a linguistic standard was irrevocably assured when Caxton set up his printing shop in the London area in the last quarter of the fifteenth century.

REBIRTH OF CLASSICAL LEARNING

When William invaded England in 1066, he led a politically well-organized power, built on a strong feudal base, able to reinforce its power on land with a system of fortifications far superior to the Anglo-Saxons' wooden walls that surrounded their wooden forts. Perched atop earthworks rising many feet above the land, Norman castles easily commanded the surrounding area. The abilities of the Norman architects are amply testified to by the Romanesque cathedrals and castles that today still tower over the English and French countryside.

But if the Norman matched the Anglo-Saxon in law and political organization and mastered him in architecture and skills of war, Normans were relative barbarians in scholarship and literature. Under Norman rule, English learning declined, until by the thirteenth century, Paris had replaced England as the center of European intellectual life. The University of Paris was world-famed; French literature was copied, translated, and admired from Norway to Spain to Italy to Jerusalem. Parisian French was not only the language of international chivalry but was challenging Latin as the language of international expression.

As Paris attracted more scholars, classical learning became more and more widely studied. Latin, of course, exceeded even French in its universality. While by the end of the fifteenth century, it was apparently no great shame for an Englishman not to know French, a clerk who knew no Latin would not be a clerk-scholar at all. Because French resembled Latin in many ways, it made borrowing from Latin into French exceptionally easy. It is certain that many of the words English borrowed from French were originally borrowed by French from Latin. In fact, it is often difficult to decide whether a word was borrowed directly from French or directly from Latin.

Paradoxically, it was probably the very resurgence of English described above in the fourteenth and fifteenth centuries that led English to adopt, with the thousands of French words it borrowed, thousands of Latin words as well. As English became more and more a language felt to equal French, indeed to be preferable to French in virtually every form of written expression, more and more translators set to translating Latin works into English, as had already been done in French. But as one anonymous writer complained in the early fifteenth century, *There ys many wordes in Latyn that we have no propre Englysh accordynge thereto*. Having no Anglo-Saxon synonym available and having apparently lost the productive means to generate new compounds for abstract words—the typically Anglo-Saxon way of meeting lexical needs— Late Middle English translators had to Anglicize Latin words. (99)

PROBLEM 4.13: Here are several late Middle English Latin borrowings. What do you conclude about the nature of the contact between Latin and English in this period?

abject, adjacent, allegory, conspiracy, contempt, custody, distract, frustrate, genius, gesture, history, homicide, immune, incarnate, include, incredible, incubus, incumbent, index, individual, infancy, inferior, innate, innumerable, intellect, interrupt, juniper, lapidary, legal, limbo, lucrative, lunatic, magnify, malefaction, mechanical, minor, missal, moderate, necessary, nervous, notary, ornate, picture, polite, popular, prevent, private, project, promote, prosecute, prosody, pulpit, quiet, rational, reject, reprehend, rosary, script, scripture, scrutiny, secular, solar, solitary, spacious, stupor, subdivide, subjugate, submit, subordinate, subscribe, substitute, summary, superabundance, supplicate, suppress, temperate, temporal, testify, tincture, tract, tributary, ulcer, zenith.

EXCESS AND REACTION

Because the rebirth of classical learning ultimately led to a new intellectual tradition in England as vigorous as it was anywhere in the early Renaissance, it is not surprising that the vogue for Latin diction finally reached excessive proportions. Beginning in the late fifteenth century, it became stylish for some to embellish a text with such borrowings as *abusion, dispone, diurne, equipolent, palestral, tenebrough, fecundius, reclinatory.* Of course, it is probably solely from our modern viewpoint that such words now seem bizarre. During the fifteenth and sixteenth centuries, words such as these and words like *compendious, delineation, dimension, figurative, function, idiom, indignity, penetrate, prolix,* and *scientific* may very well have had the same rhetorical impact. It is only because we have for one reason or another retained *compendious* and discarded *equipolent* that *equipolent* is unfamiliar and, from our twentieth century point of view, inflated.

As might be expected, this wholesale borrowing from Latin and French was (and has been) opposed by those who believe that English, after struggling back towards linguistic respectability, was able to express whatever it had to express in native English words without the help of foreign intruders. Although a good deal of the opposition was on purely practical grounds— many of the imports **were** simply opaque "inkhorn" terms which were probably unneeded—others objected to such borrowings on principle.

Sir John Cheke (1514–57) wrote, toward the end of his life: *I am of this opinion that our own tung shold be written cleane and pure, unmixt and unmangeled with borrowing of other tunges.* His attitude is shared by some modern commentators. The author of the most complete, though now outdated, history of the Norman invasion and conquest wrote "This abiding corruption of our language I believe to have been the one result of the Norman Conquest which has been purely evil" (E. A. Freeman, **History of the Norman Conquest** V. 547, quoted by Baugh).

Cheke's position led him to insist that not only should an English term be used wherever possible, but English should make much fuller use of a process of word creation that was lost to serious, scholarly writing when the Normans dominated English literature for so long. Cheke, for example, would write *foresayer* for *prophet, gainrising* for *resurrection, leechcraft* for *medicine, fleshstrings* for *muscle, likejamme* for *parallelogram,* and so on. Occasionally, he recommends a single word replacement: *mooned* for *lunatic, hundreder* for *centurion, toller* for *publican, crossed* for *crucified.* But since there are far from enough one-for-one correspondences between Anglo-Saxon derived words and all the ordinary and learned words from Latin and French, Cheke was really demanding that **compounding,** an area of English grammar that had lost much of its vitality in intellectual prose, become much more productive and vital than it was. (99)

PROBLEM 4.14: Here are several Latinate words we need (or think we need) in English to express the concepts they cover: *undiscerning, exulting, anxiety, intelligence, proud, patient, magnanimous, spiritless, despondency, precious, valiant, principle, accordant, resolute.* They all refer to some aspect of emotion or mental state. But no one piece of these words links them to a single category of meaning, as does *cogn-* in *cognition, recognize, cognoscenti, cognizant cognizance*; or *-ceive* in *receive, perceive, conceive*, and *deceive*.

In OE, on the other hand, each of the words Anglo-Saxon writers used to express any one of these ideas began with *mod-* (which ultimately gives our modern word *mood*). Here is a list of OE words with their French/Latin-derived ModE translations. The first element, *mod-*, means something approximating what is common to the concepts of mind, spirit, thought, soul. The rough meaning of the second part of the compound is in parentheses: *modblind* (-blind): **undiscerning**; *modbysgung* (-trouble): **anxiety**; *modful* (-ful): **proud**: *modleas* (-less): **spiritless**; *modcræft* (-art): **intelligence**; *modblissiende* (-joyful): **exulting**; *modgeðyldig* (-patience): **patient**; *modleast* (-least): **despondency, want of courage**. Here are some literal translations for the second part of some other *mod-* words. The meaning of the second part of the compound is in parentheses. What do the compounds seem to mean? *modrof* (-strength): _____; *modstaðol* (-fixed, basic): _____; *modleof* (-valued): _____; *modswið* (-strong): _____; *modðrea* (-menace): _____.

The capacity to compound has certainly not been lost in English. We coin new ones everyday: *moonshot, splashdown, babysit*, and so on. But by and large, we compound to create words for areas of meaning that are relatively concrete, everyday, common objects and experiences. What we have lost is the OE habit of compounding to create words for more abstract, conceptual areas of experience.

PROBLEM 4.15: (1) Make up compound words out of OE stock for five French words in each of the categories 1066–1250, 1250–1350, and post-1350 in Problem 4.10. For example: *sermon*: *churchspeech*; *mountain*: *highhill*; *combustion*: *quickburn*. (2) Make up OE compounds for an entire group of words in Problem 4.10.

Given the weakening of compound word formation in relatively formal English prose, it is a waste of time to lament the fact that we are unable to write "pure" Anglo-Saxon English. The common observation that Anglo-Saxon inheritances are short, vigorous, muscular words that communicate an idea briefly and pithily is not too far from the mark. But a good many complicated, sophisticated, abstract ideas cannot be communicated in that kind of language. In some cases, it would be rhetorically ineffective to communicate a message in blunt, concrete terms. So all in all, our French-Latin inheritance has complicated the language but not fatally.

PROBLEM 4.16: Write the paragraph beginning *Once English became . . .* , at the beginning of Chapter Five, using **only** Anglo-Saxon words.

PROBLEM 4.17: What are the national sources for words in the following semantic fields: obscenities, numbers, body parts, apologies (i.e., *I'm sorry, excuse me, pardon me, I apologize, I regret that . . .*), kitchen utensils (*pots, pans, stove, oven,* and so forth) and eating utensils (*knife, fork, spoon, saucer, goblet, platter,* and so on), astronomical bodies (*sun, moon, star, planet, meteor, comet, solar system, galaxy, universe, constellation*), days of the week and months of the year. Can you explain any pattern of national origin?

PROBLEM 4.18: Is there a way to account for the pattern of sources for the following words:

OE:	F:	OE:	F:
calf	veal	farmer	tailor, vintner
cow	beef	woodsman	butcher, poulterer
boar	brawn	fisherman	glazier, physician
swine	pork, bacon	shepherd	mason, barber
deer	venison	hunter	carpenter, attorney
chicken	poultry	skinner	painter, spicer
sheep	mutton	miller	chandler, forester
		baker	haberdasher, host
		cook	hosier, draper
		maid	mercer, merchant
			butler, servant, waiter

PROBLEM 4.19: There are several pairs of words in English, one of which we borrowed from Norman French, the other from Central or Parisian French. (1) Which do you think was borrowed first? (2) Why were both borrowed? (The first word in each pair is Central French, the second Norman French.) *chattel–cattle, chase–catch, channel–kennel, lance–launch, gage–wage, guard–ward, guarantee–warranty.*

Chapter 5

THE ESTABLISHMENT OF MODERN ENGLISH

Once English became generally accepted as the medium for official, literary, and scholarly purposes, and for most upper-class social purposes, only one element was lacking that would insure its triumph in the English Renaissance —a means to make English texts available to an increasingly literate population. But books were expensive. Because each one had to be copied manually, the twenty volumes owned by Chaucer's Clerk represented a very large and expensive library.

The missing factor was provided in 1476 when William Caxton (c. 1422–1491) introduced to England the art of printing. Within 200 years over 20,000 titles in English alone were printed in England. In the 16th century, one translation after another appeared: Thucydides, Xenophon, Herodotus, Plutarch, Caesar, Livy, Sallust, Tacitus, Aristotle, Cicero, Seneca, Ovid, Horace, Terence, Theocritus, Homer, St. Augustine, Boethius, Erasmus, Calvin, Luther. In addition to translations, a vigorous theological literature resulted from the Protestant Reformation and the debates it sparked. Works on history, rhetoric, travel, and so on made the 16th century a rich if generally unappreciated period in the history of English prose. Against those who objected that our language was too impoverished to express grand thoughts, English finally prevailed.

The continuing interest in Latin, Greek, and of course French encouraged the constant borrowing of words from those languages. During the sixteenth and seventeenth centuries, we acquired, if we did not retain, such words as *atmosphere, dexterity, expectation, appropriate, conspicuous, external, expensive, insane, adapt, benefit, consolidate, exist, mediate, ancephalize, deruncinate, illecebrous, exciccate, emacerate, eximious, mansuetude, aspectable, suppeditate.* Originally Greek words, the following were also borrowed from Latin: *caustic, chaos, chronology, critic, dogma, emphasis, enthusiasm, scheme,* and *system,* among many others.

In fact, it has been estimated that fully one quarter of the total Latin vocabulary was adopted by English speakers in some form, the majority before the end of the seventeenth century. From about 1450 through 1700, a majority of the approximately 10,000 words borrowed into English were probably Latin. Perhaps half of them have withstood the test of time to become permanent additions to the language. (7) The most important social consequence of this wholesale importation is that many of these later Latin borrowings (along with many of those borrowed earlier) have shifted from a vocabulary appropriate only to a fairly formal style to the kinds of words educated people use in their day-to-day conversation: *explain, education, scientific, function, exist, system, disagree,* and many more.

CHANGING ATTITUDES TOWARD ENGLISH

By 1400, it was clear that English would remain the language of upper-class life and most bureaucratic affairs. Latin and French would continue to be used in the law courts, and the debate would continue through the sixteenth century about the adequacy of English to express refined and philosophical ideas. But from the vantage point of the twentieth century, it is difficult to imagine any other outcome than the emergence of English as a language of intellectual and literary merit.

But other attitudes were developing too. As early as the 12th century, Englishmen were commenting on each other's speech. William of Malmesbury (1095–1143), a monk from the south of England, observed that the language of the north, particularly in York, was so crude that Englishmen in the south could not understand it. Chaucer used northern dialect for comedy in the "Reeve's Tale." He, of course, wrote in the dialect of London. In the Preface to his translations of **Eneydos**, Caxton lamented the variation and changeability of fifteenth-century English, referring to his native Kentish dialect as rough and rude. By the early sixteenth century, it was clear that the social, political, and intellectual influence of London would make its dialect a virtual standard.

PROBLEM 5.1: In the fifteenth, sixteenth, and seventeenth centuries, we find quotes such as the following. What other attitudes toward linguistic variation were developing? (42)

1. From William Caxton's 1482 version of John of Trevisa's 1387 translation of Ranulph Higden's Latin description of the state of English in 1327. This particular passage is a combination of Caxton, Trevisa, and Higden's observations:

    Therfor it is that men of mercij that ben of myddle englond as it were partyners with the endes understande better the side langages northern & sothern than northern & southern understande eyther other. Alle the langages of the northumbres & specially at york is so sharp slytying frotyng and unshape that we sothern men may unneth understande that langage I suppose the cause be that they be nygh to the alyens that speke straungely.

    And also by cause that the kynges of englond abyde and dwelle more in the south countreye than in the north countrey.

    The cause why they abyde more in the south countrey than in the north countrey. is by cause that ther is better corne londe more peple moo noble cytees. & moo prouffytable havenes in the south contrcy than in the north.

2. From Sir Thomas Elyot's **The Boke Named the Governour** (1531):

    . . . at the lest way . . . speke none englisshe but that which is cleane polite, perfectly and articulately pronounced, omittinge no lettre or sillable, as folisshe women often times do of a wantonnesse, whereby diuers noble men and gentilmennes chyldren (as I do at this daye knowe) have attained corrupte and foule pronunciation.

3. From a letter by Henry Dowes, tutor of Thomas Cromwell's (1485–1540) son: He reports that a Mr. Southwell is "dailie heringe hime to reade sumwhat in thenglishe tongue, and advertisenge hime of the naturell and true kynde of pronuntiacon thereof."

4. From John Hart's **Methode** (1570): ". . . the flower of the English tongue is vsed in the Court in London."

5. From George Puttenham's **The Arte of English Poesy** (1589):

    [The language of the poet should be] naturall, pure, and the most usuall of all his countrey: and for the same purpose rather that which is spoken in the kings Court, or in the good townes and Cities within the land, then in the marches and frontiers, or in port townes, . . . neither shall he follow the speach of a craftes man or carter, or other of the inferiour sort, though he be inhabitant or bred in the best towne and Citie in this Realme, for such persons doe abuse good speaches by strange accents or ill shapen soundes, and false ortographie. But he shall follow generally the better brought up sort, such as the Greekes call **charientes** men civill and graciously behavoured and bred . . . ye shall therfore take the usuall speach of the Court, and that of London and the shires lying about London within lx. myles, and not much above. I say this but that in every shyre of England there be gentlemen

and others that speake but specially write as good Southerne as we of
Middlesex or Surrey do, but not the common people of every shire, to whom
the gentlemen, and also their learned clarkes do for the most part condescend.

6. From Alexander Gill's **Logonomia Anglica** (1619; translated by E. J.
    Dobson 42):

    In speech the custom of the learned is the first law. Writing therefore is
    to be adjusted not to that sound which herdsmen, girls and porters use; but
    to that which the learned, or cultivated scholars, use in speaking and
    recitation.

7. From Charles Butler's **English Grammar** (1633): He takes his standard
    from the "Universities and the Citties."

8. From Owen Price's **Vocal Organ** (1665): "I have not been guided by our
    vulgar pronunciation, but by that of London and our Universities, where
    the language is purely spoken."

9. From Elisha Coles' **Schoolemaster** (1674): He bases his standards on the
    language most in use among the "generality" of scholars.

10. From an anonymous **Right Spelling** (1704): London speech is too "fine"
    and "smooth"; the speech of the Universities is preferable.

Yet another attitude that began to develop was that toward change.
Rhetoricians and others commenting on English from the beginning of the
seventeenth century began to identify the verbal energy and inventiveness of
the first half of their century with unruliness and a lack of decorum, change in
language with decay and corruption. As English came to be used increasingly
to translate the classics and as the primary language for scientific and philosophical writings, many Englishmen became uneasy over the fact that they
had nothing like a grammar of Latin to settle questions of usage, no rules to
guide those not entirely at ease in the language.

A handful of grammars, usually in Latin, appeared from the middle of
the sixteenth century, written by those who wanted to provide English with
the rules it lacked in comparison to Latin. Spelling reformers also began to
examine the orthography of their sixteenth-century English, and at the beginning of the seventeenth century, the first dictionaries began to appear. (We
shall deal with both the lexicographers and orthoepists more fully in subsequent chapters.)

The first explicit, though short-lived attempt to stem what many perceived to be a degeneration of English came in 1664. Two years before, a
group of Englishmen of letters and science founded **The Royal Society**, an
institution dedicated to the furthering of scientific interests. In December
1664, it formed a subcommittee to improve the English language. But even
though it had the successful examples of the Italian Academy (the **Accademia
della Crusca**), and the French Academy (**l'Académie Française**), to follow,
the committee met only a few times before disbanding.

But the strong belief that the English language had to be purified and "ascertained," or fixed, would not let the idea of an academy die. In 1697, Daniel Defoe (1659–1731) in his **Essay upon Projects** proposed a committee of 36 to check the "exorbitance" of writers so that "no author would have the impudence to coin without their authority." In 1712, Jonathan Swift (1667–1745) sent to the Earl of Oxford, the Lord Treasurer of England, his **A Proposal for Correcting, Improving and Ascertaining the English Tongue.** In it, he proposed an academy that would not so much prevent (though he believed that goal was desirable) as control change, admitting carefully screened new words to the language only after defective words had been improved or rejected from the language, shortened words like *mob* for *mobile* and *extra* for *extraordinary*; words with contracted inflections such as *drudg'd, disturb'd, rebuk'd,* and *fledg'd,* and "low" words such as *sham, banter, bully, shuffling,* and *palming.* Neither proposal achieved its end.

But the rational, decorous temper of the eighteenth-century mind continued to insist that the principles of order and decorum apply to language as well as to the arts and philosophy. The English language still lacked a grammar along the lines of neat Latin paradigms; low vulgar words still vied with inflated borrowed ones to corrupt the English vocabulary; speakers and writers still had no standard to appeal to beyond their own uncertain tastes.

Two Authorities

Then in 1755, Dr. Samuel Johnson (1709–84), published his **Dictionary of the English Language**, a two-volume work that followed over a dozen earlier dictionaries, but marked the beginning of serious lexicography in English. And seven years later, Robert Lowth (1710–87) published his **Short Introduction to English Grammar**, a text that went through at least 22 editions before the nineteenth century and set the tone for attitudes toward language that we still feel today. Together, they exercised a very great influence on attitudes toward language.

As Johnson described it, he "laboured to refine our language to grammatical purity, and to clear it from colloquial barbarisms, licentious idioms, and irregular combinations." He was one of the first to comment explicitly on the level of use of a word, labelling many words as "low," "cant," or "ludicrous." Despite the many scholarly defects of his work, it was justly hailed as a landmark in lexicography. English at last had an index to acceptable and unacceptable words, and a prestigious precedent for making dictionaries the final social arbiter of linguistic usage. (92, 131, 153, 202, 205)

A good many grammars had been written before Lowth published his in 1762; some even recognized that the model of Latin grammar was inappropriate to the "genius" of English, that usage by the best writers was a better arbiter of disputed points than artificial rules, no matter how apparently logical they might be. But Lowth's little book struck a responsive chord in the temper of the late eighteenth century. It provided English with a grammar along Latin lines and, it was hoped, enough advice to "teach us to express ourselves with propriety in that Language . . . Besides showing what is right, the matter may be further explained by pointing out what is wrong."

In effect, Lowth and those who emulated him set themselves up as an unincorporated Academy, deciding questions of usage not by observing how educated Englishmen actually spoke and wrote, but by appealing to the past or a kind of rationality that had (and still has) nothing to do with the real nature of language.

In the context of the entire structure of the English language, however, the points over which grammarians quarreled constituted an infinitesimally small portion of that structure. They were questions about the choice between *lie* and *lay*, *hanged* and *hung*, *I had rather* or *I would rather*, *between you and I* or *between you and me*, *who* and *whom*, *It is I* or *It is me*, *taller than I* or *taller than me*, *different from* or *different than*, *the older* or *oldest of the two*, *his* or *him doing that*, *I will* or *shall*, *backwards* or *backward*, *he need not* or *he needs not*, *averse from* or *averse to*—the questions numbered fewer than a hundred or so, most of them involving the case of pronouns, verb forms, and the choice of prepositions.

The prescriptive rules that were set down illustrate how minor features of language can be seized upon to make large social distinctions. They testify even more to the insecurities of upwardly mobile speakers. Given a finite set of rules about pronoun forms and so on, such speakers can avoid or follow those rules and know that they are not committing social gaffes that would reveal their changing social status. The advice falls into the same class as that provided by etiquette books, interior decorators, and caterers: When in doubt, rely on institutionalized advice, And equally important, knowledge of rules allows those who are insecure about themselves to judge those others who break the rules.

The most common assumption behind this advice was that language should be logical. Occasionally, Latin or the earlier meaning of a word was appealed to, but more often the advice was characterized by the logic of "two negatives make an affirmative." In algebra, such might be the case, but as we shall see later, double, triple, even quadruple negatives were the rule in earlier forms of English, and rather than cancelling one another out, they only intensified the sense of negation. Similarly, no historical justification exists for objecting to *whose* to refer to an inanimate object: *A car whose door wouldn't shut* . . . and preferring *A car the door of which wouldn't shut.* Yet eighteenth, nineteenth, and even some twentieth century prescriptive grammarians would argue that *whose* should refer only to human referents: *A man whose house burned down.* . . . Their logic defeats their powers of observation.

The same reasoning has led many to condemn constructions like *more complete* or *more unique*, or double comparatives and superlatives such as *more wilder* or *most unkindest.* The logic of Latin case led to the choice of *older than I* and *It is I.* The desire to regularize what appeared to be random variation led to the codification of the *shall–will* rule.

Some grammarians did indeed resist this kind of logic-chopping. Joseph Priestly (1733–1804), the discoverer of oxygen, wrote **Rudiments of English Grammar** in 1761. In it, he forcibly argued that the only criterion to judge usage by was the English of those who used the language most skillfully. A few grammarians and rhetoricians supported this view, but one need only scan a few modern textbooks to realize what little influence they have had. The same prescriptive rules about the same points (often with many of the same examples) are being set forth today and accepted as gospel just as they were in the eighteenth and nineteenth centuries.

In opposition to this prescriptive tone are the modern descriptive linguists (p. 26), who emerged in the early part of this century following a more objectivist, empiricist, behaviorist methodology. Because they made no assumptions about a language before they described it, they made no prior social judgements about the inherent goodness of any particular form that might occur. Because they had to confront languages whose structures bore no resemblance to languages they were familiar with, they rejected the idea that any given language should follow "rational, logical" principles. Thus for a descriptivist, if structures like *Can't nobody tell nobody nothing* commonly occur in a dialect, then those structures are grammatical **for the speakers in that dialect**. If *Nobody can tell anybody anything* commonly occurs in another dialect, **it is grammatical for the speakers in that dialect**. Neither structure is more grammatical **in itself**.

They would not disagree that social judgments condemn one form and not the other, at least the social judgments of those who are most influential in the larger community. But the condemnation, they would insist, must finally rely on conventionalized social judgments, not on any **inherent** goodness or badness of the grammatical form.

Unfortunately, this view is misunderstood by those who are not completely familiar with modern linguistic principles. It does not mean that such linguists "have no standards," that with them, "anything goes." The mistake rests on a failure to distinguish detached, objective observations from hortatory predictions of unfavorable social consequences. And that mistake unquestionably stems from the belief that grammarians and dictionary makers **should** be social arbiters in the tradition of Bishop Lowth and Dr. Johnson. But a good many social linguists look upon themselves as dispassionate observers and recorders of how people in fact do speak and write in various styles at various social levels and how they feel about how they speak and write. The linguists neither proscribe nor prescribe.

The debate that raged over the appearance of **Webster's Third New International Dictionary** (1961) illustrates this difference. Those who edited **Webster's Second** (1934) accepted the role of linguistic censor by labeling words as colloquial or vulgar, and omitted some words and definitions altogether because they were not considered to be educated or decent usage. When the average person went to that dictionary, he found advice about how to speak and write so that, in effect, he would not be scorned for linguistic uncouthness.

Those who edited the **Third**, on the other hand, looked upon themselves more as recorders, not prescribers. They included many words not found in the **Second**, and refrained from marking many others as **colloquial** or **slang**. For a great many people, this signalled a shirking of responsibility so heinous that many newspapers, libraries, and publishing houses refused to purchase the dictionary and, in some cases, specifically stipulated that it might not even be referred to. What the controversy attests to is a linguistic insecurity very little different from that recognized by the eighteenth-century grammarians and lexicographers. The difference is that those linguists and grammarians best informed about the nature of language and society today insist that every question about the usage of a particular form must be decided on the basis of actual usage in particular situations and that every answer must be phrased as follows: "Speakers of a particular geographical dialect and socioeconomic level statistically tend to select feature X rather than feature Y in social context A." Whether any speaker **should** select feature X in context A is not a question to be posed by them, but rather by those who know—or believe they know—what the consequences of that choice will be. (201)

PROBLEM 5.2: Many current grammar books claim that the following constructions are incorrect. On the basis of data you collect from writers and speakers you would consider to be educated, literate, and at least middle class, do you believe that these claims are reliable?

1. A sentence should not begin with a coordinating conjunction such as *and, but, yet, for, so, or, nor.*
2. *Their* should not be used to refer to a singular referent, as in *Everybody brought their books.*
3. *Which* should refer to a noun, never to a clause: *He left, which was too bad* is wrong.
4. One should not split infinitives, as in *He had intended to secretly enter the meeting which was planning to overthrow the government.*

PROBLEM 5.3: Dictionaries often use labels like **slang, informal, colloquial, non-standard, casual, indecent, vulgar,** and so on to advise a reader about the social status of a word. From that label, it is assumed, he should know how to use the word in the appropriate circumstances, or whether to avoid using the word entirely. Consult the introduction to the following dictionaries to determine what labels they use and how they apply them, and apply those labels as consistently as you can to the list of words provided below. Then look up each word in the various dictionaries to determine how well your judgments agree with theirs and, more importantly, how consistently those dictionaries apply their their own standards.

Dictionaries:

Webster's Third New International Dictionary. Springfield, Mass., 1961.
Webster's Second New International Dictionary. Springfield, Mass., 1934.
The American Heritage Dictionary of the English Language. Boston, 1969.
The Oxford English Dictionary. Oxford, 1933.
The Random House Dictionary of the English Language. New York, 1966.
Webster's New World Dictionary of the American Language. Cleveland, 1966.

Words:

ain't, belch, blue (sad), *claptrap, classy, crack* (sarcastic remark), *cute, egghead, enthuse, dope* (narcotic), *dumb* (unintelligent), *fart, firebug, flop* (failure), *fluke* (good luck), *hugger-mugger, infer* (meaning imply), *irregardless, jinx, kid* (joke), *kith, knock* (to criticize), *loaf* (not work), *lamb* (mild mannered person), *lush* (a drunk), *nifty, pretty* (as in pretty tired), *piss, pipsqueak, root* (cheer for), *shit, stingy, stinker, to-do, tight* (stingy), *tight* (drunk), *wangle, wisecrack*.

In labelling words in this way, dictionary makers assume that someone uncertain about style and usage will know what the effect of a sentence such as this is:

> All those pretty dumb eggheads ain't enthused about that.

Would such a person who consulted the same dictionary be able to anticipate the rhetorical affects of these sentences?

> We perambulated up the street to a restaurant. After checking our chapeaux, we perused the bill of fare and cogitated about our repast. My friend's visage was puzzled, however, because the appellations of the viands were in Chinese.

What does the fact that such words as *perambulate, chapeau, visage,* and so on are not labeled indicate about the assumptions or lack of assumptions on the part of dictionary makers?

BORROWINGS FROM OTHER LANGUAGES

The rise of a small island nation from its foggy obscurity to the commercial and military domination of a large part of the globe meant that, in many ways, the English speaker came to resemble the Roman in Britain in A.D. 45. In India, in the Near East, in the Pacific, and in the Americas, British business-men protected by British-led soldiers dominated trade and set social standards. In the eighteenth and nineteenth centuries, British wealth allowed England to develop its scientific establishment until it was, with France and Germany, the leader of the scientific and industrial world. During the pre-colonial and colonial periods, English came into contact with a variety of other cultures and languages.

PROBLEM 5.4: Here is a sampling of words borrowed from languages we have not yet discussed, grouped by language and period. Considering both the nature of the words (including style and area of reference) and the periods in which they were borrowed, could you reconstruct the kind of contact we have had with these other languages? The words in italics were borrowed through French. What does that fact tell you about English relationships with these languages?

Italian

14th–15th centuries: *florin, alarm, million, ducat, brigand, bark* (a kind of ship), *tunny* (a kind of fish).

16th–17th centuries: *race*, nuncio, *artisan*, *doge*, magnifico, mountebank, umbrella, gondola, *carnival*, mustachio, *attack*, *rocket*, *barrack*, *pistol*, *cavalier*, *musket*, *squadron*, *battalion*, *citadel*, *bankrupt*, *contraband*, *carat*, *frigate*, *porcelain*, bandit, firm (company), motto, artichoke, cupola, *cornice*, *pedestal*, piazza, stucco, portico, grotto, balcony, *corridor*, *catacomb*, dado, concert, *madrigal*, viol da gamba, *fugue*, *pastel*, fresco, *sonnet*, stanza, canto, *caprice*, regatta, lagoon, *balloon*, muslin, *mercantile*, *risk*, opera, *serenade*, sonata, *spinet*, largo, piano, intaglio, profile, vista, *cartoon*, chiaroscuro, burlesque, ghetto.

18th–19th centuries: casino, vendetta, mafia, malaria, influenza, *bronze*, lava, breccia, travertine, *mezzanine*, *colonnade*, *arcade*, loggia, studio, *baroque*, *figurine*, soprano, trombone, viola, cantata, *trio*, concerto, aria, *quartet*, finale, andante, adagio, crescendo, tempo, bravo, piccolo, prima donna, sestet, scherzo, contrapuntal, *fiasco*, *fracas*, imbroglio, *tirade*.

Spanish

Middle English: *cordwain* (a leather from Cordova), cork.

16th–17th century: peso, cask, real (a coin), anchovy, sherry, spade (on playing cards), *galleon*, *grenade*, armada, comrade, tornado, sombrero, cannibal, negro, nigger, mulatto, iguana, alligator, armadillo, sassafras, sarsaparilla, mosquito, banana, cargo, creole, desperado, matador, *lime* (the fruit), *embargo*, *parade*, guitar, siesta, peon, llama, chinchilla, cockroach, vanilla, barracuda, avocado, barbecue, tortilla, plaza.

18th–19th century: albino, stevedore, quadrille, bolero, flotilla, jade (the mineral), cigar, alpaca, hacienda, poncho, silo, cigarette, guerilla, lasso, mustang, gaucho, rodeo, stampede, lariat, quirt, cinch, bronco, pompano, bonanza, pueblo, patio, adobe, serape, vamoose, canyon, burro, dago, cafeteria, marijuana, vigilante, incommunicado, alfalfa.

Low German Languages (Dutch, Frisian, Flemish, Plattdeutsch, Afrikaans)

Middle English: poll (head), dote, dotard, luff, bounce, snatch, huckster, tackle (as in fishing tackle), boy, booze, wainscot, hobble, splint, kit.

15th–16th century: firkin (a small cask), mart, hop (the plant), pickle, spool, rack, sled, excise, buoy, hoist, hose (stockings), bulwark, boor, loiter, snap, groove, luck, placard.

17th–18th century: brandy, stoker, smuggle, keelhaul, sloop, cruise, walrus, jib, yawl, knapsack, furlough, blunderbuss, easel, sketch, stipple, decoy, slur, hanker, snort, snuff, hustle, skate, gin, schooner, pea-jacket, caboose, snow, mangle, cookie.

19th century: snoop, spook, waffle, boss, dope, aardvark, wildebeest, veldt, commando, trek.

High German

16th–17th century: junker, lobby, carouse, plunder, saber, zinc, sauerkraut, hamster.

18th–19th century: cobalt, shale, quartz, feldspar, gneiss, nickel, meerschaum, pumpernickel, waltz, zig-zag, iceberg, poodle, spitz, dachshund, vermouth, lager, zither, leitmotiv, yodel, protein, paraffin, ohm, poltergeist, rucksack, semester, kindergarten, seminar, noodle, delicatessen, frankfurter, hamburger, pretzel, poker, bum, hex, loafer, liverwurst, nix.

Slavic

16th–17th century: kvass, rouble, czar, steppe, mammoth, knout, ukase, vodka, droshky, samovar, tundra, troika, polka.

20th century: pogrom, soviet, bolshevik, intelligentsia, robot, sputnik, babushka.

Arabic

Middle English (almost all acquired through French or Italian): saffron, admiral, mattress, cotton, hazard, camphor, henna, alchemy, alembic, alkali, elixir, zenith, azimuth, almanac, syrup, cipher, sumac, antimony, alcoran, mosque, bedouin, lemon.

16th–17th century: rebec, algebra, arsenal, monsoon, assassin, jar, alcohol, apricot, sash, giraffe, hashish, coffee, sirocco, fakir, emir, sherbert, alcove, sofa, harem, minaret, gazelle, albatross, zero.

18th–19th century: allah, houri, genie, ghoul, candy, jehad, safari.

Hebrew

Old English (through Latin and Greek): amen, hemp, hosanna, manna, rabbi, Sabbath, Satan, seraphim, cherubim.

Middle English (through French): jasper, cinnamon, sapphire, babel, behemoth, leviathan, cabal, shibboleth, jubilee.

Modern English: hallelujah, shekel, Torah, kosher, kibbutz.

Persian

Old English (through Latin): pard, tiger, paradise.

Middle English (through French): scarlet, roc, checkmate, chess, azure, salamander, taffeta, arsenic, mummy.

Modern English (usually through other languages): spinach, jasmin, lilac, seersucker, khaki, caravan, bazaar, shawl.

Turkic

Various times: horde, tulip, vampire, turban, fez, coffee.

Indian Languages (Sanskrit, Hindi, Romany)

Old English (through Latin): panther, pepper, ginger.

Middle English: sandal.

17th–18th century: nabob, guru, pundit, chintz, dungaree, mongoose, punch (the drink), cot, bungalow, tomtom, juggernaut, gunny, bandana, sari, jute, chit, jungle, shampoo, myna.

19th century: thug, puttee, cashmere, pajamas, gazelle, mugger, dumdum, dinghy, loot, polo, chutney.

Dravidian (Tamil, Malay, Telegu)

16th–18th century: calico, mango, copra, curry, coolie, pariah, atoll.

Tibeto–Chinese

Old English (through Latin): silk.

Modern English: tea, ketchup, kowtow.

Japanese

17th–19th century: sake, hara-kiri, tycoon, geisha.

20th century: zen, kamikaze, judo, karate.

Malay–Polynesian/Australian Aborigine

16th–17th century: bamboo, gong, junk (the ship), gingham, cockatoo, rattan, amok (as in running amok), launch.

18th–19th century: taboo, kangaroo, dingo, caddy, sarong, boomerang, gutta-percha. (74, 95, 142, 167, 194)

AMERICAN ENGLISH

In the last quarter of the eighteenth century, there occurred an event that would diminish and probably will eventually end the prestige of the particular English dialect found in the environs of London: The American colonialists declared and won their independence. The earliest colonialists from England settled, of course, along coastal New England and the Tidewater. Generally, they probably came from the southern and midland dialect areas, from south and from north and east of London. Somewhat later, the middle Atlantic states, Pennsylvania around Philadelphia, northern New Jersey and northern Delaware were settled by Englishmen from various regions, though most of the Quakers among them were probably from north midland dialect areas. Then in the middle of the eighteenth century came large numbers of Scotch-Irish from Ulster. They had been transplanted earlier by the Crown from Scotland and northern England to Ulster to keep Ireland safe for the monarchy, but fled when they could no longer tolerate British exploitation and friction with the indigenous Irish. Many passed through the earlier coastal settlements to western New England and to the Piedmont of Virginia and the Carolinas to become a buffer against the Indians. Great numbers also settled in Pennsylvania, along the Susquehanna River and then moved into West Virginia, Tennessee, and Kentucky. Another addition to this eighteenth-century immigration were large numbers of German and Swiss from the Rhineland Palatinate. They kept very much to themselves, however, maintaining their German language and culture in Pennsylvania to become the Pennsylvania Dutch (Deutsch). Other immigrants included French Huguenots, Spanish Jews, Moravians from southeast Germany, and a scattering of other groups that have had very little linguistic influence on our speech.

After the settlement of the East, settlers from western New England pushed into upper New York State and then along the edge of the Great Lakes area into Michigan and Wisconsin. Settlers from the South Midlands pushed into Kentucky and then into southern Ohio, most of Indiana and southern Illinois. North Midland settlers later moved into central Ohio, Indiana, and Illinois. Settlement of most of the South and southwest largely originated from the western Carolinas and eastern Tennessee.

Later migrations generally followed these patterns across the United States, except that during these migrations, Americans came into contact with three other cultures which have contributed words to our language: the Indians, the French in the Mississippi basin, and the Spanish in the Old Southwest. (4, 59, 110, 114, 117, 137, 138, 145, 173, 180, 197)

PROBLEM 5.5: Here are some borrowings from American Indian languages. Comment on the kind of contact Americans have had with Indian culture.

Which borrowings from languages discussed in Problem 5.4 are these Indian borrowings most like? There is another extremely large category of Indian words many of us use every day. What is it?

> **South American** (usually through Spanish or Portuguese): *canoe, cassava, hammock, hurricane, iguana, potato, maize, petunia, tobacco, condor, chocolate, tomato, chili, avocado, cashew, cougar, ocelot, puma, quinine, coyote, cocoon.*

> **North American:** *racoon, opossum, moccasin, moose, hominy, skunk, muskrat, woodchuck, hickory, totem, caribou, succotash, chipmunk, squash, toboggan, caucus* (?), *powwow, mackinaw, podunk, kayak, chautauqua.*

PROBLEM 5.6: Reexamine the Spanish and High German words borrowed in the eighteenth–twentieth centuries. Speculate which words were borrowed through contact with Spanish and German speakers in this hemisphere and which were borrowed through contact with Spanish and German writing.

During this later settlement, of course, waves of immigrants continued to sweep across the Atlantic. The first large "new" wave began in the early 1800's when Irish who also could not tolerate British repression or subsist on the meager fertility of a stony land sailed for the United States by the tens of thousands to settle largely in the cities. Following them were the Germans who bypassed their Pennsylvania Dutch cousins to settle predominantly in the upper Mississippi River basin, in Wisconsin, in Chicago, in St. Louis, in Cincinnati. Along with them came Scandinavians who embraced the land as eagerly as the Irish embraced city life. Settling the upper Mississippi valley, they formed ethnic enclaves as enduring as those of the Germans or Irish. The last great wave of migration began after the Civil War, this time bringing millions from southeastern Europe to settle in the cities along the Eastern seaboard and the midwest, providing the lowest social layer in a fluid but stratified society. Most of these groups have contributed a few words to the general vocabulary of American English, but (outside their own dialect groups) their overall linguistic influence has been negligible.

As might be expected, British attitudes toward American English in the last three centuries have ranged from an occasional condescending admiration for its lusty exuberance to a more prevalent contempt for its alleged slovenly corruption of the language of Shakespeare and Milton. These negative attitudes had several causes. First, those most likely to defend a linguistic conservatism were probably among those most likely to condemn political radicalism. And since Americans were the radicals of the Western world, any differences in their vocabulary or pronunciation would be condemned as roundly as their politics.

Moreover, as we have seen, most British commentators on linguistic propriety condemned any unsanctioned coining of new words or new meanings. Unsanctioned change was synonymous with corruption. So predictably, the most common specific criticism of American English was that our ancestors gave new meanings to old words and invented new words for old and new meanings. It mattered little that a people making a new world would change their language with the land, that the meanings of words inevitably had to change as they were called upon to express new ideas, that new words had to be coined to express meanings—emotional and cognitive—that a citified London standard could not. And since this emerging American culture was unpolished well into this century, it was inevitable that new words and new meanings used to describe it would be judged in the same terms.

Indeed, if the English had not condemned American speech, it would have been contrary to all we know about how a group feeling itself culturally superior makes sociolinguistic judgments.

Not only our words, but our pronunciation was condemned. And even this is not surprising, considering some British attitudes towards their own dialects. Although many of the distinctive characteristics of earlier American dialects had begun to level as the migration westward mingled speakers from all dialect areas of England and America, American English west of eastern New England and the Tidewater area of the Carolinas was in some ways more like northern English than London pronunciation. As early as the twelfth century, northern British dialects were considered by many southern speakers to be barbarously unintelligible at worst, too "broad" at best. Therefore, once the upper-class educated British visitor penetrated the wilds just west of Boston or Charleston, he would have heard a speech that was probably closer to the English of his North than the English of London. And not unexpectedly, he would condemn it.

The earliest American attitudes towards American English predictably split between those who deplored its deviation from educated English usages and those who recognized that American English was gaining a character that reflected the needs of its speakers. Noah Webster (1758–1843) wrote in 1789:

> As an independent nation, our honor requires us to have a system of our own, in language as well as government. Great Britain, whose children we are, and whose language we speak, should no longer be our standard; for the taste of her writers is already corrupted, and her language on the decline. But if it were not so, she is at too great a distance to be our model, and to instruct us in the principles of our own tongue.
>
> From **Dissertations on the English Language.**

But linguistic confidence has not come easily to a people who were long overshadowed by a parent culture with a literary, philosophical, and scientific establishment much superior to their own. If Noah Webster had the confidence to revise English spelling into American spelling (a project we shall investigate later), many of his fellow Americans still suffer from an insecurity that on the one hand encourages high falutin' talk while on the other it triggers the common man's reaction against it. The nineteenth century and most of the twentieth have seen us search for a linguistic propriety in both grammar and vocabulary in ways that reveal our insecurities. One is the plethora of textbooks, correspondence courses, and newspaper columns devoted to teaching the average person how to speak "correctly." Another is a propensity (stretching back into our past) to find new terms for socially embarrassing topics: *drumsticks* and *piano limbs* for *chicken legs* and *piano legs*, *white meat* for *breast meat*, *he-cow* for *bull*, *powder room* for the place that has euphemisms for it stretching back to the sixteenth century. And how many Americans still cringe just a bit when they have to speak with someone who has what he perceives to be that educated, upper-class, la-de-da British accent?

But on the frontier, language was less self-conscious. Despite the frequent disapproval of London visitors, our forefathers coined, compounded, and converted words to fit their needs. And when they wanted to play with language, they went back to a tradition of "ink-horn" terms. What could knock out a listener better than telling him about a bodacious and splendiferous lady he once knew who obfuscated and discombobulated him with her teetotaciously grandiferous charms?

As America filled up with English speakers from a variety of British dialect areas and European countries, and as Americans began moving west, many of the original dialect areas merged until today we have dialects that correspond only slightly to what may have been the original dialects spoken by the first settlers. We can still recognize that a lobsterman from Bernard, Maine, speaks differently from a New Yorker, who speaks differently from a Charlestonian, who speaks differently from a Clevelander. And all speak differently from a Mississippian. But compared with other languages, our dialect differences are relatively slight. (And despite the persistent claim, no one in the hills of Kentucky or West Virginia speaks "pure Elizabethan.")

PROBLEM 5.7: In 1928, under the direction of Hans Kurath, the systematic study of American dialects was begun. Out of it has come a variety of publications:

> Atwood, E. B. **A Survey of Verb Forms in the Eastern United States.** Ann Arbor, 1953.
> Kurath, Hans. **Handbook of the Linguistic Geography of New England.** Providence, 1939.
> ————. **A Word Geography of the Eastern United States.** Ann Arbor, 1949.
> ————, and R. I. McDavid, Jr. **The Pronunciation of English in the Atlantic States.** Ann Arbor, 1961.

In coming years, we shall see the publication of more parts of the **Linguistic Atlas** of the United States and Canada, under the direction of Professor McDavid, and the **Dictionary of American Regional English**, under the direction of Frederic G. Cassidy.

Here are a variety of terms used in various parts of the United States. Survey students from a variety of areas to determine which terms they have used or heard used. Then try to map the areas of usage.

1. *curds* or *curd cheese, cruds* or *crud cheese, sour milk cheese, clabber cheese, Dutch cheese, pot cheese, smearcase, cottage cheese.*
2. *darning needle, snake feeder, snake doctor, mosquito hawk, dragon fly.*
3. *pail, bucket.*
4. *sick to the stomach, sick at the stomach.*
5. *quarter of, quarter till, quarter to* (as in *quarter to six*).
6. *belly-bumper, belly-slammer, belly-flopper, belly-buster.*
7. *teeter-totter, see-saw, teeter-board.*
8. *earthworm, angleworm, fishing worm, fish bait, redworm.*
9. *frying pan, skillet, spider.*
10. *snap beans, string beans, green beans.*
11. *baby carriage, baby buggy, baby coach, baby cab.*

Black English

There remains a very large movement of peoples across the Atlantic to this continent that must be included in any survey of linguistic influences on American English. Perhaps more than any other non-English group they have influenced our patterns of life. And perhaps more than any other group, they have preserved certain of the earliest influences in their present speech.

The sordid history of the slave trade need not be rehearsed here in detail. Slavery has afflicted virtually every civilization, though firearms and sailing ships made it particularly easy for Europeans to practice it for very large profits. The first slaves merchandized in the Colonies were sold to the Jamestown settlers in 1619 by a passing Dutch privateer, who had probably stolen them from some Spanish or Portuguese trader, who had probably purchased them from one of the slave ports along the West Coast of Africa, now the countries of Ghana, Ivory Coast, Liberia, Sierra Leone, and Guinea, where prisons were built to store slaves until they could be sold to European merchantmen, usually Portuguese. The word *Negro* was borrowed from Portuguese or Spanish, *nigger* from *neger*, a Middle French word also borrowed from Spanish or Portuguese. Both words ultimately can be traced back to Latin *niger* (black).

At about this time, there arose among the European traders and their African counterparts **pidgin** languages, mixtures of African and European words in a simplified grammatical structure but one still complex enough to prevent us from thinking of them as a childlike, primitive form of communication of the "No tickee, no washee" stereotype. It is very likely that at least some of the slaves learned one of the pidgins, for the diversity of languages they spoke in captivity probably would have made communication difficult enough to require some **lingua franca** to enable overseers to give the simplest orders. (40, 77)

When these slaves were herded into the loathsome holds of the slave ships, they became a highly perishable commodity, so the slavers were eager to sell them before they succumbed to starvation and disease. The nearest port in the Western Hemisphere at which a profit could be turned on their cargo was in the West Indies, where the slavers traded their passengers for sugar, rum, and other West Indian produce. The next closest North American port was Charleston, South Carolina. It became the principal American point of entry for both West Indian and African slaves. Since the economic problems of carrying them once more up the coast were generally greater than finding a profitable way to work them in the area where they first arrived, it was probably geographical and economic considerations, not lower moral standards, that eventually concentrated slavery in the South.

Thrown together as at first they were into very large groups, it is likely that one of the original Atlantic pidgins became the basis for a pidgin used by the first slaves in this country. The earliest literary representations of slave dialect resemble them:

> Kay, massa, (says he), you must leave me, me sit here, great fish jump into de canoe, here he be, massa, fine fish, mass.
>> From J. F. D. Smyth, **A Tour of the United States of America.**

> Boccarorra make de Black Man workee, make de Horse workee, make de Ox workee, make ebery thing workee.
>> Quoted by Benjamin Franklin, "Information to Those Who Would Remove to America."
>> (both quoted in (39))

The use of the object form *me* as a subject, the lack of inflections, the undifferentiated *be*, the enclitic *-ee* on verbs and other parts of speech (as in the *No tickee no washee* cliché)—all are characteristics of the pidgins developed in the Atlantic area. As we shall see in subsequent chapters, some linguists have argued that certain features of Modern Black English may be descended from those earlier features. (39, 133)

One of two things happens to a pidgin: It either disappears, leaving a few traces behind, or, if it becomes the working language for a large enough group of speakers and develops a grammatical structure and vocabulary complex enough for extended communication, it becomes a **creolized** language. While the first alternative was probably the rule in this country, the second occurred in the restricted area in the islands off the Carolinas. A creole language called **Gullah** developed which preserved not only many grammatical features of pidgin but many words from African languages as well. Some words of undoubted African origin which standard English has borrowed include *goober*, *jazz*, *hoodoo/voodoo*, *tote*, *gumbo*, *banjo*, *chigger*, *juke*, and *okra*. (224)

Now, a major controversy in modern dialectology is whether this view is, in fact, correct. Can we trace the features of any dialect of Black English (excluding Gullah) back to its pidgin origins, or are most modern features, if not all, actually characteristics of early Modern English learned from white English overseers and retained in the Black community because of its social isolation? We shall examine the evidence for both claims in subsequent chapters

American English: A Summary

If the effect of America and the New World on Modern English has been socially significant, grammatically it has been very slight. The question of pronunciation we shall deal with later. The principal lexical consequence has been a relative handful of words (excluding place names) borrowed from the Indians, a good many new meanings attached to old words, and an abundance of new compound words: *space age*, *cocktail hour*, *coffee break*, and so on. But in comparison with the over half a million words in the language and the multi-million meanings attached to those words, the lexical differences between American and British English are minor, and while the number of new meanings and compounds coined on this side of the Atlantic is not inconsiderable, they are still a small minority in the total lexicon, and not a significant part of the central core vocabulary.

Perhaps the most interesting difference between American and British English is the modest degree to which American English is not more "advanced" or "modern" than British English, but occasionally more conservative, both in pronunciation and lexicon. All these next words and meanings, for example, were once common in British English. They were transported to the United States, where their form and general meaning were preserved. But they either dropped out of British English or changed to a new meaning. Thus American English often has an older, more traditional meaning for a word than does British English: *loan* (as a verb), *progress* (as a verb), *bug* (as a general word for insect), *druggist*, *wilt*, *sick* (as a general word for ill), *apartment*, *tariff* (as the narrow meaning of tax on imports), *baggage*, *raise* (as in raises vegetables), *quit* (as in quit work).

PROBLEM 5.8: After tracing as many words as we can back through OE to their Germanic and Indo-European sources or through the various other languages if they were borrowed, there remains a residue of words which the **Oxford English Dictionary** lists as of "unknown" or "obscure" origins. Here is a sampling. Comment.

clasp, clog, cobbler, cub, dandle, dodge, dumps (as down in the dumps), *gadget, hug, job, nod, kill, paddle, pang, pedlar, pelt* (throw), *pimple, lad, pick* (verb), *pie, pink, plot, plump, prod, primp, prong, puke, pun, punk, pussy, puzzle, queer, quirk, quiz, ramble, rig, rip, roam, rote, rove, row* (fight), *ruffle, rust, scads, scatter, scoop, scorch, scoundrel, scowl, sedan, shabby, shack, sham, shoddy, shrug, skid, skull, slab, slang, slog, slouch, slum, slush, slut, smug, snatch, sneak, snide, snob, smug, sprain, spree, spry, squander, squid, struggle, stroll, suds, sulk, swizzle, tarry, taunt, tic, tickle, tiddlywink, tiff, tip, toad, toast, trash, trim* (neat), *trudge, twaddle, tweek, wad, wisp, yank.*

SOME CONSEQUENCES OF A COSMOPOLITAN VOCABULARY

Word Families

One fascinating consequence of this large-scale borrowing from other languages into English is that over the years, we have built up clusters of etymologically related words that may differ considerably in their modern meaning and form, but which all go back to the same root. All these words, for example, have as their ultimate root the Indo-European *pod-*, or foot: *foot, fetter, pedigree, pew, pilot, pedestal, peon, pawn, pedal, pedestrian, podium, expedient, expedite, expedition, impediment, impeach, repudiate, octopus, trapeze, trapezoid, tripod, sesquipedalian, podiatrist, cephalopod.* Among other forms the IE root split into a Germanic *fot-*, a Latin *ped-*, and a Greek *pod-*. From that point the words began to change in form and meaning, migrating from one language to another, picking up new senses from each culture. We can roughly represent some of these relationships on a chart like Figure 5.1.

PROBLEM 5.9: Here are some other words based on the Indo-European stem *pod-*. Trace their descent. *fetlock, pawn* (as in chess), *octopus, antipodes, tripod, impeach, expedient, expedite, impediment, podiatrist, cephalopod.* Do the languages from which these words immediately come correspond to particular centuries?

PROBLEM 5.10: Here are groups of words which in part or as a whole can be traced to a common root. Pick one group and, referring to Eric Partridge's **Origins**, plot the derivations of the words, using the model in Figure 5.1.

1.   *amateur, enemy, amorous, amiable.*
2.   *camera, chum, chamber, comrade.*

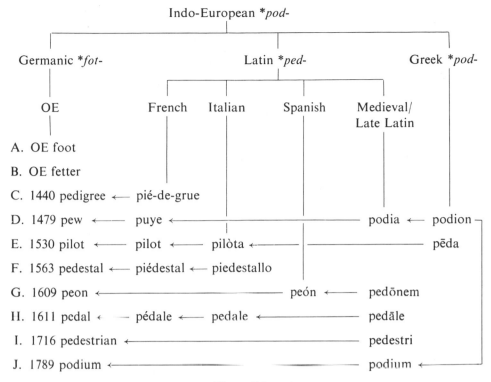

Figure 5.1

A. *Foot* comes directly from the Indo-European through Germanic.
B. *Fetter*, to bind the feet, also derives through Germanic.
C. *Pedigree* has a curious history. In the genealogical records of medieval France, a symbol of three lines, allegedly resembling a crane's foot, was used to show "descended from." This was called a *pié-de-grue*, or foot of the crane.
D. *Pew*. Greek *pous* has a genitive *podos*, which has a diminutive, *podion*, a base or pedestal. The Late Latin plural, *podia*, was apparently understood as a singular in Old French and became *puie*, a raised place. In Middle French this became *puye*, a parapet or balcony. This became in Middle English *puwe* then *pewe*, then *pew*, a preacher's raised stall.
E. *Pilot*. Greek *pous*, whose oblique stem was *pod-* gives *pēdon*, an oar blade, whose plural was *pēda*, a rudder. From this came the Byzantine Greek **pēdōtēs*, giving Italian *pedota*, then *pilòta*. Medieval French borrowed it as *pilot*, then early Modern French, *pilote*, the source for English *pilot*.
F. *Pedestal*. From Italian *piede di stallo*, for foot of stall: support for a stall for standing or sitting, becoming in early Modern French *piédestal*.
G. *Peon*. Latin *pēs*, foot, gives Late Latin (c. A.D. 200–600) *pedō*, a foot soldier. The oblique stem is *pedōn*, which in Spanish became *peón*.
H. *Pedal*. The Latin *pedāle* became in Italian *pedale*, a footstool. Early Modern French borrows it as *pédale*, and English borrows it as *pedal*, originally a treadle on a musical instrument.
I. *Pedestrian*. The Latin *pedester* with its oblique stem *pedestri-* means of the feet, or lowly. English borrows indirectly from Latin and adds the *-ian* suffix. Its first meaning was the "lowly, humble" sense, as in "pedestrian prose." Only later did it come to mean someone who could not afford to ride; i.e., someone who must walk in the street.
J. *Podium*. A reborrowing of the root for *pew*. The Greek diminutive *podion* gives Late Latin *podium*, which was borrowed directly into English. (161)

111

3. *cream, Christ, chrism, grind, cretin.*
4. *Diana, deity, diary, dismal, journal, jovial, Tuesday.*
5. *father, repair, perpetrate, patriot, pope.*
6. *general, genitals, genius, gentleman, engineer.*
7. *join, junta, jostle, yoga, yoke, zygote.*
8. *light, lucid, luna, luxury, leukemia.*
9. *lose, forlorn, analyze, palsy, solve, irresolute.*
10. *manual, manner, maneuver, manure, manuscript, commando, demand.*
11. *measure, menstruate, dimension, moon, metric, parameter, month, Monday.*
12. *nerve, needle, enervate, neurotic.*
13. *a, one, alone, none, any, atone, eleven, union, universe, ounce, inch.*
14. *ply, pliers, apply, explicate, display, employ, supplicate, simple.*
15. *sport, portfolio, export, rapport, support.*
16. *punt, pungent, punctual, point, pugilist, pygmy, pugnacious.*
17. *rapt, rape, rapture, raven, ravine, harpy.*
18. *sit, settle, sedation, size, dissident, obsess, president, reside.*
19. *stand, static, stage, ecstacy, prostrate, system, systaltic, stanza, statue, state, statistic, staid, standard, varlet, vassal.*
20. *thing, thumb, thimble, tomb, tumescent, tuberculosis, protrude, truffle.*

Semantic Families

There is another consequence of this wholesale borrowing. English perhaps more than any other language has clusters of words that, while very different in form and not precisely synonymous, are very similar in meaning. In most cases, we have at least pairs of words, one native, the other usually a French or Latin import: *hearty–cordial, help–aid, need–desire, buy–purchase, die–expire, climb–ascend, eat–dine, need–require, work–labor, teach–instruct.*

This has made it possible for English speakers more than the speakers of any other language to select words with fine nuances of meaning and association. Larger clusters of words like *help, aid, assist, succour, relieve, reinforce, support,* and so on divide the general semantic field they cover into much finer divisions than do the vocabularies of other languages.

The very richness of our vocabulary, however, makes choosing the right word more complicated than in other languages because it also makes wrong choices possible. One often reads the advice that "all things being equal," a writer can avoid the problem by choosing the Anglo-Saxon word. But this is often bad advice. These words, for example, *help–aid–assist,* do not mean the same thing. Each covers a slightly different range of meaning.

This wide-scale borrowing has created a vocabulary that allows an English speaker to modulate his tone, to control the formality or informality of his language to fit the needs of his rhetorical situation, or by using certain words, create the rhetorical situations he wants. And conversely, it allows him to make social mistakes. It is not difficult, for example, to choose which of these is more appropriate to a formal situation:

1. *The requirement that individuals present must proffer identification on request is hereby instituted.*
2. *From now on, everybody around here will have to show who they are if somebody asks them.*

The need for such stylistic possibilities, of course, results from the range of social situations we find ourselves in. The problem for most speakers is to modulate their style to fit each situation with its unique social variables. Most native speakers know how to behave in the context of their own class in the situations in which they normally find themselves. But when they move out of their class, up or down, they enter another social milieu whose speakers may use different signals, or the same signals more often or less often than in another class. In general, a lower-middle class speaker aspiring to a higher social class and sensitive to the verbal cues in that higher class is likely to overcompensate. He will use too many upper-middle class verbal cues when he finds himself in a fairly formal situation in which he is self-conscious about his language. Thus, though we have enriched the language with clusters of words that allow us to distinguish very exactly fine shades of meaning, tone, and style, we have created a complex instrument that, used badly, can have unfortunate rhetorical consequences.

Besides their inappropriate social usage, French and Latin borrowings are also used by bad writers of ModE to produce a fog of verbiage that obscures thought. Here is a passage, thick with Latinisms, from a professional journal:

> Withdrawing *positive reinforcement* and *eliminating* the *opportunity* to *obtain positive reinforcement* are *commonly employed* in our *society* as *punishments* for behavior *judged* to be *undesirable. Sentence* to *prison, dismissal* from work, loss of driver's *license*, and withheld *allowances* are a few *examples.* It is only in the last *decade*, however, that the *aversive properties* of the *removal* of *positive reinforcement* have begun to *receive* an *experimental analysis* of some depth. (28 Romance words out of 70).

The writer could have said the same thing more clearly in fewer words:

> We often *punish* those who behave badly by taking away things we give them to behave well. We lock them up, fire them, take away their driver's *license*, and withhold their *allowances.* But only in the last ten years has anyone *experimented* in depth to find out what happens when we do this. (4 Romance words out of 53).

The author was writing in what he perceived to be a very formal context on an important subject—a rhetorical situation that required a very formal rhetorical style. Unfortunately, as happens so often, he sacrificed clarity and vigor for the formal jargon of his profession, a jargon strongly dependent on French and Latin borrowings, and on the habit of turning verbs and adjectives into nouns: *withdraw–withdrawing, reinforce–reinforcement, eliminate–eliminating, punish–punishment, behave–behavior, sentence–sentence, dismiss–dismissal, lose–loss, allow–allowance, remove–removal, analyze–analysis, deep–depth.*

PROBLEM 5.11: Here are groups of rough synonyms. Can you distinguish more than two levels of style among these? Make up several sentences that mean roughly the same thing, but consistently use words from different stylistic levels. For example: *They ripped off some chintzy threads/They purloined some inexpensive attire/They stole some cheap clothes.*

1. *abduct, kidnap, snatch.*
2. *account, statement, bill, tab.*
3. *acknowledge, confess, admit, own up, sing.*
4. *addict, fiend, fan, head.*
5. *deceive, betray, double cross.*
6. *delay, procrastinate, dawdle, dillydally.*
7. *purloin, pilfer, steal, swipe, rip off, cop, lift.*
8. *dismiss, fire, bounce, discharge, sack.*
9. *dupe, trick, hoodwink, fool.*
10. *face, visage, countenance, mug, puss.*
11. *reprove, rebuke, reprimand, chide, bawl out.*
12. *chicken out, give up, capitulate, submit, surrender.*
13. *theft, larceny, burglary, robbery, rip off.*
14. *thin, skinny, slender, slim, tenuous.*
15. *guy, gentleman, person, man, fellow, chap.*
16. *rags, clothes, attire, threads.*
17. *flicks, films, movies, cinema, motion pictures.*
18. *food, grub, viands.*
19. *intelligent, smart, bright, sharp.*
20. *jock, athlete, sportsman.*
21. *dumb, stupid, dopey, unintelligent.*
22. *confused, puzzled, screwed up, troubled.*

A final possibly unfortunate consequence of these foreign imports from Latin and French is more speculative and certainly more controversial.

PROBLEM 5.12: Here are lists of Latin/French and native words. Read each list to another person, asking him to give the native synonym for the borrowed word in list (1) and then the borrowed synonym for the native word in list (2). Keep track of exactly how many seconds it takes to complete each list.

1. **Latin/French Words:** *repair, excavate, depart, velocity, rapid, decay, illumination, attempt, terminate, converse, desist, injure, prevaricate, rotate, intense.*

2. **Native Words:** *chew, eat, sell, deadly, answer, lengthwise, watch, think, sad, believable, ask, tell, raise, old, walk.*

Unless the person has an unusually ready vocabulary, it probably took significantly longer to think of the corresponding words for the native list than for the borrowed list. What consequences does this have for recognizing, and for using the vocabulary of formal English? What social consequences are there for learning or not learning the vocabulary of relatively formal English?

For the most part, serious writing—the writing of government, of much business and commerce, of education, and so on—relies on French and Latin imports over native words for **content** words, words that convey ideas rather than grammatical meanings, as do the native function words such as *in, the, may, to, of, with, will, be, though, while, for,* and so on (as the formal passage preceding Problem 5.11 indicates). This means that if a native speaker wants to take part in the intellectual, academic, or governmental life of our society, a life often characterized by formal language, he must learn a considerably larger vocabulary than speakers of many other languages.

Consequently, the most serious criticism we can make of the English vocabulary is that which the Danish linguist Otto Jespersen made: English is an "undemocratic" language. Those who want to use English for more than casual communication have to learn a very long list of separate items. Contrast this with the list of words in Problem 4.13. Each word that roughly corresponds to a Latin or French word is made up of parts semantically transparent. This means that the OE speaker had to learn many fewer individual words. He had to learn only a basic core of words and the grammatical rules for compounding and understanding them, a tacit knowledge presumably shared by every native Anglo-Saxon speaker.

This does not suggest that we should have no formal linguistic cues for formal social situations. Levels of formality in social behavior, particularly in regard to language, are an aspect of human behavior so widespread as to be very possibly a linguistic universal among even moderately complex societies. All human languages seem to have verbal cues to indicate when something serious is being said in a serious context. It just so happens that among a great many other cues, English has selected as a very important one a French and Latin vocabulary that has to be learned virtually word by word.

PROBLEM 5.13: There is a kind of borrowing not yet mentioned. The words are called **loan translations**. Rather than borrowing the words themselves, we borrow the meaning of the word or phrase and then translate it into English. Here are some examples.

> **From French**: *it goes without saying, gilded youth, castles in Spain, marriage of convenience, trial balloon.*
> **From German**: *superman, academic freedom, beer garden, world view, wonder child.*

In other cases, we borrow the words themselves and change them very little: *lebensraum* (room for living), *zeitgeist* (spirit of the times), *realpolitik* (politics of realism), *blitzkrieg* (lightning war), *weltschmerz* (pain of the world), *hors d'oeuvre, laissez-faire, savoir faire, aide-de-camp, raison d'être, tête-à-tête, pie-a-la-mode.* Why do we on one occasion borrow a word without anglicizing it: *zeitgeist* and *raison d'être*; on another borrow a word and anglicize it: *garage, menu, ration*; and on yet another, borrow the meaning without the words: *academic freedom* and *marriage of convenience*?

At this point, it might be worth distinguishing between two large categories of borrowed words. On the one hand, we borrow words to name objects uniquely associated with the culture in which the objects are found: *florin, peso, pickle, paraffin, samovar, mosque, kibbutz, chess, fez, mongoose, mango, ketchup, geisha, cockatoo, penguin, cougar, skunk.* In some cases, the object becomes entirely absorbed into our culture: *pickle, paraffin, chess, ketchup, cougar, skunk.* In others, the object remains identified with that other culture: *florin, peso, samovar, mosque, kibbutz, fez, mongoose, mango, geisha.* While it is true that these latter words are certainly part of the English vocabulary, they are used only to refer to objects still part of that foreign culture.

On the other hand, some borrowed words seem to tap concepts in our culture that, until we borrowed the words, had no names, or at least no names that captured the distinctive quality of those concepts: *blarney, slogan, creed, guess, snub, sly, inform, podunk, ghetto, vigilante, luck, intelligentsia, zero, kosher, bazaar, horde, pundit, kowtow, tycoon.* For one reason or another, these words widened their sphere of reference to include concepts and experiences in our own culture. These words now cover "psychocultural" aspects of the English-speaking world. It would be very difficult to imagine how their referents could disappear. Indeed, it is difficult to imagine how we got along without such words before we borrowed them. We certainly had other words that probably included the semantic area of these words, but no OE word that exactly represented the precise semantic reference. In fact, it may be that the word, as it were, crystallized or precipitated a semantic focus where previously there was only an amorphous sense of something in the culture that was never spoken of in precisely the right way.

Such a concept is difficult to prove, but the fact remains that in many instances, we seize on borrowed words not for what they refer to in their native culture but what they allow us to refer to in our own.

PROBLEM 5.14: In the lists of borrowed words provided so far, pick out ten words that seem to have no satisfactory synonym in our native vocabulary. (Be aware of the fact that there may at one time have been such a word in OE or ME, but that it is now lost.)

Chapter 6

CREATING NEW WORDS

So far, we have examined two sources of our current vocabulary: our **native inheritance**, those words we cannot identify as being borrowed, and **borrowing**, the most productive source of completely new forms. In other languages, German for example, borrowing is considerably less important as a source of new words. Like the Anglo Saxons, Germans make up compound words for new ideas out of their native stock. While we borrow *oxygen* from the French, the Germans synthesize *sauerstoff* (sour + stuff) out of two words they already have.

But if English has borrowed hundreds of thousands of words, yet we actively make up as many more new words out of what is available to us in our working vocabulary and patterns of sounds. There are three large categories of such word formation. In varying degrees and in different ways, all three are **rule-governed**. That is, we do not make up new words capriciously, but according to rather specific constraints that we induce as we learn English.

The first large process of word formation, which includes **compounding** and **derivation**, is very strongly rule-governed. To create new words in this way, a speaker has to know both individual words and pieces of words, called **affixes**, and the grammatical rules which tell him how to combine words or attach affixes to words, and how to change the pronunciation of both the **root** (the base word to which the affixes attaches, as in *decide–decision*) and the affix (compare *divert–diversion* and *insert–insertion*).

The second process of word formation is also rule-governed, but the rules are psychological rather than grammatical. There is in the human psyche something we can call the principle of least effort, or a "simplicity" principle. It leads to new words for old meanings and some new meanings for old words by shortening a word or phrase: *dorm* for *dormitory*, *pro* for *professional*, *taxi* for *taxi-meter cabriolet*, *jet* for *jet-propelled aircraft*. Also included are **blends** like *smog* from *smoke* and *fog*; **acronyms**, words made from the first letters of a phrase or title: *NATO*, *NOW*, *HOPE*, and so on.

The third process may also be rule governed, but the rules, also psychological, are much more difficult to formulate. These are the rules which direct us in creating new roots, completely new words that did not exist before someone, consciously or unconsciously, made them up. Included are **root creations**, words simply concocted out of thin air like *Kodak* or *nylon*; and **echoic** and **symbolic** words, words which allegedly sound like the thing they *refer to: pop, crackle, clang; teeny, grump, spit.*

TWO GRAMMATICAL PROCESSES

Compounding

As we have seen, one of the richest resources of OE, and a source that many have said has greatly weakened since then, is compounding—putting together two independent words to make one word. It is still a common process: *Green* and *house* go together to make *greenhouse*, as opposed to *a green house*.

PROBLEM 6.1: Using these next examples, suggest some criteria for distinguishing compound words (*comicstrip*) from ordinary phrases (*a comic strip*). What criterion can **not** be used? *post office, grammar school, boy friend, coal mine, gym teacher, rifle-range, horse-fly, pot-pie, water-clock, policeman, airport, bloodhound, bedtime, horsewhip, bagpipe.*

PROBLEM 6.2: All the compounds in Problem 6.1 are of the form **noun + noun = noun**. That is, a noun, *horse*, is added to another noun, *fly*, to make a new noun, *horsefly*. But if we use all combinations of parts of speech and different verb forms: **infinitive + noun** = *pickpocket*; **V-ing + noun** = *flying machine*; and **V-ed + noun** = *ground meat*, we could, theoretically, create well over 150 combinations. In Table 6.1, the vertical column at the left indicates the possible first word in the combination. The horizontal row indicates the part of speech for the second word in the combination. The vertical column at the far right indicates the part of speech that results from the combination. The entry for noun + noun = noun could be filled in with: *spot* + *light* = *spotlight*; the adjective + verb-*ing* combination with: *easy* + *going*; and the preposition + infinitive combination with: *over* + *see*. Use Table 6.1 to inventory all the possible combinations and to answer these questions:

1. Which compounds are the most productive today? That is, in which categories can we **freely** coin new compounds, not just find examples?
2. Which compounds are impossible in ModE? Which parts of speech are most productively involved in compounding? The major OE compound types are entered in their appropriate boxes with translations. Comment.
3. A count of the first 500 words under F in Hall's **Concise Anglo-Saxon Dictionary** reveals about 40 percent compound words. Count the first 500 words in any standard desk dictionary under two or three different letters. What do you conclude?
4. In a study of compounds in running lines of OE poetry, C. T. Carr counted a compound about every two lines. (26) Assuming about six words to a line, that comes to about one compound every twelve words. How does this compare with ModE poetry? ModE prose?
5. Even where the language seems to resist it, make up a new compound word. That is, verb + verb = verb does not seem natural in English, but we can imagine it: to *sneer-smile*. When you have created new types, determine whether the meaning you would assign them can be inferred by someone who hears them for the first time.
6. Does the problem of how to define a part of speech complicate this exercise? Are there any questionable categories in Table 6.1?

We might conclude from this very brief inquiry that compounding is less productive than it was in OE. There neither are as many individual compound words in the vocabulary nor do they seem to occur as frequently. Sometime between the Invasion and the end of Latin and Norman French as the intellectual languages of England, English speakers stopped casually compounding words for abstract scholarly ideas and began borrowing words for them.

That compounding is far from dead in certain styles and contexts, though, is apparent from our modern compounds and our readiness to create new ones:

> *Anchorman* Walter Cronkite has learned that *mission control* is announcing a *holdup* in the *countdown* for today's *moonshot*. The *backup crew* at the *launchpad* is on *standby*. A *follow-up story* will continue after the *station break*.

TABLE 6.1   CREATING COMPOUND WORDS

		Noun	Adjective	Verb Infinitive	Verb -ing	Verb -ed	Adverb/ Preposition	
NOUN		boc-cræft (bookcraft)						NOUN
			dom-georn (fame-eager)		sæd-berende (seed bearing)	eorð-cenned (earth-born)		ADJ
								VERB
								A/P
ADJECTIVE		god-spel (good story)						NOUN
		glæd-mod (glad-spirit)	gleaw-hydig (wise-minded)		healf-slæpende (half-sleeping)	scir-mæled (bright adorned)		ADJ
								VERB
								A/P
VERB	INF	hwet-stan (whet stone)						NOUN
	-ING							
	-ED							
VERB	INF							ADJ
	-ING							
	-ED							
VERB	INF							VERB
	-ING							
	-ED							
VERB	INF							A/P
	-ING							
	-ED							
ADVERB/ PREPOSITION		inn-gang (in-going)*						NOUN
			fela-modig (very brave)		ofer-flowende (over-flowing)	ofer-hrered (overthrown)		ADJ
				ofer-drifan (overdrive)†				VERB
						ðurh-ut (throughout)		A/P

* entrance   † defeat

In fact, the claim that compounding has weakened since OE times may be true for only certain genres of literature. If we look at OE poetry, compounds do indeed abound. But OE prose has many fewer (though still more than ModE prose). If we examine ModE prose from editorial pages, textbooks, and not self-consciously casual magazine articles about moderately abstract subjects, we find even fewer compound words. But when we turn to the sports page and other kinds of informal writing, we are likely to find more.

Indeed, since ME, the number of apparent compound **types** has seemingly increased, if we merely consider the composition of examples from various parts of speech. These types, for example, are either infrequently or never found in OE poetry and prose:

N + V	= V	*babysit*	Adj. + V	= V	*roughgrind*		
N + V-ing	= Adj.	*man-eating*	Adj. + Prep.	= V	*blackout*		
V + N	= N	*pickpocket*[1]	Adj. + Prep.	= N	*blackout*		
V + Prep.	= V	*throw up*	Adj. + V-ing	= Adj.	*easygoing*		
V + Prep.	= N	*setback*	Adj. + N	= V	*strongarm*		
Adj. + Adj.	— N	*deafmute*	Adj. + N	= N	*redcoat*[2]		

1 The compound type *pickpocket* does not follow the OE pattern where the second noun names the class of objects referred to. That is, a *horsefly* is a kind of fly, but a *pickpocket* is not a kind of pocket, but rather a kind of person. It did not occur in English until the 14th century, probably under the influence of French.

2 The type *redcoat* is like *pickpocket* in that a *redcoat* is not a kind of coat when it refers to a person. Compare *hunchback, paleface, redbreast*. These are rare before the 16th century. (97, 126, 136)

Moreover, something much like noun + noun compounding that results in a structure sharing characteristics of both a compound word and a phrase is occurring more frequently than at any time since OE, particularly in American English. Many writers of moderately technical or bureaucratic prose now quite unselfconsciously pile up strings of nouns instead of putting them into fully articulated syntactic structures. For example, a system that alerts astronauts to emergencies involving the impact of meteorites travelling at high speed becomes a *high speed meteorite impact emergency astronaut alert system*.

PROBLEM 6.3: (1) What would be the term for the board on which is posted the schedule of maintenance for the room in which planners confer about this system? The hook on which the board hangs? The salesman who sells the hook? (2) Is there any general principle by which these strings are constructed? That is, given the fully syntactic construction: *The salesman of the hook for the board on which someone posts the schedule of maintenance for the room in which conferences are held by planners of the system that alerts astronauts to emergencies involving the impact of meteorites at speeds that are high*, can we predict the order of the noun-string? (3) How would we determine whether such a string is a new word or a syntactic phrase? Does the stress pattern suggest anything?

PROBLEM 6.4: Compounds made out of noun + noun = noun constructions are common in all the Germanic languages. Examine these noun + noun = noun compounds. What sort of problem do they suggest that goes beyond merely saying that noun + noun = noun? *flower bed, waterbed, steamboat, steambath, steamfitter, shrimpboat, sailboat, sailcloth, coalyard, coalsmoke, airgun, shotgun, elephant gun, water pistol, horsepistol, horsefly, horseshoe, snowshoe, snowman, milkman, fireman, firehouse, fireplug, sparkplug.*

Derivation

Another strongly rule-governed way we form new words in English is by adding affixes to the beginning or ends of words. Consider this sentence: *The extensous destructness of the atomive bomb exemplicates the unpossiblewise task of defencement against it.* It makes sense, but obviously something is wrong. *-ous* makes adjectives out of verbs, but *extens-* takes *-ive*, not *-ous*: *extensive*. *-ness* is a noun ending, but it occurs with adjective roots: *boldness, happiness*. In short, the pieces of words, the affixes, are not properly distributed.

We must distinguish here between two kinds of endings: **inflectional** and **derivational affixes**. For our purposes a derivational affix is any non-independent element added to a word that changes its part of speech or its basic semantic meaning. For example, the plural *-s* appended to *boy* does not change the meaning of the stem, *boy*. The third person singular *-s* does not change the meaning of *walk*. Nor does the possessive *-'s* added to a noun, or the past tense *-ed*, the progressive *-ing*, or the past participle *-ed* added to a verb.

But when we add *-ize* to *final* and get *finalize*, the adjective becomes a verb. *-ment* added at the end of the verb *replace* makes it the noun *replacement*. The *-cy* added to the end of *captain* does not change *captain* to another part of speech, but it does change the meaning from the person to the abstraction. The *-ish* added to *red* does not change it to another part of speech, but the meaning of *reddish* is different from the meaning of *red*. There are other tests.

PROBLEM 6.5: Here are some words with derivational and inflectional affixes. Some are obviously incorrect. Use these data to suggest at least two more tests to distinguish them.

1. *nation–nationality–nationalities; nation–nations–nationsality*
2. *just–justify–justified; just–justed–justedify*

3. *reverse–reversal–reversals; reverse–reverses–reversesal*
4. *sick–sicken–sickening; sick–sicking–sickingen*
5. *wait–waiter–waiter's; wait–wait's–wait'ser*
6. *amusation–amusence–amusement; amused–amuses–amusing*
   entration–entrance–enterment; entered–enters–entering
   action–actance–actment; acted–acts–acting

Where do elements listed as inflections occur relative to derivational suffixes? How many inflections can be added to a word? How many suffixes? Do other characteristics distinguish inflections from suffixes?

Just as we have gained many new words through borrowing and compounding and lost many others through disuse or replacement, so have we changed how we add pieces to a word. Like compounding, affixation was a vigorous process in OE. But while a good many suffixes and prefixes have survived as fossils, not all of them are **productive** in ModE in the sense that they can still be freely combined with stems. *For-*, for example, was a very common prefix, occurring in hundreds of words. It intensified the meaning of a verb, as in *forlorn* (i.e., very lorn, or lost); or it could negate the verb, as in *forswear*. But beyond *forbid, forlorn, forbear, forswear, forget, forgo,* and *forsake*, we have no really active words in English that use that prefix. Nor can we add *for-* to any new words: *forhurt, fortake, forstand, forwork*. It is a relic form, a linguistic fossil. The OE prefix *ge-* that attached to the beginning of almost any verb has disappeared entirely, leaving only meaningless syllables in a few words like *handiwork* (from *handgeweorc*), *aware* (from *gewær*), *enough* (from *genog*), *afford* (from *geforðian*), and *either* (from *ægðer,* a contraction of *a-ge-hwæðer*). *Ge-* had a variety of meanings, among which was a perfective meaning with a sense of finished or done. If it were still active, we would say *gebroken,* to mean entirely broken up; or *ge-eaten,* to mean eaten up; or *geburnt,* to mean burnt up.

PROBLEM 6.6: What, if anything, has ModE substituted for *ge-*?

But other affixes still thrive. Among the most vigorous of those inherited from OE, for example, is the -ed in *four-legged, stouthearted,* and so on. It is **not** the past tense -*ed* or perfect -*ed*. It comes from a Germanic suffix meaning "with." We can add it to virtually any concrete object which belongs to something else: a *steel-shafted club,* a 32-*keyed typewriter,* a *six-wheeled truck,* a *two-headed giant*.

PROBLEM 6.7: A list of most of the principal prefixes that have occurred in English since the OE period is shown in Table 6.2. After the prefix is the source: E = ModE, F = French, L = Latin, Gk = Greek. If there is no source listed, then the affix is native OE. Following the source for a borrowed affix is the approximate century in which it first occurred productively in English. A second date indicates that the affix flourished much more strongly than at first. The examples are modern words if their prefixes are still found in ModE. If the prefix is completely lost, an OE example plus its modern translation in parentheses follows: *ed-* in *edwenden* (reversal), for example, is completely lost. If an OE prefix still occurs in a word but is unrecognizable, then a ModE word with whatever is left of that prefix follows in square brackets: *and-*, for example, is unrecognizable in *answer*.

As you examine Table 6.2, answer these questions:

1. What, if any, are the semantic differences between OE prefixes and the borrowed prefixes? (*Perf[ective]*) in the explanatory note means that the action is completed, as explained above.
2. What proportion of the descendants of OE prefixes are still used today **productively**?
3. What is the general proportion of productive native English versus borrowed suffixes? That is, *with* occurs only in *withstand, withhold, withdraw, withall, within,* and *without*. No other words begin with *with*. *With-* is entirely non-productive. *De-* meaning undo is extremely productive: *de-Americanize, depressurize, defuse,* and so on.
4. Are there any prefixes which have virtually become words themselves?
5. Would it be possible to give up the productive native prefixes entirely?
6. What native words can we substitute for each foreign import? For example, *inter-* could be replaced by *between,* so that *international* might be represented by *betweenland*.
7. Would the answers to any of these questions be significantly different if we decided to call the following elements prepositions rather than prefixes? *æfter, fore, forð, mid, ofer, on, to, þurh, under, up, ut, wið, wiðer, ymbe*.
8. Write a paragraph of ModE attaching OE prefixes to the appropriate ModE words. (97, 136, 175)

PROBLEM 6.8: A list of some of the principal **suffixes** that have been used since the early OE period is shown in Table 6.3. Some of the same information is provided after the suffixes as in Table 6.2 on prefixes, plus whatever grammatical change results from the suffix. The native suffixes are spelled as they were in OE. (1) What is the difference between the functions of suffixes and prefixes? (2) What OE suffixes are still genuinely **productive**? For example, *-fæst* occurs in *colorfast, steadfast, shamefaced* (originally *-fæst,* but now incorrectly reinterpreted as *-faced*). But it occurs in very few other words. *-ed,* from the Germanic **-odi,* meaning "provided with" (not the *-ed* past tense or the *-ed* past participle) is freely attached to almost any concrete noun: *a round-windowed house, a well-penciled student. -ed* is productive; *-fast* is not.

TABLE 6.2   PRINCIPAL ENGLISH PREFIXES SINCE OE PERIOD

Prefix (Source) (Meaning)	Date	Example
1. *a-* (perf./intensifier)		*afysan* (drive away) [*await*]
2. *a-* (generalizes pronouns)		*ahwæðer* (either of two) [*either*]
3. *and-* (against, toward)		*andsaca* (adversary) [*answer*]
4. *ante-* (L)	16 c.	*ante-chamber*
5. *anti-* (Gk.)	16 c.	*anti-aircraft*
6. *arch-* (Gk. but in OE)		*arch-thief*
7. *auto-* (L.)	19 c.	*autohypnosis*
8. *æ-* (without)		*ægilde* (without payment)
9. *æf-* (perfective aspect)		*æfwyrdla* (damage)
10. *æfter-*		*afternoon, aftershock*
11. *æg-* (generalizes pronouns, adverbs)		*æghwa* (everyone)
12. *be-* (around/over; intensifier; N > V)		*bedeck, befriend*
13. *bi-* (L.)	16 c.	*bi-valve*
14. *circum-* (L.)	15/17 c.	*circumnavigate*
15. *co-* (L.)	15 c.	*co-worker*
16. *counter-* (E.)	14/16 c.	*counterstatement*
17. *de-* (F.)	15/20 c.	*decontaminate*
18. *dis-* (F.)	14 c.	*disallow*
19. *ed-* (again/back)		*edwenden* (return)
20. *el-* (from elsewhere)		*elland* (foreign country)
21. *en/em-* (F.)	14 c.	*encircle, embolden*
22. *ex-* (L.)	19 c.	*ex-wife*
23. *extra-* (L.)	15 c.	*extra-terrestrial*
24. *for-* (intens./perf., negation)		*forswear*
25. *fore-* (precedence/ pre-eminence)		*foreshadow*
26. *forð-* (motion towards)		*forthcoming*
27. *ful-* (complete)		*fulfill*
28. *gain-* (against)		*gainsay*
29. *ge-* (perf./collective)		*gesceran* (cut through) [*enough*]
30. *hyper-* (Gk.)	15/17 c.	*hyperactive*
31. *in-*		*inside*
32. *in-* (intensifier)		*infrod* (very wise)
33. *inter-* (F.)	14 c.	*international*
34. *intra-* (L.)	19 c.	*intraparty*
35. *mal-* (F.)	15 c.	*maladapted*
36. *meta-* (L.)	19 c.	*metatheory*
37. *micro-* (L.)	19 c.	*microbus*
38. *mid-*		*mid-century*

continued

TABLE 6.2—continued

39. *mini-* (L.)	20 c.	*mini-skirt*
40. *mis-*		*misbegotten*
41. *multi-* (L.)	17/19 c.	*multi-colored*
42. *neo-* (Gk.)	19 c.	*neo-classical*
43. *non-* (L.)	14 c.	*non-payment*
44. *of-* (perfective)		*ofgyfan* (give up)
45. *ofer-*		*overpayment*
46. *on-* (begin/reverse action on)		*onbyrdan* (incite), *unbind*
47. *or-* (without/intens.)		*orsawle* (lifeless)
48. *oð-* (close to)		*oðstandan* (stand still)
49. *pan-* (Gk.)	17 c.	*Pan-American*
50. *para-* (Gk.)	19 c.	*para-military*
51. *poly-* (Gk.)	18 c.	*polydialectal*
52. *post-* (L.)	17/19 c.	*postgraduate*
53. *pre-* (F.)	14/19 c.	*predetermine*
54. *pro-*	19 c.	*pro-communist*
55. *proto-* (Gk.)	16 c.	*proto-Germanic*
56. *pseudo-* (Gk.)	14/16 c.	*pseudo-intellectual*
57. *re-* (F.)	13/15 c.	*reclassify*
58. *retro-* (Gk.)	14/19 c.	*retro-rocket*
59. *sam-* (half)		*samworht* (half-built) [*sand-blind*, originally *samblind*]
60. *semi-* (L.)	14 c.	*semi-circle*
61. *sin-* (extensive/lasting)		*sinnihte* (perpetual night)
62. *sub-* (L.)	14 c.	*subsurface*
63. *super-* (L.)	15 c.	*super-heated*
64. *supra-* (L.)	17/19 c.	*supra-national*
65. *to-* (motion towards)		*tocyme* (arrival) [*toward*]
66. *to-* (perfective)		*tobrecan* (break up)
67. *trans-* (L.)	16/19 c.	*trans-Atlantic*
68. *þurh-* (through/complete)		*throughway*
69. *ultra-* (L.)	19 c.	*ultra-sonic*
70. *un/in/im/il-* (OE/F.)		*unequal, insincere, impersonal, illegitimate*
71. *under-*		*understandan* (perceive), *undertake*
72. *uni-* (L.)	15/19 c.	*unicellular*
73. *up-*		*uphold*
74. *ut-*		*outlay*
75. *vice-* (L.)	15 c.	*vice-chairman*
76. *wan-* (negative prefix)		*wanhal* (sick) [*wanhope*]
77. *wið-* (away/against)		*withhold, withstand*
78. *wiðer-* (opposing/counter)		*wiðersaca* (adversary) [*withershins*]
79. *ymb(e)-* (around/about)		*ymbgang* (circuit)

What is the percentage of retention? What is the present percentage of native
vs. borrowed productive suffixes? (3) Are there any suffixes which have virtually become words themselves? (4) Would it be possible to give up the native
suffixes entirely? (5) Play the role of Saxonizer again (an example of the
productive use of -*ize* and -*er*). What native words, if any, could be substituted
for each borrowed suffix? (6) What **semantic** information is conveyed by
various suffixes? (97, 137, 175)

TABLE 6.3   PRINCIPAL SUFFIXES

Suffix	Source	Date	Grammatical Change	Example
1. -*able*	(F.)	14 c.	V > A	*breakable*
2. -*acy*	(F.)	14 c.	A > N	*confederacy*
3. -*ade*	(Span.)	19 c.	N > N	*orangeade*
4. -*age*	(F.)	13 c.	N > N, V > N	*baggage, passage*
5. -*al*	(L.)	14/18 c.	N > A	*suicidal*
6. -*al*	(F.)	14 c.	V > N	*disposal*
7. -*an*	(L.)	16 c.	N > A/N > N	*African*
8. -*ance*/-*ence*	(F.)	14 c.	V > N	*entrance, existence*
9. -*ancy*/-*ency*	(F.)	14 c.	N > N, A > N	*presidency, hesitancy*
10. -*ant*/-*ent*	(L.)	14 c.	V > N	*assistant, president*
11. -*arian*	(L.)	16 c.	N > N	*parliamentarian*
12. -*ary*	(L.)	15 c.	N > A	*fragmentary*
13. -*ate*	(F.)	13/16 c.	A > V, N > V	*activate, orchestrate*
14. -*athon*	(Gk.)	20 c.	V > N	*talkathon*
15. -*bære* (productive of)			N > A	*lustbære* (agreeable)
16. -*bora* (agentive)			N > N	*mundbora* (protector)
17. -*burger*	(Gm.)		N > N	*shrimpburger*
18. -*cade*	(Gk.)	20 c.	N > N	*motorcade*
19. -*cracy*	(L.)		N > N	*mobocracy*
20. -*cund* (has the nature of)			N > A	*godcund* (divine)
21. -*cy*	(L.)	14 c.	N > N, A > N	*captaincy, accuracy*
22. -*dom*			N > N, A > N	*sportsdom, wisdom*
23. -*e*			A > ADV	*hlude* (loudly)
24. -*ed* (provided with)			N > A	*legged*
25. -*ee*	(F.)	15 c.	V > N	*payee*
26. -*eer*	(F.)	16 c.	V > N, N > N	*auctioneer, conventioneer*
27. -*el*			V > N	*ŏyrel* (hole) [*swivel*]
28. -*els*			V > N	*byrgels* (tomb)
29. -*en*			N > A	*woolen*

continued

TABLE 6.3—continued

30. *-en*			A > V	*darken*
31. *-end* (agent)			V > N	*demend* (judge)
32. *-er*			V > N	*driver*
33. *-ery*	(F.)	13 c.	N > N, V > N	*fishery, bribery*
34. *-ese*	(It.)	15 c.	N > A, N > N	*Japanese*
35. *-esque*	(It.)	17 c.	N > A	*Kiplingesque*
36. *-ess*	(Gk.)	14 c.	N > N	*goddess*
37. *-estre*			N > N	*mobster, punster*
38. *-ett*			V > N	*bærnett* (burning) [*thicket*]
39. *-ette*	(F.)	16/19 c.	N > N	*usherette*
40. *-fæst*			N > A, A > A	*headfast, steadfast*
41. *-feald*			N > A	*fourfold*
42. *-fest*	(Ger.)	20 c.	N > N	*songfest, gabfest*
43. *-ful*			N > A	*sinful*
44. *-furter*	(Ger.)	20 c.	N > N	*fishfurter*
45. *-had*			N > N	*nationhood*
46. *-ian*	(L.)		N > A, N > N	*Austrian*
47. *-ie, -y*			N > N	*Bobby, daddy, Katie*
48. *-ie*			V > N, A > N	*movie, quickie*
49. *-iana*	(F.)	18 c.	N > N	*Shakespeariana*
50. *-ic*	(F.)	17 c.	N > A	*alcoholic*
51. *-ician*	(L.)	15/20 c.	N > N, A > N	*beautician, musician*
52. *-ify*	(L.)	15 c.	N > V	*liquefy*
53. *-ig*			N > A	*earthy*
54. *-iht*			N > A	*þorniht* (thorny)
55. *-isc*			N > A, A > A	*girlish, reddish*
56. *-ism*	(Gk.)	14/16 c.	N > N, V > N, A > N	*militarism, criticism, extremism*
57. *-ist*	(Gk.)	17 c.	N > N	*behaviorist*
58. *-ite*	(L.)	13/19 c.	N > N, A > N	*Israelite, suburbanite*
59. *-itis*	(Gk.)	20 c.	X > N	*put-it-off-itis*
60. *-ity*	(F.)	14/16 c.	N > N, A > N	*Christianity, sentimentality*
61. *-ive*	(F./L.)	14 c.	V > A	*assertive*
62. *-ize*	(F.)	13/19 c.	A > V, N > V	*finalize, crystalize*
63. *-lac*			V > N	*reaflac* (robbery)
64. *-leas*			N > A	*friendless*
65. *-læcan*			A > V	*nealæcan* (approach)
66. *-le*	(F.)	15 c.	V > V	*sparkle*
67. *-let*	(F.)	16 c.	N > N	*piglet*
68. *-lic*			A > A, N > A	*sickly, kingly*
69. *-like*		15 c.	N > A	*godlike*
70. *-ling*			N > N	*princeling*
71. *-mania*	(Gk.)	20 c.	N > N	*automania*

continued

TABLE 6.3—continued

72. *-ment*	(F.)	14 c.	V > N	*amusement*
73. *-ness/-nis*			A > N	*weariness*
74. *-ol*			V > A	*þancol* (thoughtful)
75. *-orium*	(L.)	20 c.	V > N, N > N	*corsetorium, printatorium*
76. *-ory*	(L.)	16 c.	V > A	*obligatory*
77. *-oð*			A > N, V > N	*length, growth*
78. *-ous*	(F.)	14 c.	N > A	*poisonous*
79. *-ræden*			N > N	*hatred*
80. *-s*			A > ADV	*thereabouts, days*
81. *-scipe*			N > N	*friendship*
82. *-sian*			N > V	*mærsian* (proclaim)
83. *-st*			P > P	*amongst*
84. *-sum*			A > A	*lonesome*
85. *-teria*	(Sp.)	19/20 c.	N > N	*laundreteria*
86. *-type*		20 c.	A > A, N > A	*oldtype, Chicago-type*
87. *-ung*			V > N	*running*
88. *-ure*	(F.)	14 c.	V > N	*pressure*
89. *-weard*			N > ADV	*homeward*
90. *-wende*			A > N	*halwende* (healthy)
91. *-wise*		20 c.	N > ADV, A > ADV	*educationwise, happywise*

A kind of word formation like that we have just discussed but which is largely limited to the creation of scientific terms joins two elements, neither one of which need be a complete word. These are called **bound forms** because generally they must be attached to another word or to another bound form to make a whole word. For example, we can take almost any of the elements in the first list below and attach it to almost any element in the second and get a very impressive result:

1. *electro-, duplo-* (doubling), *hydro-, eikono-* (image), *hetero-* (different), *cephalo-* (head), *andro-* (human), *idio-* (individual), *proto-* (original), *synchro-* (simultaneous), *phylo-* (racial stock), *toxi-* (poison), *pyro-* (fire), *vivi-* (alive).
2. *-clasia* (fracture), *-glyph* (carving), *-crania* (of the head), *-odyne* (pain), *-chronic* (of time), *-graphy* (writing), *-genesis* (creation of), *-tonic* (tone), *-metric* (measure), *-neural* (of the nerves), *-plex* (fold), *-tropic* (turn towards), *-vora* (to eat), *-plasm* (molded). (161)

Some of these prefixes could have been listed in the previous lists. In *protogenesis*, for example, the *genesis* is now also a word, making *proto-* a kind of prefix. The same is true with *hydro-* as in *hydroelectric* and so on. So in many cases, there is no real distinction between many of these and those listed in Table 6.2.

PROBLEM 6.9: Translate ten possible combinations into native English compounds. For example, *pyrogenesis* can be translated into *firebirth*. Then test them on someone to determine whether they can be understood in the sense of the original Greek or Latin word. Is there **anything** that *pyrogenesis* communicates that *firebirth* does not?

There was a time when one of the serious questions among critics of usage was whether it was proper, correct, decent, to combine stems from one language with affixes from another. *Scientist* was once condemned as an unspeakable hybrid, composed of a Latin stem: *scient-*, plus a Greek suffix, *-ist*. One is tempted to wax Freudian on the racial implications of the attitude reflected in the term "hybrid" and why some writers on linguistic propriety were overcome with revulsion at merging elements from different languages. Appropriately enough, the word *racial* itself was a target: it combines a Latin suffix with an Italian stem. It is an attitude that recalls some aspects of the sixteenth-century Saxonists.

In answer to such critics, we can only cite words so completely naturalized that objecting to them on principle would be simply foolish. *Beautiful* is a French stem with a native suffix, *tidal* a native stem with a Latin suffix. All these are of mixed parentage: *peaceful, successful, resentful, fruitful, merciful, doubtful; gentleness, faithfulness, promptness; paternally, royally, modestly, fortunately, certainly, allegedly; breathable, understandable, unthinkable, unbreakable; merriment, shipment; winterize.*

Like most questions of this kind, the strictures of those who would improve by purging are ignored by those who, as they use the language to express their thoughts, shape it to meet their needs. If a "hybrid" results from someone's expressing himself as naturally as he can, then the fact that he creates a hybrid is irrelevant. Some mixed creations, of course, do grate against the ear: *unusualness, drinkability, responseful.* But we might wonder whether these grate because they are hybrids, or because they are unfamiliar, or because they violate the rules of combination. *Redetoxificationability* is a Latin blueblood that follows all the rules, but it is grotesque. Whether such words become part of the language really depends little on prescriptivists and less upon historians, but almost entirely on how many speakers decide they want to use the word.

PROBLEM 6.10: (1) What requires a greater intimacy of linguistic penetration of one language into another, attaching a native suffix to a borrowed word: *graceful, spiritually, correctness,* or attaching a borrowed suffix to a native word: *beatable, amazement, oddity*? (2) How would dating the patterns of such mixed constructions support or weaken your guess? (3) Which are less restricted as to the specific words they can occur with, prefixes or suffixes? For example, how freely can we combine *re-* meaning again (as in *reset*) with verbs? How freely can we combine *-ment* with verbs (as in *amazement*)? How does this apply to the discrepancy between the number of borrowed and native prefixes we have in the language? affixes?

PROBLEM 6.11: Review the compounding chart (Table 6.1). Must we revise our description of compounding in order to take derivation into consideration? That is, what happens if we treat *-ing* (as in *oil painting* or *easy-going*) and the perfect *-ed* (or its equivalent, as in *rough-ground* or *brokenhearted*) as **derivational** endings? In what ways would we have to refine the history of compounding?

Creating by Analogy: Backformations

When a noun like *lamentation* or *obstruction* or *revolution* was borrowed into the language rather than the verb forms *lament*, *revolt*, or *obstruct*, it was virtually certain that the language would eventually increase not by one word but by two. For if we borrow *transmit* and know by the rules of affixation that we can create *transmission*, then a native speaker who comes across *exclamation* knows, without having seen *exclaim*, that *exclaim* is, by the rules of the language, a possible English word. Given *amiable*, he might not know whether the noun is *amiability* or, following his native instincts, *amiableness*. But given either of those forms, he knows that *amiable* is possible.

Once a principle of proportion is established (x : a : x as y : a : y), speakers easily extend it even to words such as these, which, strictly speaking, do not qualify: *pedlar, beggar, hawker, stoker, scavenger, swindler, editor, burglar, sculptor*. For these words, the proportion was incorrect because none of them had an active verbal root preceding the *-er/ar* ending. *Pedlar* and *hawker* are of unknown origin; *beggar* is from the name of the mendicant order, St. Beghard; *burglar* is perhaps from the OE root *burg-brechan*, or house/room-breaking. *Scavenger* is from the French for toll collected in a city and is not a verbal root. *Editor, stoker*, and *sculptor* have historical verbal roots, but they were not active when English borrowed the nouns. These are usually called **backformations**.

PROBLEM 6.12: These words were also borrowed directly into English with, originally, no verbal derivation associated with them. What modern verbs have we derived from them? *reminiscence, resurrection, pre-emption, vivisection, electrocution, television, emotion, donation, enthusiasm, jelly, peevish, aggression.* What about these words: *motion, cognizance, contempt, ambition, incursion, infraction, abeyance, imprecation, transition, insurrection, susceptible, insuperable, inquisition*? Should we have verbs for them? What would they be?

Related to the agentive backformations (*beggar–beg*) is a class of words we have already looked at, but which historically is rather new. Compounds like *firefighter, babysitter, housebreaker, bricklayer,* and so on, compounds with a **noun** + **verb-er** pattern are very old, dating back at least to the ninth century. But rather more recent is the verb compound related to them without the -*er* ending. A few of these verbs date back to the thirteenth century: *backbite,* for example, which, at least according to the **Oxford English Dictionary** citation dates, followed *backbiting* (first citation 1175) by perhaps 125 years. But it has been only in the last few centuries that the form has become genuinely productive. Many, if not all, of these new verb compounds seem to derive from backformations of three types: (1) **N** + **V-er**: *bootlicker*–to *bootlick,* (2) **N** + **V-ing**: *joyriding*–to *joyride,* (3) **N** + **V-ed**: *henpecked*–to *henpeck.*

PROBLEM 6.13: Here are some examples. Which of the three types of verb compound seems to be the most likely source for each? Check your conclusions against the dates cited in the **OED** and its **Supplement** for a sampling of these. *housebreak, shoplift, sightsee, housekeep, stagemanage, moonlight, typewrite, typeset, backpeddle, hogtie, dryclean, bootleg, sleepwalk, hitchhike, ghostwrite, pinchhit, proofread, sharecrop, babysit, chainsmoke, copyread, playact, handpick, doublepark, brainwash, breastfeed, forcefeed.*

PROBLEM 6.14: Create ten new compounds of the **noun-object** + **verb** type directly: *to houserepair, to birdfeed, to haircut,* and so on. How natural do they seem? Would this be an argument against someone who claimed that words like *bookbind, handsew, housepaint* are not backformations but rather direct compound creations? How would this influence our description of compounding in English?

Conversion

In some earlier problems, we have seen how rich English is in ways to convert one part of speech to another by adding suffixes: *decide–decision, sing–singer, orchestra–orchestrate.* But one very common way to convert one part of speech to another is for a speaker just to use a form that represents one part of speech in the **position** of another without changing the form of the word at all. In effect, he adds a zero-suffix: $\emptyset$. For example, someone who knew he could say *The lights gleam in the night,* used *gleam* as a noun, as in a sentence like *I can see the gleam in the night.* A similar process created verbs out of adjectives: *I made the desk clean—I cleaned the desk,* and nouns out of verbs: *I looked out of the window—I took a look out of the window.* All of this speakers can accomplish without adding a suffix.

While this has always been a practice in English, Shakespeare and other Elizabethans were particularly notable for their free use of such conversions:

I warrant him, Petruchio is Kated (**Taming of the Shrew**, III.ii.), *Ile Devill-Porter it no further* (**Macbeth**, II.iii.), *'Tis . . . such stuffe as Madmen | Tongue and braine not* (**Cymbeline**, V.iv.), *He words me Gyrles, he words me* (**Antony and Cleopatra**, V.ii.).

This is such a widespread phenomenon that most common content words of English occur as more than one part of speech: *man, hand, foot, eye, cloud, mouth, light.* But this may be a misleading way of speaking. To be consistent, we may have to distinguish between a **linguistic form**[1] and a **word.** *Walk* is a linguistic form. It can occur as the word we use as a verb: *He walks,* or it can occur as the word we use as a noun: *He took a walk.* When we talk about the word *walk* as either a noun or a verb, we fail to make a distinction that we have to make in other contexts. Is the word *horn* (as in an orchestra) the "same" word as the word *horn* meaning bony material? We can resolve the confusion by distinguishing between linguistic forms and words.

If English speakers have for centuries converted one part of speech to another, they seem not to have felt the same about the suitability of all conversions. A good many conversions that existed earlier have disappeared in favor of another form—or of no corresponding form at all.

PROBLEM 6.15: Here are two sets of words. (1) is a list of verbs formed from English and French nouns, (2) is a list of nouns formed from English and French verbs. Most of these conversions occurred between the thirteenth and sixteenth centuries.

Is there any difference between the stability of nouns converted into verbs and verbs converted into nouns? Is there any difference in the stability of English and French conversions? The proportions are roughly accurate.

1. **Nouns into verbs** (English): *lust, worship, child, gleam, rust, stream, master, hook, stone, word, den, blast, spark, snow, witness, fist, edge, length, head, spire, sleet, fellow, guest, chill, hammer, pin, wire, church, ring, moan, churn, filth, plough, shovel, weather, doom, knot, tail, arm, shuttle, roost, sponge, burden, riddle, share, crank, gossip, chalk, soap, whore* (50 words).

   Nouns into verbs (French): *sacrifice, curtain, fine, penalty, issue, print, treason, cement, tone, treasure, virtue, retail, exercise, plumb, dart, buckle, lure, beauty, license, robe, difference, plea, nurture, marshal, flavor, rivet, solder, liberty, farm, acquittance, accrue, experiment, motion, brush, letter, trick, safeguard* (37 words).

2. **Verbs into nouns** (English): *chew, keep, grind, steal, weep, dread, have, miss, stink, suck, look, feel, choose, hide, secrete, put, shove, crack, mourn, understand, warn, wish, blink, chide, pull, wink, build, write, skulk, fart, hunt, shake, stir, walk, stare, lap, bruise, freeze, rise, shoot, wash, like, befall, creep, grope, run, talk, clip, shut, bite* (50 words).

---

1 The term **lexeme** has also been used.

Verbs into nouns (French): *summon, escape, avow, appease, crush, disguise, pray, rescue, aim, tax, agree, arrive, elect, enforce, increase, rehearse, rush, support, depose, launch, piss, defence, enter, mock, praise, esteem, restrain, strain, acquit, approach, avoid, complain, discharge, furnish, presume, rejoice, remain, maintain, flourish, redeem* (40 words). (125)

PROBLEM 6.16: Here are some early French/Latin borrowings. Why would a speaker of ME be unlikely to convert these directly with no formal change in spelling or pronunciation into verbs: *arrival, guidance, improvement, organization, reverence, reference*? If you had to speculate, would you say that direct conversions are more likely among native or among imported words? Why?

Words (or forms) have been changing their part of speech since OE, but a pattern of change which has suddenly flourished in recent times after its fourteenth-century origins is the conversion of the verb + particle combinations like *hold up* (to rob), *set back* (delay) to the noun class with the typical compound word stress pattern: *hóldùp, sétbàck, láyùp, rúndòwn, wríte ìn*, and so on.

PROBLEM 6.17: Review the compounding chart (Table 6.1) again. How would we have to refine our description of compounding to take into consideration both derivation and conversion?

Words from Names

A very special kind of conversion occasionally combined with derivational suffixes involves only a relative handful of words in the language, but they have some of the most interesting histories of any of our words. These are words made out of proper nouns, words from names for people and places. Strictly speaking, many of these are not conversions since a word like *watt*, derived from the name *James Watt*, is still a noun when used to mean the measure of electricity. But since many others do involve grammatical change, we will discuss them all here.

In some cases, we can instantly recognize the source: *machiavellian, spartan, odyssey, quixotic, shylock, judas, platonic, sodomy, hamburger, frankfurter*. In other cases, the original referent has disappeared from our lives or the word has changed so much from the original that all sense of its source has disappeared: *guy, gin, canter, pants, copper, money, slave, bedlam, place, weiner*.

These groups of words usually have a relatively short half-life compared to most derivations and conversions. These next words, for example, have all been used in earlier histories of the language to illustrate how we derive common from proper nouns: *plimsoll, belcher, victoria, lewisite, hansom, pinchbeck, bant, lisle, daguerreotype, tram, anderson, morrison, burke, brum-*

magem. Almost all of these are at best only dimly familiar as something out of the past or—more likely, perhaps—entirely unknown.

Words are derived from proper names for about the same reasons they are borrowed. Recall that we have distinguished between borrowing and using words like *ketchup* (the brine of pickled fish, incidentally) and words like *taboo*. The word *ketchup* is necessary if the stuff is on the table. The word would disappear if the product became unavailable, with no consequent loss in our ability to express our feelings and ideas. This is exactly what happened to words like *bant*, *tram*, and *lisle*. For most of us, what they refer to no longer exists. Having no need for the words, we have allowed them to fall out of use, just as *wergild* and *scora* disappeared.

Taboo on the other hand refers to a significant area of semantic space in our culture, a space that had no exact name, perhaps, until we borrowed *taboo*. It refers not to an object, but to a way of behaving, a way of thinking and feeling and responding that is deeply embedded in our most basic behavior and attitudes. Thus it is difficult to imagine any circumstances in which a word like *taboo* would become useless and disappear from our vocabulary.

Here are some of the words from proper names that refer to objects or elements that are so specific and so limited that they have not become "psycho-cultural" words: *watt, ampere, farad, ohm, volt, curie, bunsen, fahrenheit, derrick, silhouette, zeppelin, shrapnel, derringer, pistol, davenport, bowler* (hat), *derby, stetson, cardigan, mackintosh, pants, condom, bloomers, levis, bikini, calico, cashmere, millinery, damask, china, cologne, copper, sandwich, weiner, frankfurter, hamburger, cereal, gin, bourbon, sherry, sauterne, champaign, xerox*.

PROBLEM 6.18: Can you generalize about the kind of referent most likely to acquire its name from a proper noun? Look up these words. What kinds of proper nouns are involved?

PROBLEM 6.19: These next words have become part of our "culture" vocabulary. They all originally referred to one specific place, individual, or group of individuals, real, fictional, or mythological. As you read this list, determine when you can the nature of the original referent that made it a source for the more general concept. You will have to refer to a dictionary for many of these words.

Nouns: *dunce, guy, maverick, lunatic, genius, hero, slave, assassin, thug, nemesis, quisling, mentor, solon, philistine, amazon, turk, chauvanism, masochism, sadism, enthusiasm, sodomy, onanism, cupidity, comstockery, fury, grace, babel, blarney, bunk, panic, nightmare, sacrifice, odyssey, bedlam, harmony, music, mystery, magic, fate, fortune, mint, money*.

Verbs: *mesmerize, tantalize, vandalize, bowdlerize, gerrymander, canter, meander, pander, shanghai, boycott, hector, lynch.*

Adjectives: *stentorian, spartan, utopian, herculean, gargantuan, lethal, machiavellian, rabelasian, lilliputian, quixotic, erotic, titanic, platonic, tawdry, maudlin, jovial.* (160)

Grammatical Word Formation: A Summary

At this point it should be clear that arbitrarily dividing grammatical processes of word formation into mutually independent categories of compounding and derivation (including conversion and backformation) over-simplifies the problem. Both processes are at work in creating many words like *easy going, ironing board, rough ground*, nouns like *output* and *setup*, and verbs like *hotdog* (as in skiing), *spotlight*, and *babysit*. Grammatically-based word formation must be understood more as two interlocking processes or sets of rules which together or individually may generate words.

The history of the process is then phrased in terms of how the rules for compounding and derivation have **together** changed through history. Although a detailed analysis of those changes would be out of place here (indeed, it scarcely exists even in outline form yet), we have suggested the outstanding changes. The flow of the processes might be represented like this:

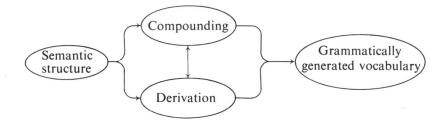

We begin with a semantic structure to be communicated. To represent that semantic structure, speakers can occasionally choose which path to take first. *Firebirth* and *pyrogenesis*, for example, are not synonyms, but at one level of meaning, their semantic structure is very similar. The derivational route overlays the meaning "scientific" on *pyrogenesis* while the compounding route overlays the more general meaning of "poetic" or "expressive" on *firebirth*. In other cases, a speaker must follow one or the other path: Only *doghouse*, for example, will serve to represent the semantic structure behind that term. No unselfconscious derivation lets us produce something on the order of *canicile* (though *caniculture, caninal*, and *caninity*, have been used for *dog-raising, doggy*, and *doggishness*).

The fact that arrows point in both directions between compounding and derivation indicates that word formation often allows recursive functions. That is, we can compound: *outhouse*; then derive: *superouthouse*; then compound again: *superouthouse salesman*; then derive again: *superouthouse-salesmanship*; then compound again: *superouthouse salesmanship award*; then derive again: *superouthousesalesmanship awarder*, and so on. Or we can first derive: *seller*; then compound: *bookseller*; and so on.

Rule changes in the past 1000 years allow a few new compound forms: *pickpocket, throw up, deafmute, roughgrind, redcoat*. One permissible sequence has been lost: Adjective + Noun = Adjective (*glæd-mod*–gladhearted). A more general change is the loss of many native prefixes that communicated semantic information, particularly in regard to the state of an action indicated by a verb. That function has been taken over by a preposition like *up* or the auxiliary verb *have*. Many borrowed prefixes have been introduced that very regularly correspond with native prepositions: *interperiod* = *between times*. Many borrowed suffixes came in with borrowed nouns, verbs, and adjectives, and for the most part, they continue to co-occur primarily with borrowed words. A very significant change is the marked increase in our tendency to convert one part of speech to another without any affixation: A person who *chairs* a meeting can suggest that a motion be *tabled* and *floor* his opponent. A unique kind of rule sequence was introduced with the simultaneous compound-derivation formation of forms like *backbiting, typesetter,* or *handpicked* followed by the backformation of the verbs *backbite, typeset,* and *handpick*. We have also introduced in a somewhat jocular sense units that share the characteristics of both root words and derivational suffixes: *-burger, -furter, -athon, -mania, -orium, -teria, -type*.

ROOT MODIFICATION

The second large category of word-formation is illustrated when a speaker consciously or unconsciously manipulates the phonetic shape of words already in the language. Frequently, these new words will exist side-by-side with their sources, but with a slightly different denotative or connotative meaning.

Clipping and Shortening

The most frequent kind of change creates new words by **clipping** a part of a word, leaving only a piece of the old word. (The technical term for dropping an initial syllable is **aphesis** (*defend* > *fend*); for a syllable inside a word,

syncope (*ægeðer* > *either*); for a final syllable, **apocope** (*master* > *mas*).) But frequently, it is a piece that goes on to become a new word in its own right. The earliest clips go back at least to the sixteenth century, probably much earlier: *coz* from *cousin*, *gent* from *gentleman*, *mas* from *master*, and *chap* from a word we have now lost except as a name: *chapman* (salesman).

PROBLEM 6.20: Here are the original forms for some clips. What words have we derived from them? Keep in mind that the resulting meanings will be fairly close: *apply, brandywine, defend, hackney, example, disport, periwig, cabriolet, omnibus, automobile, caravan, advertisement, amend, doctor, attend, pantaloons, defence, veteran, laboratory, envy, mathematics, gymnasium, examination, mistress, dormitory, professor, estate, professional, fanatic, wizard, submarine, distillery, photograph, geneva, escheat, customer, influenza, espy, benzedrine, acute, Chevrolet, etiquette, fadaise, despite, cocaine, co-education, affray, history, espice, university* (two clips from this one), *alcoholic, quadrangle, accloy, graduate, estrange, penitentiary, rumbullion, abet, nuclear, turnpike, psychology, a(d)venture, sergeant, helicopter, convict, umpire, referee, communist, bookmaker, confidence man, women's liberation, detective, homosexual.* (1) Generalize about what part of a word is retained and why. (2) In some cases, the clip and the source still refer to the same thing: *dormitory–dorm.* Is it correct to say that the two words are **identical** in meaning? Is there **any** difference between them? Are *dorm* and *dormitory* one word or two?

Shortening, of course, also operates on compound words and longer syntactic constructions, but the outcome is in some ways quite different. *Mob* comes from *mobile vulgis*, *pub* from *public drinking house*, *zoo* from *zoological garden*, *movies* from *moving pictures*, *narc* from *narcotics agent.* (Coincidentally, there is a much older word, *nark*, for a police informant in general.) More often, the shortening of the phrase leaves an entire word, often the adjective modifying the deleted noun: Through repeated association, for example, *private* comes to stand for *private soldier*. The single word replaces the meaning of the entire phrase. And when this occurs, of course, the adjective becomes a noun, an automatic conversion.

PROBLEM 6.21: What are some other clip-conversions of this kind?

Blends

Another source of word formation which combines clips and something not entirely unlike compounding is called **blending**: *smog, brunch, twirl, smaze, chortle, motel, sprig, gerrymander.* Each of these is made up of the first part of one word and the second part of another: *smoke + fog = smog, breakfast*

+ *lunch* = *brunch, twist* + *whirl* = *twirl, smoke* + *haze* = *smaze, chuckle* + *snort* = *chortle* (in this one, the second word has been inserted inside the first), *motor* + *hotel* = *motel, spray* + *twig* = *sprig*. This sort of word creation is common in the prose genre that includes **Time** magazine and various nationally syndicated gossip/society columnists: *infanticipating, blobstetrician* (for a reducing adviser), *stupidents* (for student demonstrators), *rapresentative* (someone to "rap" with), *blaxploitation* (exploiting blacks). Blending has supplied relatively few words. (165)

Acronyms

Another form of word creation resembles blending, but is considerably more useful in a bureaucratized, politicized, advertised society where organizations and movements have names too long to fit conveniently into a commercial or a headline. When talking about the Congress of Racial Equality, the National Broadcasting Company, the North Atlantic Treaty Organization, the American Federation of Labor—Congress of Industrial Organizations, we find it too difficult to give the full name every time we mention it. So we shorten them to their letters: Some are pronounced as letters: *AFL-CIO, NBC, KKK, LSD*. Others are pronounced as words: *CORE, NATO, HUD*, and so on.

Most acronyms refer to organizations, but a few refer to scientific or technological referents: *radar* = *radio direction finding and range*; *laser* = *light amplification by stimulated emission of radiation*; *lox* = *liquid oxygen*. Very few of these have entered our "cultural" vocabulary. Perhaps the only ones to transcend the specific original referents are from World War II:*gestapo* = *Geheim Staats Polizei*; *nazi* = *Nationalsozialistiche Deutsche Arbeiterpartei*; *flack* = *Flieger Abwehr Kanon* (anti-aircraft); and perhaps *snafu* = *situation normal, all fouled up*, though this last one is now mildly archaic.

Historically, the principle of acronyms goes back at least to medieval times when words were invented as mnemonic devices, much as a student today might memorize *roy g biv* to remember the order of colors in the rainbow. A similar principle operated in the Middle Ages when Jewish names were blended out of the initials of a title, a personal name, and a father's name: Rabbi Schelomo Jizchaki becomes *Raschi*. In the nineteenth century, chemical substances were named by blending the initial syllables of their constituents: *aldehyde*, for example, from *alcohol dehydrogenatum*. (136)

PROBLEM 6.22: What conclusions about conversion do you draw from these sentences? *Can I have your* OK? *I already* OK'*d it. Then it goes* OK *now? Yeah it's really* OK. OK, *let's get going.* OK! (OK, incidentally, does not come from an 1840 political slogan, *The People is Oll Korrect*; or from a Choctaw word, *okeh*, meaning it is so; or from the name of a Sac Indian chief, *Old Keokuk*; or from the initials of an Irish freight agent, *Obadiah Kelly*; or from *Aux Cayes*, a Haitian port; or from any number of other sources. It seems to be from *Old Kinderhook*. *Kinderhook* was the name of Martin Van Buren's (1782–1862, eighth president of the United States) native village, a name which was made into an appelation for Van Buren, then into a political rallying cry, then into the name of a political organization: *The O.K. Club*. When the members of this organization got into a brawl with an opposition club, *o.k.* became a kind of password.) (145)

PROBLEM 6.23: *NASA* (*the National Aeronautics and Space Administration*), pronounced as a word means nothing more than the meaning of the words it stands for. How do you suppose the genesis of these acronyms differed from that of *NASA*? *HOPE, HELP, JOIN, WAVES, NOW, PUSH*?

ROOT CREATION

Direct Sound Symbolism

Our last category of word formation is in some ways the most basic kind, quite unlike anything we have discussed so far. Earlier, we said that one characteristic of human languages which distinguishes them from many animal languages is that the acoustic image of a word does not resemble the message it conveys. That is, a bee encodes how distant a flower is from the hive by dancing along a scale of intensity that inversely matches the scale of distance from the hive. The more intense the cry of danger from an ape, the more intense the danger.

Except when we raise our voices along a scale that matches a scale of anger, surprise, fear, and so on, nothing in our language seems to have any unequivocal iconic correlation to conditions in the objective world. We do not, for example, have words like *bloob*, which, when uttered slowly: *b l o o b*, means slow, and when uttered quickly: *bloob*, means fast, or alternatively, high and low, weak and strong, fat and thin, and so on. A fundamental characteristic of human speech is that it is arbitrarily symbolic. We do not call a striped horse *zebra* because it looks like the sound of *zebra*.

Now, after making that generalization, we must immediately qualify it, because there may be some limited areas of our vocabulary where sounds in words may correspond with the sound of their referents in more than an accidental way. The most directly onomatopoetic words in the language are those which attempt to represent ejaculations. Many have a fairly long history: *ouch* (first cited in 1654), *hah* (1000), *hoho* (1150), *phoo(ey)* (1672), *ugh* (1765), *hmmmmm* (1854), *phew* (1604), *huh* (1608), *hurrah* (1686), *rah* (1894). Some not cited in the **OED** are *unhunh, yippee, tsk tsk. Teehee* goes at least as far back as Chaucer's Alisoun in "The Miller's Tale":

> "Tehee!" quod she, and clapte the wyndow to,
> And Absolon goeth forth a sory pas.
>
> Fragment A, 11: 3741–2

Tush and *twish* we can find in the fifteenth century. More recently, *wow* was the all-purpose ejaculation.

PROBLEM 6.24: The representation of naturalistic conversation at a very colloquial level is relatively rare outside of a few early plays from the fourteenth and fifteenth centuries. What does this fact have to do with the dating of these ejaculations?

PROBLEM 6.25: What do you make of the way these interjections are now being used: (1) *You can't pooh-pooh that.* (2) *You wowed them, baby.* (3) *We hurrahed him home.* (4) *I hate a rah-rah attitude.* (5) *I don't like a lot of ho-hoing around here.* (6) *I got an owie, mommy.*

One step away from representing in words the sounds we make with our vocal apparatus is representing in words non-human sounds.

PROBLEM 6.26: **The Oxford English Dictionary** lists these next words as "echoic" or "imitative." Comment. *clatter, hiss, pop, sizzle, buzz, hum, bump, squeak, crash, snort, sob, howl, whistle, bleat, snicker, snore, snort, roar, boom, twitter, jabber, flash, fuss, throb, dump, jerk, job, knock, pat, splurge, squelch, blab, blurt, jump, lull, flick, flimsy, flip, gag, gush, gulp.*

PROBLEM 6.27: Write down new words for the following sounds: (1) chalk screeching on a blackboard, (2) a suitcase bumping down a flight of stairs, (3) tinkling crystal, (4) someone sniffling, (5) a door slamming, (6) cloth ripping, (7) trees rustling in the wind, (8) automobiles crashing, (9) an electric motor humming, (10) the horn on a diesel locomotive, (11) someone typewriting. Are there any generalizations to be made? You will have to combine your results with your fellow students or yourself take a large sample to get enough data.

PROBLEM 6.28: What are the differences in the sounds referred to by *bong–bonk, thrum–thrump, clang–clank, clunk–thunk, smack–thwack. Dunt, dindle,* and *dirl* are British dialect words which refer to sounds. Before you look them up in the **OED**, guess what they refer to.

Synesthetic Sound Symbolism

When we move from words referring to sounds to words referring to other dimensions of physical phenomena, we are on even less certain grounds. The iconic dimension is still relevant, but now the relationship is **synesthetic**: the use of one sense, sound, to represent another perceptual dimension—size, movement, hue, emotion, for example. In "echoic" words, sounds are used to represent sounds; but many psycholinguists have tried to make a case for sounds representing size, movement, color, and even emotions.

All physical experience can be scaled: movement, dimension, sound, color, tactile consistency, temperature, and so on. Most have several simultaneous dimensions: sounds are measured by pitch, volume, overtones; color by saturation, intensity, and hue; dimension by height, breadth, and depth; movement by velocity, acceleration, and direction. The problem is to determine whether any of these scales can be consistently correlated with any of the scales we can devise for the way we pronounce words referring to those phenomena.

PROBLEM 6.29: Figure 6.1 shows pictures of four animals. Ask several people to make up names for them without using parts of recognizable words. That is, do not call (a) something like a *mousaphant*. Collect the names and tabulate the length of each word according to the size of the animal, and the kind of stressed vowel. That is, if (a) were called a *blorgey*, the stressed vowel would be an "aw" or "o" sound. Use Table 6.4 to tabulate the sounds. High means a sound made with the tongue bunched up high in the mouth. Front means the tongue is pushed forward. Thus a high front sound is /i/ or /ī/ as in *fit* and *feet*. A low back sound is /ɔ/, as in *bawd* or *bought*.

TABLE 6.4   VOWEL CHART

		Front		Central		Back
HIGH	/ī/	*feet*			/ū/	*pool*
	/i/	*fit*			/u/	*pull*
MID	/ē/	*bait*	/ə/	*but*	/ō/	*boat*
	/e/	*bet*				
LOW	/æ/	*bat*	/a/	*hot*	/ɔ/	*bought*

These are **diphthongs**, sounds made of two parts: /ai/ as in *hide*, /au/ as in *loud*, /ɔi/ as in *boy*.

PROBLEM 6.30: Here are descriptions for several actions. Ask several native speakers to make up words for them. Can any generalizations be made in

(A)

(B)

(C)

(D)

Figure 6.1

regard to the kind of consonant sounds they choose? The kind of syllable structure? (1) Rapid movements of the hands to indicate nervousness, (2) slow and steady pulling a load uphill, (3) thousands of lights blinking on and off, (4) tickling someone on the back of the neck, (5) punching someone in the stomach, (6) a fine rain, (7) an avalanch of snow, (8) fog drifting through the streets, (9) the circular movement of a mosquito in the air.

PROBLEM 6.31: Here are some pairs of words. One refers to a very small animal, the other to a very large one. Which is which? *weeg–wog, gleep–gloop, dobe–dabe, fam–fawm, spant–spint, fozzle–fuzzle, scug* (pronounced like the *-oo-* in *took*)–*scawg* (as in *ought*). Use the same pairs to associate with very light colored and very dark colored animals; very stupid and very smart animals, very beautiful and very ugly ones, very slow and very smart ones. Generalize about the nature of the vowels associated with the various concepts. Why is the likelihood of the "right" answer greater when one is given a word than when one is asked to create one?

PROBLEM 6.32: Ask several English speakers to associate meanings of their own choosing with the words in Problem 6.31. Is it possible to generalize about the kinds of meanings they associate with various vowel sounds?

From these problems it is apparent that—conventionally in English, at any rate—we associate certain sounds with other phenomenal scales. When making up words, we are perhaps somewhat more likely to choose low back vowels to refer to large objects, slow movements, dark colors, low sounds, sad emotions. Conventionally, we associate high front vowels with the opposite concepts.

PROBLEM 6.33: Does the natural vocabulary of this semantic field support this generalization? *dumb, stupid, dope, dull, foolish, idiotic, moronic, dim, silly, obtuse, simple, imbecilic, intelligent, keen, bright, quick, slow, sharp, genius, witty, smart, shrewd, astute, clever, wise.*

PROBLEM 6.34: Pick a category entry in **Roget's Thesaurus** that would lend itself to synesthetic interpretation: size, speed, weight, and so on. Tabulate whether the stressed vowel in the words that indicate large size or quick movement or whatever tend to select vowels of a particular phonetic shape. What statistical problems present themselves in such a problem? (19, 136)

None of this implies, of course, that all low back vowels mean dark, low, sad, slow things and high front vowels the opposite: *big* and *small*, *dim* and *glowing*, *tearful* and *joyful* testify to that. It only means that in English when we make up new words or are forced to associate nonsense syllables with certain phenomena, we conventionally draw upon certain groups of sounds.

Phonesthemes

Some linguists have gone one step further in phonetic symbolism.

PROBLEM 6.35: Here are some common words beginning with various consonant clusters. Is there any sub-group among them that is related in meaning? If so, how would you explain it?

GL-: *glacé, glacier, glad, glade, gladiator, gladiolus, glamour, glance, gland, glare, glass, glaucoma, glaze, gleam, glean, glee, glen, glib, glide, glimmer, glimpse, glint, glissade, glisten, glitter, gloaming, gloat, globe, gloom glory, gloss, glottis, glove, glow, glue, glum, glut, glutton, glycerine.*

FL-: *flail, flame, flap, flare, flash, flaunt, flee, fleet, flick, flicker, fling, flit, float, flog, flop, flip, flounce, flourish, flout, flow, fluent, flute, fluid, flume, flurry, flush, fluster, flutter, flux, fly, flat, flaccid, flatulent, flea, flint, floor, flour, flower, flunkey.*

SP-: *spat, spatter, spew, spirit, spit, spout, spray, spume, spurt, sputter, spurn.*

SN-: *snarl, sneer, sneeze, snicker, sniff, sniffle, snigger, sniffle, snoop, snore, snort, snout, snuffle, snuggle, snob, snub.*

-UMP, -UNK, -UG, etc.: *bump, thunk, hump, glump, dump, clump, clunk, sunk, funk, hunk, gunk, frump, glum, crumple, junk, lump, lunk, mump, punk, plunk, plump, rump, sump, stunt, stump, trunk, tug, ugh, mug, hug, dug, rug, tug, jug, lug, pug, rumble, tumble, humble, fumble.*

Are any of these words echoic? Look up groups of these words in other languages. What do you conclude? Look up various initial consonant clusters in other languages. What do you conclude?

Much of what we call phonetic symbolism in this area is still specific to the conventions of English. Linguists have a word for combinations like *fl-*, *gl-*, *sp-* and so on that seem to have a kind of diffuse meaning: **phonesthemes**. About all that can be concluded from them is that if English speakers coin new words, they will very likely follow the sound patterns that have become conventionalized for the referent. (16)

PSYCHOLOGICAL AND SOCIAL MOTIVES IN WORD CREATION

We borrow, create, transform, and derive words in these ways for reasons that are semantic, social, and psychological. Some words are created and borrowed to fit new artifactual and culturally restricted phenomena: *wombat, lewisite, WPA, motel, smog.* Other words seem to cover an area of psychic space that, as it were, existed in our conscious or subconscious mind and thereby needed words to objectify it: *taboo, gestapo, vandalize, spartan.* Words like these did not originally refer to broad areas of our cultural or psychological lives. But once these words were made available and precipitated or crystallized those amorphous psychological areas into the consciousness of language, the words both reflected part of English/American culture and directed the attention of its speakers to the concepts they refer to, thereby making those concepts more accessible.

The social consequences of borrowing, creating, compounding and so on, though, are equally important in the way we adapt to or create a social situation. If we postulate two poles: formal and intimate, we can roughly assign different kinds of word sources to different situations:

More Intimate	More Formal
Native inheritance	French, Latin, and Greek borrowings
Clips and compounds	Full forms, few compounds
Underived forms	Heavily derived forms

Compare two admittedly extreme examples:

1. *I think I'll cut 'cross the quad back t' the dorm 'n hit the books for the psych final with my roomie.*
2. *My decision is to traverse the quadrangle to return to the dormitory to study for my psychology final examination with the individual with whom I share a room.*

The general interaction between social class and style can be represented very roughly as follows:

Higher Class   Lower Class

Formal —— Formal
Informal —— Informal
Casual —— Casual
Intimate ——————— Intimate

That is, the frequency of features characterizing a formal style will in the (relatively) lower social dialect class generally be shifted statistically down relative to the styles in the (relatively) higher class dialect, except perhaps at the most intimate level where half-finished sentences, murmured words, and tone of voice convey information in much the same way in both classes.

But there occurs a frequent exception to this generalization. In some cases, the very formal style of someone in the most upwardly mobile group will display **more** formal cues in formal situations than does the upper middle class speaker in the same social situation. This gives us a relationship something like this:

Upper-Middle Class   Lower-Middle Class

```
                              ┌Formal
Formal┐            ┌──────────┘
Informal└──────────┴─────────┐ Informal
Casual┐            ┌──────────┘ Casual
Intimate────────────────────── Intimate
```

This may explain why so many French (and later Latin) words shifted into more casual as well as formal English after social classes began to shift. The rule for the distribution of Romance words in various styles of upper-middle class social dialects might originally have looked something like this:

1. **Intimate:** Native words$_{\text{sets } A-B-C-D}$ + French words$_{\text{set } W}$
2. **Informal:** Native words$_{\text{sets } A-B}$ + French words$_{\text{sets } W-X-Y}$
3. **Casual:** Native words$_{\text{sets } A-B-C}$ + French words$_{\text{sets } W-X}$
4. **Formal:** Native words$_{\text{set } A}$ + French words$_{\text{sets } W-X-Y-Z}$

(This says nothing about the relative sizes of any of these sets. A would certainly be the largest, however.) As a speaker moved from an intimate to a formal style, he probably successively replaced native English words with borrowings: Casual $X > D$, informal: $Y > C$, formal: $Z > B$, or more accurately perhaps, increased the frequency of one category and decreased the frequency of another.

But just as a child overgeneralizes and uses -*ed* too frequently—*hugged, goed, singed*—so perhaps the upwardly mobile Anglo-Saxon speaker used too many French words too often where they did not belong, in less than very formal contexts, by inappropriately using the largest subset of French words, *W–Z*, that characterized a formal style of a particular social dialect. It may have been this pattern of word choice that John of Salisbury had in mind around the middle of the twelfth century when he observed that it was fashionable for English speakers to use French words in English conversation. In this way, French words worked their way into the informal and casual speech of native Englishmen.

A complete study of word borrowing, derivation, and creation would probe much more deeply into grammar and phonology. Stress patterns are a test for compound words. But how we assign stress finally depends on the grammatical processes involved in compounding, a problem much more complex than we have described here. Derivation includes more than just adding an ending: *revise–revision* differ in the vowel change from pairs like *resist–resistance.*

But we have discovered some important facts about our words and their sources. The wide range of borrowing and processes of word creation gives us a flexibility and exactness of expression rivaled by few other languages. Our lexical resources allow us to modulate our style, to express fine nuances of denotative and connotative meaning, to distinguish among social dialects, and even to control the rhythm of our sentences. Its possibilities range from the Anglo-Saxon monosyllabic simplicity of the **King James Bible**:

> In the beginning was the Word, and the Word was with God, and the Word was God. The same was in the beginning with God. All things were made by him; and without him was not any thing made that was made. In him was life; and the life was the light of men. And the light shineth in darkness; and the darkness comprehendeth it not.
>
> John 1:1–5

to the rolling polysyllabic Latinate chords of Dr. Johnson:

> That praises are without reason lavished on the dead, and that the honors due only to excellence are paid to antiquity, is a complaint likely to be always continued by those who, being able to add nothing to truth, hope for eminence from the heresies of paradox; or those who, being forced by disappointment upon consolatory expedients, are willing to hope from posterity what the present age refuses, and flatter themselves that the regard which is yet denied by envy will be at last bestowed by time.
>
> **Preface to Shakespeare**

OUR VOCABULARY AND ITS SOURCES: A SUMMARY

In Table 6.1, we sketched the outlines of the processes involved in grammatical word formation. Now that we have reviewed several other processes, we can suggest a more comprehensive system. There are three sources of roots, three kinds of root-modifications, and an interlocking process of two kinds of grammatical word formation. The entire system can be approximated like this:

ROOTS

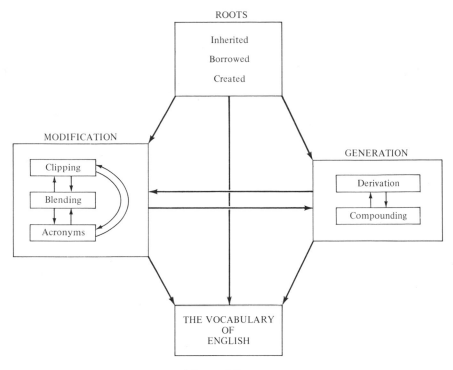

Figure 6.2

PROBLEM 6.36: Provide examples for the following processes plus five more of your own device. The root-source is in brackets; the process follows.

1. [Native]_____
2. [Created]_____
3. [Borrowed]_____
4. [Native] clipped_____
5. [Borrowed] clipped_____
6. [[Native] + [borrowed]] blended _____
7. [[Native] + [borrowed]] compounded _____
8. [[[Native] derived] + [native]] compounded _____
9. [[Borrowed] clip] derived _____
10. [[[Borrowed] derived] + [borrowed] clip] compounded _____

Chapter 7

SEMANTIC CHANGE

Unlike changes in pronunciation, syntax, or usage, the ways in which meanings change open up such interesting bypaths on social, political, and cultural history that one is tempted to wander aimlessly through historical semantic space, turning from one etymological curiosity to the next. *Surly*, for example, comes from ME *sir-ly*, from Old French *sire*, which came from *seoir*, from the slurred pronunciation of *senior*, the comparative of Latin *senex*, or aged one. A *Sir* (i.e., a sire) apparently acted sir-ly. The re-spelling hides the fact that English Sirs—or those who styled themselves such—in the fifteenth and sixteenth centuries apparently were not a generally likable lot.

Christ, cream, cretin and *grind* are all related. An Indo-European root related to *grind*, **ghrei-*, became in Greek *khrisma*, or the anointing oil produced by grinding. *Christ* comes from *khristas*, past participle of Greek *khrein* (to anoint), since he was the one anointed with oil produced by grinding. *Chrisma* (oil) also gives Old French *cresme*, which when borrowed in ME became *creme*, or the most desirable liquid that separates out from milk, or *cream*, any whitish semi-solid substance that is rubbed on something. *Cretin* is a Swiss patois word ultimately from Latin *Christianum*, which meant human creature, apparently a euphemism for those who suffered from the condition found so frequently in the Alps.

Dope comes from Dutch *doopen*, to dip, hence any sauce that is dipped.

153

It then came to mean any viscous fluid. Then in the later nineteenth century, it came to mean any opium preparation, then a specific one used on race horses, hence *dope-sheet* (information about horses), hence *dope* first as spurious information, then any information (i.e., *the straight dope* and to *dope something out*). The opium meaning then generalized to any narcotic, to pills, powders, or fluids, and also shifted to the person who is doped, a doped person, hence *a dope. Airplane dope* is a relic from the viscous fluid meaning.

And in one of the more curious results of meaning change, it has been seriously proposed that *whip*, *viper*, and *wife* are all related.

One could go on and on listing histories like these. But it would be only that—a list of anecdotes. It would give us no insight into the general processes of language, into any principles of semantic change, into how and why semantic changes occur, into the regular patterns of change and what we can discover through semantic change about our language, possibly about our society, and perhaps even about our mental processes.

THEORIES OF MEANING

As we have emphasized, however, we cannot explain how meaning has changed without an adequate theory of how words have meaning. Unfortunately, of all the areas of linguistics, meaning is the least well understood. Not only are linguists unclear about how a theory of meaning should explain what a word means; they are not even certain that when they ask what a word means, they know what they want to know. The meaning of "meaning" has been debated at least since Plato, and the semanticists exploring that question in the last decade have raised more questions that they have answered. But as in physics, biology, and all the other lively sciences, progress in linguistics can be measured by how much we discover we do not know.

Older theories of meaning have proved to be irrelevant to problems of linguistic meaning. Not too many decades ago, psychologists and philosophers talked about meaning as the images that words stimulated in their minds. Unfortunately, no one was able to describe these images in a way that let the listeners perceive how they might be similar to their own images. And under any circumstances, it is difficult to imagine what images, if any, spring before us when we hear a sentence like *Relational concepts presuppose perceptual processes.*

When behavioral psychologists came to dominate psychology in the twenties and thirties (as to a great extent they still do), it became unfashionable to introspect about what went on inside one's head. They began quantitatively describing what a word meant in terms of what they could objectively observe about the way people behaved after hearing it. Preoccupied with stimulus-response-reinforcement schedules and the like, they naturally reformulated the problem of meaning in their own theoretical terms. A referent (object) stimulates us to respond in certain ways. One is to utter a word that has, through conditioning, become associated with that referent. As the word becomes attached to the referent through conditioning, we transfer our responses from the referent to the word. Thus when we hear or read the word, we respond to it as we would to the referent. But obviously, when anyone utters the words *red-hot poker*, none of us claps his ears in pain. So behaviorists had to qualify this simpleminded stimulus-response-transference theory to say that we respond with a **partial readiness to respond**, selecting out only certain aspects of the red-hot-poker-experience to associate with the word and respond to. (156, 157, 191, 199, 207)

Unfortunately, even if this does accurately describe what happens when we hear a word, it does not tell us very much about the meaning of *Relational concepts presuppose perceptual processing*. It is not at all clear what our response to the referents (whatever **they** are), of those words would be; less clear how we are supposed to be "ready" to respond to the words referring to those referents; and less clear yet how we are supposed to be ready to respond to the words in the context of a sentence. How is it that we know that when someone says something as simple as *The door is open* he might intend us to create in our minds the meaning I-locked-the-door-when-I-left-so-someone-has-opened-it-and-we-must-be-careful?

PROBLEM 7.1: Among the ways psychologists have tried to measure meaning objectively are these: (1) **Word association.** A speaker gives all the words a particular word makes him think of. (2) **Sorting.** A speaker puts together words that seem to go together. Then he subdivides them again and again. Or he groups the groups into higher order categories:

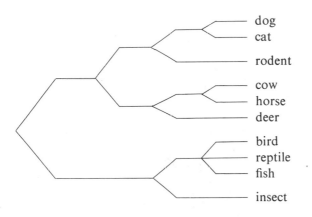

- dog
- cat
- rodent
- cow
- horse
- deer
- bird
- reptile
- fish
- insect

(3) **Semantic differential.** A speaker is asked to rank a word along scales that link several pairs of polar adjectives: *warm_____cold, hard_____ soft, fast_____slow,* and so on. Given this admittedly incomplete description of the three theories, what is wrong with each of them? (38, 157, 203)

At about the same time that the stimulus-response psychologists were working out their behavioral theories, linguists were trying to identify the smallest observable units of linguistic meaning. And impressed with the apparent successes of their fellow social scientists, the linguists adopted the same objectivist, empiricist stance in their analysis of language. Asked the meaning of a word, a linguist would be likely to answer with an empirical definition based on what he could see and categorize, a definition that in more recent years sounded something like *The meaning of a word is the sum of its linguistic environments.* That is, the meaning of a word is the sum of all the sentences the word might appear in. (84, 156, 208, 233)

PROBLEM 7.2: What is wrong with this definition?

And at about the same time, philosophers were also wrestling with the problem of meaning, equally unsuccessfully. The definitions ranged from meaning being what is necessary to make a proposition true, to what the words refer to, to how a word is used, to the method of proving the truth of an assertion, to the "picture" a sentence makes. (191)

But the principal weakness in all these definitions is that none of them allows us to deal with the specific meaning of a word in the context of a specific sentence and how that specific meaning might become a new meaning. Nor do they give us a useful way to represent a meaning in formal terms. Claiming that the meaning of *book* is the sum of its linguistic environments or the way it is used or the words elicited by it in free association yields a definition that no one can do anything with. Indeed, it yields no definition at all.

We have already suggested in Chapter Two the outlines of a theory of meaning we shall use to describe how meaning changes. We shall define the meaning of a word as the sum of the elemental components of meaning that we abstract from all the experiences we necessarily associate with the use of a word. On the one hand, it is easy enough to say now that the meaning of *boy* is the sum of [+object, +count, +animate, +human, +male, −adult]

because these are the common characteristics of virtually all the ⚇ 's we have experienced. But the same criticisms we level against word-association-ists or semantic differentials or word-sorters might appear to be valid here: What is the meaning of [+human] or [−adult]? Must we define the components of meaning in order to have a legitimate theory of meaning?

On the other hand, we have the example of the rest of the scientific and philosophical world. There are, in every constructed system of knowledge, undefined primitives. Euclid's **Elements** has as its first definition *A point is that which has no part.* But what is the definition of *part* or of *no* or of *has*? In number theory, not every concept can be defined. What is the meaning of "more than"? What is the meaning of "one"? In short, we may have to be ready to accept the idea that some of the elements, perhaps a relatively few components of meaning, are simply to be accepted as undefined primitives in the system, exactly as some mathematicians accept the idea of **number** as an undefined primitive.

But even if we do this, we are faced with an equally difficult question: Given these undefined semantic components, how do they relate to one another and how should those relationships be represented? Several ways have been proposed. One resembles the model of syntactic relationships. A fairly simple word like *girl*, for example, can be represented as a series of modifying structures providing more and more specific details. That is, the meaning of the word *girl* is a noun that is concrete, animate, human, not male, and not adult.

A more complex word like *confess* has a more complex structure. That is, one meaning of *confess* is roughly representable as the diagram on page 159.

Human$_1$ states to human$_2$ that 1 acknowledges that 1 is responsible for an action which 2 presumably did not know that 1 performed and which 1 believes 1 should not have previously revealed. This omits a good deal of secondary information such as the internal structure of *state*, *acknowledge*, *responsible for*, *action*, and so on.

PROBLEM 7.3: In a very general way, without relying on the very formal tree structure in the examples, sketch the semantic structure for these words: *admit, acknowledge, deny, brag, criticize, accuse, blame, praise.*

For our purposes here, however, we cannot possibly represent every word we discuss in such detail, even though describing the precise nature of a semantic change on **trees** such as these would reveal a good deal about historical processes. The components will instead be merely listed after each word in a purely suggestive way, as only very informal outlines of what kinds of components are relevant to certain historical changes. Eventually, perhaps, semanticists and psycholinguists will discover ultimate particles of meaning, the true primitives in the system. At the moment, however, we are in the position of yesterday's physicist. We know there are molecules (like *man*) made up of atoms [+ object, + animate, + human, + male, + adult] organized into structures. We also know that perhaps these atoms are made up of smaller but rather obscure particles organized in ways that are not at all clear. (29, 101, 102, 143, 237)

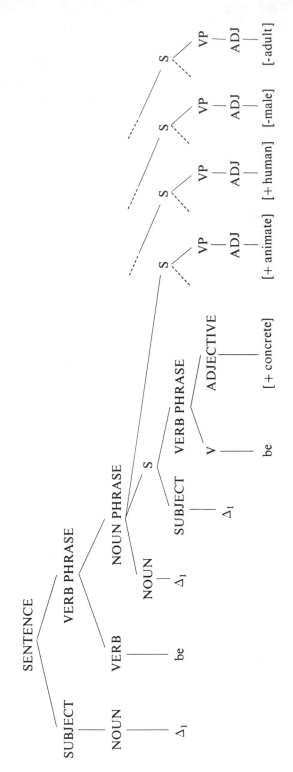

A rough paraphrase: A noun is some noun that is concrete, animate, human, not male, not adult.

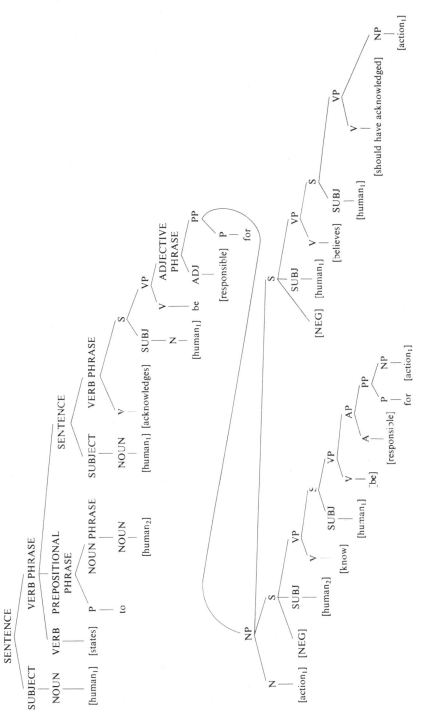

A rough paraphrase: Human₁ states to human₂ that he acknowledges that he is responsible for an action₁ which h₂ did not know h₁ was responsible for and which h₁ does not believe h₁ should have acknowledged.

WORDS, MEANINGS, AND THOUGHTS

It is easy to assume that we can abstract from our experience components like concreteness, animateness, and so on, because that is what reality out there is like. Words refer to areas of experience that have a natural discreteness and independence in objective reality. But if for a moment we can imagine our total perceptual and cognitive experiences as a finely meshed screen of perceptions and responses and potential ideas, then we will see that the words of our language cover only a relatively few areas on that screen, and that it is possible to divide that screen into many kinds of areas and subareas.

There are ways of structuring areas of our experience for which we have no words, no single words, but for which other cultures do. We have *brother* and *sister* to subcategorize siblings, but Hungarian has four: *batya*, for older brother; *öcs*, for younger brother; *néne*, older sister; and *hug*, younger sister. Malay, on the other hand, has one word that covers not only siblings but cousins as well: *saudara*. We have no single word to cover both *aunt* and *uncle* as we have a single word, *parents*, to cover *father* and *mother*, and *children* to cover both *son* and *daughter*. Nor do we have words to distinguish male and female cousins as we do to distinguish male and female siblings: *brother* and *sister*.

Some languages have basic color terms for only black and white; others for only black, white, and red; others for only black, white, red, and either yellow or green. Some languages have as many as eleven basic, nonmetaphorical color terms. In some languages, a single color term covers an area of the spectrum we would refer to with three words: *red–orange–yellow*. (9)

PROBLEM 7.4: Here are the great majority of OE words, including compounds, that refer to color. How does this semantic field differ from the color field of ModE? Keep in mind that the English translations cannot be considered entirely reliable.

hwit (white), *mærehwit* (pure white), *snawhwit* (snow white), *scir* (white, bright), *beorht* (bright), *leoht* (bright), *searohwit* (brilliant whiteness), *torht* (clearness, brightness), *leoma* (radiance, gleam, glare), *scima* (brightness), *bleobrygd* (scintillation), *glæd* (shining), *glæm* (gleam), *hador* (clearness, brightness), *hlutor* (bright), *blican* (to glitter, shine), *scinan* (to shine), *bierhtan* (to brighten), *lyman* (to shine), *scimian* (to shine), *scimerian* (to shimmer), *tytan* (to shine), *spircing* (sparkling).

geolu (yellow), *scilfor* (yellow, golden, glittering), *goldbleoh* (golden hued), *crog* (saffron hued), *geoluread* (reddish gold), *read* (red, gold), *rudu* (red), *healfread* (halfred), *bocread* (vermillion), *wealhbaso* (foreign red, vermillion), *blæhæwen* (light blue), *grene* (green), *hæwengrene* (cerulean).

pæll (purple), *purpure* (purple), *basu* (purple, scarlet, crimson), *brunbasu* (brownish-purple), *bleoread* (purple), *readbasu* (reddish purple), *wyrmread* (purple, scarlet), *weolocbasu* (whelkred–purple), *weolocread* (whelkred–scarlet, purple), *hæwen* (purple, blue, azure, green), *hæwmænged* (mixed purple), *wæden* (purple, bluish), *teafor* (purple, red, vermillion), *cynewaðen* (of royal purple), *fiscdeah* (fishdye–purple).

fealu (yellow, tawny, grey, dusky, dark), *dunn* (brown, dingy), *hasu* (dusky, grey ashen), *healfhwit* (halfwhite), *græg* (grey), *har* (hoary, grey), *deorcegræg* (dark grey), *brun* (dark, dusky, metallic, lustre), *dungræg* (dark, dusky), *æhiwness* (pallor), *wann* (dark, dusky, livid), *brunwann* (dusky), *æscfealu* (ashyhued), *aescræg* (ashygrey), *assedun* (ass-colored), *sinderhæwe* (cindergrey).

blac (bright, pallid, wan), *blat* (livid, pale, wan), *mirce* (murky, dark), *blæc* (black, dark), *deorc* (dark), *dimm* (dark), *hoðma* (darkness), *hærfnsweart* (raven-black), *þeostor* (dark), *dimhiw* (of dark color), *ælmyrca* (entirely black).

brigd (play of color), *bregdan* (change of color), *cylu* (spotted), *fah* (dappled, stained).

PROBLEM 7.5: How has ModE expanded its vocabulary of color words? What have been the sources of such color words as *orange, pink, chestnut, olive, violet, lavender, scarlet, vermillion, carmine, maroon, magenta, puce, azure, indigo, auburn, hazel, fawn, russet, chocolate, tan, emerald, chartreuse, rose, cherry, plum, salmon, citrine, lemon, navy, ochre, apricot*? What area of the spectrum had the richest vocabulary in OE? What hue area of the ModE spectrum has the richest vocabulary? The poorest? Where will we find new color terms? Predict one for each of the following areas: red, orange, yellow, green, blue.

SEMANTIC STRUCTURE

But if we cannot always be sure that all languages divide experience into the same categories, yet the way they assign words to experience is similar enough from language to language to suggest that some semantic universals may characterize all human languages, perhaps even human cognition itself. All languages, for example, distinguish nouns that categorize abstract from concrete experience; animate from inanimate referents; human from non-human; male from female. Individual items might be classified differently from language to language, but all languages systematically classify experience along these and other lines.

All languages also have ways to classify objects and experiences into higher and lower categories. *Animal* names the class to which fish, birds, and other creatures belong. *Bird*, in turn, names the set to which belong the subsets *pigeon*, *eagle*, *ostrich*, *chicken*, and *duck*. And in turn, *duck* names the set referred to as *canvasback*, *mallard*, and so on. Beyond this, we have to form subsets periphrastically, by making up complex phrases: *the mallards in my pond*, *that mallard flying past*, and so on. For these subsets, our language provides us with no individual word or term because they are not important enough in our culture to require a name.

Thus, when words communicate meanings, they name not individual experiences, but **classes** of experiences. The more we assign experiences to the categories our language gives us, the more we refine and abstract the characteristics of those categories. The linguistic meaning of a word is the set of abstracted characteristics (which we shall call **semantic features**) necessary to distinguish the category which the word names from all other categories. Thus one minimal meaning of *girl* must include [+young] and [−male] to distinguish the class that *girl* names from the classes that *woman* and *boy* name.

Words for more general categories require fewer semantic features than words referring to more specific categories. The meaning of *tree* is composed of the features we might call [+concrete, +live, −animate, +vegetative, +trunked]. The category named by *pine* would add at least one more feature, perhaps something like [−leafed]. *Plant*, on the other hand, would have one fewer feature, lacking [±trunked]. (All these features, be aware, are purely *ad hoc* inventions. A thorough investigation of the semantics of plant names in English is a book-length study itself.)

Certain features also imply other more general features. Anything [+animate], for example, must also be [+live] and [+concrete]. Anything [+male] must be [+live]. But some features cut across categories. Although [±male] may imply [+live], it does not necessarily imply [+human] because [±male] also distinguishes [−human] words like *bull–cow* and *boar–sow*.

PROBLEM 7.6: Analyze the prefixes in Problem 6.7 into semantic features. *Hyper-* and *sub-*, for example, must differ by at least something we can approximate as [±above], *pre-* and *post-* by [±before]. How do the OE prefixes differ in their semantic makeup from borrowed prefixes? Can features describe colors?

So far, our description of meaning has emphasized logical categories. But we respond to objects and experiences not only rationally and logically but emotionally as well. Compare the emotional responses to the words *filth* and *love*. Unfortunately, it is very difficult to do much more than categorize these responses along a scale of favorable–unfavorable. Nonetheless, [±favorable] may be a legitimate characteristic of a linguistic experience because we distinguish words by it. Compare *do-gooder* and *philanthropist*, *intellectual* and *egg-head*, *promiscuity* and *swinging*.

Related to this aspect of meaning is another we have already touched on. We have many pairs of words which differ by social level:

My instructor postponed the short unannounced examination.
My teacher put off the pop-quiz.

We classify the same experience in different categories named by words that reflect how we relate to our context and to our audience. In this sense, meaning inheres not just in the relationship between the word and the referent isolated from its context, but in the total relationship between word, referent, social context, speaker, and his audience. The meaning of *rip-off* is different from the meaning of *steal* precisely in the different ways the speaker relates to his audience and his subject at the moment he is speaking.

Yet another kind of meaning that can only be defined by the grammar of the language is grammatical meaning. What for example, is the meaning of *do* in *He does not need it*; of *to* in *He wants to leave*; of *of* in *Some of the people left*; of *be* in *He was being helped*; of *have* in *He has gone*. These are grammatical words, **function words**, that indicate grammatical rather than semantic information. Some words hover between grammatical and semantic information: *a* in *a boy left* is grammatical in that it indicates a noun that can be counted (Contrast *a boy* and **a chaos*) and that has not been mentioned in the previous discourse. But it also indicates singleness, a concept which is both semantic and grammatical.

A truly global theory of meaning, however, would move into even more amorphously defined areas of meaning. In addition to using words, we also communicate through our tone of voice, the speed we speak, our gestures, our posture, even how close we stand to the person we are speaking to. All these features overlay the words we speak to communicate messages about our emotions and attitudes. But while **paralinguistics** (tone of voice and so on) and **kinesics** (posture, gestures, and so on) are probably as systematic as the more formally defined areas of grammar and phonology, they are much less well described and certainly beyond our ability to re-create for speakers who lived before the phonograph and the movie camera.

THE RECOVERY OF MEANING

Complicated as all this may seem, it is part of the semantic competence of a native speaker of English. But recovering even a fraction of this information from the past is difficult, to say the least. Since we have no native speakers of Old or Middle English available, we have to rely on indirect ways to recover meaning. And from the outset, we have to acknowledge that we will recover only a narrow range of the global meaning of any given message. We will have nothing to say about intonation, relatively little to say about the way particular words might have meant different things in different contexts. We have already touched on the social prestige of French and Latin words. Given the probable attitude of Anglo-Saxons toward kinship and war, we can make some reasonable guesses about the affective meaning of a word like *broðor* (brother) or *fæderencnosl* (father's kin), *guð* (battle), or *sweord* (sword). For the most part, though, we shall restrict ourselves to the most traditional areas of meaning of individual words and how their meanings have changed.

Dictionaries

The first and most obvious way to recover meaning would be to refer to old dictionaries. Unfortunately, the first dictionaries of English (excluding glosses on Latin and French words and bilingual dictionaries) did not appear until the beginning of the seventeenth century.

PROBLEM 7.7: Listed below are the first fifteen words from the letters: *do-* in six early dictionaries. What kinds of concerns do these dictionaries appear to have had? For Minsheu, Phillips, and Bailey, the number of words from the fifteenth word to the entry for *dog* is also listed in order to suggest the degree of completeness each lexicographer strived for. Comment. Compare the same span in a modern dictionary.

> John Bullokar. **English Expositor** (1614). *Docility, docible, docibility, dock, docket, doctoral, doctrinal, document, dodrantal, dogmatical, dollar, dolorous, dolphin, doom, doomsday-book.*

> John Minsheu. **Ductor in Linguas** (1617). *Do, doat, doater, doating, dobchicke, dobeler, doblet, doced, docible, docilitie, docke, docke, docked, dockes* (plus 15 more to *dogge*).

> Henry Cockeram. **The English Dictionarie** (1623). *Dodechaedron, docible, docility, document, dogdaies, dogmaticall, dogmatist, dole, dolefull, dolorificall, dolorous, domable, domesticke, domesticall, domineere.*

Thomas Blount. **Glossographia** (1656). *Docket, docible, docibility, docilize, doctiloquent, document, dodecatemorie, dodechadron, Dodona, dodrantal, dog-days, Doge, dogdraw, dogmatical, dogmatist.*

Edward Phillips. **New World of Words** (1658). *Dobeler, dobun, doced, docility, dock, docket, doctoral, document, dodded, dodder, dodecaedrie, dodecagon, dodecatemorie, dodkin, Dodona* (plus three more to *dog daies*).

Nathan Bailey. **An Universal Etymological English Dictionary** (1721). *Dobuni, docible, docile, docility, docilize, dock, dock, dry dock, wet dock, to dock, to dock, dock, docked, docket, docket* (plus 27 more to *dog*).

PROBLEM 7.8: Below are entries for *explode* from several early dictionaries. What information can we recover from each entry? What appears to be the intentions of each dictionary? What information is provided? What information is not provided?

1. Bulloker. Explode: to drive out with clapping the hands.
2. Minshew. (no entry for *explode*)
3. Cockeram. Explode: to drive out with clapping of hands.
4. Blount. Explode [explodo] publikely to disgrace, or drive out by hissing or clapping of hands.
5. Phillips. (no entry for *explode*, but under *explosion*) explosion, [Lat.] an exploding, a sleighting, or hissing off from the Stage.
6. Bailey. To EXPLODE [Explodere, L.] to decry or cry down; to mistake absolutely.
7. Samuel Johnson. **A Dictionary of the English Language** (1755). To EXPLO'DE. v.a. [explodo, Latin.] (1) To drive out disgracefully with some noise of contempt; to treat with open contempt; to treat not only with neglect, but open disdain or scorn. "Him old and young / *Exploded*, and has seiz'd with violent hands, / Had not a cloud descending snatchd him thence / Unseen amid' the throng." Milton. "Thus was th'applause they meant / Turn'd to *exploding* hiss, triumph to shame, / Cast on themselves from their own mouths." Milton. "Old age *explodes* all but morality." Roscom. "There is pretended, that a magnetical globe or terrella, being placed upon its poles, would have a constant rotation but this is commonly *exploded*, as being against all experience." Wilkins. "Shall that man pass for a proficient in Christ's school, who would have been *exploded* in the school of Zeno?" South. "Provided that no word, which a society shall give a sanction to, be antiquated and *exploded*, they may receive whatever new ones they shall find occasion for." Swift. (2) To drive out with noise and violence. "But late the kindled powder did *explode* / The massy ball, and the brass tube unload." Blackmore.
8. William Kenrick. **New Dictionary** (1773). To EXPLO'DE—EX-PLODE. [Note: Kenrick used the numbers to indicate pronunciation] v.a.

[explodo, Latin.] To drive out disgracefully with some noise of contempt; to treat with open contempt; to treat not only with neglect, but open disdain or scorn.—To drive out with noise and violence.

9. John Ash. **The New and Complete Dictionary of the English Language** (1775). Explo'de [v.t. from the Lat *ex* out of, and *plodo* to clap the hands] To drive out with disgrace, to reject with contempt, to reject with noise and violence.

10. Noah Webster. **Compendious Dictionary of the English Language** (1806). EX-PLŌDE', v.t. (1) To decry or reject with noise; to express disapprobation of, with noise or marks of contempt. (2) To reject with any marks of disapprobation or disdain; to treat with contempt, and drive from notice; to drive into disrepute; or, **in general**, to condemn; to reject; to cry down. (3) To drive out with violence and noise.

Look up *explode* in the unabridged **Oxford English Dictionary**, in **Webster's Third New International**, and in any modern desk dictionary. Compare these ModE meanings with those of the early dictionaries.

PROBLEM 7.9: Samuel Johnson notes after each of these words that it is "low" or "ludicrous" or "cant." Comment. *coax, budge, sensible* (meaning reasonable), *gambler, clever, fun, belabor, cheery, doings, dumfound, ignoramus, job, shabby, slim, stark, visage, tiny, volunteer, width, hanker, fuss, scrape, squabble, tiff, touchy, bang*. What do modern dictionaries have to say about these words?

All dictionaries, however, particularly earlier ones, have severe limitations. By and large, they record the meanings assigned to a word by upper-middle class speakers. Dr. Johnson's dictionary and a few others are exceptions. Only recently have those two master obscenities of English, *fuck* and *cunt*, been included in any of the modern standard reference dictionaries. (We might note, however, that *fuck* and *cunt* did appear in Bailey.) Many dictionaries now regularly include dialectal, slang, and some indecent words. But one has only to think of any piece of current slang—*spaced out*, for example— to realize that in some ways, dictionaries are always out of date. And if modern dictionaries cannot include all the meanings of a word used by upper and lower classes, older dictionaries limited to "hard" words, as they were called, will help even less. It was not until Bailey attempted to create an etymological dictionary in 1721 that a lexicographer felt any reason to include all the words of the language.

So we cannot rely on older dictionaries for more than a fraction of what we want to know, both because the earliest dictionaries go back no further than the beginning of the seventeenth century and because they do not include all the information about the vocabulary that we would like. A handful of brief glossaries and collections of thieves' cant were assembled from the end of the sixteenth century on, but even they are far from adequate. Consequently, we must turn to more indirect means for reconstructing meaning.

Reconstruction

A more important source of information about the distant history of a word is in the common core of meaning retained by cognate words from different languages. All these words, for example, are cognate: From Latin: *Magna*, as in *Magna Carta*, *magnate*, *magnitude*, *magnifier*, *magnificence*; from French, *maistre*, which gives English *master*, *mister*, and by analogy, *mistress*; from Germanic, *much*. Given these forms and others and their meanings, we can triangulate back to a hypothetical IE root, **mag-*, which very likely meant something close to big or large.

As a single example of how components of meaning can endure through time, here is a collection of cognate words from a variety of Indo-European languages, all of which descend from the IE root, **kel-*, a root that is at least 5000 years old.

Sanskrit: *çāla*, a house or shed.
  Greek: *kalia*, hut; *kulon*, eyelid; *Calypso*.
  Latin: *calyx* (f. Gk.) seed-vessel; *calix*, a cup; *clam*, secretly; *clandestīnus*, secret; *cilium*, eyelid; *supercilium*, eyebrow; *superciliōsus*, disdainful; *celāre*, to conceal; *cella*, a store-room; *cellārium*, a larder; *cellārius*, a butler; *occulere*, to hide; *occultātio*, a concealment; *cucullus*, a cowl; *color*, color.
Romance: Old French: *chalice*, a cup; *calc*, a kind of cap.
  Italian: *cellario*, cellar; *cuculla*, cowl.
  French: *conceler*, conceal.
  Provence: *cella*, cell.
Germanic: Gothic: *huljan*, cover; *helms*, helmet.
  Old Norse: *hulstr*, holster.
  Scottish: *howk*, dig out.
  Anglo-Saxon: *helan*, cover; *healle*, hall; *helm*, helmet; *hol*, hollow; *hel*, hell; *hulu*, hull; *hold* (as in hold of a ship).
  Celtic: Old Irish: *ceall*, cell.
  Welsh: *celu*, to hide.

Among the words we have borrowed with the same root include *calyx*, *Calypso*, *apocalypse*, *clandestine*, *cilia*, *supercilious*, *cellule*, *occult*, *chalice*, *cell*, *conceal*, *cellar*, *cowl*, *helmet*, *halberd*, *color*, *caul*, and the *Kil-* (church) in *Kilpatrick*, *Kilkenny*, *Kilchrist*, and so on.

PROBLEM 7.10: *kel- was originally a verbal root. What meaning would you assign to it, based on the cognate words?

A roughly analogous technique for recovering meaning within a contemporary language is to examine the variant meanings of a single current word. The noun *play*, for example, now primarily means active diversion or recreation, or a theatrical performance or its script. But there are other meanings: the play of light on the water, the play (looseness) in a wheel, foul play, sword play. Merely from this information, we cannot be certain that the most general meaning (movement or action) came from the more specific (recreational activity) or vice versa. But from fixed phrases like *sword play*, *gun play*, and the specific sense of *play of light on the water*, we might suspect that the more general meaning, quick movement, is the older one. When we find relatively fixed phrases like *play of light* or *play in a wheel*, they are often the older meanings left behind, frozen in specific contexts, while the more common meaning is a more recent development.

PROBLEM 7.11: Here are pairs of phrases, one illustrating an older meaning, the other a more recent. Assuming that older meanings are often restricted to a narrow range of set phrases or special senses and that newer meanings can occur more freely, decide which phrase contains the older meaning and what that meaning was.

1. We *assumed* he was innocent. The Virgin Mary was *assumed* into heaven.
2. Police try to catch *crooks*. The shepherd's *crook* was in the barn.
3. . . . *deliver* us from evil. *Deliver* this package.
4. Get right with God for *Doomsday* is coming. You are *doomed*, so give up.
5. The outlines were very *faint*. *Faint* heart ne'er won fair maid.
6. There is a *ghost* in the house. Father, Son, and Holy *Ghost*.
7. It's an *ill*-wind that blows no good. I became *ill* from the food.
8. We must *keep* the Sabbath. You can *keep* my money.
9. I'm *mad* at you. He belongs in the *mad*house.
10. You must leave on *pain* of death. I have a *pain* in my leg.
11. You are a *pest*. *Pest*houses are awful places.
12. My friend is a chief *petty* officer. Don't bother me about *petty* things.
13. The flagship *struck* its pennant in surrender. The union *struck* the company.
14. We'll *trip* the light fantastic. We took a *trip* to Mexico.

Citations

The most reliable way to discover the earlier meanings of a word, though, is to collect and study example after example of a word in its linguistic context. For example, consider the meaning of *deor* (the ancestor of ModE *deer*) in these sentences:

c. 950: "Se camal þæt micla dear" (The camel that large *dear*)
c. 1000: "Unicornis, anhyrne deor" (Unicorn, one-horned *deor*)
c. 1200: "Shep is . . . stille der" (Sheep is . . . quiet *der*)
c. 1200: "Lamb iss soffte & stille deor" (Lamb is soft and quiet *deor*)

And consider these compounds: *deorfald* (*fald*–fold), *deornett* (*nett*–net), *deorhege* (*hege*–fence), *deorcynn* (*cynn*–kind), *deorgeat* (*geat*–gate), *deormod* (*mod*–mind, soul) and phrases like *mere deor* (*mere*–sea) and *sæ deor* (*sæ*–sea). It would be odd if all these references were limited to the Cervidae. And when we find citations such as these

Ratons and myse and soch smale dere . . . was hys mete
Rats and mice and such small deer . . . was his meat

it is certain that *deor* originally meant something close to animal or beast, and that our modern meaning of *deer* results from a **narrowing** of *deor's* original semantic range.

When we combine these ways of working back into the semantic history of *deer* with the way Latin words meaning *animal* were translated into OE and with the meaning of cognate words from other languages (Old Frisian *diaar*, Old High German *tior*, Modern German *tier*, and Gothic *dius* all mean animal or beast), we can be fairly certain that the *deor* of OE and ME named a more general category than our modern *deer*. (143)

PROBLEM 7.12: What can you tell about the meaning of these words in *bold face* from their occurrence in the following citations. How have the meanings changed?

1. Ye know the house of Stephanas, that it is the first fruits of Achaia, and that they have **addicted** themselves to the ministry of the saints (1 **Corinthians**, 16.15).
2. And well beseems all the knights of noble name / That **covet** in th'immortal book of fame / To be eternized (Edmund Spenser, **The Faerie Queene**).
3. Better be with the dead / Whom we, to gain our peace, have sent to peace / Than on the torture of the mind to lie / In restless **ecstacy** (**Macbeth**, III.ii).
4. But with an angry wafture of your hand / Gave sign for me to leave you: So I did; / . . . Hoping it was but an effect of **humour**, / Which sometime hath his hour with every man (**Julius Caesar**, II.i).

5. He shall **reward** evil unto mine enemies (**Psalms** 54.5).
6. . . . Irish ladies of Strict virtue and many northern lasses of the same **predicament** (Henry Fielding, **Tom Jones**).
7. They love to **retaliate** kindnesses, and hate any should think they are of a churlish nature (Thomas Tryon, **The Way to Health**).
8. . . . with the most beautiful **stench** [of Paradise] . . . the holy **stench** . . . , . . . delightful **stench** . . . (translated from "The Dream of the Rood," an OE poem).

TYPES OF SEMANTIC CHANGE

Schemes for describing kinds of semantic change are as numerous as those who have investigated the problem. The categories number from three up into the dozens. Part of the problem depends on how we initially approach the question. Should the principal categories arise out of the **reasons** for meaning change, out of the **mechanism** of the change, or from the semantic **consequences** of the change? The theory of meaning we have adopted here—of meaning being represented as a structured configuration of semantic components—leads us to describe change of meaning in those terms. Our categories will depend on how those structured configurations change when a new meaning is associated with a linguistic form. On these grounds, we can set up four basic categories of semantic change.

The first is **narrowing**: A word originally naming a larger category changes to name only a subcategory of the original category: *deer* (animal) > *deer* (family **Cervidae**).

The second is **widening**, the reverse of narrowing: *go* (walk) > *go* (any intended or directed movement or operation).

The third is traditionally called **metaphor**: The form of a word naming a category with a particular characteristic is transferred to name a seemingly very different category, but one which shares that specific characteristic: *grasp* (enclose in the hand) > *grasp* (understand).

The fourth kind of semantic change we shall call **shift**: A form naming a category related by contiguity to a complex of items shifts to a discrete identifiable element in the complex: *bureau* (coarse woolen cloth over a desk) > *bureau* (the desk itself) > *bureau* (the organization that uses such desks).

Narrowing

If we list the major semantic features that roughly define each of the following words and invent some others to account in a shorthand way for those aspects of meaning which are rather complex, we can represent what happens when a word like *deor* narrows from meaning any animal to meaning just the family **Cervidae.** (We shall assume that all the more general features following the entry are implied in the semantic descriptions.)

deor (deer)	liquor	mete (meat)	disease	stol (stool)
⋮	⋮	⋮	⋮	⋮
[+concrete]	[+concrete]	[+concrete]	[−concrete]	[+concrete]
[+animate]	[−animate]	[−animate]	[+state]	[−animate]
[−human]	[−solid]	[+solid]	[+animate]	[+solid]
	[+fluid]	[+consumable]	[−favorable]	[+fabricated]
				[+for sitting on . . .]

That is, *deor* was any non-human animate entity; *liquor* was any liquid; *mete* was any solid consumable; *disease* was any unfavorable state; *stol* was any fabricated object for one person to sit on.

For a variety of social and cultural reasons which we shall not touch on, speakers of English added to each of these bundles of components at least one more feature or complex of features as they used the word to refer to a specific member, to a specific kind of the original larger set, thereby narrowing the range of reference:

deer	liquor	meat	disease	stool
[. . .]	[. . .]	[. . .]	[. . .]	[. . .]
[. . .]	[. . .]	[. . .]	[. . .]	[. . .]
[+mammal]	[+consumable]	[+flesh]	[+systemic]	[−arms, back
[+**Cervidae**]	(later)		[−accident]	+ visible legs]
	[+alcoholic]			
	[+spiritous]			

(Be reminded again that these are inexact and unstructured features.)

PROBLEM 7.13: Here are some words with older meanings in parentheses. In a very general way, suggest the kinds of features you would add to give the words their modern sense: *fowl* (any bird), *shroud* (an article of clothing), *thank* (from the general word for think), *vice* (a flaw), *corn* (any grain), *hound* (any dog), *artillery* (any large implement of war).

In these examples, the narrowing has virtually eliminated the original, more general meaning. But other words **radiate** meanings: A new meaning does not completely replace the older one. Instead, several lines of meaning can develop from a single form. The problem again is whether a new sense means a new word, homonymous with the word that spawned the new meaning. *Execute*, for example, is a form (or a word, depending on whether we decide each different meaning requires us to speak of a separate word) that retains the original general meaning of performing any determined action, even though another meaning also developed, a more narrow one referring to the performance of one particular kind of action: to execute a death sentence, and hence by shift, to execute a man.

PROBLEM 7.14: A question about a word like *execute* is whether we are dealing with one word with different meanings or with homonymous words, each with a different meaning. Given the two methods of dictionary-making we have explored so far—the traditional theory illustrated in all the standard dictionaries where several etymologically related definitions are listed after a single entry, and a theory that lists the semantic components represented by a word, how **would** we decide whether we are dealing with one word with many meanings, or with many words, each with one meaning, all of the same form? What difference does it make?

PROBLEM 7.15: Here is a longer list of words which have narrowed. Can you generalize at all about the kinds of words that might predictably narrow? About the way in which they might narrow? (In some cases, an earlier and later meaning is provided, separated by >. The ModE meaning is not provided for those words, only an earlier meaning.)

1. *admonish* (advise)
2. *affection* (the act of being affected > any affection of the mind)
3. *arrest* (stop)
4. *argue* (make clear)
5. *accost* (come alongside in a boat > to approach anyone)
6. *addict* (someone who devotes himself to anything)
7. *accident* (an event)
8. *carp* (talk)
9. *cunning* (knowledge, skill)
10. *condemn* (pass sentence)
11. *censure* (judge)
12. *denizen* (a citizen of a country or city)
13. *damn* (pass sentence)
14. *deserts* (whatever one deserves, good or bad)
15. *doom* (judge)
16. *effigy* (any likeness)
17. *ecstasy* (beside oneself with any strong emotion: fear, joy, pain)
18. *erotic* (relating to love)
19. *esteem* (put a value on, good or bad)
20. *fame* (report, rumor)

21. *filth* (dirt)
22. *fortune* (chance)
23. *fiend* (the enemy)
24. *grumble* (murmer, make low sounds)
25. *ghost* (spirit)
26. *immoral* (not customary)
27. *lust* (desire in general)
28. *leer* (look obliquely out of the side of the eye)
29. *manure* (v., hold land > to cultivate land)
30. *molest* (trouble or annoy)
31. *orgy* (secret observances)
32. *odor* (anything perceptible to the sense of smell)
33. *pill* (any medicinal ball)
34. *predicament* (any situation)
35. *proposition* (a statement set forth for discussion)
36. *peculiar* (belonging to or characteristic of an individual)
37. *praise* (from (*ap*)*praise*: set a value on, good or bad)
38. *reek* (smoke from burning matter > produce any vapor)
39. *retaliate* (repay for anything)
40. *scheme* (horoscope > diagram > plan)
41. *success* (any outcome)
42. *stink* (any odor)
43. *starve* (die)
44. *seduce* (persuade someone to desert his duty)
45. *smug* (trim, neat)
46. *syndicate* (a group of civil authorities > any group of businessmen pursuing a common commercial activity)
47. *smirk* (smile)
48. *suggestive* (that which suggests something)
49. *sanctimonious* (holy, sacred)

Does any of these words retain its earlier meaning?

PROBLEM 7.16: Illustrate how any ten ModE words might narrow.

Some Causes of Narrowing

Why words narrow, though, cannot be discovered from purely linguistic data. But we might gain a possible insight into one reason some do from the way *pill* has recently narrowed from its original general category of small medicinal ball to the more specific meaning of birth control pill. Two forces, one social, the other psychological, have brought about the change. First, since birth control has become important in our society and therefore frequently discussed, a category of objects like pills that control birth (actually, they should be called *conception control pills*, but that, perhaps, is a bit too explicit) requires a name, not a phrase. Second, since the principle of least effort always operates to create the shortest convenient term for a useful meaning, the full compound phrase, *birth control pill*, became shortened to *The Pill*. Using a theory of semantic features, we can say that the semantic components originally attached to the individual words shifted to the last word, the word that originally named the superordinate set. Schematically, the change can be represented like this:

$$\text{birth} \quad \text{control} \quad \text{pill} \quad > \quad \text{The Pill}$$
$$[+A \dots] \quad [+B \dots] \quad [+C \dots] \quad [+C, +B, +A]$$

It is as if the underlying syntactic structure of the phrase becomes the semantic structure of the word:

$$\text{pill} \quad \text{controls} \quad [\text{someone} \quad \text{gives-birth-to} \quad \text{baby}]$$

That is, the pill controls someone's ability to give birth to a child, a sense compressed into *birth control pill*, and even further into *The Pill*. The meaning seems to have a syntactic structure.

PROBLEM 7.17: In Chapter Six under **Conversion**, we discussed how adjectives can convert to nouns by the same principle of economy. How would you formally describe how the meaning of such words change? What difficulties arise? Demonstrate with these terms: *criminal person, private soldier, chemical substance, vegetable plant, general officer, mortal person.*

In other cases, the narrowing of one word may have been influenced by the fact that two words were available for roughly the same meaning A. When one of the words already has two meanings, A and B, it is often the case that it will lose one of them, say A, if the other word available for A is more prestigious. *Deer* and *beast*, for example, both meant animal in ME, but by this time, another meaning of *deer* was the animal we now associate with that word. Since *beast*, a French borrowing, was undoubtedly more socially prestigious, it probably helped force *deer* to lose the general meaning of animal. The same thing may have happened with *spirit–ghost, odor–stench, table–board, chair–stool, desire–lust*. The first word in each pair is a Romance word, probably more prestigious at a time when the native word had two meanings (or more). The Romance word monopolized one of the meanings while the native word narrowed to one of its more restricted meanings. In some instances, the French word may have helped speed the disappearance of the native word altogether: *face–hleor, voice–stefn, peace–frið, people–leod.* (188)

In other cases, however, a native or borrowed word was available to replace the original semantic space of the narrowed word. Thus instead of a word being pushed toward a narrowed meaning, the empty semantic space left by a word that had already begun to narrow created a kind of semantic vacuum that pulled another word into its space: *dog* replaced the narrowed *hound*; *bird* replaced the narrowed *fowl*; *smile* replaced the narrowed *smirk*; the Danish *die* replaced the narrowed *starve*.

Widening

The opposite of narrowing, logically enough, is **widening.** And it is obvious how a theory of semantic features would represent the simplest examples of this process. The least linguistically based kind of widening occurs when a culture adding radically new objects or processes to the experiences of its speakers uses an old name for a new object. *Picture*, for example, once meant only a painted picture, then also a drawing, then a photograph, a cinematic picture, an X-ray picture, a TV picture, and now even a radio-telescope picture. Where the referent was once a fixed stable object, *picture* now names a class of things that can break up and reassemble themselves, dissolve, and in the case of laser holography, even be three dimensional.

Sail once meant to cross water propelled by windpower. Now we can "sail" under the ocean in nuclear powered submarines. *Pen* once meant a feather used as a writing instrument. It now covers ball point pens, fiber tip pens, fountain pens, drawing pens, electrical styluses for drawing on cathode ray tubes. A *barn* was once a place to store barley (from *bere-ern*, or "barley-place"). The word now covers almost any large agricultural building. *Holidays* were once "holy-days": Christmas, Easter, and so on. Now holidays include Labor Day, Veterans Day, and for school children, even the days when the teachers go out on strike.

All of these meanings have changed because our culture has changed. For the most part, such changes are close to the "artifactual" meanings attached to borrowed and created words that name items of commerce, natural flora and fauna and so on. The meanings have widened because a wider set of referents has gradually appeared to expand the semantic space the word must cover.

PROBLEM 7.18: We can probably assume fairly safely that when words widen they lose semantic features. *Bird*, for example, once meant only young or small fowl. The widening to mean any feathered creature, the modern sense, can be represented like this:

bird₁ [+concrete, +live, +animate, −human, +avis, −adult].

bird₂ [+concrete, +live, +animate, −human, +avis].

Without trying to specify all the features for the following words try to be moderately specific about the components that have been lost. Can you generalize at all about widening? About some kinds of words that widen?

1. *box* (a small container made of boxwood)
2. *allude* (mock)
3. *bend* (bring a bow into tension with a bow string)
4. *aunt* (father's sister)
5. *aroma* (the smell of spices)
6. *butcher* (one who slaughters goats)
7. *bird* (young of the family avis)
8. *carry* (transport by cart)
9. *chicken* (a young hen or rooster)
10. *divest* (remove one's clothes)
11. *dirt* (excrement)
12. *deplore* (weep for)
13. *detest* (condemn, curse)
14. *elope* (run away from one's husband)
15. *frantic* (madness)
16. *frenzy* (wild delirium)
17. *fact* (a thing done)
18. *go* (walk)
19. *gang* (a set of tools laid out for use > a group of workmen/slaves)
20. *harvest* (reap ripened grain)
21. *holiday* (a holy day)
22. *journey* (a day > a day's trip or day's work)
23. *magic* (the knowledge and skill of the Magi)
24. *mess* (a meal set out for a group of four)
25. *mystery* (divine revealed knowledge)
26. *mind* (memory > thought, purpose, intention)
27. *manner* (the mode of handling something by hand)
28. *picture* (a painted likeness)
29. *plant* (a young slip or cutting)
30. *oil* (olive oil)
31. *ordeal* (trial by torture)
32. *start* (move suddenly)
33. *scent* (animal odor for tracking)
34. *surly* (sir-ly, that behavior which characterizes a "Sir")
35. *silly* (deserving of pity > frail > simple, ignorant > feeble minded)
36. *sail* (cross water propelled by the wind)

37. *stop* (fill or plug up > prevent passage by stopping up > prevent the movement of a person)
38. *sanctuary* (a holy place)
39. *slogan* (the battle cry of Scottish clans)
40. *uncle* (mother's brother)

It is harder to find a pattern for widening than it is for narrowing. It is not entirely certain, but meanings seem to widen somewhat less frequently than they narrow. As a culture becomes more diversified and more complex with more areas of knowledge and activity, those areas require a vocabulary. Because every language has a finite number of words and because speakers are not inclined to coin completely new forms for new concepts, the simplest way to deal with new areas of knowledge is to use the current vocabulary. Borrowing, derivation, compounding, and so on operate here. But perhaps even more frequent is narrowing.

But on the other hand, it can also be difficult to talk about the most ordinary activities of daily life as they diversify. Once it becomes possible to drive (*drive* originally meaning to force an animal along), or ride (*ride* originally meaning to go on horseback), or walk (originally meaning to travel about in public), then talking about getting some place without specifying how becomes difficult. The word *go*, originally meaning to walk, generalized so that an English speaker can now say *I am going to town this morning* without having to specify how he gets there. *Carry* generalized from transporting specifically in a conveyance of some sort to transporting by bearing up in general: *The wind carried the seed*, and so on.

Like narrowing, widening also leaves behind relic forms. For the word *sanctuary*, we have bird sanctuaries, fish sanctuaries, political sanctuary, the notion of safety in general. But a good many Christian denominations still call the main meeting room in which the congregation gathers for general worship *the sanctuary*. One meaning of *start* is still what we do when we hear a loud sound. *Mind* still means memory in *remind*. *Scent* still means animal trace in *on the scent*.

PROBLEM 7.19: What are the relic forms for these words: *fact, gang, mess, mystery, stop*?

PROBLEM 7.20: Take any ten words from the list that widened in Problem 7.18 and ten from the list that narrowed in Problem 7.14. Narrow those that have widened and widen those that have narrowed so that they mean something different from what they originally meant. For example, *erotic* narrowed from a general reference to love to mean sexual love. Conceivably, it could widen past love to mean any strongly sensual experience: *erotic food, erotic sounds*, and so on.

Transfer

A third process of semantic change usually goes by the term **metaphor**. To keep our terms consistent, though, we shall use the term **transfer** to parallel the other two spatial metaphors of **narrowing** and **widening**. Transfer is a kind of sideways leap of a word through semantic space. It occurs when two categories of actions or objects resemble each other in at least one feature and one of them has a name while the other does not but needs one. The name of one is then transferred to the other unnamed category of experience.

This kind of transfer often results in a large gap between the meaning of the original word and the new meaning. There is, for example, no immediately obvious connection between what happens when the muscles of the hand contract the fingers around an object and what happens in the mind when it understands a concept. But not later than 1680, someone who saw a connection transferred *grasp* from the category referring to clutching to name the category that includes the conceptual experience. The similarity is probably in the outcome of the actions (encouraged, perhaps, by the parallel history of Latin *comprehend*).

In many cases, of course, the connection is instantly apparent. The vertical members that support the flat surface of a table look somewhat like legs, partially function like legs, so having no peculiar name of their own, they are called *legs*. But in most cases, the connection is not immediately apparent. What, for example, were the original shared features behind the literal and metaphorical meanings of *strung out* or *groovy*? And in some cases, the original sense has been entirely lost. *The idea fizzled out* contains a dead metaphor whose source we can recover only from dictionaries that supply complete etymologies.

PROBLEM 7.21: Here is a passage of straightforward expository prose. What are the obvious metaphors? What are the borderline cases? When does a word cease being a metaphor?

> Once the Nazis were beaten, many of us were glad to forget those issues [the open and covert approval of anti-Semitic activities in Germany from 1933–1945], or leave them to theologians, moral philosophers (sometimes masked as novelists or playwrights), and, not least, social scientists. Of the latter, some were traditional scholars: economists, political scientists, they had the task of sifting through the rubble of this century's destroyed dreams and realized nightmares—in the hope of finding answers to all sorts of persisting questions. How deliberate was Hitler's rise, how much the product of right-wing intrigue, left-wing myopia and ideological rigidity, popular indifference,

rising unemployment, a long tradition of fear and hate that goes back, say, to Martin Luther's later years.

From Robert Coles "Understanding White
Racists," **The New York Review of Books**,
December 30, 1971, p. 12.

But if metaphor is so common, it is hard to describe, for the process is immensely complex. No one has yet offered a theory of metaphor that satisfactorily explains how it happens, much less how it is possible to understand one. Most linguists deal with it as a bastardized form of language, concentrating instead on what they believe to be the central problem, its ordinary, literal use. But any phenomenon that occurs as frequently as metaphor, that is so important a source of linguistic change cannot be treated as anything except central to our ability to use language. Consequently, metaphor must test any theory of meaning designed to account for how humans use and respond to words.

We might initially approach metaphorical transfer something like this:

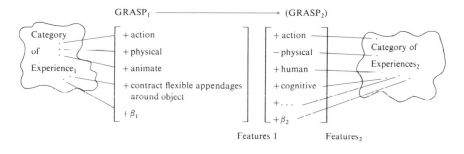

We have a Category of Experiences$_1$ from which we abstract a characteristic set of defining Features$_1$ and associate with the utterance form GRASP$_1$. The Features$_1$ become the meaning of GRASP$_1$. Then around 1680 perhaps, there was for someone a distinct though unnamed Category of Experiences$_2$ which were characterized by a set of Features$_2$. But this Category of Experiences$_2$ and its Features$_2$ had no Word$_2$ to represent them. *Understand, apprehend, comprehend, realize* elicited meanings that were all close, but did not quite include certain Features$_2$ that were crucial to Category of Experiences$_2$. But enough of those Features$_2$, specifically those features we shall represent as [β], were also among Features$_1$ abstracted from Category of Experiences$_1$. So some speaker who consciously or unconsciously recognized the shared features [β_{1-2}] shifted GRASP$_1$ from Category of Experiences$_1$ to name the unnamed Category of Experiences$_2$ and represent the Features$_2$.

But now the problem arises of how to represent the features in common, [β]$_{1-2}$. Most of the Features$_1$ were, of course, left behind. GRASP$_1$ is physical and not necessarily [+human]. GRASP$_2$ is mental, limited to humans, entirely an intellectual experience. Indeed, the shared features, $[\beta]_{1-2}$, are so abstract and so amorphous that it is difficult even to state them prosaically. They must include something like a successful completion of an intention, the at least temporary "connection" between subject and object. But when we try to become more specific than this, we fall into yet other metaphors: encirclement in the mind, seizing an idea, firm control, and so on. Or we chase synonyms down a path that takes us away from the unique meaning of GRASP$_2$. Metaphor, in fact, often seems to highlight aspects of meaning that no dictionary can hope to capture.

Here is another example: *to nitpick*. The original meaning was to pick lice-eggs from the body or clothes, an operation which, we might assume, requires a close, searching examination for tiny objects that have to be painstakingly plucked out with the fingernails. (*Nitty-gritty* may come from the same source. *Nitty* means filled with lice eggs; *gritty* is probably a rhyming reduplication of *grits*, or coarsely ground grain. Thus grits filled with nits would be the infested remnants of the grain, the last and least palatable part: *the nitty-gritty*.)

Now when we try to specify exactly what Features$_1$ we should include in the literal sense of NITPICK$_1$ that also belong to the group of Features$_2$, features that characterize the "cavil" sense of NITPICK$_2$, we discover that our original ideas about meaning may be inadequate. Let us assume that these two lists of features very roughly and very inadequately define the two words:

NITPICK$_1$: [+action, +physical, +animate, +human, +search to remove nits.]
NITPICK$_2$: [+action, −physical, +animate, +human, +cognitive, +cavil over small details].

This, however, does not specify how they are **essentially alike**. We lack the notions of the extreme tininess of the objects searched for, of their unimportance or of performing this action over an unnecessarily long period of time, of the unfavorable associations with both activities, of the judgment we make about the person who engages in such tasks.

Or consider this final example. The words *muscle* and *mussel* are both metaphoric transfers from a word meaning "little mouse." These words presumably transferred because a muscle contracting under the skin and the crustacean in the shell reminded someone of the referent of the Latin word for mouse. But precisely what common features would we have to create to reveal the similarity between the fibrous tissue moving under the skin and the rodent or the shellfish?

To solve this problem, we must distinguish two kinds of meaning. The features so far chosen to attach to words have been selected (1) to predict how the word they associate with behaves in a sentence and (2) to distinguish one word from another. Thus *resemble* would have to be marked something like [−voluntary] or [+stative] because the action referred to is a state beyond voluntary control. We do not say **He was busy resembling his father*, as opposed to *He was busy imitating his father*. On the other hand, *mimic* and *ape* can occur where *imitate* occurs: *He was busy imitating/aping/mimicking his father*. But they are not precisely synonymous. Thus we would have to formulate some other features that would distinguish *imitate* from *ape* from *mimic*.

But once we have postulated features to accomplish both of these goals, we have not necessarily exhausted a word's **global meaning**. One meaning of a word like *salt*, for example, could be defined as crystallized sodium chloride, a definition that could be reduced to features to distinguish it from other substances. But in addition to this basic level of meaning, we know a good deal about salt that is not necessary to distinguish it from other referents or to know how to use the word *salt* in a sentence. We know that it is mined, that the sea is full of it, that it is necessary to life, that it burns if it gets into a cut. . . .

If we decide that all this is also part of the cognitive network associated with *salt* and that we want the word *meaning* to name that cognitive network, then we will have to distinguish at least two categories meaning. But while semantic features appropriately structured might conceivably describe the minimal meaning and distribution of the word *salt*, that is, its **linguistic meaning**, such features cannot easily account for the second kind of meaning, the **encyclopedic meaning** of *salt*.

The Structure of Metaphor

The answer is not to exclude encyclopedic meaning as a kind of meaning, because we have to recognize that metaphoric transfer depends usually, if not always, on our ability to incorporate the encyclopedic meaning of a word into its transferred linguistic meaning. At one time part of someone's encyclopedic knowledge about the category named *nitpicking* was that literal nitpicking was boring and unpleasant; about the category named *grasp* that when we grasped something we often firmly controlled the object. But none of this would have been relevant to the original core linguistic definition of literal *nitpick* or *grasp*. In fact, the crucial aspect of $grasp_{physical}$ transferred to $grasp_{cognitive}$, the feature indicating some kind of "firm control over," is only occasionally associated with $grasp_{physical}$: Consider *He grasped the tiger by the tail*.

By testing our theory of meaning, metaphoric transfer forces us to modify it. Apparently, part of our linguistic ability lets us incorporate our virtually unformalizable encyclopedic knowledge into our more or less formalizable linguistic knowledge. Schematically, the process seems to operate something like this:

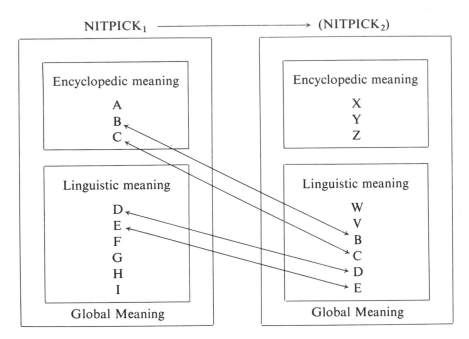

NITPICK₁ ⟶ (NITPICK₂)

The—as yet—unnamed experience on the right, which we can roughly paraphrase as "cavilling over details," includes in its central core of **linguistic** meaning the features that would represent the allegedly unnecessary and unpleasant painstaking search for small details. Part of this meaning, searching for something (features D and E, let us say) is also part of the linguistic meaning of literal NITPICK₁. Another part, the sense of unpleasant and painstaking, is part of the encyclopedic meaning of NITPICK₁ (features B and C, let us say).

Whoever wanted to express the exact quality of distaste for the unnecessary cavilling over details in a single, expressive word decided that NITPICK₁ had enough linguistic and encyclopedic features to qualify it as the name for the category of experiences. So he transferred it.

A question which always arises in discussions of metaphor and linguistic change is how metaphor of the kind we have discussed here differs from poetic metaphor. Some have argued that poetic metaphor is more intense, more emotive, more extreme. Thus a metaphor like the following is "poetic": *There might you heare her kindle her soft voice | In the close murmur of a sparkling noyse.* (Richard Crashaw, "Musick's Duel.") But synesthetic metaphors of this kind have characterized the development of English since the earliest texts of OE. *Bright sounds* is a phrase whose metaphoric origins are still alive, but it could be used in either poetry or ordinary language.

Perhaps a more basic distinction lies in the perceived **intention** of the speaker who creates the metaphor and the context in which it occurs. If in order to express a new concept one creates a metaphor like *His deep voice was also rather narrow*, the metaphor operates within the limited context of that sentence. The speaker ordinarily does not intend that his audience will respond to every possible nuance of meaning in terms of the total context. If it somehow taps an area of semantic space the listener and enough others feel must be named, *narrow* might well permanently transfer from spatial reference to aural reference.

But a poet who wrote *The narrow voices that escape the red-lipped | lipless mouths that . . .* often intends that the metaphor be part of a larger cognitive and emotive whole, that his audience understand that behind it is a rather different intention, that his audience be sensitive to implications, that they develop them in ways no audience can in ordinary discourse. Thus the same apparent metaphor, *a narrow voice*, must be responded to in very different ways, depending on whether the audience understands it to be in the context of a poem or in ordinary language.

A difference that has come to characterize much modern poetry is the degree to which some poets rely almost exclusively on private encyclopedic knowledge as the source of the similarity between two cognitive spaces:

> I am soft sift
> In an hourglass—at the wall
> Fast, but mined with a motion, a drift,
> And it crowds and it combs to the fall;
> I steady as a water in a well, to a poise, to a pane,
> But roped with, always, all the way down from the tall
> Fells or flanks of the voel, a vein
> Of the gospel proffer, a pressure, a principle, Christ's gift.
> From Gerard Manley Hopkins, **The Wreck**
> **of the Deutschland**

Whatever the shared semantic features of the metaphors are in these lines, they are not immediately obvious.

PROBLEM 7.22: Here is a list of words, most of them with multiple meanings, all of which have at least one metaphoric sense. *High*, for example, in *a high sound* is a metaphor transferred from the literal spatial sense of *high*. If the metaphoric meaning is not immediately apparent, a phrase illustrating the original nonmetaphoric sense follows in parentheses. In other cases, an earlier literal meaning is preceded by *f*. As you inspect the list, consider the following problems: (1) Pick at random four or five different kinds of words and try to state in non-metaphorical language precisely what features the original sense and the metaphorical sense share. (2) Are there any generalizations about how certain classes of words are susceptible to metaphorical transfer? (3) Are there any metaphors that characterize certain kinds of activities, social contexts, personal relationships? Which of these metaphors are likely to be the most durable? Which the most transient? Why? Which have lost all sense of their metaphorical origins? Why?

1. *abstract* (f. draw away from)
2. *advert* (f. turn to)
3. *affirm* (f. make firm)
4. *analysis* (f. separate into parts)
5. *animal* (You animal!)
6. *bright* (a bright idea)
7. *bitter* (sharp to the taste: He is a bitter person)
8. *brow* (the brow of a hill)
9. *bewitch* (a bewitching aroma)
10. *bat* (You old bat!)
11. *bread* (I have no bread to spend)
12. *blast* (We had a blast at the party)
13. *blow up* (He blew up in anger)
14. *cold* (She was cold to me)
15. *cool* (Cool it, man)
16. *conceive* (f. to catch)
17. *conclude* (f. to enclose)
18. *concrete* (f. to grow together)
19. *connect* (f. to tie together)
20. *cut* (She cut me dead)
21. *crane* (the derrick that resembles the bird)
22. *compose* (f. to put together)
23. *comprehend* (f. seize)
24. *cat* (She's a cat)
25. *dig* (I dig that idea)
26. *deep* (deep thoughts)
27. *dark* (I'm in the dark on that)
28. *define* (f. place limits on)
29. *depend* (f. hang from)
30. *dog* (You dog!)
31. *dirty* (a dirty mind)
32. *dough* (money)
33. *drip* (He's a drip)
34. *drag* (This class is a drag)
35. *eye* (the eye of a hurricane)
36. *exist* (f. stand out)
37. *explain* (f. make flat)
38. *enthrall* (f. to make a slave of)
39. *foot* (foot of a mountain)
40. *fuzzy* (I'm fuzzy headed)
41. *finger* (a finger of land)
42. *fascinate* (f. enchant by witchcraft)
43. *flat* (a flat note)
44. *get* (I don't get it)
45. *grasp* (I grasped the concept)
46. *guts* (He has a lot of guts)
47. *groove* (I'm in the groove)
48. *gas* (It was a gasser)
49. *grab* (How does the idea grab you?)
50. *high* (He got high on dope)
51. *hang* (He's always hung up)
52. *heavy* (I had a heavy time)
53. *hot* (a hot idea)
54. *heart* (the heart of the problem)
55. *head* (head of the line)
56. *hands* (hands of the clock)
57. *home* (drive the point home)
58. *jazz* (f. sexual activity)
59. *jive* (I don't dig this jive)
60. *intelligent* (f. bring together)
61. *keen* (f. intelligent)
62. *load* (a load off my mind)
63. *long* (a long time)
64. *loud* (a loud color)
65. *lip* (lip of the glass)

66. *lamb* (She's a lamb)
67. *mouth* (mouth of a cave)
68. *mouse* (You're a mouse)
69. *milk* (He milked the job dry)
70. *pagan* (f. civilian, in distinction to Christians, who called themselves soldiers of Christ)
71. *pig* (You pig)
72. *quiet* (a quiet color)
73. *rip-off* (It was a big rip-off)
74. *rough* (a rough voice)
75. *ribs* (the ribs of a ship)
76. *report* (f. to carry back)
77. *result* (f. to spring back)
78. *shallow* (shallow ideas)
79. *soft* (a soft wind)
80. *sharp* (a sharp dresser)
81. *smooth* (a smooth operator)
82. *solve* (f. to break up)
83. *spirit* (f. breath)
84. *snake* (You snake!)
85. *straight* (He's a straight guy)
86. *square* (He's a square)
87. *split* (Let's split)
88. *turn on* (He turns me on)
89. *trip* (It was a bad (drug) trip)
90. *thick* (a voice thick with anger)
91. *thin* (a thin sound)
92. *tongue* (a tongue of land)
93. *translate* (f. carry across)
94. *warm* (a warm color)
95. *wrestle* (I wrestled with the problem)
96. *wild* (a wild idea)

These exercises should also demonstrate that metaphors can function with varying degrees of liveliness. A completely dead metaphor is a word that is no longer a metaphor, one like *result*, from the Latin *salire*, to leap. *Result* earlier meant to bounce back. From the same root are *salmon* (the leaper), *somersault*, *assailant* (someone who leaps on one), *assault*, *resilient*, *exult* (from L. *exsultāre*, to leap, *ex-* is an intensifier), *insult*, and *insolent*. The specific notion of leaping is dead in many of these, but becomes immediately apparent once we know that *salire* lies behind them. Other metaphors become apparent if we think about them for a moment: *sweet music, dopey people, grasp*, perhaps even *understand*. These are the metaphors that are well on their way toward becoming dead metaphors. And finally, there are those transfers that instantly present themselves as metaphors, indeed, whose metaphoric power depends on our recognizing them as such: *rip off* for *steal*, *cracked* for *crazy* (which itself once meant cracked or broken, as in *crazed pottery*), *nosey*, and so on. Most of these, of course, are slang words, a kind of vocabulary we shall deal with later.

PROBLEM 7.23: Take any five nouns, verbs, or adjectives and describe how they might metaphorically transfer to a new meaning.

Shift

A fourth way we associate existing forms with new meanings occurs when some **discrete** element within a larger structure of related or connected objects, events or operations part of either the linguistic or encyclopedic meaning:

1. takes its name from the name of the larger structure;
2. gives its name to the larger structure;
3. shifts to or takes its name from another element within the larger structure.

We shall call this process **semantic shift**.

Changes of this kind give us some of our most unusual histories of semantic change. We have already mentioned the etymology of *pedigree*. The individual element, the three marks that looked like the foot of a crane, gave its name to the abstraction connected with the larger whole: the quality of descent. *Hearse* is another word of this kind. It first meant a triangular harrow or plow. Then it metaphorically transferred to a triangular frame that held church candles. Then it began to shift: to the framework that held candles over a coffin while it was being carried into the church, to the framework that held tapestry curtains or the pall over the tomb or coffin, then loosely to the coffin or tomb itself, then to the conveyance that transported the coffin (and later, metaphorically, to the conveyance that transported pianos in nineteenth-century London). This is a case where discrete elements within a larger whole required special names and the most readily available one was attached to another element within the whole.

Toilet is a yet more complicated example. It began with Latin *tela*, a weaving or web. It gave Old French *teile* then *toile*, a cloth, which narrowed to the cloth in which clothes were wrapped. The meaning then shifted to the cloth used to protect clothes while a woman was setting her hair. The diminutive of *toile*, *toilette*, then was attached to the little cloth cover for the dressing table, then to the items on the table, then to the piece of furniture containing them, then to the room in which the object stands and in which one dresses himself, then to the action of grooming and dressing, making *toilet* both concrete (furniture) and abstract (dressing). Thus we should not be taken aback when we read that it was once fashionable for eighteenth-century women to entertain their callers during their toilet.

Then apparently a social change occurred. Classes of speakers other than upper class used the word for the room in which they performed their dressing and grooming. But at this social level, the room had to serve more functions than just a place to dress. With the spread of indoor plumbing, the room came to include the bathtub, the washstand, and the convenience earlier known as the *close-stool* (cited as early as 1410), *jakes* (1530), the *john* (c. 1650), the *closet of ease* (1662), *watercloset* (1775—now often shortened in Great Britain to *W.C.*), *lavatory* (1845), *commode* (1851), and in less polite contexts as the *can*, *head*, etc. Since this most frequently used object required a polite name, it is not surprising that earlier it attracted to itself the name for the piece of furniture in which it was kept and then once it achieved the technological level of being built in as part of the room, the name for the room itself. Television seems to have seized on *bathroom bowl* as the latest term.

Thus *toilet* was almost certainly at first a euphemism for the plumbing fixture we now call that name. When *toilet* became too closely associated with the object (as the other names did before it), it left no name for the room containing it that many speakers could use without embarrassment. So the room was re-named after the least frequently used object—the bath. Most of us now prefer to say we have a toilet in the bathroom (even if it contains no bath) than a bath in the toilet, which would be "historically" correct but now socially impossible.

Another example: The word *bead*, which now means the little round ball strung on a string, derives from OE *gebed* or *bed*, meaning prayer. When a bedesman says his pater noster or rosary, he keeps track of the prayer by counting the small balls. Sentences such as *How many beads have you said*, *Have you finished your beads*, and so on could all be construed as referring either to the little round balls or to the prayers. Since the speakers apparently sensed a need to name the particular little round balls used in their prayers, they shifted the word for prayer, spelled *bede*, at the time, to the little round balls. (The word then generalized to include all little round balls, then to all little round shiny objects: *beads of sweat*, *beads of glass*. Then it partially narrowed to the name of the round ball at the end of a gunsight; thence, *to take a bead on someone*. And that has widened again so that we can say *Arnold Palmer took a bead on the PGA title today.*)

PROBLEM 7.24: How is the kind of shift described for *bead* different from widening? How is the shift of *toilet* different from narrowing? Narrow, widen, and transfer *toilet*.

PROBLEM 7.25: Pick several words that name elements within a larger whole and speculate how they might shift to name unnamed elements in that whole.

PROBLEM 7.26: Reconstruct the context and process by which the words in bold face derived their meaning in these phrases: *a drinking* **glass**, *a six*-**iron**, *a* **nickle** *candy bar*, **rubbers** *and galoshes*, *bed* **linen**, *a pencil* **lead**, *an expensive* **fur**, *jockey* **silks**, *sheer* **nylons**, *a* **cork** *for a bottle*, *Woolite for your* **woolens**, *read the* **paper**.

PROBLEM 7.27: The following words are ambiguous. Explain the ambiguity and the process by which the ambiguity arose. How regular a process of word creation is this? What generalization can you make? *report, illustration, building, discovery, finding, statement, description, explanation, account, announcement, invention, creation, production, representation, supplies, assembly.*

PROBLEM 7.28: Using the model we presented in the discussion of metaphoric transfer for the representation of linguistic and encyclopedic meaning, explain how the formal mechanism by which shift takes place differs from metaphoric transfer. That is, the linguistic meaning of *bede* was once that required by the meaning we now associate with *prayer*. The encyclopedic meaning included everything we know about prayers—where they were said, who said them, and what was used in association with them: little round balls.

The usual terms for these shifts come from classical rhetoric: **Metonymy**, when the name for an attribute or adjunct shifts to name what it is adjunct to: *king* = *crown*; and **synecdoche**, when a part names a whole or a whole a part: *worker* = *hand*. But this distinction is irrelevant when we recognize that a single cognitive operation is occurring here. We perceive complexes of parts of groups or events as wholes, not as unstructured collections of discrete parts. Gestalt psychology concentrates on this aspect of mental activity. We perceive and conceive of aspects of experience in a Gestalt, a figure comprised of parts in a specific relationship. When the Gestalt is significant in the culture, when it recurs in essentially the same form, we inevitably give it a name: *war, graduation, marriage, trial*, and so on. Sometimes we create the Gestalt for others by creating a name: *Establishment* is a word that pulls together a diverse range of elements into a single cognitive structure that may not have "existed" in the minds of many speakers before the meaning was explained.

Sometimes, of course, the Gestalt exists but does not yet have a name. Not too long before 1885, for example, the Gestalt of two persons, usually of the opposite sex and unmarried, meeting at a particular time for a shared entertainment, had no distinctive name, partly because the event as we now know it did not exist until relatively recently. *Rendezvous, appointment, tryst, engagement, assignation*, were not quite right. Since a time and date had to be set for the meeting, the element *date* in a phrase like *We have a date* **shifted** from the time of the event to the event itself.

Drift

There is a kind of semantic change that at first glance may appear to constitute a fifth class: When a word naming one area of meaning **drifts** into an adjacent and coordinate area of meaning. For example, *naughty* once meant wicked and depraved. Today, it means only mild mischief. *Mischief* itself once meant wicked behavior. Today, it can apply to a merely naughty child. At one time, *shrewd* meant depraved or wicked. (It comes from the noun *shrew* or a wicked and malignant man, the meaning it had before it meant a nagging woman. But before it meant wicked man, it referred to the small animal, which was believed to be a viciously evil creature.) Today, *shrewd* is somewhat complimentary.

If we lay any of these pairs of meanings on a scale, we can see how it is possible for a word to move from one point to the next by a series of small steps through overlapping semantic areas:

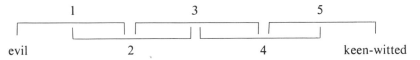

We might postulate sets of components in overlapping steps that would result in the semantic changing from one sense to the next:

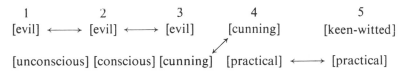

Each stage shares at least one putative feature with the next, allowing the word to "slide" through semantic space.

But this kind of gradual change can probably be explained better by successive widenings and narrowings. For example, the last citations of the evil sense of *mischief* date from the nineteenth century. The earliest citations of the merely vexatious meaning date from at least 1784. We can say, then, that at least by 1784, the sense of *mischief* widened to include vexatious actions as well as evil actions, to a class of actions including both. Only the use of *mischief* with, say, *children* or *the devil* would specify the exact nature of the action. Then in the nineteenth century, at least for many speakers, *mischief* narrowed to designate only the class of vexatious actions.

The same thing probably happened with *shrewd* (though the number of meanings multiplied greatly, as well). It meant malignantly wicked from the fourteenth through the seventeenth century (with a few citations into the nineteenth). The clever/keen-witted meaning is cited first in the sixteenth century. We might wonder whether during that period of overlapping reference, *shrewd* did not have two meanings, but rather a single wider one that could refer to both a slightly weakened sense of evil and keen-wittedness. Then in the seventeenth century, *shrewd* apparently narrowed to exclude the wicked sense, leaving only the modern sense.

PROBLEM 7.29: Here are some words, followed by their earlier meanings. Suggest how drift might explain their current meanings.

1. *mischief*: evil plight > harm.
2. *moody*: brave > proud > angry.
3. *pretty*: craft/cunning > proper appearance.

4. *grin*: draw lips back in pain or anger.
5. *quick*: living.
6. *gaudy*: luxurious.
7. *uncouth*: unknown.
8. *sly*: skillful.
9. *cunning*: learned.
10. *coy*: quiet.
11. *crafty*: strong.
12. *surly*: imperious.

PROBLEM 7.30: Show how five modern words might drift in the future.

Some Causes of Drift

The conditions for this kind of drift are found in the way we think and speak. Very few of our named semantic areas comprise sharply defined categories. Most blur at the edges. That is, while conceptually a triangle is a triangle is a triangle, real objects like streams tend to shade off into rivers at one extreme and into rivulets at another.

This kind of indeterminacy should disturb no one who is sophisticated about language, for there will always be cases where we cannot be certain whether any particular object qualifies for membership in a particular set. The naturally blurred edges of categories and the infinite variety of experiences we have every day allow such words to drift through semantic space.

Why words should drift in the specific direction they do, however, is not always easy to predict or, even after the fact, to explain. There are, however, some generalizations. Words susceptible to value judgments generally drift toward less specifically unfavorable meanings, probably because a speaker tends to exaggerate and use a word that is too strong for the situation he refers to. Through constant overstated association with a situation less extreme than the word originally referred to, the once-strong word drifts to a less strong meaning. The drift of *mischief* from evil to almost lovable annoyance almost certainly began when actions that were almost but not quite malignantly evil were called *mischief*. Once *mischief* became attached to that lessened sense of badness, it was used once again in an exaggerated way for something less serious yet, perhaps for only mindless vandalism. Once attached to that meaning, it again was used to refer perhaps to only potentially serious fun. And once attached to that, it was used again in an exaggerated way to refer, perhaps, to a baby pulling pots and pans out of a cupboard. Almost the same change has occurred with *naughty*.

PROBLEM 7.31: There is in English a class of words called **intensifiers** that illustrates this tendency to drift perhaps better than any other group of words. Intensifiers all modify adjectives; in the sixteenth and seventeenth centuries they were frequently used without their -ly endings: *horrid embarrassed*, for example. Examine the following list of intensifiers and consider these questions. (1) Why have there been so many? (2) Which are still active? (3) What sort of semantic meaning did they have originally? (4) What has become of the semantic content of these words today? How do the example phrases prove that in many cases the words are entirely lacking in any of their original semantic content? Following the example phrase is its earlier meaning.

TABLE 7.1   INTENSIFIERS

Intensifier	Example Phrase	Earlier Meaning
1. abominably	abominably tired	(excite disgust)
2. amazingly	amazingly dull	(cause to lose wits)
3. astonishingly	astonishingly minor	(stun with a blow)
4. awfully	awfully unimpressive	(cause dread or awe)
5. confounded	confounded happy	(bring to perdition)
6. damned	damned pleased	(doomed)
7. dreadfully	dreadfully small	(excite dread or awe)
8. enormously	enormously good	(abnormally evil)
9. excessively	excessively happy	(go beyond just limits)
10. extraordinarily	extraordinarily normal	(beyond the ordinary)
11. extravagantly	extravagantly unambitious	(wander beyond bounds)
12. extremely	extremely limited	(uttermost)
13. fabulously	fabulously cheap	(fabled)
14. fantastically	fantastically real	(exist in imagination)
15. full	full weary	(complete)
16. frightfully	frightfully boring	(full of horror)
17. grandly	grandly expensive	(great)
18. greatly	greatly exhausted	(great)
19. hideously	hideously expensive	(excite terror)
20. horribly	horribly expensive	(excite horror)
21. horridly	horridly embarrassed	(excite horror)
22. hugely	hugely amused	(immense)
23. immensely	immensely unimportant	(large beyond measure)
24. immoderately	immoderately hungry	(beyond limits)
25. incredibly	incredibly real	(not to be believed)
26. intensely	intensely tired	(stretched)
27. magnificently	magnificently pleased	(greatness of achievement)
28. marvelously	marvelously stupid	(miraculous)
29. might(il)y	mighty weak	(power)
30. monstrously	monstrously excited	(deviating from natural)
31. outrageously	outrageously ordinary	(exceeding limits)
32. perfectly	perfectly stupid	(complete in all senses)
33. pretty	pretty ugly	(firm, nice, proper)

continued

TABLE 7.1—continued

34. powerful	powerful tired	(force, influence)
35. really	really imaginative	(objective existence)
36. right	right foolish	(what is good)
37. simply	simply confusing	(without complication)
38. sore(ly)	sore(ly) afraid	(cause pain)
39. stupendously	stupendously alert	(struck senseless)
40. tremendously	tremendously calm	(excite trembling)
41. terribly	terribly pleased	(excite terror)
42. terrifically	terrifically happy	(excite terror)
43. vastly	vastly insignificant	(of great dimensions)
44. very	very false	(true, real)
45. violently	violently opposed	(producing injury)
46. wonderfully	wonderfully boring	(causing astonishment)
47. wondrously	wondrously tedious	(causing astonishment)

(And of course, there is the chief obscenity of English whose meaning has so faded that it could modify *chaste*.)

Minor Types of Semantic Change

There are some minor types of semantic change that are more curiosities than anything else. They have contributed a relative handful of new meanings to the language. Here are three of them.

Folk Etymology

Often, a speaker who misunderstands or fails to recognize a strange or foreign word will change it to one he does recognize, introducing elements of meaning from the known word into the meaning of the original word. Thus *samblind* (half-blind) became *sandblind*. *Shamefast*, meaning fast in shame, became *shamefaced*; *angnægl* (*ang* = tight, painful + *nægl* = iron nail) became *hangnail*; *berfrey* (tower) became *belfry*; *umble pie* (a pot pie made out of the umbles, i.e., the entrails of deer) becomes *humble pie*.

PROBLEM 7.32: Here are some original words that have changed to a new form with a modified meaning resulting from the English associations of that new form. What are the new forms and how do they influence the meaning of the words? *cucaracha*, *crevice* (a kind of crustacean that looks like a tiny lobster), *femelle* (little woman), *coutelas* (little knife), *koolsla* (*kool* = cabbage + *sla* = salad), *brydguma* (*bryd* = bride + *guma* = man), *otchek* (Algonquian for a little forest animal), *sur loin* (*sur* French for above), *pentis* (from Old French *apentis*, a small building dependent on another building, a lean-to), *mus-quash* (Algonquian for a small water animal), *chaise longue* (long chair), *techy* (from Old French *tache*, spot or blemish, meanings which changed to peevish or vicious), *wealhhnutu* (*wealh* = foreign + *hnutu* = nut), *sursis* (past participle of *surseoir*, to pause or leave off). (It has been claimed that *woman* is compounded from a phrase that meant woe + man, a folk etymology which reveals more about the etymologizer than the language. It derives from *wif* + *mann*.)

Semantic Replacement

In our linguistic history, there have been cases in which the reverse of metaphor occurred. Instead of borrowing a foreign word for a new semantic space, late OE speakers transferred certain Danish meanings to English words which phonologically resembled the Danish words and shared some semantic space with them. The native English word *dream*, meaning to make a joyful noise, for example, was probably close enough to the Scandinavian word *draumr*, or sleep vision, to take on the Danish meaning, driving out the English meaning. The same may have happened with the words *bread* (originally meaning fragment); and *dwell* (OE meaning: to hinder or lead astray).

Mistakes

Another very minor source of new meanings attaching to old words is in the way meaning shifts from one to the other of a pair of words that are frequently confused. Thus *What are you inferring?* now frequently means *What are you implying? Uninterested* takes on the meaning of *disinterested. Affect* becomes *effect*. Others include *continuous/continual, compare/contrast, flaunt/flout, anxious/eager, principal/principle, fortuitous/fortunate, fulsome/full.* Some observers of the language expend great amounts of energy decrying such mistakes. It is not clear that their concern is commensurate with the semantic confusion that may or may not result from the loss of a formal distinction.

Chapter 8

SEMANTIC CHANGE IN ITS SOCIAL CONTEXT

When we discussed the nature of borrowed words at the end of Chapter Five, we mentioned two kinds of forces at work in determining whether such words are retained in the language. The first kind of words are **artifactual** words, words to cover the categories that include objects and activities borrowed virtually intact from other cultures. Thus *coconut, allegro, shah*, and *atoll* reflect little about our society beyond the fact that we are interested enough in the referents of those words to need names for them. The same can be said of certain kinds of word derivations: *derrick, shrapnel, macadam, motel, radar*. The second kind of words we called **psycho-cultural**, usually abstract words that reveal areas of meaning that penetrate to the psychological texture of our society: *taboo, luck, ghetto, morale, chauvinism, bowdlerize, gestapo*, and so on. Such words become an index to what is latent in our cultural psyches.

We can distinguish some of these same processes in semantic change. Some meanings change because of artifactual reasons, because new objects come into being. *Ship, sail, pile* (as in atomic), *broadcast, program, satellite, jet*—all cover a wider category of technical referents, or artifactual referents, than they did a hundred years ago. We can discover a good deal about our technical progress if we examine the way such words have changed, but not very much, perhaps, about those unnamed semantic spaces that exist in our collective lives.

VALUE JUDGMENTS

Other kinds of changes do illuminate social and cultural aspects of our lives. The wholesale transfer of words in Western European languages that refer to physical actions to name cognitive processes (*comprehend, explain, conclude, grasp, get, understand,* and so on) suggests a good deal about the importance of self-conscious cognition in our culture. When words narrow to specify a particular kind of dog: *hound*; or animal: *deer*; or food: *meat*; or dope: *grass*; and so on, it suggests something about what many speakers are preoccupied with. The transfer of sense words (*sharp, sour, low, bright,* for example) to personality suggests something about our need for a rich vocabulary to discuss how we feel about one another. The extensive vocabulary, largely metaphorical in origin, that describes sensations of taste, hearing, touch, and so on indicates how important that kind of experience is to us. A relatively significant increase in the metaphorical words for sounds in the last two centuries reflects a heightened interest in music.

PROBLEM 8.1: Here are some words that cover semantic space in the field of female reference. Following each word is one or more earlier meanings. Comment.

1. *shrew*: a malicious, evil, cunning man
2. *termagant*: a male Saracen idol
3. *harlot*: a young, base fellow
4. *hoyden*: a boorish male peasant
5. *scold*: from Old Norse, a poet or lampooner
6. *baggage*: a worthless fellow
7. *frump*: a derisive snort > a jeer > ill humor > a cross, dowdy man or woman
8. *brothel*: a worthless debased fellow > a prostitute > hence *brothel house* > *brothel*
9. *bordello*: originally *bordel*, a villein of the lowest rank, hence *bordel house*, hence current meaning
10. *bawd*: a male or female procurer
11. *chit*: a young boy or girl
12. *witch*: originally either male or female
13. *gossip*: godsib, or god-relative > a familiar acquaintance
14. *jade*: a worn-out horse
15. *tart*: short for *sweetheart*
16. *virago*: "The Woman" (Biblical) > manlike heroic woman > bold, impudent woman
17. *quean* (obsolete): woman > whore
18. *wench*: a young girl or woman

19. *hussy*: shortened form of *housewife*
20. *courtesan*: a woman attached to a royal court. (This was the original Italian meaning. The ModE meaning has been the dominant one in English.)
21. *mistress*: feminine of *master*
22. *madam*: *ma* (my) + *dam* (dame)
23. *dame*: from Latin *domina*, a woman of rank heading a household
24. *girl*: a child of either sex
25. *boy*: a fettered person > a servant (with vague contemptuous meaning) > lower class male
26. *cuckold*: allegedly from the cuckoo bird, a bird which lays its eggs, in another's nest. (But the word refers to the husband of the unfaithful wife, not the male who is the cuckolder. Note that we have no current word in the language for the betrayed female, though at one time we did have *cuckquean* to refer to the gulled wife.)

Here are some other insulting terms for women: *broad, chippy, drab, floozy, slattern, slut, strumpet, trollop, trull, trot, doxy, hag, harridan, crone, biddy, harpy, vamp, nag, whore, bitch, piece, lay, tail, trull, hen, old maid, wallflower, unladylike, unfeminine.* (1) What aspects of feminine reference do these words focus on? (2) What are the masculine counterparts for these words? Are there as many insulting names for men as for women? (3) What kinds of semantic changes are at work here? (4) In what ways can *lady* be insulting (as opposed to *woman*)?

PROBLEM 8.2: These words have been used to express social judgments, usually of men. Earlier meanings follow each one. Comment.

1. *boor*: peasant
2. *knave*: a boy, servant
3. *churl*: lowest rank of freeman
4. *varlet*: an attendant or servant
5. *clown*: a rural person
6. *rascal*: rabble
7. *pariah*: from the Tamil language in India, an outcast of the untouchable class
8. *idiot*: ignorant
9. *blackguard*: scullery assistant
10. *lewd*: of the laity, not a member of a religious order > ignorant
11. *common*: shared by all
12. *vulgar*: ordinary language > persons belonging to the ordinary class
13. *villain*: a low born person
14. *surly*: Sire-ly
15. *mean*: held by two or more (the sense intended here is of a mean hovel)
16. *coarse*: common

17. *henchman*: hengest (horse) + man (a groom)
What kinds of semantic changes probably created these meanings?

PROBLEM 8.3: What animal terms have been used to express value judgments?
Ask someone who speaks another language to compare the derogatory and
laudatory animal terms in his language and in English. Do other cultures
choose animal terms for athletic teams?

When the meaning of a word narrows toward an unfavorable meaning,
it is called **pejorative** change. When the meaning narrows toward a more
favorable meaning, it is called **elevation** or **amelioration**. We have already
seen this happen with words like *merit, praise, fortune, fame*, and so on, words
that originally implied only neutral judgment, then gradually narrowed in the
direction of [+favorable]. A process similar to this has occurred with words
that refer to various occupations and social roles that have elevated through
history: *knight* originally named only a boy or youth; *constable*, the head
groom; *queen*, a woman; *minister*, a servant; *marshall*, a stable servant;
lady, a kneader of bread (?); *steward*, possibly overseer of the sty, i.e.,
sty + ward; *ambassador*, a messenger; *engineer*, a plotter or schemer; *baron*,
a feudal thane. Any of these could have changed in an unfavorable direction.
(189, 226)

EUPHEMISM

There is another kind of linguistic amelioration specifically directed toward
finding socially acceptable words for concepts that many people cannot easily
speak of. It is called *euphemism*, from the Greek for "to speak favorably."
It recalls an earlier attitude toward language—that somehow between the
word and the thing there exists a bond so strong that the word is virtually
equivalent to the thing. So instead of calling cancer *cancer*, we call it *a growth*,
almost in fear that calling it *cancer* will make it so. A liquid which a woman
sprays on her genitals in the belief that they will then not smell bad becomes a
feminine hygiene spray. An invasion in Southeast Asia becomes an *incursion*;
retreat is called *mobile maneuvering*. A person does not lie in his box where
people can come and look at him before the undertaker puts him in a hole in
a graveyard. The departed rests in his casket in a slumber room where friends
may visit with him before the grief therapist assists the dear one to his plot in
a memorial garden.

Euphemism is such a pervasive human phenomenon, so deeply woven into
virtually every known culture, that one is tempted to claim that every human
has been pre-programmed to find ways to talk around tabooed subjects. One
of the oldest known euphemisms is the word we use for bear. It once meant

"the brown one," and goes far back into Indo-European prehistory when animals were probably totems and their names forbidden. The biological foundation is probably in the remaining connections between man's limbic system and his speech system. (Review pages 18–20.)

PROBLEM 8.4: Here are some words selected by speakers of English as substitutes for more offensive or insufficiently prestigious words. What areas of our culture are involved? Try to discover the semantic and grammatical processes by which euphemisms are created. If the meaning is unclear, a definition follows.

1. *little girl's room*
2. *pass on* (die)
3. *social disease*
4. *expectorate*
5. *glow* (perspire)
6. *growth* (cancer)
7. *memorial park* (cemetery)
8. *human waste* (feces, urine)
9. *exceptional child* (moron)
10. *sleep with*
11. *grief therapist* (undertaker)
12. *central city* (slums)
13. *go to the bathroom*
14. *lady of the evening* (prostitute)
15. *sanitary engineer* (garbage man)
16. *senior citizen*
17. *have to go* (need to excrete)
18. *sexual relations*
19. *void* (urinate)
20. *culturally deprived*
21. *building engineer* (janitor)
22. *comfort station*
23. *expire* (die)
24. *capital punishment*
25. *inter*
26. *seat* (buttocks)
27. *washroom*
28. *funeral home*
29. *upchuck* (vomit)
30. *terminal case*
31. *blossom* (pimple)
32. *hickey* (pimple)
33. *casualty* (killed in action)
34. *garment* (girdle)

35. *dental plates* (false teeth)
36. *bridge* (false teeth)
37. *bra*
38. *panties*
39. *monthly difficulties* (menstruation)
40. *male organ* (penis)
41. *Hansen's disease* (leprosy)
42. *hairpiece* (wig)
43. *dentures*
44. *heart condition* (heart disease)
45. *tipsy* (drunk)
46. *disabled* (crippled)
47. *special student* (retarded student)
48. *job action* (strike)
49. *love child* (bastard)
50. *plump*
51. *know* (have sexual relations with)
52. *pre-owned* (second hand)
53. *sanitary napkin*
54. *slumber robe* (shroud)
55. *fix* (castrate)
56. *swinger* (promiscuous)
57. *irregularity* (constipation)
58. *matter* (pus)
59. *VD* (gonorrhea/syphilis)
60. *BM* (bowel movement)
61. *final solution* (extermination of Jews)
62. *criminal assault*
63. *fanny* (buttocks)
64. *wee wee* (urinate)
65. *put to sleep* (kill)
66. *underprivileged*

To create euphemisms like these, we can rely on any one of five processes. The first process is **widening**. This blunts the impact of the semantic features being communicated in a single word by moving up one level of generality to name the superordinate set, usually omitting the specific feature that would unequivocally identify the referent. The specific *cancer* becomes the more general *growth*; the specific *pus* becomes the more general *matter*; the specific *urination* becomes the more general *voiding*; the specific *girdle* becomes the more general *undergarment*.

In some cases, the general features are split between two words. Hitting someone on the head is a *criminal assault*, but by convention, we know that this very general term refers to rape. Many diseases are *social diseases* if we contract them through social contact. But syphilis and gonorrhea are particular kinds, and by convention we know *social disease* means VD, itself a euphemism for venereal disease, another euphemism for the names of the diseases themselves. Expired breath, heat and sweat are all human waste products. But *human waste* usually means only urine and feces, themselves euphemisms for *piss* and *shit*. In other cases, the two or more words do specify the exact subset, but splitting the semantic features between them still softens the impact: *hairpiece, male organ, capital punishment, mental retardation*.

Schematically the difference between one word and a more general construction can be illustrated like this:

$$
\begin{array}{cccccc}
\text{solid} & + & \text{human} & + & \text{waste} & = & \text{feces} \\
\left[\begin{array}{l} +\text{concrete} \\ -\text{animate} \\ +\text{solid} \end{array}\right] & & \left[\begin{array}{l} +\text{concrete} \\ +\text{animate} \\ +\text{human} \end{array}\right] & & \left[\begin{array}{l} \pm\text{concrete} \\ +\text{produced} \\ -\text{wanted} \end{array}\right] & & \left[\begin{array}{l} +\text{concrete} \\ +\text{solid} \\ +\text{human/} \\ \quad\text{produced} \\ -\text{wanted} \\ +\text{organic} \end{array}\right]
\end{array}
$$

Should there be doubt that spreading semantic components across several words rather than delivering them in a single word lessens the impact, one need only compare the relative emotional effects of *feces, solid human waste,* and *that material of a non-fluid, non-gaseous nature which is the byproduct of metabolic and digestive processes in higher order primates.*

The second process owes much to our propensity for **borrowing** words from Greek and Latin. There is a scientific or learned word for every bodily and social function we can think of. Even bad breath has been renamed *halitosis. Expectorate, perspire, expire, abdomen, penis, defecate, urinate, eructate, crepitate, vagina*—all carry strong clinical scientific, medical overtones that render them, if not completely inoffensive to many, at least usable when speakers cannot avoid talking about their referents.

The third process is identical to **semantic shift**. A word naming a part of the larger complex in which the element named by the distasteful word operates shifts over to re-name that element. Thus we *make love* or *sleep with* or *go to bed with* instead of *copulate* or *fornicate* (which has a curious history). Such terms name what comes, one might presume, before, simultaneously with, or after the act in question. A *grief therapist* may attend to the emotions of the bereaved, but his main job is to dispose of the corpse. Thus a name for an element within the larger process diverts attention from the central element in the complex of dealing with dead people. The *memorial park* to which he drives the body is "really" a *graveyard*, a place for graves. But the subsequent action of "memorial" or remembering gives its name to the location. Going to the bathroom precedes the act referred to while a comfort station is identified by the condition resulting from the act performed there.

The fourth process, **metaphorical transfer**, may not be as common as it once was as a source for the most frequently used euphemisms. *Glow* for sweat and *blossom* for pimple are clear examples, along with *slumber robe* and *swinger*. *Belly button* and *break wind*, themselves once euphemisms, now need their own. Actually, a good many of our current vulgarisms and obscenities for which we now need euphemisms may themselves have originally been euphemistic metaphors. *Cock* is a metaphorical transfer from the spigot on a barrel; *prick* is self-evidently derived from the action. *Cunt* may ultimately derive from a word related to Latin *cunnus*, related to *cuneus*, a wedge, though the source of the *-t* at the end of the word is a puzzle. A more likely source is a Low (no pun intended) German word, *kont*, the female pundendum. *Pussy* seems self-evident, but it may also be simply a shift following a transfer since *pussy*, a sixteenth-century term of endearment for a girl or lady, may not have acquired its vulgar sense until the seventeenth century. (*Bunny* and *coney*, another word for rabbit and pronounced *cunny*, went through the same series of changes.) The origin of *twat* is obscure, but it may be from *twachylle*, or a passage. Finally, *fuck*, that vulgarism of vulgarisms, is probably related to German *ficken*, to strike or knock. It may have been borrowed from Scandinavian. Norwegian has a *fukka* and Swedish a *focka*, meaning to copulate. In any event, it definitely is not an acronym for *For Unlawful Carnal Knowledge* allegedly written over those put in stocks for that act in Puritan New England.

With the permissiveness of the seventies, the rich vocabulary of expletives and swear words available to speakers at least from Chaucer's time has dwindled away until we are left with the tedious repetition of that one last Anglo-Saxon obscenity that can still infuriate most of middle America. Some have claimed that we need a new vocabulary, suggesting we try out words like *sphagnum, flocculate, surd, fuscous, lingulate, ort, scutum, pismire, fruticose*, and *nard*. But like pronouns, articles, prepositions and other function words, we just cannot grow new obscenities like hothouse tomatoes. They have to ripen naturally into the full richness of true scatalogical and sexual indecency, a process that requires centuries.

The last catch-all process, **phonetic distortions**, abbreviations, clips, and so on, is most amply represented by our words for *Christ*, *God*, and a few obscenities: *Shucks, shoot, cripes, gosh, golly, gad, darn, doggone, drat,* *crimanentlies, for crying out loud, son of a gun, gol durned, gee whiz, for Pete's sake, for the love of Mike, jimminy cricket, jeepers creepers, dang, dad-blame, dad-burn, sam hill, land's sake.* The seventeenth century had a richer set than we because the "real" name of God was banned from use in stage plays or in jest; so new ones were required: *'zounds* (God's wounds), *'zblood* (God's blood), *'sfoot* (God's foot), *'sbodies* (God's body), *'sdeath* (God's death), *'sheart, by gog, by cocke, by crackey,* and so on.

Other kinds of phonetic distortions draw on the diminutive *-y/ie* ending: *panty, tummy, hicky, fanny,* or on the reduplication of high vowels: *pee-pee, wee-wee, poo-poo, doo-doo.* And finally, there are the acronyms: *VD, TB, BO, GD, SOB, BVD, BM, WC, SNAFU.*

Some Psychological Causes of Euphemism

The meaning of anything can be psychologically (not linguistically) defined as the sum of our responses to it, whether the "it" is an object or an abstraction. Thus the meaning of *lion* could be defined as our response to one. We have already noted the problems with this kind of psychological explanation for a linguistic theory of meaning. But it may give us an insight into this particular problem of the constant turnover of euphemisms.

The simple S → R theory was modified to claim that the responses to a word was a "disposition" to respond rather than the response itself, a claim that was modified again: Rather than a disposition to respond, meaning became a **mediated** response. That is, after a word has been associated with the stimulus long enough, the word picks up aspects of the response elicited by the stimulus object itself. This response, in turn, stimulates a speaker or hearer to respond further to the word in some explicit or implicit way. Schematically, it looks like this:

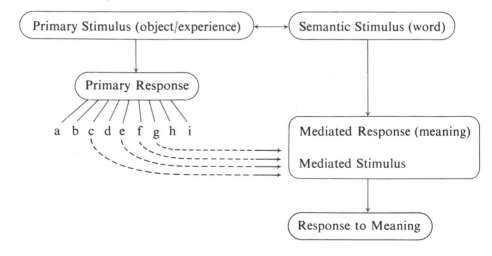

For example, the action of vomiting elicits a primary response composed of elements a–i. The word *vomit* becomes firmly associated with the experience vomit, becoming a new stimulus that elicits some of the elements of the response that vomiting itself elicits; let us say c, e, f, and g. This meaning becomes, in turn, a stimulus which causes us to respond in certain strong ways not only to vomiting itself but to the word *vomit*.

Euphemisms arise when the nasty elements of a response attach so strongly to a particular word that the word elicits too many of the same responses as the thing. *Puke* and *vomit* elicit distinctly unpleasant responses. So we substitute a word or phrase that has not yet gathered to itself those associations: *upchuck*, *sick to my stomach*, and so on, But eventually, through continued association, too many of the unpleasant responses to the referent will attach to these words and yet new euphemisms will have to be found.

PROBLEM 8.5: What would be the nature of language if it were **totally** independent of our limbic system?

PROBLEM 8.6: Assume that for some reason, eating and all its associated objects, actions, and ideas become a tabooed subject. Make up euphemisms, using **all** the processes discussed above to substitute for words like *mouth*, *teeth*, *fork*, *dinner*, *food*, and that ultimate obscenity, *eat*.

SLANG, ARGOT, CANT, JARGON

Just as some words are used by certain social classes to label other classes, so other groups of words are used by certain speakers to identify—though tacitly—themselves. We have already seen how English lets us modulate tone through two or three styles by choosing different words:

1. Professor Smith gives failing grades to all lackadaisical athletes.
2. Smith flunks every lazy player.
3. Smitty axes any jock who goofs off.

From the point of view of someone in or out of college life, the difference between *fail*, *flunk*, and *ax* is more than just a difference in style. *Flunk* is more likely to be used by students than by teachers; and *ax* (or *fox*, meaning "F") has been, or was, used almost solely by some students among themselves.

Other terms have also been used to identify words associated with particular groups. Along with **slang**, they simultaneously identify a vocabulary and implicitly judge it. **Cant** (related to *chant*, and originally the whining pleas of beggars) is often used to refer particularly to the language of thieves, gypsies, and such. But it has also been used to refer to the specialized language of any occupation, particularly to the mechanical and mindless repetition of special words and phrases.

Argot (a French word of unknown etymology), usually refers to the secret language of the underworld, though it too has also been used to refer to any specialized occupational vocabulary—the argot of the racetrack, for example. **Jargon** (once meaning the warbling of birds) is usually used by someone unfamiliar with a particular technical language to characterize his annoyed and puzzled response to it. Thus one man's technical vocabulary is another's jargon. *Feature, shift, transfer, artifactual, narrowing, acronym, blend, clip, drift*—all these words belong to the vocabulary of semantic change and word formation, the vocabulary of historical linguistics. But for anyone ignorant of the subject and unfamiliar with the terms, such words would make up its jargon. Thus *cant, argot,* and *jargon* are words that categorize both by classing and by judging.

Slang (of obscure origin) has many of the same associations. It has often been used as a word to condemn "bad" words that might pollute "good" English—even destroy the mind. For Oliver Wendell Holmes, the use of slang was "at once a sign and a cause of mental atrophy." For George Kittredge and James Greenough, authors of a classic work on English words, (74) slang "has a taint of impropriety about it which makes it offensive . . . slang is ill-adapted to serve as a medium of intercourse and therefore is unsuitable for adoption into legitimate speech . . . ; the unchecked and habitual use of slang (even polite slang) is deleterious to the mind."

But for others, *slang* is a technical term like the terms *grammatical* and *ungrammatical*—a neutral term that categorizes a group of novel words and word meanings used in generally casual circumstances by a cohesive group, usually among its members, not necessarily to hide their meanings but to signal their group membership. It is in this second sense that we shall use *slang* here.

Since the same processes at work in "respectable" word formation and meaning change are also at work in slang, slang is probably as old as language and a source of meaning change. Some of the earliest recorded instances of slang go back to Aristophanes (c. 448–c. 388 B.C.). In his play **The Frogs**, a character is said to be "cracked." Certain words in Homer (c. ninth century B.C.) have been identified as possibly slang. Among the classical Roman writers, slang can be found in Plautus, Horace, Juvenal, and Petronius. It can be traced through Vulgar Latin to the Middle Ages. In France, the earliest records of slang date from about the middle of the fifteenth century. In the late fifteenth century, a glossary of **Rotwalsh**, or German thieves slang appeared.

In England, the earliest vocabularies of thieves' slang appeared in the sixteenth century: Copland's **The Hye Waye to the Spyttel House**; John Awdeley's **Fraternitye of Vagabondes**, and Thomas Harman's **Caveat for**

Common Cursetours. By the end of the sixteenth century, Robert Greene was recording thieves' argot in his **Coney-Catching Pamphlets**. And by the eighteenth century, Dr. Johnson was noting in his dictionary his judgment of a word's social propriety.

PROBLEM 8.7: Collect twenty or so words that you would consider to be your contemporary slang. Why do you identify some words as slang: *It's a groove* (if that is still fashionable) and others as not: *It's a bore*. Using the model of meaning change and word formation provided in the foregoing pages, explain the processes by which your slang came into being. Are there any slang words you cannot explain using that model? What areas of meaning are most frequently referred to? What areas of meaning have few or no slang words associated with them? Why?

PROBLEM 8.8: Here are some American "slang" words that are listed in Eric Partridge's **Slang: Yesterday and Today** (New York, 1970). Words that require explanation have a meaning in parentheses. What sorts of questions does this list raise?

1.	*artillery* (beans)	**27.**	*divvy up*
2.	*bangup* (exactly right)	**28.**	*dough*
3.	*chuck* (food)	**29.**	*dude*
4.	*darb* (a popular person)	**30.**	*flirt*
5.	*fade* (a poorly dressed person)	**31.**	*fuzz*
6.	*goof* (sweetheart)	**32.**	*dope* (foolish person)
7.	*hipe* (cheat)	**33.**	*straight*
8.	*ivories* (teeth)	**34.**	*bleachers* (uncovered grand-
9.	*charge* (injection of narcotics)		stands)
10.	*kale* (money)	**35.**	*bluff*
11.	*lilies* (hands)	**36.**	*blurb*
12.	*mess* (dull person)	**37.**	*booster*
13.	*nines* (the limit)	**38.**	*boss*
14.	*peach* (pretty girl)	**39.**	*camouflage*
15.	*all in* (tired)	**40.**	*catch on*
16.	*all set* (ready)	**41.**	*close up* (as in movie making)
17.	*beef* (complain)	**42.**	*fade out* (as in movies)
18.	*big shot*	**43.**	*still* (as in movies)
19.	*baloney* (nonsense)	**44.**	*fake*
20.	*brainstorm*	**45.**	*insider*
21.	*broke* (out of money)	**46.**	*frolic*
22.	*buddy*	**47.**	*gadget*
23.	*butt in*	**48.**	*hike* (walk)
24.	*chow*	**49.**	*hoodlum*
25.	*crap*	**50.**	*leak* (tell a secret)
26.	*crasher*	**51.**	*phony*

52. *prom*   **54.** *prowler*
53. *proposition* (matter to be con-   **55.** *turn down*
sidered)

PROBLEM 8.9: What ultimately happens to slang words? Consider the fore-going list and Johnson's list of "low" words in Problem 7.9. Is there any other list or lists of words provided so far that might conceivably be relevant to this problem of slang?

Given the short life of any given set of slang words and their appropriate-ness to rather narrowly defined social situations and social groups, it is not surprising that slang should be condemned by most teachers. For they are almost exclusively concerned with teaching a kind of standard language appropriate to communicating with an unknown audience that may be reading a piece of prose long after it was written. Despite the lively, vivid quality of much slang, if it is too evanescent to be understood after a relatively short time, it fails to communicate clearly. And even if the reader under-stands the words, nothing bugs a dude like a cat who lays slang on you after it is out of date.

Whether slang, like syphilis or heroin, atrophies the mind is, of course, another question. Slang not only satisfies a quite legitimate desire to play with language (why else puns, tongue-twisters, palindromes and so on?), it also often provides a word or phrase for a category of meaning that "respectable" words fail to cover. It is true that *mug, lilies, dogs, schnozzola, peepers, gams, balls, yap, ivories*—all current or dated slang words for parts of the body—express no new referential area. But they do invest the category of items with a particular affective tone. If we lost these words, we would still have *face, hands, feet, nose, eyes, legs, testicles, mouth, teeth,* and so on. But without slang terms for them, we would be unable to express the affective meaning we invest in them.

But some words name a category of experience that no standard word covers: *graft, fan, doodle, leak, turn off, dig, hip, frisk*. In such cases, if the word really does meet a felt or even unfelt need that is not just a temporary part of the cultural vocabulary of a limited group, then the word stands a good chance of being absorbed into the more permanent vocabulary of the lan-guage. In fact, when we consider the original metaphorical transfers of words like *result, explain, comprehend, grasp,* and so on, we might suspect that even they were not as formal and academic when they were first used as their literal use is for us now. They have become necessary words because the semantic space they now occupy is important to a society preoccupied with thinking. And because thinking is important, the words have become respect-able.

Thus what may begin as slang may take one of four courses. First, and most likely, it may disappear entirely: *skidoo* is kept alive only as a trite example of archaic slang; *goof* for sweetheart, *grummy* for low spirits, *rake* for comb have almost certainly disappeared everywhere. Second, a slang word may move into a limbo between slang and very casual speech: *booze, dude, mob, junk, chintzy, fire* (dismiss from a job), *dumb* (stupid). Third, other words that once may have been slang-like may move more into the permanent casual vocabulary of the language: *cab, taxi, bus, blight, nag, fun, wail, banter, bigot, flimsy, flippant, sham, shuffle.* Even the most fastidious speaker would be unlikely to boggle at using such words in casual moments.

And finally, there are those words that have been completely absorbed into the language, into an English appropriate to writing of this sort. Only the most super-sensitive soul would object to words like these: *A* **sensible** *student does not* **gamble** *on a future* **job** *by dressing in a* **shabby** *manner. Nor does he appear* **touchy** *when asked to* **volunteer** *for extra work.* The words in boldface were listed by Dr. Johnson as "low" or "ludicrous" or "cant" words. Other words he condemned included *bolster, abominable, desperately, finesse, fragmentary, slim.* Others have condemned *banter, fop, flippant, bigot,* and *flimsy.* Yet today we would not be shocked to find all these words in quite elevated prose. (52, 75, 159, 162)

SEMANTIC LAWS

Historical semanticists have searched for laws, or rules of semantic change, much as historical linguists studying sound patterns and grammatical structures have. In the nineteenth century, a group of Germanic philologists were able to formulate laws of phonological change in the Germanic languages that were of very great explanatory power, laws we shall explore in Chapter Thirteen. Inspired by their success, semanticists set about looking for equally powerful laws of semantic change.

Unfortunately, they have met with very limited success. There are a few tendencies that we can discover in the previous data:

1. Words for abstractions will generally develop out of words for physical experience: *comprehend, grasp, explain,* and so on.
2. Words originally indicating neutral condition tend to polarize: *doom, fame, predicament, luck, merit.*
3. Words originally indicating strong emotional response tend to weaken as they are used to exaggerate: *awful, terrific, tremendous.*
4. Insulting words tend to come from names of animals or lower classes: *rat, dog, villain, cad.*
5. Metaphors will be drawn from those aspects of experience most relevant to us: *eye of a needle, finger of land*; or most intense in our experience: *turn on, spaced out, freaked out,* for example.

But these only approximate statistical tendencies. They are not laws fulfilling the usual requirements of a law: that it not only explain relevant past events, but predict future events as well. The odds are that a word for an abstract cognitive or emotional process will develop out of an earlier concrete reference, but we cannot take any given word with concrete reference: *rock* or *push* and predict that it will evolve into a word referring to abstract experience. And the reverse has happened with originally abstract words like *dull, blunt, keen*, and *soft*. All originally referred to nonphysical referents.

A change that has been given the name of "law" and often cited as one of the best examples of a law is that suggested by Gustaf Stern: Adverbs meaning *rapidly* before 1300 developed into adverbs meaning *immediately*. Adverbs meaning *quickly* after 1300 did not. This, of course, is peculiar to English and limited to a particular point in time. At best, it is a restricted generalization about the past, not a law than encompasses the future. (208)

We must, however, distinguish two kinds of predictions: (1) In some cases, we have to base a prediction on relevant external forces. A culture will invariably assign meanings it **must** develop to the words it uses most frequently or can create most easily. Thus a generalization about, say, euphemism, is entirely culture-dependent in regard to the tabooed and non-tabooed areas in which euphemisms will be used. (2) On the other hand, there may be universals of change which, because they are so regular and so general, reflect internal influences either peculiar to the particular language or to human language and cognition in general. It has been claimed, for example, that all human languages obey a very general law for the development of color terms. (9) The development has seven stages and each stage must be passed through in sequential order. The order can be represented like this:

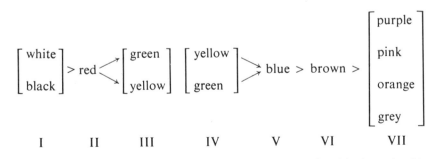

That is, all languages have nonmetaphorical words for black and white. Such words may exhaust the spectrum. If there are only three terms, the third one will be a word for something approximating red. Stages III and IV may occur in either order: green and yellow will be the next words to develop, but they may develop in either order. Once those five words have developed, then blue and brown will follow, themselves to be followed by the next four in no particular order.

As the authors of this research have suggested, there are eleven universal potential color categories, and those colors develop in a fixed order. If they are correct, this is surely an example of cognitive-linguistic interaction and a very powerful semantic "law" dependent not on any particular cultural organization but rather only a particular level of cultural complexity.

There may be another law of semantic change in English where mental processes interact with a cultural milieu to create new meanings for old forms. Words for sensory experience fall into five basic categories.

Tactile: *mild, soft, smooth, even, hard, rough, harsh, coarse, dull, dry, keen, sharp, hot, cold, warm, cool, heavy, light, dry, bland, hard.*

Gustatory/Olfactory: *piquant, pungent, tart, bitter, cloying, acrid, acid, sweet, sour, vapid, tangy.*

Visual (dimension): *high, low, thick, thin, deep, shallow, wide, broad, narrow, full, big, little, flat, steep, small, level.*

Visual (color): *clear, light, bright, brilliant, fair, dark, dim, faint, pale.*

Aural: *quiet, loud, shrill, strident.*

We can expand these basic categories by transferring words from one category to another: *hot music, loud colors, sharp tastes, sour smells,* and so on. But not all metaphors are equally comfortable: *loud heights, wide smells, bright edges, low tastes* (i.e., parallel to low sounds on a sensory dimension not the sense of vulgar tastes). At first glance, we might assume that we randomly select our metaphors, since many of these are perfectly clear even though we never or rarely use them. A loud height is certainly higher than a quiet one.

But the historical development of these metaphors in English reveals a pattern that approaches the regularity of a law that might be represented like this:

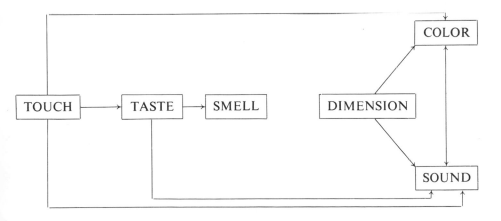

That is, in English (and possibly many other languages), words referring primarily to tactile sensations will, if they transfer at all, transfer to taste (*sharp tastes*), color (*harsh colors*), and sound (*soft sounds*). Taste words will transfer to smell (*sour smell*) or to sound (*sweet sounds*). There are no primary, non-metaphorical smell words in English (or in many other languages, interestingly enough). Dimension words may transfer to color (*deep red*) or to sound (*high sound*). Color and sound words trade metaphors (*dark sounds, quiet colors*).

There is a second regularity: Each successive transfer follows the same sequence. That is, once *dull* transferred from tactile to vision, it transferred on to sound, but not back to taste/smell or dimension. Each successive transfer of a word is determined by the most "advanced" meaning of the metaphor.

And there is a third regularity: If a sense transfer violates either of the first two regularities, that sense development tends to disappear. For example *soft taste*, a sense not usual in standard English, was active for a time after *soft sounds* had developed, a violation of the "most advanced sense" constraint. That taste meaning subsequently disappeared. *Shrill* developed touch and taste senses, contrary to the main principle. Neither sense has maintained itself in the language.

There are a very few exceptions to this generalization: *Mellow* developed senses out of the predicted order; *faint* developed a smell/taste sense after earlier transferring from the meaning "feigned" or "simulated" to color. *Sharp* transferred to angles, perhaps on the model of Latin *acute*. *Flat* and *thin* transferred to taste. But when all the transfers are taken into consideration, these exceptions constitute less than one percent of the total data.

This kind of research into the semantic development of an entire field of words as opposed to tracing the history of a single word is little explored at the moment, largely because the data is so difficult to assemble. We require what we do not yet have for any language: An historically organized **Roget's Thesaurus**, a resource that would list every word that has ever referred to any sense listed under the category of that sense along with the earliest and latest citations of that word with that sense. Without such a resource, historical semanticists are forced to read dictionaries entry by entry, searching for senses and words that at one time may have referred to a particular referent but no longer do. How, for example, would we discover all the words that at any time have ever referred to, say, taste? These have: *aspre, coarse, cold, poignant, rough, smart, soft, warm, acrid, austere, dulcet, eager, acute, high, small, loud,* and *shrill.*

PROBLEM 8.10: Here are some sense words with their etymological sources. Does this information confirm or contradict the generalization about sense transfer? *sweet* (pleasing to any sense), *bitter* (from biting), *acid* (from *ac-* = sharp), *acrid* (from *ac-* = sharp), *tart* (sharp pain), *cloy* (prick with a nail), *piquant* (piercing or stinging), *pungent* (to prick), *shrill* (rasping or grating, earlier to scrape or abrade), *quiet* (calm, peaceful), *dulcet* (sweet to taste or smell), *blunt* (unclear of sight), *keen* (intelligent), *soft* (producing agreeable sensations), *coarse* (ordinary), *dull* (unintelligent), *harsh* (rough and hard to touch, then to taste). How do these fit in: *eager, poignant, austere, brisk*?

PROBLEM 8.11: Many of these words also apply to abstract situations and to personality: *a dark moment, a rough time, a warm personality, a dry humor,* and so on. Are there any generalizations to be made regarding the sequence of development of these transfers? You will have to consult the **OED** for dates.

PART III

GRAMMAR AND SOUND

Chapter 9

BETWEEN SEMANTICS AND GRAMMAR

Between questions that are purely semantic—the origin of insulting names for women, for example—and purely grammatical questions, whether *-tion* or *-ness* goes with *happy*—is a kind of language change that seems both semantic and grammatical. *Starve*, for example, originally meant simply to die. It later narrowed to mean to die from hunger, but it changed in another way. In its original sense, it was always **intransitive**. That is, it was possible to say *He starved*, but according to the **OED** not until the sixteenth century do we find *starve* used in its **transitive** sense: *Someone starved him*. Before that time, presumably, it would have been ungrammatical to utter that sentence, just as it is now ungrammatical for a ModE speaker to say, *He laughed him*, meaning he caused him to laugh. In order to understand this kind of change— and to understand even more complex problems of grammatical change—we have to pause for a moment to explore some of the ways in which such grammatical-semantic problems are dealt with in a modern grammar, and how their solutions bear on problems of historical linguistics.

GRAMMATICAL STRUCTURE

Verbs are conventionally grouped into **intransitive** or **transitive**, depending on whether they take an object:

1. *The man disappeared.*
2. *The man fixed* **the piano**.

But most verbs in English are neither strictly transitive nor intransitive:

3a. *The people ate.*
3b. *The people ate* **food**.
4a. *The man watched.*
4b. *The man watched* **the parade**.
5a. *The bird sang.*
5b. *The bird sang* **songs**.

Dictionaries usually list these transitive and intransitive senses separately, as different meanings for the same word. Yet the differences may not be in the meaning of the word but in whether the word occurs before an object, before a noun phrase.

PROBLEM 9.1: Suppose we were concerned only with surface grammatical structures, with what we can observe about the order of words in sentences as they are actually spoken or written, with no concern for the meaning of a sentence. Would that attitude toward these next sentences lead us to some misleading conclusions about the notions transitive and intransitive?

6a. *Tom pours wine.*
6b. *Tom pours.*
6c. *Wine pours.*
7a. *George cooks eggs.*
7b. *George cooks.*
7c. *Eggs cook.*
8a. *Bill drives cars.*
8b. *Bill drives.*
8c. *The car drives easily.*
9a. *Jack reads books.*
9b. *Jack reads.*
9c. *The book reads well.*

If we were concerned only with surface patterns, we would conclude that the (a) examples were transitive verbs, verbs with objects; (b) and (c), intransitive verbs grammatically identical with the intransitive verbs in (10)–(13):

10. *He exists.*
11. *Tom grew.*
12. *Jack waited.*
13. *The star twinkled.*

But the intransitive verbs in the (b) sentences are very different from those in (c), and both differ from (10)–(13): Those in (b) are implicitly transitive because in each case, we could put something after the verb, making it transitive without really changing the meaning: *Tom smokes* (*something*). But we cannot say *Eggs cook (*something*) or *He waited (*something*).[1]

And the (c) sentences differ from both (b) and (10)–(13): In each case, the subjects, *wine, eggs, car,* and *book,* are in some sense like the **objects** of the action. That is, they are being caused to do or undergo the action indicated by the verb: *X causes eggs to boil—Eggs boil.* The subjects in (b) and (10)–(13), on the other hand, are not being acted on. So what appear to be grammatically similar sentences are really quite different in ways that we have to explain in grammatical terms, not just semantic terms.

We thus have three kinds of transitive and intransitive verbs:

1. Pure intransitive (no object possible): *George exists.*
2. Intransitive with implied object: *The man eats.*
3. Intransitive with subject as implied object: *The eggs cook.*
4. Pure transitive (object generally required): *George fixes things.*
5. Transitive with optional object (see (2) above): *The man eats something.*
6. Transitive related to (3) above: *Someone cooks the eggs.*

One new and very influential school of linguists has tried to account for these questions by assuming two levels of grammatical structure. One is the obvious sequence of overt elements we respond to in a sentence. The other level of structure represents the deeper grammatical and semantic relations that lie behind the surface of a sentence, relations we can describe independently of the overt, perceptible word order. The overt level we will call **surface structure**; the deeper level we will call the **deep structure** of a sentence.

We can represent or "generate" one kind of simple deep structure behind sentences with formula-like rules something like the following:

1. $S \rightarrow NP\ VP$ S = sentence, NP = noun phrase, VP = verb phrase

               V = verb

2. $VP \rightarrow V \begin{pmatrix} \begin{Bmatrix} NP \\ AP \\ PP \end{Bmatrix} \end{pmatrix}$ AP = adjective phrase, PP = prepositional phrase

3. $NP \rightarrow ART\ N$ ART = article, N = noun
4. $PP \rightarrow P\ NP$ P = preposition

Rule (1) says that the abstract idea of a sentence is at the simplest level of organization made up of a subject noun phrase and a predicate verb phrase: *Tom left, The boy saw the dog, A girl seemed happy, The man was in the house.*

---

1 In the next three chapters, * will mean not a reconstructed root but an ungrammatical construction.

Rule (2) says that the predicate verb phrase can be made up of just the verb: *left*, in *Tom left*. Or it can be made up of the verb and any one of the three elements in parentheses. Parentheses mean that whatever they embrace is optional. They may or may not be selected. The three elements are (in boldface) a noun phrase: *The boy saw* **the dog**; an adjective phrase: *Mary seemed* **hungry**; or a prepositional phrase: *The man was* **in the house**. The braces enclosing the elements in rule (2) mean that one and only one of these elements may be selected if any are selected. Rule (3) indicates that the noun phrase is made up of an article and a noun: *the boy, a man, an apple*. Rule (4) indicates that a prepositional phrase is made up of a preposition and a noun phrase: *in the house, by the road*.

These choices and the resulting structure can be represented on "trees." If only V is chosen in rule (2), then the tree would look like (a). If the NP were chosen in rule (2) along with the V, then the tree would resemble (b):

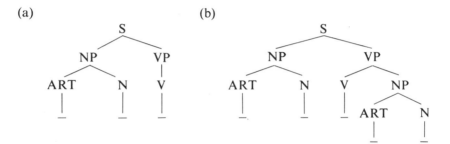

(a)   (b)

PROBLEM 9.2: What would the trees look like if AP had been chosen for one and PP for another?

Of course, these are only grammatical skeletons. We need semantic units, words, to fit under the nodes that specify parts of speech, under noun, article, verb, preposition, and adjective. These we can list in a dictionary that accompanies the base rules. In addition to the meaning of the words (indicated in the form of semantic components) we list restrictions which determine whether the verb must or may occur before an object: *fixed the chair*; before an adjective phrase: *seemed old*; before a prepositional phrase: *was in the house*; or before none of these: *He disappeared*. The dictionary component (minus the semantic features) might look like this. The position, specified by _____, indicates the position of the verb relevant to any other part of speech:

disappear: V; _____ #	*fix*: V; _____ NP
become: V; _____ NP/AP	*be*: V; _____ NP/AP/PP

(The slashes without parentheses indicate an obligatory choice of one element.)

That is, *disappear* occurs under a V but because it is purely intransitive, it may occur only without a complement. This restriction is symbolized by #. (This ignores modifiers of time and place, and so on, which we shall omit for now): *He disappeared #*. *Find*, a transitive verb, **must** have an object NP after it: *He found money*. *Become*, a copula verb, may have either an NP **or** an AP after it: *He became king/tired*. And *be*, another copula, may have after it any of the three: *He is a king/old/in the house*. (31, 94, 132, 143)

PROBLEM 9.3: Here are several words to add to the dictionary. Specify very simple restrictions for the verbs. Generate four or five deep structures, picking words **at random**. Where must the dictionary information be modified, added to, expanded? How might we do it?

> N: *man, cars, piano, food, parade, songs, wine, people, bird, Tom, George, Bill, Jack, eggs, books, star, he.*
> V: *was, pours, drives, reads, exists, grew, waited, twinkled, became, cooks, exists, disappeared, fixed, ate, watched, sang.*
> AP: *old, heavy, smart, straight, hard, square, good.*
> P: *in, on, at, by.*
> ART: *the.*

PROBLEM 9.4: Add a rule that would account for these patterns: *old, very old; tired, somewhat tired; sick, quite sick; intelligent, rather intelligent.*

Now the rules and the dictionary would let us generate the sentences mentioned above, (1) to (13). But if we just list all the different verbs and their possibilities under different entries in the dictionary, we will not capture a generalization about the differences and similarities among them, that *He reads* and *He reads (something)* are somehow related, that *Someone cooks eggs* and *Eggs cook* are related. So even if any intransitive sentences such as *He reads, Eggs cook*, and *They exist* have the same **surface** structure, we also know that they differ from one another in very basic ways.

Transformational generative grammarians try to account for all this by postulating transformations that change the deep structures generated by the kinds of rules described before Problem 9.2 into surface structures, into the grammatical strings we understand in an actual sentence.

The problem is to decide how surface and deep structure relate to one another. Consider *Tom hunts*, for example. It always implies *Tom hunts something*. We can capture that insight by assuming that the structure of *Tom hunts* is **transformationally** related to the structure of *Tom hunts something*, through a **transformation** that **deletes** the indefinite object in the deep structure. This produces a surface structure superficially like that of an intransitive sentence.

We can represent the transformation rule like this:

OBJECT DELETION: V   NP   (if NP is indefinite)
                  → V   ∅

The first line refers to the relevant elements in a tree, the verb and the object, and by implication, anything under those nodes. The second line represents the change, the elements in the new tree created by the transformation. In this case, the whole NP node has been deleted.

But if we applied this rule to all verbs that had an NP after them, we would delete any indefinite object after the verb. This would generate sentences like *Tom fixed*, *Bill found*, *George earned*. So we have to indicate that some verbs cannot have objects deleted. Since most verbs **do** allow their objects to be deleted, it is simpler to stipulate the exceptions, those which may **not** undergo object deletion.

We can do this by adding to the dictionary a fourth item of information. We already include (1) part of speech, (2) semantic definition, (3) the syntactic environment in which the verb may occur. We add (4), the transformations a verb may or may not allow. Thus for *find*, *eat*, and *exist*, we would have dictionary entries roughly like this (semantic information is omitted):

> *eat*: V; _____ NP.   *exist*: V; _____ #.   *find*: V; _____ NP;
> −OBJECT DELETE.

That is, *find* may not have its object deleted, while *eat* may; *Tom found*, *Tom ate*, *Tom found something*, *Tom ate something*.

Thus a complete grammar would look something like this:

PROBLEM 9.5: One kind of transformation is DELETION: *They eat something* → *They eat*. There are other kinds of transformations. Here are some other pairs of sentences that might be transformationally related. How? Which sentence **form** is derived from which? Note: Do not assume that the first sentence structure is the source of the second. (Strictly speaking, one sentence is **not** transformed into another. The abstract structures behind sentences are transformed. We will use sentences here as a shorthand for that structure.)

1.   *He looked the number up. He looked up the number.*
2.   *I know that he is there. I know he is there.*

3. *It is easy to do that. To do that is easy. For someone to do that is easy.*
4. *The man in the house left. The man who was in the house left.*
5. *He usually leaves. Usually, he leaves.*
6. *Down the street came a truck. A truck came down the street.*
7. *All of the people were there. All the people were there.*
8. *John and Mary married. John and Mary married each other.*
9. *For someone to do that is bad. To do that is bad.*
10. *Tom is older than Jack. Tom is older than Jack is.*

HISTORICAL IMPLICATIONS

The historical importance of these patterns when we describe them by this kind of grammar is this: Many individual verbs move from one class to another, thereby allowing a previously prohibited transformation. For example, as purely transitive verbs have been born or borrowed into English, they have generally lost restrictions against deleting objects. The change in the grammar would mean that we simply remove the restrictions against object deletions. Verbs like *paint, hunt, cook, read, eat, kill*—once obligatorily transitive—may now have their objects deleted.

But here we have to distinguish between the **consequences** of grammatical change and its **causes**. The consequence of the change is a new pattern for certain verbs. The cause of the change lies in us. Strictly transitive verbs regularly shift to optionally transitive verbs probably because we operate on a combined principle of economy and generality. If a verb **requires** an object, we cannot speak of doing whatever the verb indicates unless we specify a particular action or add an indefinite object. In ModE, for example, most of us do not ordinarily say *He is fixing around the house, but we may say He is painting around the house.

Given the principle that we all unconsciously strive for grammatical economy where it does not interfere with communication, we can understand why verbs referring to the most common and hence important actions are optionally transitive. Were they not, we could not in the most economical way speak in general about eating, drinking, reading, writing, and so on. On the other hand, verbs which still do not allow their objects to be deleted are often too general to communicate anything without an object: *He finds/ determines/prefers/mentions/keeps, and so on.

Since only exceptional verbs are marked against OBJECT DELETION, we might also consider whether another aspect of the principle of least effort, the simplicity principle, operates here. If the few verbs which may not lose their objects have to be specially marked in our internalized grammar, then a child, as he learns verbs (or most adults as they use them, perhaps), may learn to use them without their accidental and often unpredictable restrictions, much as irregular verbs like *help–holp–holpen* lost their exceptional status and regularized to *help–helped–helped*.

But simple object deletion does not explain patterns like those in sentences (6c)–(9c). In a sentence like *The eggs cook*, the apparent subject is a noun phrase that can be interpreted as the understood "receiver" of an action or as a deep-lying subject that is caused by some unstated agent to undergo or perform the action of the verb. If this is so, then we have to assume a different deep structure behind *George cooks* on the one hand and *eggs cook* on the other. We can get at the differences, perhaps, through history.

PROBLEM 9.6: Actually, four kinds of changes have created new transitive and intransitive verbs. The deletion of the object, as we have seen, is one. Compare these next groups of sentences. At an earlier time, the verbs in (1) and (2) were **strictly intransitive**; those in (3) **strictly transitive**. What would you speculate were the intransitive sentences historically related to those in (1) and (2); what would have been the transitive sentences related to those in (3)? Why did they change?

1. *He whispered the words. They sang the lyrics. He answered his critics. He argued the case.*
2. *He grows corn. He starved millions. We work our animals hard. She dined several friends.*
3. *The situation developed. The material disintegrated. The news continued. The troubles resumed. The waters separated. The oil spread.*

Those sentences in (1) were originally pure intransitives, but eventually attracted an object, probably because the action referred to always involved some concept besides the subject, on the analogy of *say something*. Modern pure intransitives such as *sparkle, kneel, disappear, exist*, and *die*, on the other hand, ordinarily involve only a single noun phrase element, which is the subject.

Those sentences in groups (2) and (3) historically constitute mirror images of each other. The verbs in (2): *grow, starve, work*, and *dine*, were originally intransitives: *Tomatoes grow, people starve, employees work, friends dine*. Conversely, those in (3) have been cited as transitive before they were cited as intransitive: *Someone developed the situation | disintegrated the material | continued the news | spread the oil*, and so on. We have to explain the changes in two different but related ways.

There is a large class of verbs called **causatives**. Their subjects cause the objects to perform the action indicated by the verb. Compare the sentences in (a) with those in (b):

a. *He rolled the ball* (that is, he caused the ball to roll) / *moved the box* / *broke the dish* / *fried the eggs* / *rocked the cradle*, and so on.
b. *He saw the ball* / *bought the box* / *found the dish* / *felt the eggs* / *painted the cradle*, and so on.

The subjects in (b) do not cause the objects to move or change, as they do in (a).

In a generative theory of language, each verb of the *roll, cook, move, break* kind would have associated with it a feature we might call [causative]. Ordinarily, such a verb allows a transformation in which **the underlying object is shifted to the subject position in the surface structure and the original indefinite subject is deleted:**

> someone/thing   breaks   the dish
> → the dish   breaks

More recently, this has been modified to change the direction of the transformation.

> someone/thing ⟨causes⟩ [the dish (to) break]
> → someone/thing breaks the dish

The verb written here as ⟨cause⟩ is in this theory an abstract entity in the deep structure that is not a real "word," but rather an abstract "operator" or theoretical element not unlike certain related elements in algebra and calculus. There are a good many arguments in favor of this analysis, but for historical purposes, the simpler transformation will better account for the change. For we would otherwise have to assume an underlying intransitive *break* before it actually was attested to in the history of the language.

Some transitive verbs like *commence, circulate, increase, dissolve, continue, resume, reconcile,* and so on originally had a causative sense in that they could occur in sentences like *We continued the trial.* But these causative transitive sentences did not at first allow an equivalent intransitive sentence: *The trial continued.* Before the eighteenth century, for example, it would have been as ungrammatical to write *The situation improved* as it is now ungrammatical to write **The situation exacerbated.* At the time, *improve* had to exclude the transformation which would have shifted the object, just as *exacerbate* does now. But apparently, just as speakers simplified their grammar by regularizing the OBJECT DELETION restriction, so they frequently regularized the restrictions in regard to CAUSATIVE OBJECT SHIFTS by dropping the restrictions against it from verbs like *continue* and *improve.*

The shift from non-causative intransitives like those in (2), *flowers grow,* to causative transitives, *I grow flowers,* requires a slightly different explanation, akin, perhaps, to back-formation. Intransitive verbs like *grow, starve, work,* and *dine*, could occur in a pattern like *The man starved* or in literal causative constructions like *Someone caused the man to starve*. But originally, they did not allow an implicit causative construction like *Someone starved the man*. Presumably, however, speakers added [causative] to the verb rather than keep it in the sub-class of verbs which did not allow a transformation of the types *Someone causes the platform to turn* → *Someone turns the platform* → *The platform turns*. Thus when *Flowers grow* lent itself to a pattern like *Someone causes flowers to grow* (or the approximate idea), it could easily lead to *Someone grows flowers* on the analogy of the verbs that do allow the transformation. The modern consequence of this is two identical pairs of sentences: *He grows/ improves apples* and *Apples grow/improve*. But each sentence is historically the mirror image of the other member of the pair.

So with two transformations: OBJECT DELETION and CAUSATIVE OBJECT SHIFT, we can account for a variety of contemporary grammatical patterns. And in the terms of our theory, we can account for the historical changes in words that occur in these patterns: Speakers tend to simplify a grammar by removing unpredictable restrictions against transformations. In a sense, this is the grammatical explanation for analogy.

PROBLEM 9.7: What do these sentences mean?

1. **He existed the new element.*
2. **The child cried the woman.*
3. **She waited the people.*
4. **I disappeared the cat.*
5. **They twinkled the light.*

Find five or ten other ModE verbs of the same type.

PROBLEM 9.8: Some grammatical structures are semantically causative but their verbs do not allow the shift. For example, *I caused the man to leave* does not allow *I left the man*, as *I caused the man to trip* allows *I tripped the man*. Here are some other examples: *I caused the man to lose/succeed/sell/study/ fight/eat/spit/clean/dust/wash/confess/applaud/explain*. What might be one explanation of why these do not allow the transformation? Is this problem related to the immediately preceding one? What is the meaning of *I failed my friend*?

PROBLEM 9.9: Does any of this explain sentences like these: *This book reads easily; the car drives awkwardly; the class teaches well; the turkey carves cleanly; the wood saws hard*? Check the dates for these senses relative to others connected with same words in the **OED**. Comment.

A stylistic consequence of these changes, perhaps even a secondary cause, is a greatly increased flexibility in how we can construct sentences in English to reflect rhetorical nuances. When verbs like those we have described occur in new patterns in the language, they allow a writer to control rather carefully the rhetorical structure of his paragraphs. One organizing principle of discourse is the way a writer controls what words fill the subject position of a sequence of sentences within a paragraph. How well a writer can control his reader's attention by manipulating subjects partly determines the quality of his prose.

This discussion should also point out how different theories of grammar and meaning will lead us to different histories of the language. If we follow a theory of traditional dictionary definitions of verb meaning or the theory of those who primarily collect grammatical patterns, the kind of changes that we have described here would be represented in a dictionary something like this:

Earlier period: *teach*:   verb transitive: *I teach English.*

verb intransitive: *I teach.*

Later period: *teach*:   verb transitive: *I teach English.*

verb intransitive$_1$: *I teach.*

verb intransitive$_2$: *The children teach easily.*

The dictionary simply adds a meaning to the word *teach* as its syntactic environment changes.

A transformational generative grammar would argue that in these sentences the meaning of *teach* does not essentially change. All that change are the possible surface relationships among the noun phrases that occur with the verb in the deep structure. And these potential new relationships can be represented by minor notational changes in the dictionary. Here are four examples of notational changes. (We omit everything except the relevant information. In each pair, (a) is the earlier entry, (b) the later.)

explain: a. V; _____ NP; − OBJECT DELETION.
 b. V; _____ NP.   (OBJ. DELETE now
                                                                         possible)

study: a. V; _____ #.
 b. V; _____ NP.   (direct object now
                                                                         assumed)

improve: a. V; _____ NP; − CAUSATIVE SHIFT.
 b. V; _____ NP.   (CAUS. SHIFT now
                                                                         possible)

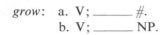

grow: a. V; _____ #.
        b. V; _____ NP.   (CAUS. SHIFT now
                                                                possible)

(In addition, we would add [causative] to *grow*.)

Another kind of linguistic change which falls between semantics and syntax is illustrated by the difference between these sentences:

    a. *It is made of stone.*   b. *It is made of stones.*
       He eats fruit.   *He eats fruits.*
       They love song.   *They love songs.*

In the (a) group, the noun is a **non-count** noun, one referring to a concrete or abstract referent without discrete shape or number. In the (b) group, the same words appear but are used as **count** nouns, nouns referring to a concrete or abstract referent that has a discrete shape and can be counted: *one song, two songs; one book, two books.*

Depending on what kind of linguistic theory we adopt, throughout its history English has either (a) added [+count] meanings to many [−count] nouns (and vice versa), or (b) has shifted a word from the [+count] category to the [−count] category (and vice versa). These nouns, for example, were at one time purely count nouns: *rock, stone, cake, pearl, brain, liver.* In the course of time, they have also come to name the material of the objects they originally referred to, thereby becoming [−count] as well as [+count]. On the other hand, these next words were originally [−count] nouns, but are now both [+count] and [−count] nouns: *brick, rice, wine, fruit, meat, paint, pain, thought.* All can now be used in the plural: *bricks, rices, wines,* and so on. While this is in one sense a semantic change, it is also a change with syntactic consequences, for we add plural *-s* and use articles differently with count and non-count nouns.

PROBLEM 9.10: Here are some noun phrases to put into the frame *I see* _____. How do the plural *-s* and the articles *a* and *the* occur with these nouns? Is there a general rule you can formulate? (Assume that those phrases and words marked * are ungrammatical when they occur in the indicated syntactic frame.)

*girl	girls	a girl	*a girls	the girl	the girls
dust	*dusts	*a dust	*a dusts	the dust	*the dusts
*car	cars	a car	*a cars	the car	the cars
chili	*chilis	*a chili	*a chilis	the chili	*the chilis

PROBLEM 9.11: The object noun phrases in *I see the girls* and *I see girls* are, respectively, definite and indefinite. It is the lack of an overt article in *I see*

girls that indicates the indefinite *girls*. We might account for this pattern with a rule such as the following: ART → [± definite]. We would then "spell" [−definite] as either *a/an* or as nothing, [+definite] as *the*. What conditions determine how [−definite] is spelled?

Now that we have explored some of the grey areas between clear-cut semantic problems and clear-cut grammatical problems, we can see that describing historical change in this area must be done on a very abstract level. In the past, most historical linguists were satisfied to collect the data and categorize the ways in which the data could be organized. But this does not get to some of the deeper problems of linguistic change, problems that depend in good part, again, on the particular way we choose to describe our own living language. For once we discover the crucial categories and processes in our own grammars, elements such as causatives and so on, we are compelled at least to try to describe dead languages in the same terms, an attempt that very quickly reveals how difficult it is to reconstruct the linguistic abilities of speakers who have been dead for over a thousand years.

Chapter 10

GRAMMATICAL CHANGE:
THE NOUN PHRASE

We have seen how transformations can rearrange the major sentence elements in a deep structure to produce a variety of surface structures. Most of these transformations delete a subject or object, or both delete and rearrange: *I saw (some unspecified object)* → *I saw. (Some unspecified agent) cooked the meat* → *The meat cooked.*

PROBLEM 10.1: How would a transformational grammar deal with the following sentences:

1. *Him I like.*
2. *Down the street came a truck.*
3. *Those questions no one can answer.*
4. *Across the way was a large dog.*
5. *Happy you may be but lucky you are not.*
6. *To grandmother's house we go!*
7. *Then came an important part.*

How would a descriptive grammar deal with them (review page 26ff)?

WORD ORDER: THE MAJOR ELEMENTS

The deep structure of these sentences, of course, would be in a basic, specified order, and transformations would then shift their elements into the desired order: (1) *I like him* → *Him I like* and so on. Transformations of this kind do not create new subjects and objects. They are **stylistic** transformations allowed by the limited freedom of ModE from the more usual subject–verb–(complement) order. (In **complement**, we include direct objects: *I saw* **Tom**; indirect objects: *I gave* **Tom** *money*; and elements after copulas like *be, seem, become, appear, feel, look*: *I am* **in the house**, *He became* **a king**, *You appear* **sick**.) The freest elements are adverbial modifiers: *I left* **yesterday** → **Yesterday** *I left*. *I* **usually** *sleep* → **Usually** *I sleep*.

Statistically, however, the order of the main elements in ModE deviates very little from an S–V–(C) order. If the order did vary, if it did allow us any sequence, we would have to rely heavily on semantic and contextual clues to understand which noun phrases were subjects and which objects. If a sentence like *John saw the house* could occur in any order: *The house saw John, Saw the house John, The house John saw, John the house saw, Saw John the house*, of course, we could be fairly certain who was seeing what. But if we substituted *bear* for *house*, we would be less certain. And if we substituted *George* for *bear*, then depending on its context, the meaning might be very unclear.

PROBLEM 10.2: In any ten consecutive sentences from a newspaper story, reverse the subjects and objects to determine whether a reader would be seriously confused if he could not tell from position alone which noun phrase was the subject and which the object in those sentences. Does this suggest anything about the importance of word order?

PROBLEM 10.3: Here are some OE and ME sentence types that represent only strong tendencies, not invariable rules. What do you conclude about OE word order? About ME? What do you conclude about the range of variations among the main sentence elements and whether we can predict those variations by any principles of grammatical context? (The translations given in (1)–(15) and (16) (20) are word for word.)

Old English

1. *Se man is god.* (The man is good.)
2. *Ne mihte he gehealdan heardne mece.* (Not might he hold grim sword.)
3. *Þa sende se cyning þone disc.* (Then sent the king the dish.)
4. *Þa he þone cyning sohte, he beotode.* (When he the king visited, he boasted.)

5. *He hi fedan sceolde.* (He them feed should.)
6. *Ne drincst þu win?* (Not drinkest thou wine?)
7. *Nu is þeos gifu eow ætbroden.* (Now is this gift (from) you taken.)
8. *Heo hine lærde.* (She him advised.)
9. *Ne habbaÞ we cyning.* (Not have we king.)
10. *He wearÞ wædla.* (He became (a) poor man.)
11. *God behead us þæt we þæt treow ne hrepodon.* (God commanded us that we that tree not touch.)
12. *He wæs ylde.* (He was old.)
13. *We eow can.* (We you know.)
14. *Þa com mæssepreost.* (Then came priest.)
15. *Hi hæfdon hira mete geboht.* (They had bought their food.)

Middle English

16. *Nu biseche ich þe.* (Now beseech I thee.)
17. *I hym folwed.* (I him followed.)
18. *I ne can ne I ne mai tellen þe wunder.* (I not know nor I not may tell the wonder.)
19. *Þa þe King Stephne to Englalande com, þa macod he his gadering æt Oxeneford.* (When King Stephen to England came, then made he his gathering at Oxford.)
20. *A leafdi wes mid hire fan biset al abuten.* (A lady was with her foes beset all about.)
21. *We redeth* (read) *i þe holi godspelle* (gospel) *of to-dai þat ure* (our) *lord Jhesu Crist yede* (went) *one time into ane* (a) *ssipe* (ship) *and hise deciples mid* (with) *him into þe see.*
22. *Nou þou hest* (have) *y-hyerd þe zennes* (sins) *þet comeþ of glotounye* (gluttony) *and of lecherie. And þervore þet zuyche* (such) *zennes arizeþ communliche ine taverne, þet is welle* (well) *of zenne, þervore ich wylle a lite* (little) *take* (touch) *of þe zennes þet byeþ* (be) *y-do* (done) *ine þe taverne.*
23. *Whan I herde hem, I was ryght glad.*
24. *And whanne* (when) *he cam, and was ny3* (near) *þe hous, he herde a symphonie and oþer noise of mynystrlcye* (minstrelsy).
25. *Al þe longage* (language) *of þe Norþhumbres, and specialych at 3ork, ys so scharp, slyttyng* (piercing) *and frotynge* (grinding) *and unschape* (unshapen), *þat we Souþeron men may þat longage unneþe* (with difficulty) *undurstonde.*

From these sentences, we can see that word order in OE was considerably more varied than in ME or ModE. Some linguists have even claimed that OE word order was almost free, allowing virtually any order among the major sentence elements as the demands of rhetorical emphasis demanded. But the order was not "free" in the sense that it was not in most cases, outside of poetry, rule governed, that it could not be predicted. Most patterns were highly regular:

1. The usual word order was that of ModE: S–V–(C).

   He geseah þone mann. (He saw the man.)
   Þet Estland is swyðe mycel. (Estonia is very large.)

2. In many kinds of dependent clauses, the typical (though not invariable by any means) order was CONJUNCTION–S–(C)–V:

   Þeah he him leof **wære**, he weop. (Though he (to) him dear were, he wept.)

3. When an adverbial element like the negative *ne* or the adverb *þa* (then) occurred initially, a very frequent order of elements with a single verb was ADV–V–S–(C):

   Ne mihte he gehealdan heardne mece. (Not might he hold grim sword.)
   þa sende se cyning þone disc. (Then sent the king the dish.)

4. When the object of a verb was a pronoun, the typical order was S–O–V:

   He **hi** fedan sceolde. (He them feed should.)
   þa burgware **hie** gefliemdon. (The citizens routed them.)

A transformational grammar would deal with these patterns through a series of obligatory transformations, transformations which (in opposition to those that would produce a sequence like *Him I like*) were not stylistic, but governed by grammatical context. In fact, the failure to observe these transformations may very well have been in OE prose a stylistic feature that would have been noted by an OE reader or listener. (150, 174, 221)

PROBLEM 10.4: Rewrite this passage of ModE prose observing these transformations. (1) OBJECT PRONOUN SHIFT: (2) VERB-ADVERB SHIFT (for negatives and þa) (For this one, you will have to rewrite ModE negatives into OE *nė* negatives and *then* into *þa*.) (3) SUBORDINATE CLAUSE VERB SHIFT.

> When a linguist studies the history of a language, he does not study it in isolation from its social surroundings. He does not ignore the society it depends on. If he overlooks this social context, then he risks turning language into a bloodless formalism. Then the study of language becomes cut off from its reason for being. When we forget the roots of language, we are no longer sensitive to the interaction between man and man through language. Then we fail to recognize the single most important cause of linguistic change. We may study it for years, all the while overlooking the real sources of its evolution—the interaction of social class which brings into contact speakers from different social levels.

Although these same transformations can be found in Early ME as well as OE, they began to occur much less frequently after the thirteenth century.

Between the years 1000 and 1500, for example, the frequency of an accusative object before a verb decreased markedly:

	1000	1200	1300	1400	1500
Accusative object before verb:	53%	53	40	14	2
Accusative object after verb:	48%	47	60	86	98

In fact, by 1350 or so, the word order of main elements in written English was virtually that of ModE. (28, 65)

INFLECTION: OE, ME, AND ModE

In order to understand why these larger patterns may have become more regular when they did and as they did, we have to examine an aspect of grammar we have touched on before.

PROBLEM 10.5: Problem 4.5 distinguishes derivational affixes from inflections. The endings we shall define as inflections for ModE are these:

1. The plural -s (or other sign of plurality: *boys, feet, men*, and so on)
2. The genitive -s (*boy's, boys', children's*).
3. The third person singular -s (*He walks; It stops*).
4. The past tense -ed of verbs (or other signal corresponding to it: *We walked; He ran; They flew; I hurt it*).
5. The past participle -ed of verbs (or other signal corresponding to it: *He has grown; She has sung; I have walked*).
6. The progressive participle -ing (*He was singing.* Distinguish this from the suffix -ing that makes a noun out of a verb: *Singing is fun*).
7. The comparative -er or superlative -est of adjectives (*bigger–biggest*).

To determine how important inflection be for ModE, take 250 consecutive word from a newspaper or magazine and delete every inflection from it. All verb will be in it infinitive form; all noun and pronoun in it singular and nominative (*he, she, I, you, it*) form; all adjective in it base form. To what degree do the loss of inflection obscure communication? Assume you can get use to reading sentence without inflection in it, what semantic information be lose when inflection be lose? Do any syntactic pattern become ambiguous? Which inflection be need much? Which be unnecessary? Now do the same thing for all affix. Which be some crucial to English, inflect or suffix? What take the place of inflect? Write you answer to this quest without any inflect. Then write it again but omit the affix.

THE NOUN PHRASE: INFLECTIONS AND STRUCTURE

Although OE had an elaborate paradigm of inflectional endings for both noun phrases and verb phrases, it was the inflectional system for the nouns and their associated adjectives and articles that is most relevant in explaining why OE word order may have changed as it did. The remnants of this system can be seen in our pronoun paradigm with its three to four forms for most of the pronouns:

I	*my/mine*	*me*	*we*	*our/ours*	*us*
you	*your/yours*	*you*	*you*	*your/yours*	*you*
he	*his/his*	*him*	*they*	*their/theirs*	*them*
she	*her/hers*	*her*			
it	*its/—*	*it*			

The function of these different forms is to specify how the noun phrases they occur in relate to the main verb, to the preposition, or to another noun. Given *I saw him, Him I saw, I him saw, Saw I him, Saw him I*, we could decide who saw whom, regardless of word order, if we were certain that we could rely on the form of the pronouns to reveal how they related to their verb: *him* = object, *I* = subject.

But in OE, not only pronouns, but nouns, articles, and adjectives displayed these distinctions. We could, for example, write *se man geseah þone hengest* (the man saw the horse), *se man þone hengest geseah, þone hengest geseah se man*, and so on, and always know which noun phrase, *se man* or *þone hengest*, was subject and which object. *Se* was a masculine singular article that always marked the nominative case, making *se man* unambiguously the subject. *Þone* always marked the masculine singular accusative, making *þone hengest* an unambiguous object. Thus word order in OE was not always crucial to identifying subjects and objects, even though it was rule-governed, because in addition to word order and semantic sense, OE had this third system that specified grammatical relationships: inflections. It was a system that would almost disappear by the end of ME.

Case, ModE and OE

Of the three distinctions this system displayed in OE—case, number, and gender—case is (and continues to be in ModE) the most complicated. Only among the pronouns in ModE do we still cross-classify by three overt cases: nominative, accusative, genitive. But when we investigate in the context of an entire sentence how ModE pronouns work, we discover that, in fact, case is a necessary implicit feature even for common nouns; even though a noun may not be overtly marked for case, our grammar must always mark it for **potential** case.

Whenever we repeat a noun phrase within a sentence (or between sentences), we ordinarily have to transform one of the noun phrases, normally (though not always) the second one, into a pronoun. If we begin with a semantically explicit deep structure that we can roughly paraphrase as

Tom left when **Tom** *saw* **Tom's** *girl walk by* **Tom.**

we recognize that in fully grammatical English the surface structure must be more like

Tom left when **he** *saw* **his** *girl walk by* **him**.

If we assume that we begin with the specific noun phrases and **then** transform them into the pronouns, then even in ModE it is clear that we have to be able to specify **potential** case relationships for every noun because it **might** become a pronoun. If the noun is mentioned in the immediately preceding discourse, for example, it is often turned into a pronoun, which must be marked for nominative, accusative, or genitive case: *he/him/his*.

How we specify these cases in a grammar of ModE is in some ways quite different from how it may have been specified in OE, a fact which indicates a major change in the grammar. At least from the written evidence, in OE, the nominative, accusative, genitive, and one more case which we have lost entirely in ModE the dative case—were determined in these two ways:

by how the noun phrases they marked related grammatically to their governing verbs or prepositions, and

by how those noun phrases functioned adverbially in their sentence.

Noun phrases that were **subjects** or **predicate nominals**, regardless of their actual position in their sentence, were in the nominative case: *ic hit eom* (I it am), *we hie sindon* (we they are). Noun phrases that were **objects** of verbs and prepositions took different cases, depending on the particular verb or preposition. Some verbs required objects in the accusative case: *He ofslog þone mann* (he slew the man): *þone* was the accusative masculine singular definite article. Some required objects in the dative case: *He ætwindeð þæm manne* (he escapes (from) the man): *þæm* was the dative masculine singular article. And some verbs required objects in the genitive case: *He ehteð þæs mannes* (he pursues the man). *Þæs* was the genitive masculine singular definite article.

In addition, many noun phrases after prepositions implying motion took the accusative case; noun phrases after prepositions implying largely static relationships generally took the dative case; there were no prepositions that exclusively required the genitive case in their noun objects, but some occasionally were followed by genitives.

This kind of case agreement requires only that in the dictionary, entries for prepositions and verbs include the notation that the noun phrases following them must be in the required case. A transformation can then attach the appropriate case to the article and noun. For example, in this sequence, the feature [dative] is transferred from the verb to the ART and N. The sum of the features is then "spelled" appropriately by another set of graphemic rules which we shall discuss briefly later:

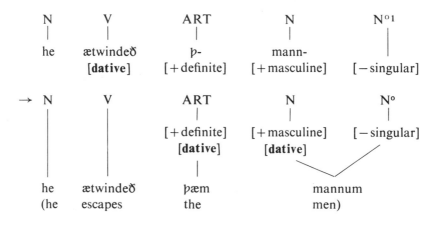

1 N° refers to "number," singular [+singular], or plural [−singular].

PROBLEM 10.6: Is there any equally simple way to specify which nouns should be in the nominative case?

The second principle by which case was assigned to noun phrases depended on how those noun phrases functioned in their sentences. Noun phrases that functioned as adverbs indicating an extent of time or space, for example, often took the accusative:

> *Þa sǽton hie **þone** winter ǽt Cantwarbyrig.*
> Then spent they the winter at Canterbury.

Adverbs of instrumentality or time often took the dative (*-um* was a dative plural ending).

> **Hwilum** *wǽs he god.*　　　　*He wǽs **wundum** werig.*
> (At) times he was good.　　　　He was (by means of) wounds weary.

Adverbial phrases of measure took the genitive (*-a* was a genitive plural ending).

> **Daga** *ond* **nihta** *drincað we meodu.*
> (Of) days and nights drink we mead.

(Note the adverbial shift in these examples.)

How a grammar would assign case for these patterns is more complicated than the means described previously. We must, of course, expand our base rules to account for these adverbial phrases:

$$S \rightarrow NP \quad VP \quad (ADV_{time}) \quad (ADV_{place}) \quad (ADV_{manner}) \ldots$$

We might assign different case features directly to these adverbial units. It has also been suggested that in their deep structure, **all** adverbials are best treated as prepositional phrases. The details of the argument need not concern us here, beyond pointing out that interrogative adverbials like *when, why, how,* and *where* can be paraphrased as: **at** *what time,* **for** *what reason,* **in** *what manner,* **at** *what place.* Since they are synonymous, some transformationalists have argued that the more general, the more powerful explanation of such adverbials would be to **begin** with the preposition and then delete it where it does not occur in the surface structure. (55, but see 94 for the opposite view.)

Such a proposal would greatly simplify how we assign case for OE adverbials, for we would then simply list the case feature for the preposition in the dictionary as described previously, shift that case feature to the noun phrase object of the preposition, and then delete the preposition. For example, in *hwilum wæs he god* ([At] times was he good), *hwilum* with its *-um* ending is in the dative plural case. In the deep structure of this sentence, we might postulate a preposition that if realized in the surface structure would be spelled *æt,* a preposition that governs a dative object. After that dative feature is transferred to the noun phrase, the preposition would be deleted leaving only *hwilum*:

Prep	N	N°
æt	*hwil-*	[−singular]
[dative]	[feminine]	
→ æt	hwil-	[−singular]
	[feminine]	
	[dative]	
→ #	hwil-	[−singular]
	[feminine]	
	[dative]	
	hwil-um	

PROBLEM 10.7: Let us assume that comparative constructions like the following result from an ellipsis of a fuller deep structure:

He is taller than George is tall.
→ He is taller than George (is).

If we do delete elements, must we be certain that in OE, the nouns following *þonne* (than) are in the correct case, the nominative case, **before** or **after** such a transformation? How does this compare with casual educated spoken ModE? With formal written ModE? Here is an OE sentence to use as an example:

He was betera þonne ic.
He was better than I.

PROBLEM 10.8: From the few examples you have seen of the dative and from these next few word for word translations, how has ModE compensated for the loss of the dative case? How would you explain the change transformationally? descriptively? (The quotes run on separate half-lines.)

1. *Eadmund æðeling, ealdorlangne tir | geslogon æt sæcce sweorda* **ecgum** ...
   Edmund (the) nobleman, lifelong glory / won at battle [with] swords'

                                                                          edges.
2. *... swa* **him** *geæðele wæs | fram cneomagum* ...
   ... so [to] him noble was / from ancestors ...
3. *... feld dennode | secga* **swate** ...
   ... field streamed [with] warriors' sweat (i.e., blood)
4. *Þær læg secg monig |* **garum** *forgrunden* ...
   There lay warrior many / [by] spears killed ...

(*ecgum*: dative plural; *him*: dative masculine singular; *swate*: dative singular; *garum*: dative plural.)

How would one decide whether, in principle, it were better for a language to have inflections or periphrastic constructions to express the kinds of syntactic relationships suggested here? (177)

Gender, ModE and OE

Another, though much less important, difference between OE and ModE is that OE formally distinguished grammatical gender in both nouns and third-person singular pronouns, while ModE signals natural or conventional gender only among third person singular pronouns: *he, him, his; she, her, hers; it, it, its*. We distinguish these ModE pronouns, of course, by whether we refer to naturally masculine humans: *boy, man, priest, waiter*; naturally feminine humans: *woman, girl, waitress, priestess;* or to nonhumans or naturally inanimate objects: *rock, book, desk, idea, pig, dog, chicken.* But we have also conventionalized certain referents as feminine: *She's an old tub, but a seaworthy one. Hurricane Alice blew herself out . . .*

In OE, on the other hand, **grammatically** masculine, feminine, and neuter nouns did not always correlate with natural gender. Among the masculine nouns were *wifmann* (woman), *stan* (stone), *að* (oath), *bat* (boat), *hlaf* (loaf), *mete* (food). Among the neuters were *mægden* (girl), *scip* (ship), *lim* (limb), *ban* (bone), *bedd* (bed), *wedd* (pledge), *spere* (spear). Among the feminine were *glof* (glove), *ecg* (edge), *hwil* (space of time), *ides* (woman), *miht* (might), *tid* (time), *sceadu* (shadow).

PROBLEM 10.9: In OE, reference back to a noun by a pronoun required gender agreement, much as in ModE: *My girl lost her glove,* not **My[1] girl lost his/its glove.* Here are a few sentences written in ModE but with pronouns as they were often used in OE. How must the rule of **grammatical** gender agreement be qualified? (221, 222)

1. *When I threw the stone, he* (referring to *stone*) *hit the window. Then I picked it up and threw it again.*
2. *The maiden helped itself* (referring to *maiden* reflexively) *to the food, but later she put it back.*
3. *The glove was too small so I returned her* (referring to *glove*) *to the store. They wouldn't take it back, though.*
4. *The woman loved the man who kissed him* (referring to *woman*) *but she didn't marry him.*

Number, ModE and OE

In Problem 9.10 we began to deal with the problem of number through the semantic-grammatical change that shifts a word like *grass* from a category of nouns that does not occur in the plural to a category that does. The syntactic consequences of this change are that such nouns may occur not only with the plural *-s* marker, but after the indefinite article *a/an*, as well: *a grass, several grasses.* The [-count] sense of grass does not take a plural and may occur without any article at all: *Grass grows everywhere.* Contrast **Car drives everywhere.*

In order to account for these distributions in ModE and to understand how OE noun phrases have changed in regard to number, we have to sketch— very briefly—how we might grammatically describe ModE number. We already have the single base rule for the NP: NP → ART N. Because every NP must be either singular or plural, we will add to this rule a symbol we have already

---

1 * means an ungrammatical construction.

used, number, N°: NP → ART N N°. We can then add another rule: N° → [±singular]. This will allow us to specify whether the noun will be singular ([+singular]' or plural ([−singular]). We need this not only to account for plurality in nouns: *boy–boys*, and so on, but also to account for the problems involved with the distribution of *a/an* and *the*.

The definite article may occur with any kind of noun, singular or plural, count or non-count: *the boy, the boys, the food*. The indefinite article *a/an* may occur only with count nouns in the singular: *a boy*, not **a boys* or **a chaos*. Indefinite count nouns in the plural may occur without any article: *Boys will be boys*, as may indefinite non-count nouns: *Food means strength*.

In order to make sure these features of count vs. non-count, singular vs. plural, and definite vs. indefinite are indicated in all of these phrases, we have to mark **every** noun phrase for [±count], [±singular], and [±definite]. Now, since noun phrases that have no articles are [−definite], that is, general, unspecified nouns, it makes sense to say that in the deep structure of phrases like *boys* in *Boys will be boys* and *food* in *Food is good for you* there **is** in fact a [−definite] ARTICLE, even though it is not pronounced in the surface structure. One simple way to account for this is to make the ARTICLE an obligatory choice in the base rule: NP → ART N N° and then add a rule for ART: ART → [±definite]. We then have yet another kind of transformational rule, not one that shifts elements about or deletes them, but spells certain groups of semantic features into words.

For example, consider these three trees:

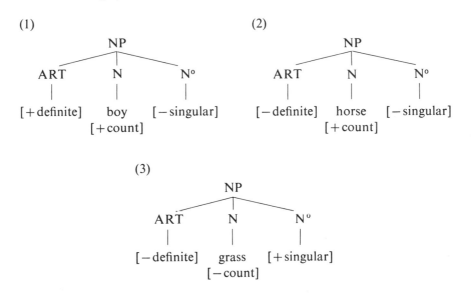

(1)

NP

ART   N   N°

[+definite]   boy   [−singular]
[+count]

(2)

NP

ART   N   N°

[−definite]   horse   [−singular]
[+count]

(3)

NP

ART   N   N°

[−definite]   grass   [+singular]
[−count]

First, we have to transfer the features of [±count] and [±singular] from NOUN and NUMBER to the ARTICLE, since the ARTICLE must reflect whether the noun is count or non-count and singular or non-singular, and NUMBER to the NOUN, since its spelling will reflect number too. Here is what happens with (1).

$$
\begin{array}{ccc}
\text{ART} & \text{N} & \text{N}^\circ \\
| & | & | \\
[+\text{definite}] & \text{boy} & [-\text{singular}] \\
 & [+\text{count}] &
\end{array}
$$

$$
\rightarrow \quad
\begin{array}{cc}
\text{ART} & \text{N} \\
| & | \\
[+\text{definite}] & \text{boy} \\
[+\text{count}] & [+\text{count}] \\
[-\text{singular}] & [-\text{singular}]
\end{array}
$$

Then a spelling rule spells the ARTICLE in the appropriate way. In this case, the ARTICLE is spelled *the* and the NOUN, because it is [−singular], is spelled *boys*.

PROBLEM 10.10: Spell trees (2) and (3). What is to be done with proper nouns like *George* in *George is here*?

The particular expression of definite and indefinite reference for noun phrases in OE differed in many respects from our own. Often, no overt article at all was necessary where we would have to use either a definite *the* or an indefinite *a/an*:

1. *In ðeosse abbudissan mynstre wæs sum broðor syndriglice mid godcundre gife gemæred . . .*
    In this abbess's monastery was a certain brother especially with divine gift famed . . .
2. *Ond for his leoðsongum monigra monna mod oft to worulde forhogdnisse . . . onbærnde wæron.*
    And for his poemsongs many (of) men's minds often to world's contempt . . . inspired were.
3. *Se Cyneheard wæs þæs Sigebryhtes broðor.*
    The Cyneheard was this Sigebryht's brother.

In (1), the singular *gift* is the first mention of the gift in Bede's story of the poet Cædmon. We should translate it as . . . *with a divine gift*. Conversely in (2), we now require *the world* instead of just *world*. On the other hand, OE could also use the definite article where we ordinarily would not—before names as in (3).

**TABLE 10.1   PARADIGMS FOR OE ARTICLES, NOUNS,
AND PRONOUNS**

Singular

	Article	*Noun ending*		*Pronoun*	*Interrog.*	*Shared element*
1. Masculine: (stone)						
Nom.:	*se*	-∅	(*se stan*)	*he*	*hwa*	—
Acc.:	*þone*	-∅	(*þone stan*)	*hine*	*hwone*	*-ne*
Dat.:	*þæm*	*-e*	(*þæm stane*)	*him*	*hwæm*	*-m*
Gen.:	*þæs*	*-es*	(*þæs stanes*)	*his*	*hwæs*	*-s*
2. Neuter: (ship)						
Nom.:	*þæt*	-∅	(*þæt scip*)	*hit*	*hwæt*	*-t*
Acc.:	*þæt*	-∅	(*þæt scip*)	*hit*	*hwæt*	*-t*
Dat.:	*þæm*	*-e*	(*þæm scipe*)	*him*	*hwæm*	*-m*
Gen.:	*þæs*	*-es*	(*þæs scipes*)	*his*	*hwæs*	*-s*
3. Feminine: (tale)						
Nom.:	*seo*	-∅	(*seo talu*)	*heo*	(no	—
Acc.:	*þa*	*-e*	(*þa tale*)	*hi*	feminine	*-(e)*
Dat.:	*þære*	*-e*	(*þære tale*)	*hire*	forms)	*-(r)e*
Gen.:	*þære*	*-e*	(*þære tale*)	*hire*		*-(r)e*

4. -*an* Group (mixed masculine, feminine, neuter nouns): (*name, heart, ear*)

Nom.:	(same	-*a*/-*e*/-*e* (*se nama, seo heorte, þæt eare*)
Acc.:	articles	-*an*/-*an*/-*e* (*þone naman, seo heortan, þæt eare*)
Dat.:	as	-*an* (*þæm naman, þære heortan, þæm earan*)
Gen.:	above)	-*an* (*þæs naman, þære heortan, þæs earan*)

On the other hand, there was no OE indefinite article corresponding to ModE *a/an* at all. Our modern *a/an* developed in ME out of the number *an* (one) as it phonologically and semantically weakened. The closest thing to an indefinite article is *sum*, which is less definite than the definite article but more definite than the absence of any article, which communicated the more specific sense of indefiniteness.

Overall, the paradigms for the OE articles, nouns, and pronouns, both interrogative and personal looked like Table 10.1. At the far left is the shared element that characterizes the particular gender, case, and number. Groups (4) and (8) are examples of some of the more common irregular nouns in OE. (25, 28, 148, 174)

PROBLEM 10.11: Is there any opposition between cases that is maintained in every gender or every number? That is, masculine and neuter dative articles and endings, *þæm* and *-e*, are identical, erasing any gender distinction in that case. In the feminine, the dative and genitive articles and endings, *þære* and

TABLE 10.1 (Continued)

Plurals

	Article	Noun ending	Pronoun	Interrog.	Shared element
5. Masculine					
Nom.:	þa	-as (þa stanas)	hie	(no	—
Acc.:	þa	-as (þa stanas)	hie	plural	—
Dat.:	þæm	-um (þæm stanum)	him	forms)	-m
Gen.:	þara	-a (þara stana)	hira		-(ar)a
6. Neuter					
Nom.:	(same	-u/∅ (þa scipu)	(same		—
Acc.:	as	-u/∅ (þa scipu)	as		—
Dat.:	above)	-um (þæm scipum)	above)		-m
Gen.:		-a (þara scipa)			-(ar)a
7. Feminine					
Nom.:	(same	-a (þa tala)			-a
Acc.:	as	-a (þa tala)			-a
Dat.:	above)	-um (þæm talum)			-m
Gen.:		-a (þara tala)			-(ar)a
8. -an Group					
Nom.:	(same	-an (þa naman, earan, heortan)			—
Acc.:	as	-an (þa naman, earan, heortan)			—
Dat.:	above)	-um (þæm namum, earum, heortum)			-m
Gen.:		ena (þara namena, earena, heortena)			-a

-e are identical, neutralizing the case distinction in that gender. How crucial were gender and case then?

PROBLEM 10.12: ModE pronouns reflect gender only in third-person singular. Create a pronoun system which would be maximally distinguished for gender and number in every person. What would be the consequences? Create a gender system that would be minimally differentiated. What would be the consequences? Can these two systems be combined? How many pronouns would each system have? (Do not count different case forms here, such as *she, her.*) Can you imagine a pronoun system based on features other than case, number, gender, and person? What would a pronoun system look like that was based on relative social position? on age? on marital status? ModE has, in fact, developed a gender-neutral singular third person pronoun, but a typical junior high grammar teacher would consider its use in that sense ungrammatical. What do they object to?

A second paradigm of articles was available alongside the one just sketched.

	masc.	neut.	fem.			
singular nom.	*þes*	*þis*	*þeos*	**plural nom.**	*þas*
acc.	*þisne*	*þis*	*þas*	**acc.**	*þas*
dat.	*þissum*	*þissum*	*þisse*	**dat.**	*þissum*
gen.	*þisses*	*þisses*	*þisse*	**gen.**	*þissa*

The difference between them is at times not always clear from the context in which they occur. Perhaps they can be best understood if we imagine our own article system reduced from the three-way opposition of

the—(this/these)—(that/those)

to a two-way opposition, with *that/those* absorbing the function of *the*.

Adjectives as well as articles had to be inflicted to agree with gender, case, and number of the noun. The agreement system, however, was further complicated by the fact that OE distinguished **weak** and **strong** adjectives, much as Modern German does. The principle was this: The distinguishing form for case, gender, and number usually had to mark the **first** element in the noun phrase and the noun. If the first element was an article (**se** *man*), then the article, *se*, had to indicate by its form its gender, case, and number. If the article was absent and the first element was an adjective, **god** *man* (good man), then the adjective has to carry an inflection (or a distinctive lack thereof) almost identical with the ending of an article. In such cases, the adjective was strong because it signalled gender, case, and number: **trumum** *folcum* (firm people): neuter, dative, plural. When the adjective followed the article: *þæm* **truman** *folcum*, then the article made the distinctions and the adjective was weak, taking a different and much less differentiated set of endings.

FROM OE TO ME TO ModE

Inflections

Long before the end of the ME period, by the thirteenth century, these inflections had considerably leveled. Among the nouns, grammatical gender distinctions had entirely disappeared, along with all noun case markings, except the genitive. Below is a schema of the ME article, noun endings, personal pronoun and interrogative pronoun that corresponds to the OE nominal system outlined in Table 10.1. With the exception of the feminine pronouns and the third person plural pronouns, we will use the Northern dialect forms (see Figure 10.1), which eventually spread throughout England. Even by very early ME, the weak-strong distinction among adjectives applied only to single syllable adjectives that ended in a consonant, like *god* (good), not to adjectives like *fre* (generous), *open* (open), or *grene* (green).

Before the end of the twelfth century, however, as the strong-weak distinction began to disappear, scribes were adding final -e's to adjectives almost indiscriminately. Some traces of case-gender distinctions can be found in Southern and Midland texts as late as the twelfth century, but disappear soon after that. (98, 150, 154) The following paradigm does not suggest the variety of forms found even within a single dialect. Over time, the second personal plural pronoun, for example, varied over *eu, ou, ȝow, ȝou,* and *you.*

Between OE and ME, the first and second person pronouns changed less drastically than the rest of the system. The earliest OE texts had a distinctive

Figure 10.1. Middle English Dialect Areas

TABLE 10.2   PARADIGMS FOR ME ARTICLES, NOUNS, AND PRONOUNS

Singular

		Article	Weak Adj.	Strong Adj.	Noun	Pronoun	Inter.
Masc.	Nom.	the	-e(gode)	∅ (god)	∅ (man)	he	who
	Acc.				∅ (man)	hine	whom
	Dat.				(-e) (man(e))	him	whom
	Acc.				-es (manes)	his	whos
Neut.	Nom.					(h)it	what
	Acc.					(h)it	what
	Dat.					him	whom
	Gen.					his	whos
Fem.	Nom.					heo/sche/scho	who
	Acc.					hir	whom
	Dat.					hir	whom
	Gen.					hir(e)	whos

(Note: *heo* is the Southern and Western form, *sche* the Midland form, and *scho* the Northern form. The third person plural pronouns below are in the same order: roughly Southern, Midland, Northern. There was no distinctive interrogative plural.)

	Article	Weak Adj.	Strong Adj.	Noun	Pronoun
Nom.	*the*	-e (gode)	-e (gode)	-es (stones)	hy/þei/þai
Acc.					hi/hem/þaim
Gen.					her(e)/hare/þeir(e)

accusative singular form, but by late OE, the dative and accusative were identical. The forms listed below separated by slashes: *mec/me*, are earlier and later forms in the OE and ME periods. The *min-mi, thin-thy* distinctions in ME were contextually determined forms, a question we shall return to.

	Singular		Plural	
	OE	*ME*	*OE*	*ME*
Nom.	ic	ich/I	we	we
Acc.	meo/me	me	usic/us	us, ous
Dat.	me	me	us	us, ous
Gen.	min	min-mi	ure	ur(e)
Nom.	þu	thou	ge	ye
Acc.	þec/þe	thee	eowic/eow	eu/you
Dat.	þe	thee	eow	eu/you
Gen.	þin	thin-thy	eower	your(e)

In addition to these forms, OE and very early ME had dual forms, *wit* and *git*, which meant "we two" and "ye two." They were inflected much like the other forms: *wit–uncit/unc–unc–uncer*; *git–incit/inc–inc–incer*.

PROBLEM 10.13: What are the major distinctions lost in the pronouns between ME and early ModE? Here are the early ModE (post 1500 or so) pronouns. (It should be noted that in many British dialect areas, *thou, thee, thy, thine,* and *ye* are still used.)

Singular				**Plural**			
I	*me*	*my*	*mine*	*we*	*us*	*our*	*our/our(e)n*
you	*you*	*your*	*yours/your(e)n*	*you*	*you*	*your*	*yours/your(e)n*
he	*him*	*his*	*his/his(e)n*	*they*	*them*	*their*	*theirs/their(e)n*
it	*it*	*its/it*	—				
she	*her*	*her*	*hers/hir(e)n*				

Our(e)n, your(e)n, his(e)n, her(e)n, and *their(e)n* are from the Midland and Southern dialects. The forms *ours, yours, his, hers,* and *theirs* are of North and North Midland origin.

PROBLEM 10.14: The source of the modern *my/mine* distinction is illustrated in the following ME and Early ModE examples. Explain what happened. But first review the OE genitive forms. *my dere hert, myn herte, thi synne* and *thyn offence, to slay mine enemies and ayde my friends, I cut mine arm, and with my blood Assume my soul.* Shakespeare has these: *Give every man thine eare but few thy voyce, my owne life, mine uncle, my hand, thy foot, thy ambition.* By the early eighteenth century, *my,* and so on, is normal everywhere before nouns; *mine,* and so on, as a pronominal possessive.

PROBLEM 10.15: In rapid pronunciation, we say *I know'm* to mean either *I know them* or *I know him.* Yet when we rapidly pronounce *I know their house* or *I know they left,* we do not drop the initial *th* sound. Might there be an historical explanation for this?

PROBLEM 10.16: *Yours, hers, ours,* and so on did not occur in OE. How would you explain their origin? They began to appear in Early ME, eventually replacing the uninflected anaphoric pronoun by the middle of the sixteenth century. One of the last examples of the uninflected anaphoric pronouns is a sentence like . . . *eternall dampnacyon is youre.*

PROBLEM 10.17: *His(e)n, our(e)n, your(e)n, her(e)n, their(e)n* developed in the South and Midland of England. What might explain their introduction? What social distinctions do they make today in this country? Where are they found? Why?

PROBLEM 10.18: Let us assume from the extant documents that OE based its case system strictly on the kinds of grammatical relationships described before and after Problem 10.6. That is, no matter where in a sentence a pronoun happened to occur, it was ordinarily in the case required by the governing verb or preposition. Here are some examples of ModE to consider. Comment. *It's me. He's better than me. Him and me left. Him I don't like. Who did you want to see? With whom did you wish to speak? You saw who? It is I. Whom did you see? Between you and I, he's a fool.*

Between OE and ME, the system of articles before nouns also changed greatly. First, an indefinite article *a/an* developed out of the number *an* (one), though its use was not as predictable as it has become in ModE. Second, the invariable *þe* developed very rapidly in the twelfth century as the replacement for the entire article system of OE. Although some remnants of gender-case distinctions can be found among articles in the South into the thirteenth century, *þe* had become the standard article in the North by 1200. (209)

PROBLEM 10.19: Where did *þe*, ancestor of *the*, come from?

The outlines of our demonstrative system had also developed. It is fairly evident that *this* descended from *þis*, neuter nominative; and *that* from *þæt*, also neuter nominative, but from the other paradigm. From *þes* had come *these*, while *those* probably descended from the plural *þa*, which by analogy developed the plural *þas*. It is not entirely clear why the article system should have developed a near-far distinction. It may be that *here–there, now–then, thus–so* provided some impetus.

Although the *thou/thee/thy* pronouns are still used among some religious groups in this country and in many parts of England, they had generally disappeared from educated usage at least by the beginning of the eighteenth century. But between their simple use as singular second person pronouns at the beginning of the ME period and their loss 600 years later, the particular use of *thee/thou* was part of a socio-linguistic event that is still felt in most of the languages of Europe. During the fourth century A.D., the second person plural in Latin, *vos*, developed a second meaning. It began to be used when addressing social superiors as a mark of respect. It may have had its origin when the Roman Empire was governed by two emperors, one in Rome, the other in Constantinople. Those addressing the Emperor as an institution were required to use the plural. Perhaps those in court personally addressing one of them also felt obliged to use the plural form. In any event, the practice spread across Europe and in the thirteenth century, to England, where in imitation of the upper-class French *tu/vous*, the English began *thee*ing and *you*ing one another.

This usage soon included another dimension of social distinction. As the *you* became the mark of respect from inferior to superior or between socially superior equals, the *thou* form came to mark intimacy between family members and lovers, then developed as a mark of solidarity between speakers who shared a set of values. It also developed one more dimension of usage—contempt. In Shakespeare's **Twelfth Night**, when Sir Toby Belch is urging on Sir Andrew Aguecheek to write a challenging letter to the disguised Viola, he says:

> Go, write it in a martial hand; be curst and briefe; it is no matter how wittie, so it bee eloquent and full of invention: taunt him with the license of Inke: if thou thou'st him some thrice, it shall not be amisse.
>
> III.ii.

PROBLEM 10.20: Discuss the use of *you*/*thou* in one of the following: (1) A fairly long scene from Shakespeare (some suggestions: **Hamlet**, III.iv; **As You Like It**, IV.i; **Antony and Cleopatra**, V.ii; **The Merchant of Venice**, IV.i; **The Two Gentlemen of Verona**, V.iii. (2) The links (including Prologues) between several of Chaucer's **Canterbury Tales**. (3) **Sir Gawain and the Green Knight** (particularly the encounters between Gawain and the Lady). Do not use modernized texts for the last two. (20, 21, 24, 51, 105, 155, 232)

PROBLEM 10.21: We are no longer able to manipulate the social tone of our conversations through pronouns. What devices are available today to express social distance, solidarity, contempt, or close emotional relationship? Do not include tone of voice, posture, expression, and so on. Consider modes of address (what do you call your instructor? what does he call you?), vocabulary, pronunciation, syntax. Write about thirty lines of dialogue which begin in a very intimate tone of solidarity, switch to contempt about line 10, then to a superior-inferior relationship at about line 20.

Relative Clauses

The rule for the noun phrase: NP $\rightarrow$ ART N N°, is still too simple to account for longer, more complex noun phrases. Nor have we adequately dealt with the genitive. For example, these relative clauses would also have to be included in any description of the noun phrase: *the man who was dead, the girl whom I saw, the man whose friend left, the book which I read, the dog that was by the door, the tree which is blowing in the wind,* and so on.

In those cases where a full relative clause is present, the relative clause has the same basic structure as a sentence. The relative pronoun stands for an element in its clause semantically identical to the noun it follows. In the noun phrase, *the boy who left, who left* has a subject *who* and a verb *left*. *Who* "stands for" or, more accurately, replaces *the boy* in the clause. If this is so, then the deep structure of a noun phrase with a relative clause would look

something like this: [*the boy* [*the boy left*]ₛ]ₙₚ. A transformation moves
the repeated article and noun in the clause, *the boy*, to the beginning of its
clause. In the case of *the boy* [*the boy left.*], they are already there. But they
must be moved in *the boy* [*I saw the boy*]. → *the boy* [**the boy** *I saw*]. The
repeated noun phrase is then transformed into a relative pronoun: *the boy*
[**the boy** *I saw*] → *the boy* [**whom** *I saw*]. In the case of a genitive, the genitive
and its following noun are moved:

the boy [I bought **the boy's** *book*]

→ the boy [**the boy's** *book* I bought]

→ the boy [**whose** *book* I bought]

So we must revise the NP rule once more and add some transformations.
Since a relative clause is only a transformed sentence embedded in a noun
phrase, we can simply add an S to the NP: NP → ART N N° (S). The
transformations (1) shift the repeated NP forward to the head of its clause
and (2) change it to a relative pronoun.

PROBLEM 10.22: Here are some additional data regarding ModE relative
clauses. Comment.

1. *The man who left was a friend.*
2. *The man whom I saw was a friend.*
3. *The man that I saw was a friend.*
4. *The man that left was a friend.*
5. **The man which left was a friend.*
6. *The man to whom I spoke was a friend.*
7. *The man who(m) I spoke to was a friend.*
8. *The man that I spoke to was a friend.*
9. **The man to that I spoke was a friend.*
10. *The man I spoke to was a friend.*
11. *The man I saw was a friend.*
12. **I talked to the man walked down the street.* (i.e., *the man who walked . . .*)
13. **The book who I read was dull.*

PROBLEM 10.23: Here are several examples of relative clause patterns from
OE, ME, and Early ModE written in ModE, except for the relative pronoun.
Sketch a very rough history of the changes in relative clauses and suggest the
kinds of transformational changes that have occurred in the last 1000 years.
If a form of a relative clause is asterisked, assume that it would have been un-
grammatical in the period; that is, an example of it has never been found. For
example, **Ic knowe the man who lefte* would not have been possible in 1300.
(In the OE examples, *þe* is an indeclinable particle.)

OE

1. *The man se was there left. The man þone I know stayed.*
2. *The ship þæt was there sank. The spear þæt you had broke.*
3. *The glove seo was there was lost. The talu þa you heard is old.*
4. *The maiden to þæm I spoke left.*
5. *The king to þæm I spoke left.*
6. *The wife to þære I spoke left.*
7. *The man þe I saw left. The ship þe was there sank. The glove þe the man looked for was lost.*
8. *The boat se þe sank was old. I have the horse þone þe you want. The land þæt þe is fertile is eastward. I saw the child þæm þe you entertained. I saw the woman þe left. The glove soe þe ripped is mine.*
9. **The man þæm I spoke to left. *The ship þæm I looked at sank. *The woman þære I spoke to left.*
10. **The man to þe I spoke left. *The ship at þe I looked sank. *The woman to þe I spoke left.*
11. *The man I saw left. I saw the man walked down the street. I have the sword killed the warrior.*

ME (pre-1450)

12. *The man þe I saw was here* (frequent).
13. *The man to which I spoke was here* (less frequent).
14. *The man whom I saw left* (less frequent).
15. *The man I saw left.*
16. *I talked to the man walked down the street.*
17. *The man þæt I saw left.*
18. **The man to þæt I spoke left.*
19. *The man whose book I read left.*
20. *The man who was here left* (very infrequent).
21. *The man whom that you saw left.*
22. *The man whose that book I read left.*
23. *The man the which was here left.*
24. *The man the which man was here left.*
25. *The man which that was here left.*
26. *I spoke to a man, which man was my friend.*

ME–Early ModE (1450–1550)

(13), (14), (20) become more frequent but disappear by 1300; (21), (22), (23), (24), (25), (26) become less frequent.

Early ModE

(13) becomes less common; (21), (22), (23), (24), (25) disappear; (26), *The man which I saw left* begins to disappear. (36, 221)

The Genitive

Constructions like *Tom's hat, my friend's defeat, the teacher's performance, Bill's weakness* are closely related to the relative clause construction. But we have to distinguish four kinds of genitives, only one of which we can correctly call possessive: *George's hat.* We might generate such a phrase in a series of transformations roughly like the following:

> the hat [George ⟨possesses⟩ the hat]
> → the hat [the hat George ⟨possesses⟩]
> → that hat [which George ⟨possesses⟩]
> → the hat [of George]
> → George's hat

That is, in the deep structure of the noun phrase, *George's hat,* is an embedded sentence which defines the semantic relationship between *George* and *hat,* a relationship that eventually will be realized as the genitive, or possessive: *George's hat.* (Whether the actual verb in the deep structure sentence is a specific word like *have* or *possess* or *own,* or whether the verb should be represented rather as an abstract bundle of semantic features that abstractly represents a deep structure meaning of possession has been debated at length and generally resolved in favor of the more abstract interpretation.)

PROBLEM 10.24: Comment on constructions like these: *George's performance, the man's escape, my disappearance, your release, his defeat, their encirclement by the enemy, our capture, her sickness, Tom's weakness, his intelligence, their strength.* (Their equivalents were found in OE.)

PROBLEM 10.25: Here are some genitives from before 1600 or so. Comment.

1. *for the wyves love of Bathe* (i.e., for the Wife of Bath's love),
2. *The Dukes wyfe of Tintagail* (i.e., the Duke of Tintagail's wife),
3. *The Archbishop's Grace of York* (i.e., the Archbishop of York's grace). This pattern was the rule before the 16th century. After, group genitives like the *Duke of York's land* became common, replacing the earlier pattern. (46)

PROBLEM 10.26: In Early ModE, patterns such as *the man his heart was broken* begin to appear. By the seventeenth century, the apostrophe possessive: *the man's heart was broken* is felt to represent a contraction. Comment.

One very important difference between OE and ModE genitive constructions is that OE did not, ordinarily, allow the *of-* paraphrase: *George's performance = the performance of George, his hat = a hat of his, the enemy's weakness = the weakness of the enemy.* Moreover, the genitive could either precede or follow the modified word: *þæs cyninges mann* (the king's man) as opposed to *sumne dæl þæs hlafes* (some part (of) the bread).

Then, between the years 900 and 1250 or so, a major change occurred in the form of the genitive, a change related to that which fixed the S–V–(C) word order and increased the structural load carried by prepositional phrases. In 900, the genitive occurred before the noun about half the time: *his feonda slege* (his enemies' defeat), and after about half the time: *ænige þinga* ([by] any [of] means). By 1000, the inflected genitive occurred after its noun only about 31 percent of the time; by 1100, about 23 percent; by 1200 about 13 percent, and by 1250, less than 1 percent. By 1300, the inflected genitive was permanently fixed before the noun it modified.

But as the genitive became fixed before the noun, the periphrastic genitive, the genitive expressed by *of*, began to increase in frequency. In 900, the *of*-construction occurred in less than one half of one percent of the genitive constructions. By 1200, it still occurred in only about 6 percent of the constructions. But then by about 1250, it jumped to about 32 percent of all genitive constructions, and then to almost 85 percent in 1300. In other words, as the position of the inflected genitive became fixed before the noun, its relative frequency decreased in favor of the prepositional phrase after the noun. (65) The change can be best seen on a graph (Figure 10.2).

PROBLEM 10.27: If Baugh's figures on the proportion of French words borrowed at various periods in ME are reliable (Problem 4.12), would they tend to confirm or contradict the claim that the *of* + NP phrase resulted from the influence of the French *de* + NP?

The periphrastic genitive may have spread so rapidly because prepositional phrases were in general becoming more important. It may also be that

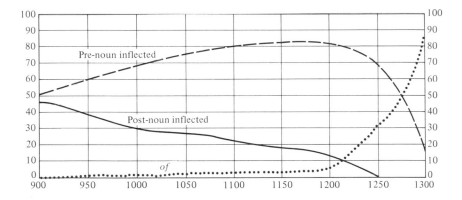

Figure 10.2. Construction of the Genitive

the French genitive construction with *de* became a strong model: *Femme de chambre*. Whatever its ultimate cause, the change further illustrates the two basic structural principles of our language after the Norman Conquest:

1. Word order was becoming increasingly fixed.
2. Inflections were decreasing in favor of periphrasis.

There is some evidence that even the inflected genitive is disappearing in some nonstandard dialects today. Both in Great Britain and in the United States, one can hear genitive phrases such as *my wife father*, *the boy hat*, and so on. Whether this inflection began disappearing centuries ago and is merely reflected in the current speech of nonstandard speakers, or whether this is a relatively recent innovation that heralds the loss of the last overt case distinction among common nouns remains to be seen.

CAUSES OF GRAMMATICAL CHANGE

Now that we have described some of the overt patterns of OE, ME, and ModE noun phrases and have a very general idea of how the grammar of these patterns has changed, we can turn our attention to **why** these patterns may have changed in these ways. Like so many other changes in the language, the replacement of a highly inflected, variable word order in OE by a slightly inflected, relatively fixed word order system in ME undoubtedly had both internal and external causes.

PROBLEM 10.28: This general change, the loss of inflections and the fixing of S–V–(C) word order, occurred between roughly 1000 and 1400, though the tendency toward this change can be detected as early as 900 in some dialects. The crucial period seems to be between about 1100 and 1300. Looking back at the external history of language during these 400 years, and more particularly at the 200 years between 1100 and 1300, speculate what causes might have contributed to such a change. What information would you particularly like to have? What do the following data suggest? In ninth century OE prose, subject and object are inflectionally distinguished less than half the time. When they are not, 94 percent of the distances are in Subject–Object order. When they are inflectionally distinguished, S–O order occurs 93 percent of the time. (Robert L. Saitz. **Functional Word Order in Old English Subject– Object Patterns**, Unpub. diss., Madison, Wisc., 1955. Quoted in Cassidy and Ringler.)

In conjunction with these external forces, perhaps in a necessary conjunction for the change to occur, was a major internal force. We have said little about how OE or ME was pronounced. But here we must point out one phonological characteristic of OE and ME that may have strongly influenced the loss of inflections, a cause that probably worked in conjunction with an increasingly predictable S–V–(C) order, even in OE.

Generally speaking, words of Germanic origin and Romance words that were completely assimilated into ME stressed the root or initial syllable, unless the first syllable was a prefix like *ge-* or *ed-*. Thus we have words like *OPen, AFter, ANimal, CAStle, FInal, ACcident, ALchemy, STANdard*. Unassimilated Romance words, mostly borrowed since Early ME, usually stress the last syllable: *maCHINE, poLICE, laTRINE, proTECT, comMEND*, and so on.

In rapid heavily-accented speech, unstressed final syllables tend to lose their distinctive vowel quality as they are reduced to a kind of indistinguishable mid-central vowel called **schwa**, a sound symbolized /ə/. It is the sound of the first syllable of *allow* or *above* or the vowel of the second syllable of *zebra* or *bolted*. In OE, however, the vowel in the endings had to be clearly distinguished in speech. Otherwise, speakers could confuse endings like *-es* and *-as*; *-an, -en*, and *-on*; *-u, -e*, and *-a*.

As early as the tenth century, speakers began to reshape the lightly stressed dative plural ending *-um* to *-un*, perhaps by analogy with the other *-n* endings. Whatever the cause, by Late OE *-un* had begun to occur as the new ending for many *-um* forms.

PROBLEM 10.29: How would this affect the oppositions among the cases and genders? Would any distinctions be lost as long as the vowel in *-un* were still clearly pronounced? (See Table 10.1.)

PROBLEM 10.30: By the eleventh century OE scribes were often writing words earlier spelled like those among the first of each of the following pairs in a new way, like those among the second of each pair. What does this suggest? *fiscas–fisces, biton–biten, truman–trumen, guman–gumen, eagum–eagem, dæda–dæde*.

PROBLEM 10.31: If *-um* endings had become *-un*, and if endings that had once had clearly pronounced vowels spelled ⟨a⟩, ⟨e⟩, ⟨o⟩, and ⟨u⟩, became endings spelled ⟨e⟩ and probably pronounced /ə/, how would the oppositions among the cases, genders, and numbers be affected? Refer to the list of endings in Table 10.1 and systematically change all *-um* to *-un*, then all vowels in the endings to ⟨e⟩.

PROBLEM 10.32: By the end of the eleventh century, the final *-n* in inflectional endings began to disappear too, leaving only a general /ə/ sound, spelled ⟨e⟩, in place of /ən/, spelled ⟨-en⟩. How would the loss of /n/ affect the distinctions among case, gender, and number? Refer again to the endings listed in Table 10.1. Change all *-en* endings to just *-e*.

PROBLEM 10.33: Strictly on the basis of these changes, what **should** the inflectional system for nouns have looked like by ME? Here is the actual noun paradigm that resulted:

	Nom./Acc.	Dative (infrequent)	Genitive
Singular	*ston*	*ston(e)*	*stones*
Plural	*stones*	*stones*	*stones*

Where are the unexpected inconsistencies? What has to be explained in a way other than by predictable phonological changes?

PROBLEM 10.34: Eventually, in Late ME, even the final unstressed /ə/ largely disappeared (though scribes added final ⟨-e⟩ indiscriminately, evidence that the system was breaking down). How did the loss of /ə/ affect the inflectional system? What would you say was the crucial point in this progressive loss of inflections?

PROBLEM 10.35: From the meter of poetry, we can tell that words like *jumped*, *kinges*, *stopped*, *dogges*, and *egges* were often two-syllable words. Examine some poetry between 1300–1800 to determine when they consistently became single syllable words. (146, 147, 148, 150)

SOME MODERN SURVIVALS OF OE INFLECTIONS

Despite the fact that most of the gender, case, and number system in OE was leveled in ME, we can find some survivals of the system in the irregularities and anomalies of ModE inflections.

PROBLEM 10.36: There is one group of nouns in English whose plurals frequently have no *-s* endings: *I saw twenty sheep, eight swine, four deer, two moose, six buffalo, five caribou, seven fish, twelve haddock, six perch, four salmon, two trout, three bass, nine tuna, four mackerel,* and so on. In ME, there were a few others: *two horse, four neet* (cattle), *six folk. Swine, sheep, deer, folk, neet,* and *horse* all descend from a class of neuter nouns whose plural ending was *-u. Fish* was a masculine with a regular plural, *fiscas. Buffalo* is a Latin word dating from 1588; *caribou* is French Canadian, 1774; *moose* is a

Narragansett Indian word adopted in the United States after colonial times. The *fish*-words come from a variety of sources, many borrowed into ME from Old French. Comment.

PROBLEM 10.37: In other phrases of measure, ModE nouns also lack a plural, though in this case, the nouns come from any OE gender: *a ten foot pole, a five dollar bill, a four year old child, a five yard gain, a twenty minute wait*, and so on. In parts of this country and in England one can also hear phrases like *It's two foot long, He walked five mile*, and so on. In OE phrases that count or enumerate a noun, the noun was typically plural genitive: *seofan mila* (seven (of) miles), *tweo feta* (two (of) feet). What happened?

PROBLEM 10.38: In ME, the plural *-en* ending was common in the Southern dialects. But the *-s* plural ending common in the North and Midlands finally pushed *-en* out of the language, leaving only three relics in ModE: *child–children* (actually double plural, the original plural being *cildru*), *ox–oxen*, and the archaic *brother–brethren*. Why might we have expected the Northern and Midland forms with *-s* to replace the Southern *-n* forms in Late ME, rather than vice versa?

Another small category of irregular plurals in English are those which indicate plurality by a vowel change: *foot–feet, tooth–teeth, goose–geese, mouse–mice, louse–lice, man–men*. The group was larger in OE. Their origin goes back to the Germanic period, before any written records. The Germanic form of *geese* was something like **gansiz*. The Pre-OE form was probably close to **gosi*. In very early OE the plural *-i* ending caused the back vowel /ō/ as in *goat* to **mutate** or **umlaut**, to become first a rounded front vowel like German ö, which then unrounded to become a front vowel /ē/ as in *gate*. When the *-i* ending was lost, only *gēs* (pronounced like *gase*) remained to contrast with *gōs* (pronounced to rhyme with *dose*).

PROBLEM 10.39: These nouns were in OE also umlaut plurals. Had analogy not put them into the regular noun class, how might we pronounce their plurals today: *oak, goat, foe, cow, shroud, book*?

PROBLEM 10.40: How do we explain these irregular plurals: *banditti, stadia, foci, cherubim, formulae, gladioli, phenomena, data, opera, agenda, stamina, stimuli, curricula*?

Adjectives and Adverbs

We have already touched on the case and gender endings of adjectives. Another kind of ending is the comparative and superlative. OE comparisons were much like some of those of today: *heardra* (harder) for masculine nominative and accusative, *heardre* for feminine and neuter nominative and accusative, *heardost* (hardest) for all genders. The common element -*r* and -*st* is retained today. But there were also significant differences.

PROBLEM 10.41: The rule generating comparatives and superlatives in OE would generate forms like *modcearigra* (more troubled in heart), *feohgifrost* (most greedy for wealth), *andgitfullicost* (most intelligibly), *wanhygdigra* (more imprudent), *bliðra* (more joyful), *blindost* (blindest), *indryhtenost* (most noble), *hatheortost* (most hot tempered). In educated ME, we find comparisons like *more wylde* (wilder), *more swete* (sweeter), *moste gracyus* (most gracious), *moost profitable* (most profitable), *older*, *lengar* (longer), *most mylde* (mildest), *mare pore* (poorer), *mylder*, *moste old*, *the most fairest damyselles*, *the more gretter king*. In Late ME and Early ModE, we find *more ruefullyr*, *pooriste*, *horryblest*, *merueyllest*, *thinner*, *famousest*, *gladdest*, *diligenteste*, *melancholiest*, *ancienter*, *more nere*, *most thyk*, *moost abiecte* (abject), *most ritch*, *more plesant*, *more auntient* (ancient), *moost adventurous*, *more fressher*, *more diligenter*, *most worshipfullest*, *most sharpest witted*, *more worser*, *more neerer*, *most cruellest*, *most finest*. From about the eighteenth century, we find comparison much as it is today. Comment.

Adverbs in OE and early ME were formed by adding -*e* to an adjective: *beorht* (bright)–*beohrte* (brightly). Our -*ly* ending comes from an adjective ending -*lice* which weakened to -*ly* and was then reinterpreted as the mark of an adverb. The adjectives *friendly*, *homely*, *earthly*, *heavenly*, and so on still use that original ending.

PROBLEM 10.42: Sentences like these are considered "ungrammatical" by many grammar teachers. *He walked slow. She sang real sweet. He talks too loud. He got up pretty quick.* Sentences very similar to these are not considered ungrammatical: *He walks fast. I work hard. They ran far.* Comment, using a historical mode of explanation.

One expression in ModE *He works nights, I work days, We live there summers*, sounds like a modern plural noun serving an adverbial function. Some historians of the language would argue that such expressions are "really" singular genitives. OE had a construction that added the genitive inflection to the noun to give a construction with the sense of *He works (of) night*. From the point of view of a linguistically naive ModE speaker, though, a sentence like *I am there weekends* can only be interpreted as having a plural noun in an adverbial function. At some point in the past, the genitive was simply reinterpreted as a plural. From the same source comes the final -*s* of *once* from *anes* (ones), *twice*, *thrice*, *homewards*, *southwards*, *sideways*, *always*, *sometimes*, *backwards*.

Chapter 11

GRAMMATICAL CHANGE: THE VERB PHRASE

Like the noun phrase in ModE, the verb phrase has also lost most of an earlier, more extensive set of inflections. And like the noun phrase, the verb phrase has also developed an elaborate system of **periphrastic** or phrasal constructions that communicate fine shades of tense, aspect, and voice: *He will have been helped*, *He has been being careful*, and so on. We will examine the history of these patterns as we did the history of the noun phrase: First we will organize the data to see how the forms of OE, ME, and ModE verbs differ. Then to understand how the grammars that generated these structures have changed, we will construct some very simple rules for them. Finally, we will speculate about what caused these changes.

The ModE verbal inflections are limited: (1) to the third person singular present tense *-s*: *He goes*; (2) to a general past tense inflection, often called the **preterit**, that we spell *-ed* for the regular form, in a variety of other ways for irregular verbs: *sleep–slept*, *think–thought*, *fall–fell*, *go–went*. Two other inflections indicate **aspect**, or the state of the action: ongoing, over, about to begin, and so on. (3) The progressive *-ing* form marks the verb after the progressive *be* and signals the ongoing but usually temporary nature of an action: Contrast *It is raining here* with *It rains here.* And (4) the perfect participle which, like the past, marks verbs in a variety of ways: *fallen, seen, gone, stopped.* It marks the verb after the auxiliary *have* that signals the bounded period of an action: *He saw the picture* vs. *He has seen the picture,* and the verb after the passive *be*: *He was seen.*

The Past and Perfect

The ModE past tense and perfect forms are difficult to describe briefly because of reasons that go back into Indo-European prehistory. A pattern that distinguishes Indo-European languages from other language families is **ablaut**, or a vowel change in verbs that signals different tense and aspects: *sing–sang–sung, fall–fell–fallen, fly–flew–flown.* Through the last ten centuries, about half of the over 300 originally strong verbs have disappeared. Over 80 originally strong OE irregular ablaut verbs have become weak, so that they now follow the regular *-ed* form of the past tense and perfect participle endings. But almost 70 strong verbs remain strong, and a handful of originally weak verbs, by a kind of reverse analogy, have joined them.

Excepting *be* and *do*, strong verbs in English have at the most three forms: infinitive: *sing, walk, hurt*; past or preterit: *sang, walked, hurt*; and perfect participle: *sung, walked, hurt.* Some OE verbs, on the other hand, had four. (1) The infinitive form served as the root for the present form: *beodan–ic beode* (I command). (2) A second form served as the form for the past singular first and third person: *ic/he bead* (I/he commanded). (3) A third form served for past plurals and past second person singular: *þu/we/ge/hie budon* (you/we/you/they commanded). (4) A fourth form served for the perfect participle: *ic hæbbe (ge)boden.* (I have commanded). *Ge-* was a typical prefix in the perfect form.

PROBLEM 11.1: Traditionally, the OE strong verbs are organized into seven classes, depending on the kind of ablaut in the vowel. For ModE strong verbs, however, such categories are largely useless for three reasons: because sound changes in the last ten centuries have obscured the original basis for classifying them, because a fairly large number of weak verbs have become irregular through other sound changes, and because inconsistent analogy has made speakers choose unpredictably from among the four OE forms to select the three forms we now use. Originally strong were the OE ancestors of all the ModE verbs listed below. First is an example of the class that is still strong: for Class I, rise–rose–risen. Then follows a list of others that are still irregular verbs: *write, ride,* and so on. Following that in parentheses are ModE verbs that were once strong in that class but are now weak: In Class I are *abide, glide,* and so on; in II are *reeked, shoved, chewed,* and so on. On the basis of the model and the other verbs, how would you guess a sampling of those weak verbs would be pronounced today if they were still strong?

Class I: *rise–rose–risen: write, ride, bestride, bite, shine, drive, slide, strike, smite (abide, glide, spew, writhe).*

Class II: *freeze–froze–frozen: creep, fly, cleave, shoot, lose, flee, choose (reek, shove, chew, rue, brew, lie* [prevaricate], *seethe).*

Class III: *drink–drank–drunk: shrink, begin, sink, sing, run, swing, ring, stink, spring, swim, bind, wind, spin, find, cling, grind, sting, swell, win, fight, burst (climb, burn, help, delve, melt, carve, starve, mourn, spurn, bark, yell, yield, swallow).*

Class IV: *steal–stole–stolen: break, bear, tear, come, shear.*

Class V: *weave–wove–woven: tread, eat, give, see, sit, lie, speak (knead, weigh, fret, wreak, scrape, reap).*

Class VI: *shake–shook–shaken: draw, forsake, stand, slay, swear, wake (fare, bake, wade, shave, wash, heave, step, gnaw, laugh, flay, engrave).*

Class VII: *fall–fell–fallen: hang, hold, know, mow, sow, grow, hew, blow, weep, read, beat (wax* [grow], *flow, dread, row, blend, crow, leap, span).*

PROBLEM 11.2: Here is an artificial example of "illiterate, uneducated speech." Comment. *I writ him that the flowers ris because he holp me last year when we clim the hill to plant them. When we sot on the top, we seed all the stones, so we flang them in the pond. The big ones we digged a hole for and hove them in.* (Note all the irregular forms like *ris, holp, clim,* and *sot* and so on have occurred in various dialects of British and American English.) (4, 174)

The kinds of judgments that prescriptive grammarians make about verb forms like these very often take on a tone of divine authority. The fact is, "correct" and "incorrect" verb forms are more a matter of historical chance than grammatical inevitability. Many originally strong verbs have become weak. Those speakers who say *He clim the stairs* happen to be using the historically attested to form. Some weak verbs, on the other hand, have become strong: *He dug the hole and flang it in.* It just so happens that *dug* has become an acceptable new past form. At one time, *digged* was the "correct" preterit. *Flang,* on the other hand, is not, even though it exactly models the preterit of *sang, swam, rang,* and others. And in many dialects, of course, some of the verbs which are strong in standard English have been regularized to become weak. Just as *knead, weigh, wreak,* and *reap* have been regularized, so have *go* to *goed, draw* to *drawed, swing* to *swinged, see* to *seed,* and so on. It just so happens that those who used new weak preterits like *weighed* and *wreaked* were apparently more socially prestigious than those who regularize and use *seed, goed,* and *drawed.* (170)

PROBLEM 11.3: Are there any irregular verbs which are in the process of becoming regular today? How do you know?

The model for regularizing strong verbs, of course, is the paradigm of weak verbs, which included by far the greatest number of verbs in OE. With some exceptions, weak verbs did not change their stressed vowels to signal preterits, but rather added a feature that distinguishes the Germanic languages: the dental preterit, the source of our *-ed* past tense ("dental" because the /d/–/t/ sounds are made by placing the tip of the tongue against the back of the upper teeth): *ic lufie* (I love) vs. *ic lufode* (I loved). In some cases the OE verbs added just *-de*: *ic deme* (judge) *ic demde* (I judged); in others, *-ede* or *-ode*: *ic trymede* (I strengthened), *ic endode* (I ended).

PROBLEM 11.4: In OE, preterit endings with vowels—*-ode* and *-ede*—were always pronounced as full syllables: *lufode* was a three syllable word, for example. Today, it is a one syllable word: *loved*. At some time before ModE, the final *-e* was lost and the penultimate (second to last) vowel was **syncopated**, or dropped. Suggest a way to determine when the final *-e* was lost and when the vowel before the /d/ was lost.

PROBLEM 11.5: Is it possible to predict the exact pronunciation of the regular dental preterit endings in ModE? Consider these words: *pushed, snapped, danced, bombed, called, buzzed, hissed, ended, lurched, judged, fitted, rubbed, ripped, longed, routed, started.* How would you explain the inconsistency between spelling and pronunciation?

(Among the irregular verbs now in ModE are these: *lead–led, speed–sped, deal–dealt, set–set, meet–met.* But these were originally weak in OE, with no vowel alternation. The ModE variations resulted from a sound change that we shall look at more closely when we discuss phonology.)

Person Endings

In addition to these vowel changes and the dental preterit to indicate tense and perfect forms, OE, ME, and Early ModE had other endings that also indicated the person and the number of the subject. Some of these can still be found in the conservative usage of the **King James Bible** (1611): *Thus saith the Lord . . . , Knowst thou not this . . . , If thou hadst . . . , When thou wast young . . . .* By this time, however, it had generally disappeared from standard written English and probably in educated spoken English. In some rural areas of England, however, it has been reported as late as this century.

If we compare the regular weak endings from OE through ModE, we can see better how they have changed. In the ME list in the table, the first form represents the Northern endings; the second the Midland; the third, the Southern.

	First	Second	Third
Singular			
OE	*ic cysse*	*þu cys(se)st*	*he cysseþ*
ME	*ich kiss(e)/kisse/kisse*	*þu kisses/kisses(t)/ kis(se)st*	*he kisses/kisseþ, kisses/kisseþ*
EModE	*I kiss*	*you kiss*	*he kisses*

Plural (same for all persons)

	First
OE	*we cyssaþ*
ME	*we kisses/kisse(n)/kisseþ*
EModE	*we kiss*
ModE	*we kiss*

Preterit

	First	Second	Third
OE	*ic cyste*	*þu cystest*	*he cyste*
ME	*ich kist/kiste/kiste*	*þu kist/kistest/kistest*	*he kist/kiste/kiste*
EModE	*I kissed*	*you/thou kissest*	*he kissed*
ModE	*I kissed*	*you kissed*	*he kissed*

Plural

	First
OE	*we cyston*
ME	*we kist/kiste(n)/kiste(n)*
EModE	*we kissed*
ModE	*we kissed*

PROBLEM 11.6: Compare the endings in the table above. What endings have completely disappeared? What endings in ME are **not** predictable from OE? What endings in ModE are not predictable from ME? How might they be explained?

PROBLEM 11.7: Go through the same sequence of phonetic changes described for noun endings: (1) Unstressed vowels level to /ə/. (2) /ən/ endings become /ə/. (3) Final /ə/ endings disappear. What contrasts are lost first? What are the exceptions to this sequence of changes?

PROBLEM 11.8: A number of explanations have been given for the adoption of the third person -*s*. Here are five. Comment.

1. The third person -*s* allowed poets more rhymes than -(*e*)*th* endings.
2. A regular sound change changed final /θ/ as in *wreath* to /s/: *kisseð* > *kisses*.
3. /θ/ is a difficult sound to pronounce in conjunction with other consonants and was simplified to /s/.

4.   The *-s* ending is an analogical extension of the third person *is*.
5.   It was borrowed from Danish.

Two minor categories of verbs that do not conform to these patterns are the **preterit-present** verbs and a very few anomalies. The preterit-present resulted from verbs that had an original past tense vowel in the present form and then added the dental preterit: *agan* (own–ought), *cunnan* (can–could), *magan* (may–might), **motan* (an archaic *mote*–must; the * means here that no actual citation has been found for the word), *sculan* (shall–should). *Will* with its alternate *would* come from a regular verb *willan*.

The most anomalous verb in English, *be*, has in its paradigm the descendants of different words: *beon*, *wesan*, and **esan*. It also varied markedly from dialect to dialect in its occurrence with various numbers and persons. In the ME examples, the slashes separate Northern, Midland, and Southern forms respectively.

OE	ME	ModE
ic eom, beo	am, be/am/am, em	am
þu eart, bist	ert, es, bes/art, best/art, best	are
he is, bi	es, bes/is, beoþ, buþ/is, beoþ, beþ	is
we sindon, beo	ar(e), es, bes/arn, beoþ, ben/beoþ, beþ	are
ic wæs	was, wes/was/was	was
þu wære	was, wes/wore, were, wast/weore	were
he wæs	was, wes/was/was	was
we wæron	wer, war(e), wes/woren, were(n)/weore, wære	were

In OE, there may have been some slight semantic differences between *beon* verbs on the one hand, and *eom*, *eart*, *is*, and *sindon* on the other. The *be* verbs frequently expressed the tense of repeated events or invariable facts, which in ModE might be rendered *They be always ready* or *The door always be open at ten o'clock*. The *eom/eart/is* verbs indicated a condition whose permanence was not emphasized: *He is here, I am happy*.

Among the other anomalous verbs were the ancestors of *have*, *live*, *say*, *do*, and *go*, whose past tense, *went*, is derived from the past of *wendan*, the ancestor of the verb *wend*, as in "to wend one's way home."

PROBLEM 11.9: Why would one suspect *have*, *say*, *do*, and *go* of being anomalous verbs in OE strictly from modern evidence?

PROBLEM 11.10: What useful comparisons can be made between the changes in noun phrase and verb phrase inflections? Why do speakers not confuse the ModE *-s* endings for plural, genitive, and third person singular? What might be an internally motivated reason why the Northern tendency to add

-*s* endings to **all** present tense verbs did not take hold when other Northern inflectional innovations did? (5, 150)

The Progressive -*ing*, a Problem

The form of the ModE -*ing* ending in the progressive now happens to be identical with the -*ing* ending we use to create gerunds: *He was singing* (progressive) vs. *His singing was awful* (gerund). This nominalizing or noun-making -*ing* goes back to the OE suffix -*ung*(*e*). The original OE progressive ending was -*ende*: *He wæs singende*. By ME, it had become -*and*(*e*) in the North, -*and*, -*ende*, or -*ing*(*e*) in the Midlands, and -*inde* or -*ing*(*e*) in the South. How -*ende* either became or was replaced by -*ing* is not at all clear.

It has, in fact, been debated whether there really was a progressive in OE on the model of ModE *be* + *V-ing*. Patterns like *beon* + *V-ende* occurred very infrequently in texts originally written in OE, and only a little more frequently in translations which attempted to render Latin periphrastic verb forms. Even in ME, the progressive was uncommon. Only in the eighteenth century do we find it occurring with the passive. *It was being built* (replacing the older *It was building* or *It was a-building*). And not until the nineteenth century do we find it occurring with *have* or *be*: *He is having a party—He is being careful*. (All these new passive usages, incidentally, usages which are entirely correct in the twentieth century, were roundly condemned by the grammarians of the nineteenth century.)

Some have suggested that during ME, certain grammatical patterns of the gerund form with -*ing* and the progressive form with -*ende* were so similar that they merged: *Thei had ben a fyghting—Thei had been fyghtende*. The *a* is a reduced form of *on* or *at* which would have as its object the gerund: *Thei had ben on fyghting*. The usage is still common today in rural areas: *He's gone a-huntin'*. From the same source comes *aboard* (on board), *away* (on way), *aside* (on side), and so on. The gerund form may have come to be reinterpreted as a progressive when the *a* weakened and disappeared. The relatively frequent occurrence of this gerund pattern and the relatively infrequent incidence of the participle -*ing*/-*ende* gives some supporting evidence to this position. On the other hand, enough cases of -*ende* progressives dated before the *V-ing* constructions have been found to suggest that the relationship may be a direct one, perhaps resulting as much from phonological confusion as from grammatical substitution. (22, 97, 151, 221, 230)

PROBLEM 11.11: The -*ing* has not yet spread to normal use with all verbs or to all instances of *be*. Try to formulate some general restrictions that would account for these next sentences:

1. **He was weighing 180 lbs.—He was weighing the chicken.*
2. **He was resembling his father.—He was imitating his father.*

3. **He is having a car.—He is having a party.*
4. **He is being fat.—He is being careful.*
5. **He is being old.—He is being helpful.*
6. **I am liking it very much.—I am studying it very hard.*
7. **I am resenting that.—I am rejecting that.*

PROBLEM 11.12: Listen closely to the pronunciation of words in ordinary conversations spelled *singing, jumping, dancing,* and so on. You can often hear something we call "dropping the *-g*" *He was singin', dancin' 'n jumpin' around.* Is this difference predictable on **any** grounds? (56)

The Imperative and Subjunctive

Finally, we might note that identifiable imperative and subjunctive verb forms have entirely disappeared. In formal ModE, we may use the same form as the past (*were,* in the case of *be*) to indicate counter-factual or conditional statements: *If he came, we would . . . , Were I he, I would . . . .* But we also say *If he comes, we will . . . , If I was him, I would . . . .* We no longer have any distinctive imperative form, but now use the infinitive form instead: *Stop that! Be good!*

PROBLEM 11.13: If we reduce noun phrases and verb phrases to componential elements such as these below, how would a transformational grammar insure that the form of a verb in OE, ME, and early ModE would be "spelled" in the correct form? (Review Problem 10.10.) Assume present tense. What is relevant to verb agreement?

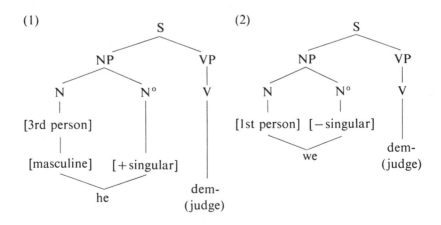

PROBLEM 11.14: Sketch a new system of verb agreement in which **gender** would be relevant to verb inflections. What other kinds of possible semantic

and grammatical distinctions among verb endings can you imagine? For example, could the age of the subject or object be reflected? His social status? Could we inflect for lies? For irony? For probability? For judgment (i.e., fortunately or unfortunately)? For emphasis? For the shape of the object? For the value of the object?

THE GRAMMAR OF THE VERB PHRASE

Now that we have outlined the formal changes in the inflections from OE to ModE, we can examine how they function in the context of their verb phrase, and how a grammar that generated OE forms would differ from a grammar that generated ModE forms.

Auxiliary Verbs

To explain how tense, -*ing*, and the perfect endings were distributed in OE and ME and how the ModE patterns emerged, we must look at the part of the verb phrase that includes the auxiliary verbs: the modals: *can, could, may, might, shall, should, will, would, must, ought*; the perfect *have*: *have gone*; the progressive *be*: *is going*; and the passive *be*: *was found,* and the combinations of these. In ModE, this structure allows several combinations:

1.	He				fixed the car.
2.	He	may			fix the car.
3.	He		has		fixed the car.
4.	He			is	fixing the car.
5.	He	may	have		fixed the car.
6.	He	may		be	fixing the car.
7.	He		has	been	fixing the car.
8.	He	may	have been		fixing the car.
9.	The car			was	fixed by him.
10.	The car will			be	fixed by him.
11.	The car		has	been	fixed by him.
12.	The car			is	being fixed by him.
13.	The car will		have	been	fixed by him.
14.	The car		has	been being	fixed by him.
15.	The car should have been being fixed by him.				

The modal, the *have*, the progressive *be* and the passive *be* combine with the main verb into fifteen different sequences, all of which have been given a good many complicated names by traditional grammarians: past perfect progressive, future perfect progressive, and so on. But just listing and naming them says little about their underlying structure, about the **grammar** of these phrases. If we note a few patterns, however, we can make some significant generalizations:

1. These elements may occur in any combination with one another, but always in the same order: **modal** (*may, will, shall, can, must*)—*have/had*—*be*_{progressive}—*be*_{passive}.

2. The tense (present/past: *will–would, have–had, is–was*, and so on) is always indicated in the **first** verb of the phrase.

3. The form of any individual verb—infinitive (*go*), progressive (*going*), perfect (*gone*), or inflected for tense (*goes, went*)—always depends on the verb (or lack thereof) immediately preceding it. That is,

   a. The verb following a modal is always in the infinitive or uninflected form (see 2, 5, 6, 8, 10, 13, 15).

   b. The verb following *have* is always marked [perfect] (see 3, 5, 7, 8, 11, 13, 14, 15).

   c. The verb following the progressive *be* is always marked with an *-ing* form (see 4, 6, 7, 8, 12, 14, 15).

   d. The verb following the passive *be* is always marked [perfect] (see 9–15). If no auxiliary verb is present, then the main verb is inflected for tense, as in (1).

We can now sketch some additional grammatical rules to explain these ModE patterns. We shall renumber the rules omitting all rules irrelevant to the question.

1. $S \rightarrow NP \quad VP$
2. $VP \rightarrow AUX \quad MV$
3. $AUX \rightarrow TENSE \quad (MODAL) (HAVE) (BE_{progressive}) BE_{passive})$
4. $TENSE \rightarrow [\pm present]$
5. $MV \rightarrow V \left(\begin{Bmatrix} NP \\ AP \\ PP \end{Bmatrix} \right)$

The parentheses around MODAL, HAVE, BE_{progressive} and BE_{passive} in rule (3) mean that any or none of them can be chosen in any combination, but that they must occur in their relative order.

Next to be accounted for is the fact that the first verb in the phrase always carries tense. If no auxiliary verb is present, tense goes after the main verb: *He goes*. If tense were listed after each of these verbs as an option to begin with, including the main verb, we would need a very complex rule to **exclude** tense from all except the correct verb. But the problem can be solved by writing a rule placing TENSE in one position and then using a transformation to transfer TENSE to the verb immediately following it. The rule would have this effect on these two examples:

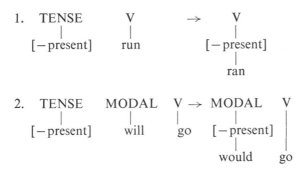

1. TENSE   V   →   V
         | | |
    [−present]   run   [−present]
                                            |
                                       ran

2. TENSE   MODAL   V → MODAL   V
         | | | | |
    [−present]   will   go   [−present]
                                       |
                                would   go

Exactly the same kind of transformation will also create the correct form of the verbs after MODAL, HAVE, $BE_{progressive}$, and $BE_{passive}$. Except for MODAL, each of these auxiliary verbs must also have associated with it an inflectional feature that shifts to the following verb: [perfect] from HAVE to whatever follows HAVE; [ing] from $BE_{progressive}$ to whatever follows it; and [perfect] from $BE_{passive}$ to whatever follows it. In fact, we can write a composite rule to include all these elements:

$$[\text{affix}] \quad \text{verb} \rightarrow \text{verb}$$
$$[\text{affix}]$$

(Affix = any TENSE, [perfect], or [ing]; verb – any MODAL, HAVE, BE, or any main verb.) The rule simply states that whatever element is indicated by [affix] should be re-attached to mark the verbal element immediately following. Therefore, we must expand the base rule for auxiliaries once again.

BASE RULE: AUX → TENSE   (MODAL) (HAVE   [perfect])
                                     $(BE_{prog.} \quad [-ing]) (BE_{pass.} \quad [\text{perfect}])$

TRANSFORMATION: [affix]   v →   v
                                    |
                               [affix]
             where [affix] = TENSE, [perfect], or [-ing].
                         v = MODAL, HAVE, BE or any main verb V.

PROBLEM 11.15: Generate four or five verb phrases, applying the transformation and spelling rules as appropriate.

PROBLEM 11.16: Very briefly suggest how a traditionalist or a descriptivist would describe these patterns.

One further question must be accounted for before we can explore the history of some of these patterns. As Rule 3 is formulated, it allows the passive BE to occur before intransitive verbs, generating ungrammatical sequences like *He was disappeared*. (1) The passive BE must occur only with transitive verbs, and (2) the passive, since it is related to roughly synonymous active sentences: *Tom saw Bill—Bill was seen by Tom*, must somehow be related to the same deep structure the active is based on.

Some transformationalists have dealt with the problem like this: The $BE_{passive}$ can be included in the AUX rule: AUX $\rightarrow$ TNS (MODAL) (HAVE) ($BE_{progressive}$) ($BE_{passive}$). But $BE_{passive}$ is limited to occurring before transitive verbs: $BE_{passive}$: _____ V NP (where V is not *be, become*, a group of other verbs like *weigh, resemble, behave*, and some others.) If $BE_{passive}$ is selected from the choices in the AUX, it automatically signals the need for a passive transformation:

$$NP_1 \quad X \quad BE_{passive} \quad [perfect] \quad V \quad NP_2 \quad by \quad \Delta$$
$$\rightarrow NP_2 \quad X \quad BE_{passive} \quad [perfect] \quad V \qquad\quad by \quad NP_1$$

$$Tom \quad TENSE \quad BE_{passive} \quad [perfect] \quad see \quad Bill$$
$$\rightarrow Bill \quad TENSE \quad BE_{passive} \quad [perfect] \quad see \qquad by \quad Tom$$

The other transformation then shifts the [perfect] inflection feature associated with $BE_{passive}$ from it to the following verb, giving

Bill was see-n by Tom

PROBLEM 11.17: Here are some OE and ME sentences that represent the possible auxiliary verb combinations during those periods. Forms that do not occur in these lists should be considered ungrammatical. For example, a form corresponding to *he was being taught* would have been impossible in OE (at least such a structure has never been found). How do these combinations differ from period to period? Try to sketch some rules that might generate each set in their period. Note that in OE, the verb following a modal has an -*an* infinitive ending. Inflections are in boldface.

OE

1. *He sceal deað swelt**an**.* (He shall death suffer.)
2. *He hafa**ð** hit onfund**en**.* (He has it found.)
3. *God bi**ð** eardig**ende** on heofonum.* (God is dwelling in heavens.)
4. *Ic sceal bid**ende** beon.* (I shall waiting be.)
5. *He sceal wes**an** Ismahel hat**en**.* (He shall be Ishmael called.)

6. *Se boda is gefaren.* (The messenger is departed.)
7. *He wæs gefangen.* (He was captured.)

ME

8. *He hath promyst it.*
9. *I kan not ben well att ese.* (I can not be well at ease.)
10. *It will not be worshipt.*
11. *We han been waitynge al this fourtennyght.*
12. *Ich mihte habbe bet i-don.* (I might have better done.)
13. *I shal be chaunged.*
14. *He hath been y-founde.*
15. *There was com another knyght.*

The most obvious difference between OE and ME on the one hand and ModE on the other is the relatively limited number of possible auxiliary verb combinations in OE and ME. OE allows only six possible combinations; ME, at least Early ME, allowed eight:

(Old English Inflections, -infinitive AN, progressive -ENDE, perfect -EN, in caps):

1.	MODAL		verb-AN	(as in (1) above)
2.	MODAL	$BE_{prog.}$-AN	verb-ENDE	(as in (4) above)
3.	MODAL	$BE_{pas.}$-AN	verb-EN	(as in (5) above)
4.		BE_{prog}	verb-ENDE	(as in (3) above)
5.		$BE_{pas.}$	verb-EN	(as in (7) above)
6.	$\left\{\begin{array}{l}\text{haf-}\\ \text{be-}\end{array}\right\}$		verb-EN	(as in (6) and (2) above)

These combinations can be derived from this rule and the same kind of affix-verb transformation rule described above.

$$\text{AUX} \rightarrow \text{TENSE} \left(\left\{\begin{array}{l}(\text{MODAL} \quad \text{-[inf.]}) \left(\left\{\begin{array}{ll}BE_{progressive} & \text{[-ende]}\\ BE_{passive} & \text{[perfect]}\end{array}\right\}\right)\\ \text{HAVE} \quad \text{[perfect]}\end{array}\right\}\right)$$

What this rule stipulates is the limited combination of modals with passive and progressive BE's, and the fact that the perfect corresponding to ModE *have* occurs without any other auxiliary. This rule must be developed further, however, because the HAVE, an abstract symbol, is manifested in two ways, depending on the kind of verb it occurs with. With transitive and intransitive verbs of motion, HAVE is spelled *haf-*, the ancestor of ModE *have*. But before other intransitive verbs, the HAVE is spelled *be-*, *wes-*, or *weorð-*. (The full infinitive form, *beon*, is the ancestor of our *be*; the full form *wesan* is the ancestor of *was/were*. *Weorðan* has disappeared entirely.)

ME has all of these OE verb forms, but also allows three more:

7.	MODAL	HAVE			verb-EN	(as in (12) above)
8.		HAVE	BE$_{prog.}$-EN		verb-ING	(as in (11) above)
9.		HAVE		BE$_{pas.}$-EN	verb-EN	(as in (14) above)

These new ME possibilities can be represented with this rule:

$$\text{AUX} \rightarrow \text{TENSE}\ \ (\text{MODAL})\ \ (\text{HAVE}\ \ [\text{perfect}])\ \left(\left\{ \begin{matrix} \text{BE}_{prog.} & [\text{-ing}] \\ \text{BE}_{pas.} & [\text{perfect}] \end{matrix} \right\} \right)$$

PROBLEM 11.18: What inflectional changes are involved here?

If we compare the rules, we can see that the perfect HAVE has been taken out of the disjunctive choice with the other auxiliaries and put into a linear order after the MODAL and before the BE$_{prog.}$ and BE$_{pas.}$. A further change in this HAVE, however, is that it is now manifested as a form of *be* before intransitive verbs of motion, as *have* elsewhere.

This rule, however, is too powerful for Early ME. It generates sentences with three auxiliary verbs like *He may have been found* and *He may have been singing*, neither of which appears to have been possible for that period. In other words, the Early ME rule would have to have a further constraint to the effect that only two out of the three auxiliary elements may be chosen in any one phrase. But that is a very "messy" kind of rule. It does not have the neatness of the OE or later ME rule. Indeed, it may be the very "messiness" that led to the grammatical change that finally allowed a sequence of three consecutive auxiliary verbs. If speakers tend to formulate the simplest set of rules, a constraint on the number of verbs in a sequence would seem to be a kind of excrescense that would disappear.

Another characteristic of ME distinct from OE is not represented in this rule. It was the emergence of *do* as a kind of all-purpose function word. In OE, *do* functioned as a main verb on the model of *He did the work*, and as an **anaphoric** or substitute verb as in *He works and I do too*. Probably out of the main verb *do* arose a **causative**-*do* pattern. *Thi soul-cnul ich wile do ringe* (Thy soul-knell I will do ring; i.e., I will cause someone to ring your soul knell.), *He dede meyk a newe trone* (he did make a new throne; i.e., he caused someone to make a new throne). Perhaps out of this causative-*do*, that often indicated the completion of action, arose what we now find in modern non-standard spoken English, particularly in the American South and in parts of Newfoundland: *I've done finished*, or more usually, *I done finished*.

Yet another *do*-form developed later in ME, perhaps out of the causative, as its semantic sense weakened. This was the semantically empty *do* that in later ME and Early ModE poetry seems only to flesh out a rhythm or in prose, was a seemingly meaningless unstressed syllable: *They did find the answer ...*, *We did leave when. ...* Out of this *do*, probably, developed the interrogative and negative *do*'s: *... why do ye wepe, they did not weep*.

The empty *do* reached the height of its use in the sixteenth century when almost any sentence, verse or prose, might contain one. The last examples of the causative *do* date from the early seventeenth century. The interrogative-*do* was developing as early as Chaucer, but the negative-*do* was a later development.

In order to include the aspectual *do* as in *He has done left* and the empty *do* as in *He did leave*, we have to expand the rules for ME auxiliaries:

$$\text{AUX} \rightarrow \text{TENSE} \quad (\text{MODAL})$$

$$\left(\left\{\begin{matrix} (\text{HAVE} \quad [\text{perfect}] \quad (\text{DO} \quad [\text{perfect}])) \\ \text{DO} \end{matrix} \right. \quad \left(\left\{\begin{matrix} \text{BE}_{\text{pass.}} & [\text{perfect}] \\ \text{BE}_{\text{prog.}} & [\text{-ing}] \end{matrix}\right\}\right)\right)$$

This will allow *He may have done been gone* from *do* + EN, and from the other *do*, *He does go* and *He may do go*, forms which have been cited. The causative *do* described earlier is not an auxiliary *do*, but more like the verbs *tell*, *want*, *promise*, and so on, that take complements of the form *I told **him to leave**, *I want **him to leave**, *I promise to leave*. It is a main-verb *do*: *I did [someone] make the house*, parallel in meaning to *I had him promoted*, but lacking the noun object.

Between ME and ModE, five important changes occurred. First, the causative-*do* disappeared entirely. Second, the aspectual *have* + *done* + V–EN (*he has done gone*) form, a form frequently found in northern British dialect areas, became stigmatized as nonstandard. It was probably brought to this continent by Ulstermen, many of whom became slave overseers and probably passed the form on to Blacks. Third, the unstressed empty *do* in sentences like *He did leave* disappeared (or merged with emphatic do: *He **did** leave*.). Fourth, as we shall see in more detail, this empty *do* may have become the source for questions with *do*, first appearing in ME: *Did he go?*, then later to negatives: *He did not go*. The earlier forms, *Went he?* and *He went not*, occurred side-by-side with the newer forms, often reflecting social distinctions, but eventually died out except in the most formal public prose: *Ask not what your country can do for you ...*, *Beats there a heart in this great land which. ...?*

Finally, the last disjunctive choice in the auxiliary rule, the choice between BE$_{\text{passive}}$ and BE$_{\text{progressive}}$ changed to a linear choice of either or both:

He is watching, He is watched, He is being watched. Before this time, before later ModE, the progressive sense of the passive was communicated in a sentence like *The food was bringing in* or *The house was a-building.* As we have seen, the origin of this construction was probably the gerund: *The house was on building.* As the *on* weakened to *a-*: *The house was a-building*, and then disappeared: *The house was building*, a form identical to the progressive appeared, perhaps even replaced the *-ende* form. But in the eighteenth century, grammarians began to object to this construction, partly because it was homonymous with the non-passive progressive: *The house/wind was building*, and partly because they felt it not to be in accord with the "genius" of the language.

One of the earliest citations of the modern finite passive progressive is from 1795: *... like a fellow whose uppermost grinder* **is being torn out** *by the roots.* .... Centuries before this time, though, what appear to be participial modifiers with progressive passives had occurred: *... he should stand in fear of fire,* **being burnt** *i'th hand for stealing of sheepe.* The potential confusion of the two forms, the earlier progressive passive (*The house was building.*) and the progressive active (*The wind was building.*) plus the earlier occurrence of this passive participial phrase led to the progressive passive as we now know it.

Another pattern that flourished in northern British dialect areas (and still does) and which was probably brought to America by Ulster Scots are sentences with multiple modals: *He may can go, I might could leave, She will can stay.* Now, however, like the *He has done gone*, also of Northern British origin, the multiple modal is stigmatized as nonstandard English. (22, 32, 47, 49, 151, 195, 220, 230)

Nonstandard English

The fact that there are these similarities between Early ModE auxiliary structures and structures that characterize what has come to be known as **Black English** strongly suggests that the one has been a strong influence on the other. Had we the space to explore some of the finer details of early ModE, we would discover other similarities.

There are some significant differences, however. One dialect of Black English seems to lack a form of the inflected *be* in sentences such as these:

1. *He in the house.*
2. *She my friend.*
3. *You a bad man.*
4. *They playing downstairs.*
5. *You covered with dirt.*

At the same time, this dialect also seems to use the uninflected form of *be* "incorrectly" in sentences like these:

6. *They be there tomorrow.*
7. *I be ready if I could.*
8. *Whenever they be there, they be happy.*
9. *She be taken care of.*
10. *They always be joking.*

And some sentences appear to be like passives, but are not:

11. *He been left.* (i.e., he has left.)
12. *She been worked.* (i.e., she has worked.)
13. *They been et.* (i.e., they have eaten.)

Some have argued that these differences in surface structures reflect deep structures in Black English that are significantly different from the deep structures of standard English, and that therefore, despite the superficial similarities between the two, Black and standard English are really two different languages, with all that that implies for education and social understanding. Indeed, the source of these differences has occasionally been attributed to the grammatical structures African slaves brought with them in the earliest days of slavery.

Actually, a rather simple deletion rule seems to explain many of these patterns. Wherever Standard English speakers **contract** an auxiliary verb or the main verb *be*, the dialect of nonstandard English illustrated by these sentences will predictably **delete** the verb:

Full form:	*I am here.*	*I have gone.*	*I will be ready.*
	V	V	V
Contracted form:	*I'm here.*	*I've gone.*	*I'll be ready.*
	V	V	V
Deleted form:	*I here.*	*I gone.*	*I be ready.*

These deletions are not invariable, any more than contractions are invariable in standard spoken English. But statistically, the contracted verbs do tend to be dropped, just as statistically, other speakers tend to contract them. The statistical trend can be charted across social classes and styles. As a speaker becomes more casual, he will, depending on his linguistic background, contract or delete more and more frequently.

In fact, the very ability of a speaker to adapt his speech to social situations requires us to conceive of a grammar as an intersection between rules of the kind we have been describing and their statistically predictable application. Some grammatical rules have 100 percent predictability: The relative pronoun will always occur as the first noun phrase in a full relative clause: *the man whom I saw* vs. **the man I saw whom.* Other rules depend on variables related to social class, social situation, and speaker-audience relationship: *the man whom I saw* vs. *the man who I saw* vs. *the man that I saw* vs. *the man I saw.*

But some other nonstandard sentence types resist this kind of explanation. One is *I be here everyday, so I saw what happened.* This does not seem to be an ellipsized version of *I'll be here everyday so.* . . . In fact, this invariant *be* appears to be a characteristic of certain nonstandard North American dialects, especially, but not exclusively, Black dialects. It appears that this invariant *be* communicates a continuous habitual sense of time. Where standard English communicates duration through time with the usual inflected form of a verb or with a verb and adverb: *He is always there,* some dialects of English seem to signal the same notion of aspect with the form of *be*: Thus *I be there* means I am regularly and predictably there.

Where this invariant *be* came from, however, is a bit of a puzzle. There was (and is) in the southern British dialect of ModE a *be* in sentences such as these: *I think he be a traitor. Where be the men? We be ready to leave. If it be as you say, then let us end it.* But these are simply the forms of the present tense of *be* used in Southern British English instead of *is* or *are*, often with plural subjects or subjunctives. By the sixteenth century, this particular form of *be* was more often found in the speech of nonprestige speakers. But none of these examples communicates the same habitual sense of time that the present nonstandard English *be* can communicate. It may be that the durative *be* has its origins in the OE *beon*, the *be*-verb that often indicated duration, that after being used in that durative sense with some frequency in OE, it submerged into a lower class or lower middle class social dialect, was brought to this continent, and is now being observed for the first time.

Support for this view and against the view that this durative meaning was brought with the slaves from their native African languages and invested in the *be* form is the fact that this invariant durative *be* has also turned up in Eastern Canada as well as in the American South, from whence it was apparently brought to the inner cities of the North. It is difficult to argue convincingly that Newfoundland Canadian whites could have adopted it from the relatively few Blacks that settled there or that exactly the same meaning could have independently evolved in exactly the same form in the two dialects.

An anomaly among these verb forms, however, seems to occur in sentences such as *He left, ain't he?* The full and "correct" form would be *He has left, hasn't he?* The contraction and deletion yield the first part of the sentence: *He has left > he's left > he left.* But the *ain't he* **tag question** seems to contradict the generalization that such tags normally repeat the subject and auxiliary verb and add a negative if the main clause is affirmative and vice versa. In *He left, ain't he? ain't* appears to be a contraction of *am not.* But that would imply the full form of *he left, ain't he?* was either **he is left, isn't he?* or **he has left, isn't he?* both of which are impossible in English.

Historically, *ain't* is a contraction of *am not*: *am not > amn't > aan't > ain't.* If it is now "ungrammatical" in some upper middle class dialects in our north central states, it was as late as the turn of the century freely used by many upper middle class educated speakers in the southern part of England and is used today in the casual speech of a good many highly educated southerners and westerners. To call it totally ungrammatical is to betray one's geographical biases. That it is now considered such is a sociological, historical accident.

But *ain't* has a second source. It also descends from a contraction of *have not*. Such forms as *ain't* in *He's got the money, ain't he?* evolved from *hasn't* to *han't* to *hain't* to *ain't*, making *ain't* a contraction of either *have + not*, *has + not*, or *am + not*. The occurrence of sentences like *He dead, ain't he?* illustrate the common tendency to generalize a form. Although *ain't* historically is derived from the contraction of *am not*, it is used as the tag for sentences with other forms of *be*. This can be demonstrated by sentences such as *He ain't dead, is he?*

Thus what at first glance may appear to be an anomaly—*ain't* occurring where we would expect *haven't* or *am not*—is, if not sociolinguistically prestigious among some speakers, historically consistent and as logical, indeed more logical perhaps than *I am here, aren't I?*, where the *aren't* suggests a plural subject **are I?*

Another grammatical form that has been uniquely attributed to Black English dialects is the use of *been* in intransitive sentences of the form: *He been et (et = ate)*. This is not a passive form, but rather a form whose meaning is probably the completion of an action in the remote past, as opposed to a form like *He done ate*, which represents the completion of an action in the less remote past. While there appear to be no citations of such verb phrases in any extant English texts from older periods, it too has been found in the speech of Newfoundlanders. (39, 40, 53, 54, 77, 119, 133, 197, 211, 212, 221, 224)

Whatever the origin of the differences between standard and Black nonstandard speech (though the weight of the arguments is on the side of British rather than African or pidgin influence), the reason for the difference today is social isolation. Example after example of preserved archaic forms can be found among groups of speakers who have been isolated from a changing standard, isolated because they have been either geographically or socially cut off from the influence of those who set the standard. Those who are geographically isolated have little opportunity to hear the standard model. Those who are socially isolated often have no expectation of moving up and out of their social class and so do not seem to imitate the speech of those in the more prestigious groups as strongly as do those who feel themselves to be upwardly mobile. (1,200)

TRANSFORMING THE VERB PHRASE

Changes in the auxiliary verb system since OE have been accompanied by some other changes in the verb phrase. They involve the way auxiliary verbs operate in questions and negatives, the way some verbs and prepositional phrases have restructured themselves into two-word verbs and direct objects, and the way one pattern in OE and ME has disappeared entirely.

Negation

Closely tied to the patterns of the auxiliary phrase are negatives. Because this is such a complex subject, we shall deal with only the major patterns and those in no great detail. ModE negatives may occur in these verb phrase patterns:

1. *I will not leave.*
2. *I have not left.*
3. *I did not leave.*
4. *I was not leaving/happy/in the house.*

The negative occurs after the first auxiliary verb (MODAL, *have*) or after any form of *be*. If no auxiliary verb is present, then a *do* is needed as in (3).
Negatives can also occur in these patterns:

5. *No flowers bloomed* (compare: Flowers did not bloom.)
6. *The man had no money* (compare: The man did not have any money.)
7. *The man never arrived* (compare: The man did not ever arrive.)
8. *He went nowhere* (compare: He did not go anywhere.)
9. *I saw nothing* (compare: I did not see anything.)

Because the negative patterns that negate a verb: *The man did not have any money* are often synonymous with negatives that negate a noun phrase: *The man had no money*, negation seems to be a kind of meaning that ranges over a whole sentence, an element that can be manifested in different places while the sentence it occurs in retains the same meaning. In other words, different surface patterns can represent the same deep structure, the same underlying semantic structure.
One way to deal with the problem is to generate the NEG(ative) element separate from the rest of the sentence and then shift it to the appropriate place in the sentence: S → (NEG) NP VP. Since the *not* may occur after an

auxiliary verb or *be* but before the main verb, we need a transformation of this sort:

NEG   X   TENSE   (v)   (where v = MODAL, BE, or HAVE.)
$\rightarrow$ X   TENSE   (v) NEG

The NEG is shifted after Tense, and if a modal, *be*, or *have* is present, then after it too:

NEG   I   TENSE   be   happy
$\rightarrow$ I   TENSE   be   NEG   happy

Once this transformation has occurred, the TENSE is then attached to the immediately following verb.

But when no modal, *have* or *be* is present, then the NEG is moved behind the TENSE, but it will not be after the main verb:

NEG   he   TENSE   go
$\rightarrow$ he   TENSE   NEG   go

In this case, the TENSE cannot move past the NEG, so we insert a *do* to "carry" the tense:

he   TENSE   NEG   go
he   do-TENSE   NEG   go
or: he   does   not   go   (assuming TENSE is [+ present])

Negatives that attach to noun phrases are more complicated to describe because they are closely associated with indefinite pronouns: *someone–anyone no one; somebody anybody–nobody; somewhere–anywhere–nowhere,* and because of a *some–any* variation (in standard English): *I have some money–I don't have any money–I have no money.* Without getting into the complexities of the problem, we will only note that the NEG, if it is not moved after the TENSE in the auxiliary phrase, may be attached to an underlying indefinite ART in a noun phrase:

NEG   I   TENSE   have   ARTICLE   money
$\rightarrow$ I   TENSE   have   NEG   money
or: I   have   no   money

This is a grossly oversimplified, incomplete, and in many ways misleading description, but it will serve our purposes here. The most important point to note is that in standard ModE, only one occurrence of NEG in a sentence is allowed (barring prefixes and suffixes): *I don't have no money* is in standard ModE ungrammatical.

PROBLEM 11.19: Here are some examples of negatives from OE, ME, and Early ModE. Translations retaining the negative pattern follow in parentheses. What kinds of rules would account for the differences between the various stages of the language? (There are other patterns in addition to these.)

Old English

1. *Ne mihte he biddan.* (Ne might he pray.)
2. *Ne þurfan ge noht besorgian.* (Ne need ye not worry.)
3. *Ne demdon we.* (Ne judge we.)
4. *Næbbe ic nænig scipu.* (Ne-have I ne-any ships.)
5. *Næs he snotor.* (Ne-was he wise.)
6. *Ne ic ne herige ne ic ne tæle.* (Ne I ne praise ne I ne blame.)
7. *Ne hit næfre ne gewurðe.* (Ne it never ne happen.)
8. *Nis nænig swa bliðe.* (Ne-is ne-any so happy.)

Early Middle English

9. *Ic ne seye not.* (I ne say not.)
10. *He ne held it noght.* (He ne held it not.)
11. *He nolde slepe in noon house.* (He ne-would sleep in no house.)
12. *There nas no man nowhere so vertuous.*
13. *Ne taketh nothing to hold of no men ne of no womman.*
14. *He ne speketh nawt.*
15. *No mon nule don hym no good.* (No man ne-will do him no good.)

Later Middle English

16. *I seye not the wordes.*
17. *He held it noght.*
18. *We sawe them nawt.*
19. *We sawe nawt the knyghtes.*
20. *A man has not all his wyll.*
21. *He wolde not come inn.*
22. *Thei may nawt singe.*
23. *I am not cold and nakyd.*
24. *It is not longes gon.* (It is not long ago.)

We can see two very significant differences among OE, ME, and ModE. First, multiple negation was once common in English. The change requiring that only one NEG appear in a sentence is a relatively recent rule in the dialect of Early ModE that has become the standard. In fact, it is one of the few instances where prescriptive grammarians may have encouraged a tendency already at work. Standard Early ModE had already begun to favor single negation before the prescription against multiple negatives appeared in usage books of the eighteenth century. When prescriptive grammars like Lowth's extremely influential **Short Introduction to English Grammar** stated that . . . *two Negatives in English destroy one another, or are equivalent to an affirmative*, the tendency was simply defined as the logically prescriptive norm for standard speakers. His advice has been repeated so often and so strongly that few English speakers who have endured our educational system can fail to recognize that *No one didn't have no money* is not a favored construction among educated speakers, despite the weight of respectable English history behind it and the testimony of numerous other languages in which multiple negation is not factored out like an algebraic formula, languages in which the more negatives there are in a sentence, the more negative it is.

The specific change we would need in a rule to generate multiple negation in OE and ME is one that would "copy" NEG in several specific places rather than one that allows only one placement of NEG. The second major change involves the loss of one option in the placement of negatives after verbs. As late as the end of the last century, the *do*-negative and the negative without *do* were not unknown: *I did not leave–I left not.* Presently, though, the *do*-less negative has largely disappeared from standard informal educated English. (53, 94, 97, 132, 221)

PROBLEM 11.20: What are we to do with the following sentences?

1a. *I haven't any money.*
1b. *I don't have any money.*
2a. *You needn't stay.*
2b. *You don't need to stay.*
3a. *He don't never be there.*
3b. *He ain't there now.*
4a. *Can't nobody tell him what to do?*
4b. **Can't George tell him what to do?*
5a. *Ain't no way he gonna find out.*
5b. **Ain't that way he gonna find out.*
6a. *Didn't nobody tell me that?*
6b. **Didn't that man tell me that?*

Why are 4b–6b wrong? What does the fact that you know they are wrong tell you about the grammaticality of nonstandard dialects?

Questions

Like negatives, questions in ModE also relate in some important ways to the grammar of auxiliary verbs. English has two kinds of questions: Those we answer with a *yes* or *no*, and those we answer with information: (1) *Can he come then? When can he come?* (2) *Has he done it? How has he done it?* (3) *Was he going there? Where was he going?* (4) *Did he see that? What did he see?* The patterns are similar. In *yes–no* questions the first element is always a modal, *have*, or *be*, or if none of these is present, then a form of *do* is required as in (4). In information questions, the first element is the interrogative pronoun. Then if the pronoun asks for information about any element in the sentence except the subject, the next element must be a modal (1), *have* (2), *be* (3), or *do* (4). But if the interrogative questions the subject, then the main verb may follow: *Who left? What happened?*

One way to explain question patterns within the framework of a transformational grammar assumes that all sentences, not just questions, begin with what is called a **performative utterance** having the force of I state, I ask, I order, and so on. Among the reasons for assuming this is the problem involved in a sentence like *Frankly, I have no time* or *Frankly, did you brush your teeth?* The adverb describes the attitude of the speaker: *I say frankly* or *I ask frankly*. . . . We have to assume in such sentences an implied subject–verb which is deleted. There is a good deal more evidence, but it need not concern us here.

We can represent the statement, question, and imperative performatives with a shorthand ST, Q, and IMP in the first rule:

$$S \rightarrow \begin{Bmatrix} ST \\ Q \\ IMP \end{Bmatrix} \text{(NEG)} \quad NP \quad VP$$

The deep structure of a question would then look something like this:

Q   he   TENSE   will   see   something

A transformation then (1) changes the element questioned into an interrogative pronoun and (2) shifts it to the beginning of its clause:

Q   he   TENSE   will   see   *something*
→ Q   he   TENSE   will   see   *what*
→ Q *what* he   TENSE   will   see

If the series of transformations stop here and the Q is realized as *I ask*, then we would have the sentence: *I ask what he will see.*

But if we go on to delete the performative, the Q, the *I ask*, then we are left with a sequence of elements, *what he TENSE will see*, needing one more transformation. In this case, the TENSE and the first auxiliary verb or *be* is moved from its position after the subject to a position directly after the inter-rogative pronoun:

	Q	what		he	TENSE	will	see
→		what		he	*TENSE*	*will*	see
→		what	*TENSE will*	he			see?
or:		what	will	he			see? (assuming TENSE is

[+ present])

PROBLEM 11.21: Perform the question transformation on these **strings** below.[1] Assume that the indefinite pronoun, whatever it is, is to be transformed into the corresponding interrogative word—*who, when, why, how, where, what.*

1.	Q	I	[−present]	be		*somewhere*
2.	Q	he	[+present]	may	ask	*someone*
3.	Q	she	[+present]	have	-en	buy	*something*
4.	Q	they	[−present]	be	-ing	work	*sometime*
5.	Q	you	[−present]	shall	say	that	*for some reason*

But if the first verb after the TENSE is not an auxiliary or form of *be*, but rather the main verb, then only the TENSE can be moved:

| what | | he | TENSE | find |
| what | TENSE | he | | find |

This leaves TENSE without anything to "carry" it, and we insert the *do* again, just as we did with negatives.

what		TENSE	he	find
what	do	TENSE	he	find
or: what		did	he	find	(assuming TENSE is [−present])

PROBLEM 11.22: The lack of a *do* after the interrogative in a sentence like *Who saw the boy?* seems to be an anomaly in the pattern. Go through exactly the same transformations described above: (1) Indefinite pronoun becomes a WH-word. (2) WH-word shifts to beginning of clause, after Q. (3) Q is deleted. (4) TENSE and, if one is present, the first auxiliary verb shifts to a position directly after the WH-word. (5) Attach TENSE to the following verb. (6) If some element intervenes between the TENSE and a verb, insert a *do*. Perform those operations on this string:

Q   someone   [−present]   see   the boy

1 A string is a sequence of symbols generated by base rules.

PROBLEM 11.23: If we assume that questions of the WH-word form follow the pattern described above, what would be the parallel derivation for yes–no questions? *Did you leave?* and *Did you leave or not?* are semantically if not stylistically identical. Presumably, they are related to a common deep structure. How does this fact bear on the problem of generating *yes–no* questions?

PROBLEM 11.24: Here are some questions based on OE, ME, and Early ModE sentence patterns. How do they differ from ModE question patterns? How would the rules suggested for ModE have to be revised?

OE

1. *Eart þu se cyning?* (Are you the king?)
2. *Hwæt sægst þu?* (What say you?)
3. *Hwilce fixas gefehst þu?* (What fishes catch you?)
4. *Hæfst þu ænige gefangen?* (Have you any caught?)
5. *Is þes of þinum geferum?* (Is this (one) of your friends?)
6. *Ne canst þu huntian buton mid nettum?* (Ne can you hunt except with nets?)
7. *Hu gefehst þu fixas?* (How catch you fishes?)
8. *Hæst þu hafoc?* (Have you hawk?)
9. *Hwæt canst þu scieppan?* (What can you create?)
10. *Wille ge beon beswungen on leornunge?* (Will you be beaten in learning?)

ME

11. *Hwat is þe light?* (What is the light?)
12. *Gaf ye the mann anythyng?* (Gave you the man anything?)
13. *Hard ye not?* (Heard you not?)
14. *To wom shuld he speke?* (To whom should he speak?)
15. *Is that sothe?* (Is that truth?)
16. *Shal I tellen more?* (Shall I tell more?)
17. *Has he a long snowte?* (Has he a long snout?)
18. *Who shal hunte here?* (Who shall hunt here?)
19. *Is youre chyld a knave?* (Is your child a knave (boy)?)
20. *How mow þey þan shryve þat synne?* (How may they then shrive that sin?)

Early ModE

21. *Ride you far today?*
22. *Is this your friend?*
23. *Will you be there?*
24. *When left he?*
25. *What think you now?*

26. *Who goes there?*
27. *Do you hear, porter?*
28. *Shall we go draw our numbers?*
29. *How many hast thou killed today?*
30. *Why dost thou bend thine eyes upon the earth?*
31. *What sayst thou to her?*
32. *What seem I that I am not?*
33. *Who did strike out the light?*

PROBLEM 11.25: Compare the rule changes for negatives and questions.

Why the rules changed in the way they did is difficult to determine. In the case of negatives, it may have been that speakers felt negatives should always occur before the element that carried the main semantic content being negated, the difference between *He came ← not* and *He did not → come*. We find negatives always preposed in noun phrases: *no man, not a single person*, for example, rather than **man no* or **a single not person*. We must also place negative adverbs of frequency before rather than after the verb: *He hardly slept – *He slept hardly. He had scarcely left when . . . – *He had left scarcely when. . . .* On the other hand, we can place non-negative frequency adverbs either before or after the verb: *He often slept – He slept often. He usually left. – He left, usually.*

In regard to questions, it may have been felt that the principal semantic verb should always occur directly after the subject, as it normally did when the first verb was an auxiliary:

Early ModE: *Will you go? Have you gone? Are you going?* **Went** *you?*
ModE: *Will you go? Have you gone? Are you going? Did you go?*

PROBLEM 11.26: What might explain why speakers wanted the semantic verb to follow the subject?

PROBLEM 11.27: What are we to do with the following sentences (Review Problem 11.20)?

1a. *Have you any money?*
1b. *Do you have any money?*
2a. *Need I stay?*
2b. *Do I need to stay?*
3a. *Do he always be there?*
3b. *Is he there now?*

Whatever the internal and external causes that triggered the change, by the end of the eighteenth century, the negative and question had settled into relatively stable patterns. The negative now regularly occurs before the element being negated: *No money, not enough, did not leave.* The main verb in questions remains after its subject: *Did he* **come**? Both patterns were created simply by redefining what went into the v in the transformational rule.

Restructuring the Verb Phrase

So far, we have examined several grammatical constructions that were once quite different in OE or ME and have completely changed in ModE. But in some other cases, the change is one that is constantly affecting areas of the grammar. Many individual nouns, for example, are still being converted into verbs: *The satellite is in* **orbit**. → *The satellite is* **orbiting**. And many verbs are still converting from one class to another: *The satellite* **orbits**. → *They* **orbit** *the satellite.* → *The satellite* **orbits** *around the moon.* → *The satellite* **orbits** *the moon.* → *The moon was* **orbited** *by the satellite.*

These are changes involving the distribution of individual words. Other syntactic changes involve new transformations. These we have seen in new negative and interrogative patterns. More basic changes involve the deeper structures of a language, such as those we have seen in the rules for the auxiliaries. There we saw a simplification of rules stretching over 1000 years.

A somewhat more abstract change involves the restructuring of a group of elements so that their sequence is not changed but their constituent structure is. For example, a sequence of elements like X Y Z could be restructured either X (Y Z) or (X Y) Z:

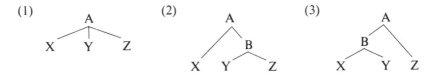

Each of these three structures is represented by the order X Y Z, but they have different structures underlying them.

One example of a structural change like that from (2) to (3) is illustrated by sentences like *He talked over the problem.* While in OE there were **verb + particle** constructions, many of those in ModE have evolved from **verb + preposition** constructions. Until about the fourteenth century, while there was still some degree of flexibility in where the preposition could occur relative to the noun-object, it was possible to place the preposition (or particle) either before or after the noun. The earlier tradition of separable prefixes with verbs much as in Modern German, also contributed to this variable placement. As a consequence, some prepositions have become semantically more and more closely associated with the preceding verb until they become a semantic unit. In conjunction with the variable preposition placement, we developed a pattern in English allowing either *I held up the man* or *I held the man up.* Thus *hold up* is **semantically** a unit but still **grammatically** composed of two parts. The fact that we also require *He was holding up the man* rather than **He was hold upping the man* is further evidence of the semantic-grammatical ambivalence. The grammatical restructuring that went on—and is still going on with many other such pairs—can be represented like this:

Earlier: Later:

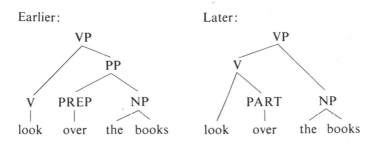

(We rename the PREPOSITION a PARTICLE because as part of the verb, it is no longer a preposition.)

This sort of construction differs from VERB + PREPOSITIONAL PHRASE in some important ways, but much the same kind of restructuring is going on with modern verb + prepositional phrase sequences like *He looked at the man.* VERB + PARTICLE constructions allow passives: *Somebody held up the man → The man was held up by somebody.* But VERB + PREPOSITIONAL PHRASE of the following sort does not: *He lives in Cleveland → *Cleveland is lived in by him. He arrived at noon. → *Noon was arrived at by him. He sings off key. → *Key is sung off by him.* But prepositional phrases after verbs of this next kind **do** allow passives: *He looked at the man. → The man was looked at by him. He asked for my friend. → My friend was asked for by him.*

The beginnings of this passive with the preposition go back at least to Caxton and Malory in the late fifteenth century: *I wylle that my moder be sent for . . . , . . . that he is thus complayend on.* But it is a pattern that has become much more common in modern times. The change undoubtedly was encouraged by the semantic restructuring of VERB + PARTICLE passives, so that now, virtually any VERB + PREPOSITIONAL PHRASE that communicates an action directed toward the object of the preposition seems to allow a passive, suggesting that the combination is becoming a semantic unit. Compare *He held onto the box* and *He stood beside the door.* We can say *The box was held onto* but **The door was stood beside* seems much less likely. Those VERB + PREPOSITIONAL PHRASE constructions that do not allow passives are ordinarily verbs followed by adverbial prepositional phrases of time, place, and manner—prepositional phrases in which the noun is not semantically "acted on" by the verb. Compare *He arrived at Cleveland*

and *Cleveland was arrived at* as opposed to *He arrived at a conclusion* and *A conclusion was arrived at*.

One way to account for this grammatical difference is to assign some adverbial prepositional phrases—those not closely tied to the main verb—to a position in the tree by means of the base rules we have been discussing that would represent the less close connection:

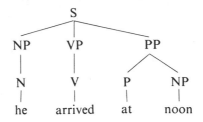

To distinguish this from *He arrived at conclusions,* we have to associate *at* with the verb, but we must at the same time insure that *at* is still classed as a preposition. For like prepositions, it can be brought forward in questions and relative clauses:

What time did he arrive *at*?
The time which he arrived *at* . . .

At what time did he arrive?
The time *at* which he arrived . . .

What conclusions did he . . .
The conclusions which he . . .

At what conclusions did he . . .
The conclusions *at* which he . . .

But the *at* in *arrive at conclusions* is still not as free as a particle:

*He arrived conclusions *at*.

One possible solution is to write a new base rule that would generate a deep structure of roughly this form (compare above):

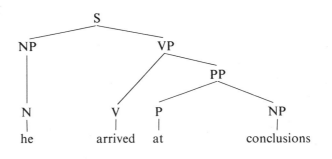

We would be asserting that *at noon* is **not** part of a verb phrase but that *at conclusions* **is** part of the verb phrase. And it is that closeness to the verb that allows the passive transformation.

Along with the great increase in verb + particle constructions, this is a change that is quite in keeping with the kind of general changes we have seen in English over and over again through the last thousand years: English is continually becoming a more **periphrastic** language. The auxiliary verb combinations have multiplied; prepositions have taken over the function of the dative case and the genitive case; articles have become obligatory for singular count nouns. Comparison with *more* has become more frequent than comparison with *-er*. And now, we see two-part verbs developing out of verb + prepositional phrases.

PROBLEM 11.28: We ordinarily make agent nouns out of verbs by adding *-er*: *rob* > *robber*, *fly* > *flyer*, and so on. What are the agentive forms for these: *someone who picks up*: *He is a* _____. *Someone who fixes up*: *He is a* _____. *Someone who sets up*: *He is a* _____. Comment on the claim that *fix up* is grammatically two words, that the past tense form: *fixed up*, not *fix upped*, shows that they have to be considered grammatically un-synthesized.

The Impersonal

A construction that has entirely disappeared in ModE is the **impersonal** sentence, a pattern that with certain verbs apparently lacked a subject:

Hine nanes þinges ne lyste. (Him no things ne desired.)
Me sceamað. (Me shames.)
Him þyrstede. (Him thirsted.)

It is clear from the case of the pronouns (*hine*—accusative, *me*—dative or accusative, *him*—dative) that none of them can be the subject of the sentence. Two things happened to bring about the disappearance of this pattern. First, in Late OE, *hit* (it) began to occur more frequently in the subject position, particularly when the verb took a **sentence complement**:

Hit sceamað me þat he me syhð. (It shames me that he sees me.)
Hit licode him þat ic eode. (It pleased him that I left.)

It is from that pattern that we have ModE sentences such as *It seems that . . .*, *It appears that . . .*, *It pleases me that. . . .* The second cause of its disappearance was in the loss of case distinctions between nominative and accusative/dative among common nouns. So long as the case of the common noun was apparent, it was always clear that the first noun phrase in such sentences was not the subject:

> *Þæm gumum hungrede.* (The men [dative] hungered.)

But when these inflections were lost and the noun was in the singular (impersonal verbs always occurred in the singular), there was no overt indication that the first noun phrase was not the subject:

> *Þe mann hungered.*

On the basis of the overwhelming frequency of the subject-verb order, the first noun phrase was naturally reinterpreted as the subject. (The pattern endured into the sixteenth century in the limited structure *meseems, methinks, me had rather.*)

SUMMARY

The major grammatical changes in Modern English are these:

1. The Nominal system:
    a. Inflections are greatly reduced.
    b. Prepositions largely assume the function of the dative and genitive cases.
    c. *A/the* develop as articles, *this/that – these/those* as demonstratives.
    d. The rules for relative clauses are simplified.

2. The Verbal system:
    a. The auxiliary system greatly expands.
    b. All person endings except third person singular disappear.
    c. Many ablaut verbs become regular.
    d. Many regular verbs (as we shall see) become irregular.
    e. *Do* develops in negative and interrogative patterns.
    f. Many new verb + preposition and verb + particle patterns appear.

3. The Adjectival system:
    a. Comparison evolves from strictly inflected to mixed periphrastic-inflection.
    b. Strong-weak distinctions disappear along with inflections.

4. The Sentence:

    a. Words order settles into S–V–(C).
    b. Negation precedes the negated.
    c. The impersonal pattern disappears.

Chapter 12

BETWEEN GRAMMAR AND PHONOLOGY

SOUNDS

We have seen how semantics and grammar interpenetrate in the continually changing patterns of transitive and intransitive verbs, of new distributions for verbs like *grow*, *spread*, *whisper*, and *teach*. We have also seen how sound patterns and semantics merge in phonetic symbolism, creating words like *teeny*, *boom*, *tinkle*, and *splash*. And we have briefly seen how phonology and grammar have impinged on one another with some very important consequences to the history of the language: When in Late OE, inflectional endings on nouns began to level because they were so lightly stressed, the elaborate case and gender distinctions of OE began to disappear too. And as case distinctions disappeared, English speakers came to rely more and more on an already increasingly regular word order to understand how sentence elements related to one another. And this loss of inflectional complexity and greater reliance on word order very likely encouraged other periphrastic expressions to develop throughout the language, further weakening the need for inflectional distinctions.

Phonology and grammar have interpenetrated in other, less obvious ways. When in the fifteenth century, syllabic inflectional endings on nouns and verbs were well on their way to dropping their vowels in most contexts:

cártĕs > *cárts, ványsshĕd* > *vánished,* the remaining consonants varied according to the kinds of sounds they occurred after. They **assimilated,** became like those sounds. With a few exceptions, voiceless word-final sounds determined voiceless inflectional endings: *bank, banks, banked.* Voiced word-final sounds determined voiced endings: *bag, bags, bagged.* Thus a minor phonological change resulted in a more complicated way to express grammatical distinctions.

Other sound changes have resulted in more obvious grammatical and semantic differences. At one time, English verbs were, with some exceptions, clearly split between those with the regular **dental preterit** ending: *name, named, named,* and those irregular verbs with **ablaut,** or vowel changes: *sing, sang, sung.* But in late ME a number of once regular verbs joined the irregular group. Because of certain conditions which we shall explore in Chapter Fourteen, a sound change modified the vowel quantity in the past tense of many verbs from **long** to **short.** Then a second sound change altered the quality of the vowel in the present tense, raising it to a higher vowel (review page 144). This created two different vowels in present and past tense verb forms. Thus from once regular verbs we now have the following irregular verbs, verbs whose irregularities are quite different in origin from the Indo-European ablaut verbs: *feel–felt, slide–slid, bleed–bled, speed–sped, meet–met, feed–fed, mean–meant, leave–left, hide–hid.* Had the first sound change not occurred, we would pronounce the vowel in the past tense of these verbs as we do the ModE present: *feeled, slided, bleeded, meeted, hided,* and so on. (25, 28, 174)

A yet more extreme kind of sound change has created what we now perceive to be completely different, though grammatically related words. In West Germanic, before the earliest written records, even before the Anglo-Saxons left the Continent, there was a derivational suffix that changed nouns and adjectives into verbs: **-jan.* It gave the new verb a sense of bringing about what the noun or adjective indicated. Thus to the Germanic stem **blōd-* (blood), the suffix **-jan* produced **blōdjan,* meaning to bring about or cause to produce blood. The **-j-* in the ending represents a sound not too different from the first sound in *yet.* It caused the rounded back vowel in the first syllable, the /ō/ in **blōd-,* to **umlaut,** to be pronounced more toward the front of the mouth in anticipation of the front /y/ sound. The /ō/ **assimilated** to the /y/ sound, giving a rounded front vowel we can write as /œ̄/. Not too long after this, the **-j-* disappeared. Then in OE, the rounded front vowel unrounded to /ē/. The whole sequence went like this:

stem	stem + affix	fronting	loss of *-j-	unrounding
*blōd- >	**blōdjan*	> **blœ̄djan* >	*blœ̄dan*	> *blēdan*

We thus have ModE *blood* from *blōd* and *bleed* from *blēdan,* both from the root **blōd.*

PROBLEM 12.1: The same kind of change gives us ModE pairs like *food–feed, knot–knit, doom–deem, drop–drip, stunt–stint, foul–(de)file, brood–breed, tooth–teethe, full–fill.* Sound changes have created other pairs. Match up the pairs, which have been separated into groups (1) and (2):

1. *slack, pass, beacon, holy, day, brass, grass, glass, prize, batch, breach, match, stick, stink, watch, web, learn, do, blithe, fleet, rise, cold.*
2. *deed, make, wake, pace, praise, brazen, float, dawn, slake, bliss, graze, lore, weave, beckon, bake, rear, hallow, cool, stitch, glaze, stench, break.* (97)

What kinds of meaning changes have also occurred?

The pronunciation of words can also change from semi-grammatical causes when grammatical word boundaries are misunderstood. Thus in English, we have *newt, nickname,* and the now archaic *nuncle* because speakers mistakenly attached the *-n* from *an: an ewt, an ekename, an uncle,* to the beginning of the following word. The opposite occurred with earlier *napron, nadder, nauger,* and *numpire.* The ModE *orange,* borrowed from French, differs from its earlier source, Spanish *naranja,* because Old French speakers made the same mistake in the noun phrase *un naranja.*

PROBLEM 12.2: The same mistake has changed the form of a number of foreign borrowings. Two words, often an article and a noun, merged. Here are some borrowings. What are the ModE words?

> **Spanish:** *el lagarto* (the lizard), *la reata* (the rope).
> **French:** *la crosse* (the bishop's crook), *dis mal* (days unlucky), *a las* (oh, weary!).
> **Dutch:** *de kooi* (the cage—for catching birds), *de affodil* (from Latin *asphodelus*).
> **German:** *gar aus!* (all out!—i.e., my beer stein is empty).
> **Arabic:** *al iksīr* (the powder), *al jabr* (a shortening of a longer phrase meaning the reduction—to another form), *al kīmiyā'* (the extracting and mixing of juices), *al kuhl* (the powder), *al qilī* (the ashes of the salt wort), *al manākh* (the weather), *amīr al barh* (commander of the seas—the *barh* was dropped when the word was borrowed by the French), *al ilāh* (the god). In many of these, the second word was borrowed by the Arabic from Greek. All except the last were borrowed into English through French, Latin, or Italian.

STRESS

Unfortunately, a history of the most crucial area where syntax and phonology interact cannot be written with any certainty. When we utter a sentence in

ModE, the pitch of our voices rises and falls in intonation patterns. When we make a statement for example, our voices rise and then almost immediately fall to a pitch below that from which the rise began:

1 = low pitch

2 = middle pitch

3 = high pitch

PROBLEM 12.3: Plot the intonation contour for these sentences:

1. *He went home.*
2. *He went there.*
3. *He went to it.*
4. *Did he leave?*
5. *Did he leave it?*
6. *Did he leave it there?*
7. *What did he leave?*
8. *What did he leave there?*
9. *What did he leave there for?*
10. *Did he leave or stay?*

Use ordinary intonation. Can you predict grammatically when the pitch begins to rise and fall?

As our voices rise and fall in these contours, we stress some parts of words more than other parts, some words in a sentence more than other words. Ordinarily, the pitch begins to rise on the word we stress the most in a phrase, and the word we stress most tends to be the last content word in a grammatical phrase or clause.

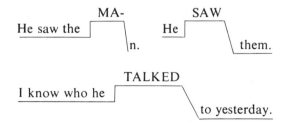

PROBLEM 12.4: What words bear phrase stress in the problem above?

In utterances longer than just a few words, we tend to retard the rhythm of our speech at major syntactic junctures, usually rising one pitch level, from 2 to 3, and then falling not to 1 but back to the original 2, still stressing the last content word of a phrase:

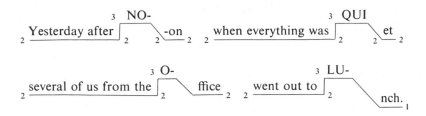

PROBLEM 12.5: Plot the pitch and stress patterns in these sentences. Numbers (6) and (7) have pitch patterns we have not described above.

1. *Unfortunately, everyone who was there on time decided to stay for lunch.*
2. *My friend George, the guy that lives next door, wanted to meet you.*
3. *If you decide you want it now, tell me about it.*
4. *He was therefore unable to decide what to do.*
5. *Therefore, we were unable to decide what to do with all the money.*
6. *George, Bill, Mary, and Nancy were all there.*
7. *I gave him a book, a pen, a piece of paper, and a piece of cardboard.*

In all these cases, stress, pitch, and juncture clearly depend on part of speech and syntactic structure. Unfortunately, we can say relatively little about whether such rules may have been significantly different in OE or ME because the textual evidence is insufficient. (59, 70, 86, 219)

PROBLEM 12.6: We do know that many words we borrowed from the French were stressed on the last syllable: *parDON, paLAIS* (palace), *hoNOUR avenTURE* (adventure), *graMAIRE* (grammar). Here are some verses from Chaucer. Comment on the stress patterns of the words in boldface, citing your evidence.

1. And songen, everych in hys wyse
   The moste solempne **servise**
   By noote . . .
   (And sung, each in his way
   The most solemn service
   By note . . .)
   From **The Book of the Duchess**, ll. 301–3.

2. And Cleopatre, with al thy **passyoun**
   Hyde ye your trouthe of love and your **renoun**;
   From **The Legend of Good Women**, ll. 259–60.

3. This Somonour bar to hym a stif **burdoun,**
   Was nevere trompe of half so greet a soun.
   (This Summoner bore to him a stiff burdoun (*burden*, or bass accompaniment to singing)
   Was never trumpet of half so great a sound.)
   From **The Canterbury Tales**, The General Prologue, ll. 673–74.

4.   But trewely to tellen atte laste,
     He was in chirche a noble **ecclesiaste**.
                    From **The Canterbury Tales**, The General Prologue, ll. 707–8.

We know from metrical evidence that compound words in OE and ME were also stressed on the first syllable. And from metrical evidence, we can be certain that the second root word of a two-word compound was less strongly stressed than the main syllable, but based on spelling evidence, also more strongly stressed than any of its non-root syllables. Thus there were certainly three distinct levels of word-stress in compounds like *tungerefa* (district officer), *beadurof* (bold in battle), and *manslaga* (murderer). Beyond this, we can say relatively little, particularly about the complex patterns of intonation, or about sentence and phrase stress.

In ModE, three **distinctions** in stress seem to be fairly clear. There is primary stress—the loudest stress we hear in monosyllables uttered alone or in the first part of a compound word: *dog, man, house, tree, flophouse, steamboat, highway*. The second degree of stress is most clearly heard in the second half of compound words: *doghouse, steamboat, highway, hambone, foot-sore*. It is also heard in some non-compound words: *Plato, transcribe, remit, elbow, antique*. If the vowel quality is clear, the stress is usually one of the first two degrees. A light degree of stress is more common in polysyllabic words, the one associated with the obscured /ə/ vowel: *allow, except, awful, occur*. All three stresses can be hard in *housekeeper, accidental, takeover, sleighriding, transcribing, inducement, remitted, ecumenical*.

PROBLEM 12.7: Transcribe these words including stress: *antagonisms, pacification, extrasensory, disestablished, carcarriers, protruberances, polydialectal, revisionism, entymology, railroading, encyclopedias, floorcoverings, transportation, telephonically*.

PROBLEM 12.8: What can you tell about sentence stress from the fact that *ne habban* (ne have) was often written *nabben*; *ne eom* (ne am) as *neom*; *ne wylle* (ne will) as *nylle*; *ne wat* (ne knew) as *nat*? What can you tell about stress from the fact that *on* in gerundive phrases like *on hunting* was often written as *a-hunting*, and then dropped entirely? What can you tell about stress from the fact that the OE *ich* (I) became *I* pronounced like the short *i* in *is*, that *art thou* was often written *artow*, *hast thou* as *hastow*, *wilt thou* as *wiltou*; that *he* and *hit* (*he* and *it*) were occasionally written just *a*, that *hit* became *it*; from the fact that in ME the perfect auxiliary *have* was written occasionally as *a*? What do you conclude from these sentences from Early

ModE: *Th'hast found me out, Y'are a scondrel, H'is gone, Let's see't, He looked from one t'other, He'le discover't, Hee'ld tell'm so*?

Phonology has also influenced grammar indirectly when two patterns are so phonologically similar that they could easily be confused and therefore either began to differ or to fall together. The former may have happened when English adopted the Danish third person plural pronouns: *they*, *them*, and *their* to replace the OE *hi/hie*, *him*, and *hira*. Had the initial *th-* sound not replaced the OE initial *h-*, the third person masculine singular, the third person feminine singular, and the third person plural would have become too similar to one another to be easily distinguished:

	nominative	accusative	genitive	dative
Third person masculine singular:	he	hine	his	him
Third person feminine singular:	heo	hi(e)	hi(e)re	hire
Third person plural:	hi(e)	hi(e)	hira	him

The same underlying need to maximally distinguish easily confused forms may have contributed to the development of *she* to replace *heo*. Had it not, the ModE masculine and feminine nominative pronouns would have been too similar to distinguish easily. Of course, this in no way tells us where *schee* came from originally. It seems to have originated in the Northeast Midlands in the twelfth century. (209)

The opposite occurred when the similarity between the OE and ME progressive ending *-ende/-ande* and the gerund *-unge* ending, caused the two to merge, ultimately leading, perhaps, to a much wider use of the progressive. In this case, the structural load carried by the two was not great enough or distinct enough to prevent them from falling together.

Those sound changes which most profoundly affect the phonological structure of a language, though, usually occur independently of the grammar of that language. When a sound changes—or more accurately—when on certain occasions certain speakers begin to use one sound in a word rather than another sound—that sound will ordinarily change in all words, regardless of whether they are nouns, verbs, adjectives, or prepositions. And unless there are predictable conditions or unpredictable analogies, the sound will change in all grammatical contexts. Therefore, the discussion in the next chapter on the ways English sound patterns have changed will largely ignore grammatical and semantic questions.

Chapter 13

PHONOLOGICAL CHANGE

THE IMPORTANCE OF PRONUNCIATION

Linguists and fifth graders alike have labored over a problem that originated sometime during the Middle English period. It was then that sound changes in the language began to lay the groundwork for our present orthographic confusions, so that today the way we spell words no longer accurately represents how we pronounce them. In most other European languages, spelling is more regular. Those who grow up speaking Spanish, German, or Italian, can learn to read and write those languages with fewer of the problems facing an English-speaking child. Those linguists who try to discover how English was pronounced as little as two centuries ago wrestle with many of the same problems: The "fit" between English orthography and pronunciation is at best imperfect and occasionally chaotic. The ways in which our speech has changed can shed some light on these problems.

But the way we pronounce words is important to more than just understanding how we spell. Perhaps more than any other characteristic, our accent assigns us to a geographical area, to a social class in that area. It tells a listener whether we are being formal or informal, casual or intimate. We judge and are judged in turn by how we pronounce our words. Indeed, pronunciation has been a social criterion at least since the first quarter of the twelfth century, no doubt earlier. If we can understand something about how these judgments have come about, about the history of our attitudes toward our pronunciation, more importantly about how our pronunciation has changed, we shall perhaps better understand our own responses to those who speak differently from us.

Because spelling is a major source of evidence of sound changes, we have to understand not only how it has changed in the last 1500 years, but also the principles and history of writing and how they relate to phonology. **Fit** is how well the letters in an alphabet match the significant sounds of a language. An alphabet can have too many symbols[1] for the number of sounds: ⟨qu⟩, ⟨k⟩, ⟨ch⟩, ⟨ck⟩, and "hard" ⟨c⟩, for example, can all represent a /k/ sound: *clique, kid, chorus, sick, cap.* Or an alphabet can have too few symbols to represent sounds: English, for example, has no unambiguous single symbol for the /ž/ sound at the end of *rouge* or the middle of *leisure*; or for the sounds represented by ⟨th⟩ in *thin* or the ⟨sh⟩ in *ship.* And perhaps worst of all, symbols can represent sounds inconsistently: Compare ⟨ough⟩ in *cough, though, tough, hiccough, through,* and *ought.*

THE PHONEMIC PRINCIPLE

PROBLEM 13.1: Here are some words which illustrate the significant sounds in a common dialect of American English, the one spoken around the Great Lakes, and extending more west than east: *dot, pub, crag, this, quit, keg, sad, fawn, wool, thing, hive, chose, shame, rouge, joy, year, wow, zip, ax.* (1) What letters could we drop from the alphabet? (2) What sounds have no individual letter to represent them? (3) What are some of the obvious inconsistencies between letters and sounds?

PROBLEM 13.2: Listen carefully to the sound ⟨t⟩ in these words: *eighth, ten, Bertram, button, butter.* Say *eighth,* but when you get to the /t/ sound, hold your tongue in that position and say *train.* Do the same and say *team.* Are the three sounds the "same"? Are the /t/ sounds in *button* and *butter* the same? How do they differ from the /t/ sounds in *train* and *team*? How many perceptibly different sounds are represented by ⟨t⟩ which we still call /t/

---

1 We shall use three notations in this chapter. Angles, ⟨ ⟩, will enclose letters of the alphabet. Slashes, / /, will enclose categories of sounds. Square brackets, [ ], will enclose specific sounds within a category, a concept which will be fully explained in the next few paragraphs.

sounds? If we require a different symbol for every different sound, why do we not require a different symbol for these different /t/ sounds?

If we listen closely to the sounds we make, we quickly realize that the number of different sounds we can hear exceeds the letters in the alphabet. Indeed, with a little training, we can distinguish literally hundreds of different sounds. But in ordinary listening, we consciously discriminate considerably fewer. Even though physiologically, we produce them in different ways, the /t/ sounds in *Bertram, eighth,* and *ten* are psychologically the "same." Yet even though we unconsciously articulate these /t/ sounds more differently than we do the initial sounds in *sip* and *ship*, we consciously discriminate them much less readily than the initial /s/ and /š/ in *sip* and *ship*.

Actually, all sounds differ. For at a sub-molecular level, no two events or objects are **precisely** alike. As the differences become more gross, we can, if we sharpen our ears, distinguish phonetic characteristics that an untrained observer would not detect. But for the purposes to which the sounds are put, they might still be considered functionally equivalent. It is at this level that the /t/ sounds are functional "sames," or more accurately, are responded to as functionally equivalent members of the same class of /t/ sounds. We respond to the critical class characteristics rather than to the individual differences within the class.

PROBLEM 13.3: At a somewhat different level of analysis, all /t/ sounds are not entirely functionally equivalent. How do we recognize a foreign accent? Does such a speaker substitute different sounds for native sounds? If he does, how do we understand him?

At some level, however, differences do become important enough to make us distinguish sounds as belonging to different significant classes. The ordinary speaker has thresholds of sensitivity for different sounds that require him to distinguish differences according to the rules of the language, rules that he has subconsciously learned. An English speaker must learn to group the very different /t/ sounds into one class, to discriminate them from a similar class of /d/ sounds. He must learn to distinguish the class of /s/ sounds (as in *sip, swing,* and *bus*) from the slightly different class of /š/ sounds (as in *ship, bush,* and *mission*).

The minute differences among the members of these sound classes, however, are not random. We can predict that for a /t/ in *Bertram*, we will retract the tongue slightly to adjust to the /r/ sounds that surround the /t/ sound. In *eighth*, we push the tongue forward to make a /t/ sound, because the following segment which we spell ⟨th⟩ and pronounce /θ/ is made with the tongue between or against the teeth. Each class of significant sounds, all the sounds which taken together as a group we perceive as "sames," are called **phonemes**. The individual members of a phoneme, of the class of sounds, are called **allophones**. Phonemes are written between slant lines, allophones within square brackets. Some of the allophones of the phoneme /d/, for example, are these:

[ḍ] A retracted sound that occurs before or after /r/, as in *droop*.

[ḍ] A fronted sound that occurs before or after sounds spelled ⟨th⟩, as in *width*.

[d̥] A segment made with rounded lips that occurs before or after a sound made with rounded lips, as in *dwindle* or *rude*.

[d] An unrounded alveolar segment (made at the ridge behind the upper teeth) that occurs in environments not specified above, as in *dig* or *rid*.

PROBLEM 13.4: What are some allophones of /k/, /h/, and /n/? Test these categories of sounds in different phonetic environments.

Phonologists have tried to formalize how they discover phonemes and their allophones in any language: (1) They collect thousands of words, recording them in detailed phonetic script. (2) They determine whether any given segment can be predicted on the basis of its environment. (3) Those segments which are roughly alike and (a) can be predicted on the basis of their environments, (b) do not ordinarily occur where the others occur are grouped into the categories called phonemes. In English, for example, the front, middle, and back allophones of /t/ are roughly alike, can be predicted on the basis of their environment, and do not ordinarily occur where any other occurs. On the other hand, the segments [s] and [š] are roughly alike. But their occurrence cannot be predicted because each may occur where the other occurs: *sip–ship*. They therefore belong to two different phonemes. (14, 59, 78, 84, 86, 219)

PROBLEM 13.5: Here is a sample problem in an imaginary language. How many phonemes are in this language? The letters represent sounds as in English. /g/ as in *gun*, /e/ as in *pep*, /o/ as the [ō] in *pope*.

[pemp]–boy	[font]–hill	[tovemf]–cat	[kevek]–door
[pebep]–man	[fenze]–sun	[pombo]–duck	[tont]–cloud
[kont]–house	[sezok]–dog	[sezes]–river	[pedek]–foot
[kogomp]–tree	[poge]–hand	[konde]–apple	[kemve]–nose

This language has two vowel phonemes: /o/ and /e/. We cannot predict where either will occur. The language has six consonant phonemes. (1) There are two allophones belonging to a phoneme we shall symbolize as /N/: [n] and [m]. [n] occurs only before sounds made where [n] is made—on the alveolar ridge behind the teeth, before [t], [d], [s], and [z]. The [m] allophone occurs only before sounds where it is made, at the lips: [p], [b], [f], and [v]. They are roughly alike. Neither occurs where the other does. When one of them does occur, its environment is entirely predictable. Therefore we have one phoneme, which we can symbolize as /N/.

The other six segments can be predicted according to where they occur in a word. The voiceless sounds, sounds made when the vocal cords are not vibrating, [p], [t], [k], [f], and [s], occur only at the beginning and end of words. The corresponding sounds, [b], [d], [g], [v], [z], occur only in the middle of a word. Roughly alike are [b] and [p], [d] and [t], [g] and [k], [f] and [v], [s] and [z]. Neither occurs where the other does. They constitute the pairs of allophones in phoneme classes which we can arbitrarily symbolize as /P/, /T/, /K/, /F/, and /S/. We can now write the first five words in the problem like this: /PeNP/, PePeP/, /KoNT/, /KoKoNP/, /FoNT/.

PROBLEM 13.6: Write five more of the words in phonemic notation. Translate these into allophonic notation: /PeKeNP/, /KoKoK/, /TePoNT/.

PROBLEM 13.7: Suppose by a process similar to what happened in ME, final vowels were lost in this language.

PROBLEM 13.8: Suppose that [p] after [m], and [t] after [n] were also lost. Suppose just one were lost.

PROBLEM 13.9: Suppose that **before** these final vowels and consonants were lost, these words were borrowed into this language: [vedep], [zogop], [vovof], [zozok].

The rationale behind organizing individual sound segments like these into classes of sound segments is three-fold. First, phonemes may have a psychological existence. Asked if *keep* and *cool* begin with the "same" sound, English speakers will answer yes. Asked if *keep* and *cheap*, or *cool* and *tool* begin with the same sound, they will answer no. Speakers of certain other languages will answer differently if their phonology organizes their phonetic segments into different classes. Second, the overall **patterning** of sounds in a language can be better perceived if we study how phonemes rather than individual phonetic segments are organized in a language. As we shall see, English phonemes, the classes of sounds, arrange themselves into a highly symmetrical relationship that would be obscured if we simply cited all the allophones of English. Third, it is more economical to represent sounds phonemically than with individual phonetic segments. English requires fewer than 35 symbols to represent its pronunciation, if we choose to represent that pronunciation phonemically. If we choose to represent it with phonetic segments, we would need as many symbols as there are sounds our ears can detect, and that number reaches into the hundreds. (81)

Modern linguistic science has probably expended more effort in the last two centuries on phonology than it has on any other aspect of linguistic research. The nineteenth century was distinguished by those Scandinavian and German linguists who successfully systematized the regular phonological relationships among a wide variety of related languages across Europe and parts of Asia, the group of languages that has come to be known as the Indo-European family. In this century, linguists have developed elaborate techniques to describe the phonological structure of modern languages. In the last decade, generative linguists have extended the bases of generative grammars to the description of deep and surface phonological structures. (33, 106)

Although generative phonologists have described English sound patterns with considerable generality and have contributed greatly to the study of historical English phonology, it would require too much space to develop the needed background in this text. Therefore, we will rely here on a more conservative theory of phonology. (219)

THE PHONOLOGY OF MODERN ENGLISH

The place to start in a traditional description of English phonology is the physiology of the vocal apparatus. (See Figure 13.1.) Although each part of the anatomy that helps us talk functions primarily in some other capacity (the teeth to bite, the tongue to swallow, the diaphragm to breathe, and so on), we have evolved until those separately functioning organs now also integrate into a complex speech mechanism. As we contract the intercostal muscles along the ribs in short pulsations to push the air through the pharynx and past the glottis, or vocal cords, we allow the cords to vibrate, producing a humming sound, or not. This gives us two large categories of phonological segments: **voiced** and **voiceless** sounds. The vibrations of the vocal cords can be felt by placing the thumb and forefinger on either side of the adam's apple and alternately pronouncing *ss–zz, ff–vv, shh–zhhh*.

PROBLEM 13.10: What are the voiced segments in Problem 13.1? What are the voiceless segments?

Voicing is an important phonological environment. In many languages, including the artificial one in Problem 13.5, segments at the beginning and end of a word are voiceless, while segments between vowels are voiced.

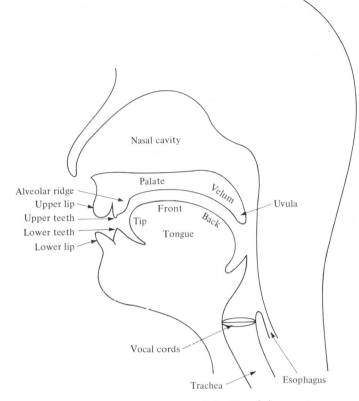

Figure 13.1. The Physiology of the Vocal Apparatus

Consonants

Once the column of vibrating air reaches the oral cavity, its harmonics are modified by the tongue, teeth, tension of the muscles in the mouth and throat, and the volume of the cavity. If there is little or no constriction in the oral cavity, then **vocalic** or vowel sounds are produced. If there is constriction, then **non-vocalic** sounds.

Where and how much we constrict segments allows us to define non-vocalic sounds more exactly. The **consonantal** sounds can be defined by whether we completely stop the air, then release it, giving a group of sounds called voiced and voiceless **stops**: /p/, /b/, /t/, /d/, /k/, /g/ (as in *gun*); or whether the air is allowed to escape while the sound is produced, giving us a class of **continuants**. The continuants can be subdivided by a number of features. If we constrict the passage enough to produce audible friction, then we have a class of voiced and voiceless **spirants**: /f/, /v/, /θ/ (as in *thin*), /ð/ (as in *this*), /s/, /z/, /š/ (as in *she*), /ž/ (as in *leisure*). A combination of a brief top and a spirant is called an **affricate**: /ǰ/ (as in *judge*) and /č/ (as in *church*).

If we let the air escape through the nasal passage instead of through the mouth, then the continuant sounds are **nasal** segments: /m/, /n/, and the sound we usually spell ⟨ng⟩ as in *sing* or as ⟨n⟩ before ⟨g⟩ or ⟨k⟩, as in *think* and *finger*, a sound symbolized /ŋ/. In the context of nasal consonants, vowels take on nasal coloring. In some English and American dialects, the vowels become so nasalized that the nasal consonant disappears: [mæ̃] for *man*, for example. Nasals also tend to obscure the quality of a vowel, often changing it. In some dialects, for example, /e/ before /n/ tends to become /i/, making *pen* and *pin* homonyms.

Because these next sounds are so full of acoustic resonances, they have been classified by some as having both vocalic and consonantal characteristics: /l/, a **lateral** made with the air escaping over the side of the tongue, and /r/, a **retroflex** sound made in a variety of ways, one by humping the back of the tongue up close to the roof of the mouth for medial or final /r/ sounds, another by slightly curling back the tip of the tongue for initial /r/ sounds.

Three segments, **semi-vowels**, are very similar to vowels in their quality of resonance: The /y/ in *yes* and *boy* is close to the vowel we spell ⟨ee⟩ in *eel*. The same is true with the initial /w/ in *wow*, which is close to the vowel we spell ⟨oo⟩ as in *ooze*. The third semi-vowel is /h/. Always voiceless, it takes on the articulatory shape of the following vowel: *heat, head, hat, hut, hot, hoot.* You can demonstrate this by starting to pronounce the /h/ in *heat* but saying *hot* instead.

/r/, /l/, /y/, and /w/ strongly influence the vowels around them because they are so much like vowels. For example, ME ⟨a⟩ historically symbolized the "ah" sound, /a/, as in *father*. By the sixteenth century, this sound changed to an /æ/ sound as in *cat*. But in the environments of /w/, /r/, and /l/, various changes occurred in various dialects: Before /r/, it moved back to /a/, as in *barn* or *start*; after /w/, it also moved back to /a/: *quad, wad*; between /w/ and /r/ or before /l/, it changed to a vowel even further back: *war, quarrel, call, malt, talk*.

The point in the mouth where the speaker most constricts the articulation is the last criterion. Constriction at the lips gives **bilabials**: /p/–/b/–/w/–/m/. Constriction between upper teeth and lower lip gives **labio-dentals**: /f/–/v/. Constriction with the tip of the tongue between or against the teeth gives **interdentals**: /θ/ as in *thick* and /ð/ as in *this*. Constriction with the tongue on the alveolar ridge gives **alveolars**: /t/, /d/, /s/, /z/, /n/, and /l/. Constriction by placing various parts of the tip and blade of the tongue behind the alveolar ridge just at the edge of the palate gives **alveo-palatals**: /ǰ/, /č/, /ž/, /š/, /y/ and /r/. Constriction at the back of the tongue with the soft velum gives the **velars**: /k/, /g/, /ŋ/, /h/ is glottal.

The consonants are arranged schematically in Table 13.1.

PROBLEM 13.11: Transcribe the following words phonemically. Use the vowel

TABLE 13.1   A SCHEMATIC REPRESENTATION OF THE CONSONANTS

	Bilabial	Labio-dental	Interdental	Alveolar	Alveo-pal	Velar
Stop						
vcls	/p/			/t/		/k/
vcd	/b/			/d/		/g/
Spirant						
vcls		/f/	/θ/	/s/	/š/	
vcd		/v/	/ð/	/z/	/ž/	
Affricate						
vcls					/č/	
vcd					/ǰ/	
Nasal	/m/			/n/		/ŋ/
Lateral				/l/		
Retroflex					/r/	**Glottal**
Semi-vowel	/w/				/y/	/h/

symbol /i/ for the letter ⟨i⟩, the vowel symbol /e/ for the letter ⟨e⟩, and the vowel symbol /æ/ for the letter ⟨a⟩. *tip, sin, fill, wet, vend, spend, stack, chest, gyp, thick, lapsed, chin, chink, gem, gym, swing, yelped, hang, is, that, thanks, banged, flange, stripped, script, quit, squelched, glimpsed, hinge, limb, damn, baths, shrink, hatched.*

Vowels

The vowels are classified differently from the consonants. The first distinction is between simple and complex vowels, or between **monophthongs** and **diphthongs**. The monophthongs, or simple vowels, have only one major segment, as in the vowels of *pit, pet, pat, putt, pot, put,* and *ought.* Diphthongs have two clearly perceptible segments in *boy, house,* and *by*; less clearly perceptible in *eat, aid, food,* and *road.*

We produce vowels by shaping the oral cavity with the tongue, so the categories of simple vowels can be defined by where in the mouth we bunch the tongue. Three vowels are **front vowels**: /i/ as in *bit,* /e/ as in *bet,* and /æ/, called **asch**, as in *bat.* Two vowels are **central**: /ə/, called **schwa**, as in *but* or *allow*, and /a/ as in *father.* And three are **back vowels**: /u/ as in *put,* /o/ as in the Eastern New England pronunciation of *boat*, a sound not often heard any more, and /ɔ/, called **open-o**, as in *bought.* These vowels can also be classified by height: /i/ and /u/ are **high**; /e/, /ə/, and /o/ are **mid**; /æ/, /a/, and /ɔ/ are **low**.

A characteristic of the back vowels is lip rounding. Unlike a language like German, rounding is not a significant feature of the English vowel system, whose main contrasts are between back-front and high-low. No two vowels contrast only because one is rounded and the other not. German, on the other hand, has two rounded front vowels: /ü/ and /ö/. They roughly correspond to /i/ and /e/ in frontness and height, but are produced with rounded lips. They contrast with German /u/ and /o/ which are also round, but back.

Using a three-by-three system, we can classify the simple vowels like this:

	Front	Central	Back
High	i		u
Mid	e	ə	o
Low	æ	a	ɔ

Other systems attempt to represent the shape of the oral cavity more graphically and use something that more closely resembles a vowel triangle:

That is, as physiologically /æ/ sounds are both more front and higher than /a/ sounds, so the vowel triangle represents that fact.

PROBLEM 13.12: Transcribe these words using the system outlined above: *pods, coughs, runs, puts, canned, checked, squashed, gnats, axed, odds, as, clucked, width, chinks, jawed, thwacked, strong, this, whizzed, cents, sieves, wronged, chalked, throngs, munch, scratched, crunched.*

PROBLEM 13.13: Consonants can be conditioned by vowels as well as by other consonants. How do the allophones of /k/ differ in *keep* and *cool*? Why do they differ? Consonants can also condition vowels: How do the allophones of /a/, /i/, /æ/, /ɔ/, /u/, and /e/ differ in these words: *hot–hod, bit–bill, bat–bang, bought–bawd, put–pull, pep–pen.* Why do they differ?

Diphthongs have two distinct parts, a **nucleus** and a **glide**. The most obvious diphthongs in English are in *buy, bough,* and *boy.* They begin with a stressed nucleus then glide off into a more constricted vowel: /bay/ or /bai/, depending on how we choose to represent the sound; /baw/ or /bau/; and /bɔy/ or /bɔi/. How we choose between /au/ and /aw/, /ai/ and /ay/, /ɔi/ and

/ɔy/ depends on considerations which need not concern us here. For our purposes, we shall use /i/ and /u/ to represent the ModE offglides.

The less clearly perceptible diphthongs in English are the vowels in these words: (1) *beet*: /bīt/; (2) *bait*: /bēt/ or /beit/; (3) *boot*: /but/; (4) *boat*: /bōt/ or /bout/. The way we use symbols to describe these sounds can become complex because some systems of descriptive phonology use symbols for long vowels to represent what in ModE are diphthongs. But strictly speaking, length alone is not a significant feature that distinguishes one category of English sounds from another. Everything else being equal, diphthongs are temporally longer than monophthongs. But we do not use length as the feature which distinguishes diphthongal *beet* from monophthongal *bit*. It is rather an off-glide and a quality of **tenseness** in a word like *beet* not found in the more lax and monophthongal pronunciation of *bit*. (You can detect this tension by holding the muscle below your jaw directly under your tongue and alternately pronouncing *beat–bit*, *pool–put*, *bate–bet*. The muscles tense for the first sound, but not for the second.)

In this study, however, we will use the unitary symbols to represent these latter diphthongs: /ī/ for the vowel in *eel*, /ē/ for the vowel in *ail*, /ū/ for the vowel in *pool* and /ō/ for the vowel in *pole*, because in OE, ME, and Early Modern English, these were still probably long monophthongs.

$$\begin{array}{ccc} \bar{\imath}/i & & u/\bar{u} \\ \bar{e}/e & \mathrm{ə} & o/\bar{o} \\ & a & \end{array}$$

PROBLEM 13.14: Transcribe these words: *chides, choice, squeezed, sleighs, plowed, speeds, horse, cleared, pears, joked, voiced, through, pierced, though, psyched, veins*. Are there such things as **triphthongs**?

Diphthongs are by far the least stable category of sounds. In the history of English, they have appeared and disappeared more frequently than any other kind of segment. A great variety of diphthongs other than the ones we have been examining here can be heard from Eastern New Englanders, New Yorkers, Cincinnatians, and so on, a fact which testifies to the geographical biases of this text.

PROBLEM 13.15: Find someone raised outside the dialect area we have been illustrating and describe some of his diphthongs.

One characteristic of English phonology requires special, if too brief mention here. The schwa symbol, /ə/, has been used not only for the vowel sound in *but*, /bət/, but also has been used with /r/, /l/, /m/ and /n/ to symbolize the syllabic quality of the final syllables in words like *bother, barrel, bottom*, and *button*; and the stressed vowel quality in words like *burr, sir*, and *her*: /baðər/, /berəl/, /batəm/, /bətən/, /bər/, /sər/, /hər/. A more exact phonetic transcription has a special symbol for the /ər/ sound: [ɚ], and for the stressed /ə/ it has /ʌ/. Thus *but* can be transcribed /bʌt/, while *allow* is transcribed /əlau/. We shall use /ə/ in /ər/ and instead of /ɚ/. Under light stress, the vowel quality of most syllables is also symbolized as /ə/, though sometimes it may tend toward [i] or [ɨ] (a central high vowel), as in the last syllable of *fitted*.

PROBLEM 13.16: Transcribe the following words: *firs, birds, bottomed, rotten, squirrels, earls, fathomed, woolens, squirters.*

PROBLEM 13.17: Transcribe the sentences in Problem 12.5 into phonemic notation, including stress patterns for individual words.

THE DEVELOPMENT OF WRITING

The spelling system that Western Europeans use to represent all these sounds has descended through Latin and Greek from a Semitic system dating from perhaps the seventeenth century B.C., a system which may have had its conceptual origins in the hieroglyphics of ancient Egypt, dating back to c. 3500 B.C. Its successive adaptations from language to language to fit different phonological patterns makes its history a complex one.

The most primitive way to represent an idea, the way that certainly must have led to the invention of writing, is in pictographic representation. Virtually all cultures draw pictures for purposes ranging from telling a story to magic. Many have adapted their pictures to sending or leaving messages. The simplest picture represents in one frame an entire semantic complex. Traffic signs use this system: a picture of a deer or a child represent warnings we can instantly translate into ideas without using intervening words. More complex pictures represent more complex messages:

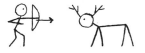

No single element in this message need specifically represent or be represented by any word, though a word can be attached to each element. The total picture simultaneously represents the message.

Because there are several writings systems whose exact origins are unclear, it is impossible to say how many times, once or many, it was realized that part of a picture could represent not only an idea or a physical referent, but the word associated with that referent as well. But at least one person in

the history of the human race recognized that a picture like

represented an idea that need not but might be verbally translated into **words**, into something like *A deer is running*. A picture like this can then be abstracted into components which, by convention, might be attached to words associated with its idea or referent. We could, for example, abstract out of this picture a symbol for the word *deer* and a symbol for the word *running* and write it left to right in English word order:

Graphically, the change from pictographs to ideographs looks like this:

Pre-writing

Words
⟶ Ideas   Ideographic writing
Pictures   Pictures → (symbols) → Words → Ideas

Unfortunately, while this intellectual leap equals any in man's history, a writing system based on ideographs is so unwieldy that only a few members of a culture ever have the time to learn it. Every distinct word needs a different symbol. The problems the Chinese are now having in achieving national literacy are so acute that they are in the process of changing their largely ideographic writing system to an alphabetic one. But they are able to step over an intermediate stage in the development of writing that our ancestors had to pass through.

That next stage was the development of a **syllabic** writing system. Syllabic writing systems arise when particular ideographs become associated with the sound of a particular word, and the symbol shifts from the idea the word represents to part of the word itself. The process is identical to the way we create a **rebus**:

= *I see cartons of milk.*

But this development can occur in two ways. The less efficient way, the way chosen by the Sumerians, was to have a distinctly different symbol for every different syllable. It would be as if we had a completely different symbol for each of these syllables: /ap/, /sap/, /tap/, /stap/, /spat/, /pats/. Although there are many fewer syllables in a language than there are words, such a syllabary would still be exceedingly large.

Another way was devised by the Egyptians and then developed by the

Semitic tribes. Because syllables in the Semitic languages are very simple— often consisting of just CONSONANT + VOWEL, the Egyptians developed a syllabary (to complement their ideographic hieroglyphics) that represented only the first consonant of the syllable. It would be as if the ideograph

represented /bī/, /bē/, /bā/, /bū/, /bō/ and so on. The vowel was

not specifically identified. This was a great advance over the Sumerian syllabary because it isolated one symbol for one sound plus a very limited number of possible second sounds. Since the number of consonants in a language is much smaller than the number of syllables, a syllabary of this sort is much more efficient than one with a distinct symbol for every syllable.

PROBLEM 13.18: Develop both kinds of syllabaries for ten ModE syllables out of an ideographic system of your own device. Then conventionalize the ideographs for easy writing. Why is a syllabary on the Semitic model so much more difficult for a language like English? Choose one of these writing media for your symbols: stone, wood, clay, paper. What difference would media make?

When around the tenth century B.C., the Greeks adopted this Semitic (or as they called it, Phoenician) writing system, they improved on it in one important way. They recognized how useful it would be to have sounds for both consonants and vowels in their language, whose syllables were more complex than just the CONSONANT + VOWEL of the Semitic languages. They used the consonant symbols representing Semitic sounds that did not occur in Greek to represent Greek vowels. The first symbol of the Semitic alphabet, 'aleph, represented a syllable beginning with a glottal stop consonant (like a catch in the throat), a sound useless to the Greeks. But they adapted aleph to represent the vowel now known as *alpha*, our ⟨A⟩ to represent /a/.

The instant this change was accomplished, the Semitic syllabary became our modern **alphabetic** system, a system even more efficient than a syllabary. For now there is no ambiguity about how a syllable is to be pronounced and hence what it is supposed to mean. Thus **beth**, from which **beta** and our ⟨b⟩ derive, no longer stood for any possible syllable beginning with /b/, but by default for only the single segment /b/. Any vowel following /b/ would be overtly represented by its own symbol.

This system was then brought to Southeastern Europe and the Italian peninsula and passed along to various Italic cultures. The Romans modified several letters to meet the needs of Latin phonology and then passed it on once more to the civilizations they dominated and later to those Slavs now in Poland, Czechoslovakia, and Rumania who followed the Roman Catholic

Church. The Russians, Bulgarians, and Serbians adopted the Greek-Cyrillic alphabet from Greek missionaries.

When the Germanic invaders succeeded the Roman legions in fifth century Britain, they brought with them an alphabet they had probably borrowed from some northern Italic culture in the second or third century B.C., an alphabet similar enough to both the Roman and Greek alphabets to indicate its derivation, but distinctively different both in form and in the order of the letters. The Germanic tribes called it **runic** writing, or secret writing. The letters, called **runes**, were believed to have magical properties. The alphabet was called the **fuðarc** after the first six letters: ᚠ ᚾ ᚦ ᚨ ᚱ ᚲ The letters were very angular, presumably because they most often had to be cut into stone or wood. A good many runic inscriptions and documents survive, the most famous perhaps being passages of a religious poem, "The Dream of the Rood [cross]" engraved on the Ruthwell Cross, a large stone monument erected in Dumfriesshire, Scotland, around the end of the seventh century or beginning of the eighth.

When the Christian missionaries from the Continent converted Britain in the seventh century, they naturally enough brought with them their Latin script, which quickly replaced the pagan-tainted fuðarc. But when somewhat later the Irish missionaries replaced Roman missionaries, they brought with them a modified Latin script called **Insular** script, which became the form of writing used in most OE documents.

The later Anglo-Saxons, however, did adopt two symbols from the runic fuðarc: After earlier using the **digraph** (two letters representing one sound) ⟨th⟩ to represent Greek words with **theta**, [θ], they replaced it around A.D. 900 with the rune ⟨þ⟩, **thorn**, which represented either [θ] or [ð]. They also borrowed **wynn**, ⟨ᵽ⟩, which at first represented the sound now symbolized by ⟨w⟩. They also adapted a Latin letter, ⟨d⟩, with a line through it, ⟨ð⟩, and called it **eth**. It also came to represent the two interdental spirants, ⟨ð⟩ and [θ].

Other major differences in the inventory of OE letters from ModE included the presence of the Latin **ligature** (two letters written as one) called *asch*: ⟨æ⟩, representing /æ/ as in *cat*. Also present was an Irish form, **yogh**: ⟨ʒ⟩, first used to represent a high front sound close to the /y/ in *yes*, later some other sounds, all usually represented in modern OE texts with ⟨g⟩. Rare or entirely absent from the OE alphabet were the letters for ⟨q⟩, ⟨z⟩, ⟨x⟩, and ⟨w⟩. ⟨k⟩ was infrequent. Originally, the English used ⟨uu⟩, "double-u" to represent the /w/ sound, but later replaced it with wynn. But the double-u convention was adopted on the Continent, the letters turned into a ligature, and reintroduced into England by Norman scribes. ⟨qu⟩ was also introduced later by Norman scribes to transliterate OE ⟨cw⟩. ⟨x⟩ occurred in OE, but only in foreign words.

The Norman scribes were also responsible for introducing (or re-introducing) various digraphs: ⟨th⟩ for /ð/ and /θ/; ⟨sh⟩ for /š/; ⟨ch⟩ for ⟨c⟩

when pronounced /č/; ⟨ph⟩ for the /f/ sounds in Greek words and the ⟨gh⟩ for ⟨h⟩ in words like *riht–right, cniht–knight,* and so on. They also reversed the ⟨hw⟩ to ⟨wh⟩ in words like *hwil–while.*

By the end of the Middle English period, under the influence of continental scribal practice, the symbols ⟨æ⟩, ⟨ð⟩, ⟨þ⟩, and ⟨p⟩ had disappeared and a new set of spelling conventions had replaced them. ⟨z⟩, ⟨q⟩, and ⟨w⟩ had also been introduced. Not until the 16th century, however, did ⟨u⟩ and ⟨v⟩ come to be distinguished from one another. Earlier, for example, words like *ever* and *until* were spelled *euer* and *vntil.* ⟨j⟩ was originally an elongated version of ⟨i⟩ in numbers like *xiij.* A word like *just* was spelled *iust.* Not until the seventeenth century did ⟨j⟩ consistently come to have its modern value of /ĵ/. (41, 69, 225)

SOUND AND SPELLING

In order to understand how the relationship between spelling and pronunciation has evolved and how to interpret older spellings, we have to distinguish between two ways that spelling can relate to sound: By **symbols** and by **markers**. The **symbols** directly represent a sound segment. Some symbols are simple: ⟨t⟩, ⟨o⟩, and ⟨p⟩ in *top* each represents a significant class of sounds: /tap/. Other symbols are complex digraphs: ⟨sh⟩ represents /š/; ⟨th⟩ represents either /ð/ or /θ/, for example. Among the vowels, ⟨ee⟩, ⟨ea⟩, ⟨ei⟩, ⟨ie⟩, and so on, can all function as units to represent diphthongs.

Markers do not directly represent their own sounds, but rather indicate the sounds that preceding or following symbols stand for. The "silent-e" in *tide* is a marker indicating the ⟨i⟩ is to be pronounced not /i/ but /ai/. Either ⟨i⟩ or ⟨e⟩ after a ⟨c⟩ are both symbols and markers: They symbolize the /i/ or /e/ sound in *city* and *cell* and mark the ⟨c⟩ as /s/. ⟨a⟩, ⟨o⟩, or ⟨u⟩ after ⟨c⟩ would indicate both their own vowel quality and mark the ⟨c⟩ as /k/: *cut, cot, cat.* The same letters after ⟨g⟩ generally mark whether it is to be pronounced /g/ or /ĵ/: *gasp, got* and *gum* vs. *gem* and *gin.*

Double consonants perform the same double function: They redundantly mark their own quality and mark the monophthong before them: *biter* vs. *bitter.* The double consonant convention reflected phonetic reality in Early ME, because in OE, double consonants were actually pronounced longer than single consonants. And in ME, short vowels inevitably occurred before doubled consonants.

The silent-e convention arose in Late ME. Because many words with a final ⟨e⟩ had long vowels preceding, there arose the practice of adding ⟨e⟩ to indicate any long vowel, even where the ⟨e⟩ did not etymologically belong: *ham > home, pin > pine.* On the other hand, final ⟨e⟩ in some words of

Latin derivation do not mark a diphthong: *doctrine, infinite, private, resolve, obdurate* (though Milton dropped the ⟨e⟩ in all these).

Other letters which are neither symbols nor markers are merely excrescent. The ⟨b⟩ in *debt*, the ⟨h⟩ in *hour*, the ⟨b⟩ in *lamb*, the ⟨p⟩ in *psychology* serve no phonetic purpose. Some letters, though, only appear to serve no purpose: The ⟨n⟩ in *condemn, hymn*, and *damn* seems to be useless, but it represents a phonetic segment that is realized in derived words: *hymnal, condemnation, damnation*. The same is true with the ⟨g⟩ in *sign*, for it is a symbol in *signify*. (228).

PROBLEM 13.19: Identify whether the letters in boldface are symbols, markers or excrescent. You should consider how words derived from these words are pronounced:

> **g**host, ta**l**k, **q**uit, bui**l**d, lea**t**her, gau**g**e, p**l**aid, resi**g**n, frui**t**, maneu**v**er, t**w**o, t**h**yme, ba**k**e, **g**uard, **g**uest, **sc**ene, dis**c**ern, pat**c**h, **j**udge, hi**gh**, lea**r**n, bott**l**e, **ch**oir, **g**uise, a**cc**ent, gli**m**pse, of**t**en, recei**p**t, **k**now, t**h**umb, deb**t**, **g**nostic, ba**ck**, sie**v**e, jump**ed**.

By the end of the ME period, roughly during the late fifteenth century, the inventory of letters and most conventions of English spelling had been introduced. Many of the conventions would be used erratically for some time to come, since writers generally felt no obligation to spell consistently. Francis Bacon's **Essays** (1625), for example, has several instances of inconsistently spelled words: *betwene–between, frendship–friendship, wisdom–wisedome*. Not until the eighteenth century did printers finally begin to impose the consistency we adhere to today.

Unfortunately, several events conspired to disturb what might eventually have developed into a truly consistent spelling system. Close to the time when printing was introduced into England, the last quarter of the fifteenth century, English speakers in most dialect areas had begun to change the way they pronounced certain vowels. But over the next three centuries, printers, a notoriously conservative group, were fixing the general rules of spelling according to earlier conventions. Moreover, many of the early printers had learned their trade on the Continent and were not always entirely familiar with English spelling. At just about the same time, the prestige of classical learning prevented scholars from thoroughly Anglicizing the Latin and Greek spellings of those many words which they were importing into the language. So as a consequence of Continental spelling conventions imposed on a Germanic language filled with Latin and Greek words at a time when pronunciation was beginning to change drastically while printers, often foreign trained, were fixing their conventions on the basis of earlier pronunciations, English spelling achieved its present state, much to the grief of fifth graders and historical linguists alike.

RECONSTRUCTING THE PAST

We can now consider how we deduce from different kinds of evidence the way English speech and writing have related to one another through the last 1500 or so years. To understand these changes, we have to understand how linguists reconstruct sound systems, what kinds of evidence and logic they use when they try to describe how an Anglo-Saxon would have pronounced a word fifteen centuries ago.

Start with some assumptions: When a sound changes, it changes in similar environments in the same way unless special circumstances dictate otherwise. That is, if an /a/ sound changes to an /ɔ/ sound, then all /a/'s ordinarily change to /ɔ/'s in all similar environments. Inconsistencies can be explained in a number of ways: First, a word that still has, for example, an /a/ instead of the expected /ɔ/ might have been borrowed from a dialect in which the sound change did not occur. For example, certain words spelled with ⟨a⟩ in OE began to turn up in ME spelled with ⟨o⟩ or ⟨oo⟩, indicating that an /a/-like sound was changing to something more like an /o/-like sound. Thus OE *hal* became ME *hool*, which became ModE *whole*. But the word *hale*, as in *hale and hearty*, also descends from *hal*. The ⟨a⟩ in *hale* contradicts the generalization that /a/-like sounds became /o/-like sounds. The explanation is that standard English, generally descended from East Midland dialects north of London, borrowed *hale* from the more Northern dialect areas where the ⟨a⟩ did not change to ⟨o⟩.

PROBLEM 13.20: Since we know *hale* was borrowed, can we conclude that it was borrowed before or after the change from ⟨a⟩ to ⟨o⟩? What information about dating changes do such facts give us? What date do we want concerning *hale*?

Second, a word that still has a segment that should have changed might be based by analogy on another form of the word in which the change did not occur. The /č/ in *chosen*, for example, is based on the analogy of the present tense pronunciation of *choose*. The original perfect participle in OE, *gecoren*, had a hard /k/ sound, quite in accord with the phonological rules, and would not have changed to /č/. We "should" now pronounce the perfect participle of *choose* as something like /kurən/ or /kərən/: *He has cooren it.*

Third, a sound ordinarily lost or changed might be reintroduced into a word because of a spelling pronunciation. *Balk* was for many years rhymed with *walk*, both having lost their /l/ before /k/ in accord with a general loss of /l/ between /ɔ/ and /k/. But it is not uncommon to hear it now pronounced /bɔlk/. Or a sound might be inconsistently changed by **false etymology**: The ⟨th⟩ in *author* and *throne* was introduced by ME scribes because they thought they were Greek words and should have the ⟨th⟩ spelling. The Old French words were *autour* and *trone*.

Finally, some words just defy explanation because we do not have enough solid evidence to decide on any answer. Most words spelled ⟨ea⟩ are now pronounced /ī/: *weak, read, meat, seat*, etc. But four are pronounced /ē/: *steak, break, great*, and *yea*; and several are pronounced /e/: *head, bread, death, breath*, etc. All were at one time pronounced /ē/. We can invent explanations: The four /ē/ words were borrowed from a dialect in which /ē/ did not change to /ī/. The /e/ words resulted from a sound change that often shortened /ē/ to /e/ before alveolar or dental sounds. But finally, these are *ad hoc* statements made simply to account for exceptions.

But unless we assume that sound changes are basically regular, we cannot hope to generalize about phonological change. We would otherwise be left with only a mass of random changes. Both historical evidence and our aspirations to formulate scientific "laws" deny this as a possibility we can seriously consider.

PROBLEM 13.21: In some cases, it is possible to reconstruct hypothetical forms of earlier pronunciations even when evidence from writing is not available. Imagine a cataclysm has cut off communications around the world for 500 years, destroying all forms of writing that might have recorded pronunciations both before and after. Here is some evidence about pronunciation collected from languages for the year 2550. We are fairly certain these languages are related and that each set of words all descend from some common ancestor word we are trying to reconstruct. Argue for your interpretation of the data.

	British	Irish	Ameri-can	Cana-dian	Austra-lian	New Zealander	Jamai-can	Bermu-dan
1.	/drī	dri	trī	tərī	trē	trī	ri	ti
2.	dap	dap	tab	tab	tɔp	tɔp	ap	ta
3.	zdik	zdik	stig	sətig	stek	stek	stek	sti
4.	guk	guk	kug	kug	kok	kok	kuk	ku
5.	gēn	gen	kēn	kēn	kæŋ	kēŋ	kēn	ken
6.	bōst	bost	pōzd	pōsəd	pɔst	pōst	pōst	pos/

In this kind of analysis, in external reconstruction, we try to discover cognate words from different languages by formulating regular phonological relationships among the words. Once we discover these relationships, we can be fairly certain that the words descended from some roughly common source. We can then reconstruct that hypothetical earlier form by piecing it together out of those sound features which correspond most frequently and most widely. No single entire word identical to an ancestral form need now exist.

The most widespread phonological form or feature (voicing, spirancy, nasality, for example) that cannot be attributed to borrowing is a strong candidate for being closest to the original form. In (1) in Problem 13.21, for example, the common segments in (1) could be reconstructed as /t/, /r/, /ī/, or /trī/. (3, 14, 91, 128, 188)

PROBLEM 13.22: Here are some cognate words from several modern and ancient languages that we shall assume we already know are related. Reconstruct the phonologically earliest form for only the sounds in boldface. When you have sorted out the relationships, phrase them in this way: Sound X > sound Y. Then using the kinds of categories of sounds listed in Table 13.1, group the sound changes into **categories** of sound changes. Keep in mind that we are not assuming that any of the sounds in the words listed here came from any of the other listed words. Rather, all these sounds in boldface in all the words descended from some earlier unrecorded sound in some unrecorded word, a sound and word that may be identical to any of the relevant sounds or words or quite different. But assume that that earlier sound is probably similar to the more geographically widespread one or the one found in a much earlier language. The ⟨bh⟩, ⟨dh⟩, ⟨gh⟩ initial sounds in Sanskrit (the earliest records date from c. 1500 B.C.) are voiced stops followed by a slight puff of breath. Unless otherwise stated, the non-English word is Latin. The words are spelled in ordinary orthography, not in phonemic or phonetic transcription. Give the boldfaced consonants their ordinary values. ⟨th⟩ spells either /θ/ or /ð/. (Lith. = Lithuanian, Old Bulg. = Old Bulgarian, Sans. = Sanskrit, Gk. = Greek, Russ. = Russian, Pers. = Persian.)

thorp–**troba** (Lith. house)
yoke–**yugam** (Sans.)
bear (carry)–**bhr.** (Sans.)
nephew–**nepos**
deep–**dubus** (Lith.)
five–**pente** (Gk.)
fee–**pecu** (cattle)
have–**capere**
fish–**piscis**
lip–**labia**
thunder–**tonāre**
knee–**genu**
three–**trēs**
foot–**pēs**
flood–**plōtós** (Gk.)
apple–**abhal** (Old Irish)
cold–**golotu** (Old Slavonic–ice)

sleep–**slabŭ** (Old Bulg. slack)
tooth–**dentis**
mead–**madhu**–(Sans.)
hundred–**centum**
brother–**bhrātr**–(Sans.)
two–**dva** (Russ.)
father–**pidar** (Pers.)
ten–**decem**
do–**dhā** (Sans.)
acre–**ager**
hemp–**cannabis**
head–**caput**
kin–**genus**
heart–**cridhe** (Irish)
çardhas (Sans. crowd)–**herd**
hump–**kumpas** (Old Slavonic)
grind–**ghr̥shati** (Sans.)

PROBLEM 13.23: If the change had not occurred, how might we now pronounce these next words? *cake, fat, feed, fight, hawk, hunger, teach, throw, thing, town, true, heal, holy, finger, deed, deft, dare, gate, goose, ghost, comb, quick, club, care, both, hope, hobby, pear, pine.*

PROBLEM 13.24: There seem to be in English a good many exceptions to these sound changes. We have not only tooth with /t/ derived from IE */d/,[2] but also from the same root, *dentist, dental, indent,* and so on with the unchanged /d/. We have *heart* with /h/ derived from IE */k/, but also the related cognates *courage* and *cardiac* with unchanged /k/. Why?

The law which Problem 13.22 suggests was formulated by Jacob Grimm in 1822. But a number of nagging exceptions seemed to contradict his generalization. Where the rule predicted the IE /p/, /t/, and /k/ should become the voiceless spirants /f/, /θ/, and /h/, they instead became Germanic voiced spirants, /ƀ/ (a bilabial spirant), /ð/, and /ɣ/ (a velar spirant), which in OE became /b/, /d/, and /g/. In addition, /s/ in some cases seemed to become /r/, a change apparently not related to Grimm's Law:

/t/ in IE *pater did not become /θ/ but /d/ in OE *fæder* (father).
/p/ in IE *sept did not become /f/ but /b/ in German *sieben* (seven).
/k/ in IE *swekrus did not become /h/ but /g/ in Old High German *swigar* (mother-in-law).
/s/ in IE **wes-* did not remain /s/ but became /r/ in OE *wæron* (were).

In 1875, Karl Verner discovered that the reason for the discrepancy had been obscured by another, subsequent change. In IE, two syllable words could be stressed on the first or a subsequent syllable: IE *pater > (father) vs. IE *bhráater (brother). This difference disappeared in the Germanic languages when the stress in all words shifted to the root syllable: Thus IE *pater > Gmc *faðer (the /t/ > /ð/ change was an intermediate stage before /d/). Verner discovered that if a relevant consonant were in a syllable **following an unstressed syllable**, then Grimm's Law did not operate. It is for this reason we have pairs today like *seethe/sodden, was/were, raise/rear, lose/ (for)lorn.* In each case, the second word of the pair was originally a polysyllabic word stressed on what was earlier, a second syllable. The first word in each pair had initial stress. The same IE sounds, */s/ and */t/ became two different sounds, */s/ or */r/ and */ð/ or */d/ because of that difference.

PROBLEM 13.25: Assume again the year is 2550. You have just discovered in the ruins of a city once located on the southern tip of Lag Nizhian a chest

---

2 Here, we return to the use of * to symbolize a root.

full of books, letters, diaries, newspapers, and so on dating from about the last third of the twentieth century. Here are some excerpts from the materials. Assuming we can understand them and many other documents we have found, what kinds of tentative judgments can you make about pronunciation from them?

1. A letter from a seven-year-old to a friend:

Deer Jim, wel, it luks lighk them sientists hav dun it at last. Thei sed that they new how to fiks up the woter in the leyk so that it wood nat meyk poyzin gass eny mor. They are goin to pump it ful of orinj jus. I hope they are rite becaus I shoor am tird of livving undergrawnd like thiss. My father sez that it wasn't becauz of hiz fakteries pellutin the wauder. It was al the hippyz takin baths in it. The sientists say that evrythin will be OK in just a fyu munths. I hope so. Yer frend in Ellinoy, Tom.

2. A poem:

I think that I shall never see / A bug as lovely as a flea, / A flea who hops around all day / And never has to ride a sleigh / A bug whose passion burns all night / And never bites you out of spite. / So every constellation's sun / should shine its brilliance on such one.

3. Some jokes:

a. When the three children of a rancher inherited his ranch, they called it "Focus" because that's where the sons raise meat.
b. Why did the fly fly? Because the spider spied her.
c. Knock knock. Who's there? William. William who? Will y' meet me 'round the corner in half an hour?
d. What's black and white and red all over? A newspaper.

4. Advice from a spelling book:

Do not confuse the spelling of these words: *affect–effect, principle–principal, accept–except, emigrant–immigrant, compliment–complement.*

What other books, documents, and so on, would you like to have?

This kind of evidence is used for internal reconstruction. Linguists use spelling, particularly by those who are uneducated, or better yet, half-educated. There are two kinds of spelling errors, however. First, simple misspellings. If someone writes *dum* for *dumb*, we know the ⟨b⟩ is not pronounced. Second, there are **reverse spellings**. If someone writes *plumb* for *plum*, we know that the final ⟨b⟩ is probably not being pronounced in *dumb*. Otherwise, he would not use the *dumb* spelling for a word like *plum* which never had a /b/ at the end (at least in Modern English).

Linguists also use poetry, if it can be established that the poet was a strict rhymer and that he was not using conventional rhymes like *rain–again*; puns, quibbles, jokes, and other kinds of word-play that depend on pronunciation; spelling manuals and for English, at any rate, the vast amount of printed advice from orthoepists of the sixteenth century on, those who write about spelling and pronunciation. It is not always possible to specify exactly how a word was pronounced, but it is often possible to estimate whether two words were pronounced almost alike, which is almost as good. And if a good rhymer never rhymed two words that were spelled alike, we also know when two were probably not pronounced alike.

PROBLEM 13.26: Here are some rhymes and puns from Shakespeare (c. 1600), Pope (c. 1700), and Wordsworth (c. 1800). Comment.

> Shakespeare: *tears* (noun)–*hairs, case–ease, eate–hate, say–sea, shape–sheep.*
> Pope: *weak–take, eat–state, shade–dead, speak–take, sea–obey.*
> Wordsworth: *trees–please, revealed–steeled, heal–feel, peers–years, dreams–seems.*

PROBLEM 13.27: Here are a few dated spellings with OE and ModE related words. Comment on the consonants. *behaf*–1400 (OE *bi-healfe*, ModE *behalf*); *bight*–1500 (OE *bitan*, ModE *bite*); *faul*–1450 (OE *ful*, ModE *foul*), *doombe*–1598 (OE *dom*, ModE *doom*), *wore*–1350 (OE *werre* ModE *war*).

Another, more complex way to reconstruct phonological history from internal, contemporary evidence is to examine how current sounds are distributed in the words of a language. For example, /v/ never occurs as the initial sound in ModE words derived from native OE words (with the exceptions of *vat, vixen, vent* (as in *coat vent*), and perhaps *vane*). Unless a sound change devoiced all initial /v/ sounds, we can assume that all OE words had only initial /f/ sounds.

PROBLEM 13.28: Examine the linguistic sources of words beginning with /j/ and /z/, or which have /ž/ anywhere in them. Comment.

PROBLEM 13.29: What is unusual about the distribution of /ŋ/ in English?

It should be noted here that the data in the following Problems are rather misleading. They are neat, clear, and consistent. But in perhaps no other area of historical linguistics is it more difficult to interpret the data. Beginning with the mere decipherment of the often dim and illegible handwriting on a crumbling manuscript, the problems of interpreting the relationship between spelling and pronunciation abound. What were the conventions for representing sounds? Were only phonemic distinctions observed? What do vowel digraphs like ⟨io⟩ or ⟨ea⟩ represent? Who was the original author of the manuscript? What was his dialect? What was his social class? How old was he? When did he write the manuscript? Did he write it in his native dialect area? Or was he influenced by another dialect area? How educated was he? If he was badly educated, how can we know whether misspellings were the result of attempts at phonetic writing or of ignorance?

Is the manuscript a copy? Who copied it? What was his dialect? His education? How old was he? Was the scribe a consistent speller? Were there historically two forms for a single word? In regard to poetry, did a particular poet rhyme accurately? Did he choose variant forms of words for rhyming purposes? Did those commenting on spelling and pronunciation really know what they were talking about? There is some evidence to suggest that many did not.

In short, there is very little in the following Problems to suggest the practical difficulties a historical linguist faces in the attempt to reconstruct from the best texts pronunciation that has long since disappeared. (214)

THE PHONOLOGY OF OLD ENGLISH

We have available several different kinds of evidence to help us reconstruct the phonological patterns of a dead language, but we must have a key to the system to begin with. If we discovered a completely unknown language written in a completely unknown orthography, no amount of purely written evidence would suggest how to pronounce it. At one time, scholars had no idea how to read Egyptian hieroglyphics. But the discovery of the Rosetta Stone in 1799 with its simultaneous translations of the same passage in Greek, Egyptian demotic script, and Egyptian hieroglyphics gave them the key. Unfortunately, no such key has been found for the writings left by various South and Central American cultures, making them largely indecipherable.

Fortunately for those investigating the history of English, however, the Latin-based script used by Latin and Irish monks corresponded rather well with the spoken Latin on which it was based, a language we **do** know how to pronounce. Thus given the Latin letter ⟨I⟩ and our knowledge that in Latin it represented only either short /i/ or long /ī/, we can conclude that the OE word written *lim* was certainly not pronounced like the ModE descendant of the form, not like the ModE *lime* /laim/, as in *bird-lime*.

Vowels

The letters used for vowel sounds in Late OE (c. 900–1100) were these: ⟨e⟩, ⟨æ⟩, ⟨a⟩, ⟨i⟩, ⟨o⟩, ⟨u⟩, ⟨y⟩. Earlier manuscripts (c. 800) used ⟨œ⟩ as well, but this letter disappeared before Late OE. We can assume that the sounds these letters represented roughly corresponded to their Latin equivalents:

$\langle$a$\rangle$ = /a/ or /ā/ $\langle$ æ$\rangle$ = /æ/ or /$\bar{æ}$/ $\langle$e$\rangle$ = /e/ or /ē/
$\langle$i$\rangle$ = /i/ or /ī/ $\langle$o$\rangle$ = /o/ or /ō/ $\langle$u$\rangle$ = /u/ or /ū/

(The letter $\langle$y$\rangle$ we shall deal with in a moment.)

PROBLEM 13.30: Unfortunately, Anglo-Saxon scribes did not use diacritical marks (lines over letters, strokes, dots, and so on) to distinguish long vowels from short. Indeed, the lack of any such marks unambiguously indicating length means that we do not know from OE orthography alone whether long-short distinctions even existed in OE. Here, however, are some data that will suggest whether long-short distinctions did exist. You can use both internal and external methods of reconstruction. (Assume that doubled letters and two-letter sequences like $\langle$ei$\rangle$, $\langle$au$\rangle$, $\langle$ui$\rangle$ are diphthongal or long in the non-English examples. Length marks have been supplied in some cases.)

OE *lim* > ModE *limb–limr* (Ice.), *lem* (Dan., Swed.)
OE *lim* > ModE *lime lijm* (Dut.), *līm* (Ice.), *liim* (Dan.), *leim* (Ger.)
OE *ham* > ModE *home–heim* (Dut.), *heimr* (Ice.), *heim* (Ger.)
OE *ham* > ModE *ham–hamme* (Ger.), *höm* (Ice.), *ham* (Dut.)
OE *clif* > ModE *cliff–klif* (Dut., Ice.), *klippe* (Swed.)
OE *wif* > ModE *wife–wijf* (Dut.), *vīf* (Ice.), *weib* (Ger.)
OE *ful* > ModE *foul–vuil* (Dut.), *fūll* (Ice.), *fuul* (Dan.), *faul* (Ger.)
OE *ful* > ModE *full–vol* (Dut.), *fullr* (Ice.), *full* (Swed.), *voll* (Ger.)
OE *ded* > ModE *deed–daad* (Dut., Dan.), *dāð* (Ice.), *dēds* (Gothic)
OE *bed* > ModE *bed–bed* (Dut.), *bett* (Ger.), *badi* (Gothic)
OE *bot* > ModE *boot–boete* (Dut.), *bōt* (Ice.), *bōta* (Gothic)
OE *top* > ModE *top–top* (Dut., Dan.), *toppr* (Ice.), *topp* (Swed.)
OE *dæl* > ModE *deal–deel* (Dut., Dan.), *dails* (Gothic), *theil* (Germ.)
OE *æt* > ModE *at–at* (Ice., Gothic), *ad* (Dan.)

From the external evidence, from comparisons with other languages, we can conclude that OE had long and short vowels. The evidence shows that for the most part, cognate words in Germanic languages have corresponding long-short distinctions: Danish *lem–liim*. Since it is unlikely that this difference developed independently in Modern Danish, German, Swedish, Dutch, Icelandic and in Gothic, but not in OE, we can assume that OE also inherited length from its Germanic ancestor.

On the basis of the internal evidence (though there are many exceptions to this generalization which we shall explore below), words which had long vowels in OE correspond to ModE words with diphthongs: OE *lim* > ModE *lime*. Words with short vowels in OE have monophthongs in the descendant

ModE words: OE *lim* > ModE *limb*. Apparently then, ModE diphthongs are the regular modern reflex of OE length.

If we can trust these conclusions, then we assume these OE vowels:

The precise quality of any of these sounds is impossible to reproduce of course, but they must have been close to these: /i/ as in *sit*; /ī/ as in a monophthongal pronunciation of *seat*; /e/ as in *set*, /ē/ as in monophthongal *sate*; /æ/ as in *cat*; /ǣ/ as in *cad*; /a/ as in *hot*, /ā/ as in *hod*; /u/ as in *pull*, /ū/ as in monophthongal *pool*; /ɔ/ as in *bought*, /ō/ as in *boat*.

PROBLEM 13.31: Because for a time, the letter ⟨y⟩ was consistently used only in certain words where we now have ⟨i⟩, we might suspect that it represented a sound not yet discussed. Here is a body of data. Using both internal and external methods of reconstruction, what might that sound represented by ⟨y⟩ have been like?

OE hyd > ModE hide–huid (Dut.)   OE fyr > ModE fire–vuur (Dut.)

OE cyssan > ModE kiss–koss (Ice.)   OE cyning > ModE king–konung (Swed.)

OE synn > ModE sin–sünde (Ger.)   OE bryd > ModE bride–brūðr (Ice.)

OE yfel > ModE evil–übel (Ger.)   OE fyllan > ModE fill–fulljan (Goth.)

OE fyst > ModE fist–vuist (Dut.)   OE dynnan > ModE din–dön (Dan.)

The cognate languages have rounded vowels, front or back, where OE had ⟨y⟩. But in most ME texts, this ⟨y⟩ came to be consistently respelled ⟨i⟩, indicating that the sound it represented had by then merged with the high front /i/ and /ī/. Therefore, in OE ⟨y⟩ almost certainly represented a sound that originally shared both rounded and front qualities. It was a rounded high front vowel, an umlauted vowel that approximated an /i/ with rounded lips. The umlauting resulted from the change in pre-historical OE which we have already described. The digraph ⟨œ⟩ in Early OE represented a rounded mid-front vowel corresponding to /e/. It derived from Gmc */o/: *domjan > dœman > deman (deem). Since for both ⟨y⟩ and ⟨œ⟩ long and short reflexes occur in ModE, we can assume four more vowel sounds in Early OE:

$$\begin{array}{ccc}
\text{ī/i} & \text{ǖ/ü} & \text{u/ū} \\
\text{ē/e} & \text{ȫ/ö} & \text{ɔ/ō} \\
& \text{ǣ/æ} & \\
& \text{ā/a} &
\end{array}$$

By 900, /ŏ/ had coalesced with /e/. There is no evidence of a significant /ə/ phoneme, either stressed or unstressed in OE.

PROBLEM 13.32: Suggest a way to determine when the rounded front vowels became unrounded.

PROBLEM 13.33: From the data in Problem 13.30, we can also see a great many other changes in the quality of vowels. One meaning of OE *lim* /līm/ is now pronounced /laim/; the other is *limb* from short OE /lim/. OE *hus* /hūs/ is now pronounced /haus/ (except in Scots English where the /ī/ > /ai/, /ū/ > /au/ change never occurred. Scots thus has *hus* for *house*, *ee* for *eye*, and so on). Plot the changes between OE long vowels and ModE diphthongs.

The dialect of OE we are describing here, West Saxon, may also have had eight diphthongs, four long and four short. They were written ⟨ie⟩, ⟨io⟩, ⟨ea⟩, and ⟨eo⟩. By A.D. 900, ⟨ie⟩ had simplified to ⟨i⟩, and ⟨io⟩ had merged with ⟨eo⟩. There is considerable debate about the phonetic values of these segments, even whether there were short diphthongs. But on the basis of subsequent changes in these words, they were probably close to these values: ⟨ea⟩ = /æə/; ⟨ie⟩ = /iə/; ⟨eo⟩ = /eə/; ⟨io⟩ = /iə/. (25, 28, 89, 111, 148, 175, 209)

Consonants

Describing the OE consonants is somewhat more difficult than describing vowels because the consonants were less consistently represented. The letters used to represent OE consonants were these: ⟨f⟩, ⟨b⟩, ⟨p⟩, ⟨t⟩, ⟨d⟩, ⟨c⟩, ⟨ʒ⟩ (yogh), ⟨þ⟩ (thorn), ⟨ð⟩ (eth), ⟨s⟩, ⟨m⟩, ⟨n⟩, ⟨r⟩, ⟨l⟩, ⟨ƿ⟩ (wynn), and ⟨h⟩. ⟨x⟩, ⟨z⟩, and ⟨k⟩ were rather rare. Modern ⟨w⟩, it may be recalled, was represented as ⟨uu⟩ or ⟨ƿ⟩.

Because the relationship between the following OE letters and ModE letters has been extremely stable over the years and because the ModE letters still correspond to Latin phonetic values, we can assume that in OE, they represented sounds very close to the same sounds in ModE: ⟨p⟩, ⟨b⟩, ⟨d⟩, ⟨t⟩, ⟨m⟩, ⟨n⟩, ⟨l⟩, and ⟨w⟩. ⟨r⟩ was probably different only in quality, very likely being more like the trilled /r/ in Modern Scots.

PROBLEM 13.34: Transcribe these OE words. You will have to work backwards from ModE to determine vowel length:

> *bæð* (bath), *bitan* (bite), *cu* (cow), *cwic* (quick), *dæl* (deal), *dæd* (deed), *hus* (house), *deman* (deem), *dom* (doom), *dwellan* (dwell), *endian* (end), *fæt* (fat), *fedan* (feed), *fif* (five), *fyllan* (fill), *glæd* (glad), *gos* (goose), *hal*

(whole), *halig* (holy), *helpan* (help), *frogga* (frog), *land* (land), *lim* (limb), *lus* (louse), *meltan* (melt), *bulla* (bull), *sæ* (sea), *sittan* (sit), *swete* (sweet), *tellan* (tell), *broð* (broth), *þus* (thus), *tid* (tide), *þyn* (thine), *we* (we), *wis* (wise), *glæs* (glass), *writan* (write), *god* (God), *ramm* (ram).

Some of the earliest changes in the inventory of English consonants involved the sounds represented by ⟨c⟩ and ⟨ʒ⟩ (represented by ⟨g⟩ in ModE texts, recall, the symbol we shall use here).

PROBLEM 13.35: Here are some data from OE and some related cognate languages. (1) On the basis of the cognates, what probably was the earliest pronunciation of the OE digraph ⟨sc⟩? Of ⟨c⟩? (The sequence of letters ⟨sh⟩ and the sound /š/ did not occur in Early OE.) (2) Is there any way to predict which OE words would come to have initial /š/, /k/, and /č/?

OE *sceacul* > ModE *shackle* (*skagle*, Dan.)

OE *sceaft* > ModE *shaft* (*skapt*, Ice.)

OE *sceacan* > ModE *shake* (*skaka*, Swed.)

OE *sceap* > Mod *shape* (*skapa*, Swed.)

OE *cece* > ModE *cheek* (*käk*, Swed.)

OE *corn* > ModE *corn* (*kaurn*, Gothic)

OE *cin* > ModE *chin* (*kind*, Dan.)

OE *cat* > ModE *cat* (*katze*, Germ.)

OE *calf* > ModE *calf* (*kalf*, Swed.)

OE *scrift* > ModE *shrift* (*skript*, Ice.)

OE *scip* > ModE *ship* (*skib*, Dan.)

OE *sceoh* > ModE *shy* (*skygg*, Swed.)

OE *sceafan* > ModE *shave* (*skave*, Dan.)

OE *ceaf* > ModE *chaff* (*kaf*, Dutch)

OE *cropp* > ModE *crop* (*kroppr*, Ice.)

OE *clif* > ModE *cliff* (*klippa*, Swed.)

OE *ciele* > ModE *chill* (*kala*, Ice.)

OE *cicen* > ModE *chicken* (*kjūklíng*, Ice.)

PROBLEM 13.36: If in OE, all sequences of [sk + front vowel] became [š + front vowel], how does it happen that we have /sk-/ sequences in ModE like *skip, skim, sky, skin, schedule, scale, skid, skill, skit*?

PROBLEM 13.37: Are any of these words apparent exceptions? Comment: *keep, kettle, kelp, kitchen, kith, kin, kipper, kiss, kit, kink, chocolate, choke, coach, pooch, catch, pouch, touch, roach, brooch, hootch*.

PROBLEM 13.38: Roughly the same thing happened with the /g/ phoneme, though this is even more complicated because ⟨g⟩ (that is, ⟨ʒ⟩) represented several different sounds. Here are several OE words with their modern descendants. Comment.

1. *þegn–thane*	11. *weg–way*	21. *god–good*
2. *slægen–slain*	12. *boga–bow*	22. *gnæt–gnat*
3. *twegen–twain*	13. *gear–year*	23. *stigrap–stirrup*
4. *ge–ye*	14. *geoc–yoke*	24. *manig–many*
5. *sorgian–sorrow*	15. *geon–yon*	25. *gold–gold*
6. *glæd–glad*	16. *græg–grey*	26. *grund–ground*
7. *dæg–day*	17. *agan–own*	27. *dragan–draw*
8. *folgian–follow*	18. *halig–holy*	28. *sægde–said*
9. *lagu–law*	19. *fuglere–fowler*	29. *glowen–glow*
10. *gast–ghost*	20. *gat–goat*	30. *geolu–yellow*

The letter ⟨g⟩ represented at least three sounds, but only two phonemes. One phoneme consisted of the allophones [g], the **voiced velar stop**, and [ɣ], the **voiced velar spirant**, two sounds which never occurred in the other's environment: [ɣ] occurred only inside a word before or after a back vowel: *lagu* [laɣu] (law). Initially before back vowels or consonants, ⟨g⟩ represented the other allophone, the [g] we hear today: *gast* [gast] (ghost), *god* [gōd] (good). The third sound represented by the letter ⟨g⟩ was a **voiced palatal spirant** that was probably very close to a strongly aspirated [y],[3] as it·might be stressed in *year*. It normally occurred before or after front vowels: *stigrap* [stiyrāp] (stirrup, literally "ascent-rope").

In one environment, initially before certain front vowels, [y] contrasted with [g], thereby making [y] a distinct phoneme, /y/. In those words which at one time had a back vowel that mutated forward to become a front vowel, the letter ⟨g⟩ still represented the sound [g]: *ges* [gēs] (geese) from Germanic **gansiz*; *gylt* [gilt] (guilt) from Germanic **gultiz*; *gyrdan* [girdan] (to gird) from Germanic **gurdjan*. After the vowels mutated, OE had pairs like *gylt* [gilt] and *gist* [yist] (yeast). Since in these two words [g] and [y] contrast in identical environments, they must be considered different phonemes, /g/ and /y/. Finally, in combination with a preceding /n/, the ⟨g⟩ was pronounced [g]: *singan* [siŋgan] /singan/ (sing); *hring* [xriŋg] /hring/ (ring).

PROBLEM 13.39: This does not account for these words. Comment. *get, give, ginko, guess, big, cog, dog, dig, fig, hag, jig, lag, leg, nag.*

The phonemic symbol /n/ used above in /singan/ and /hring/ should not be interpreted as [n]. Before the velar consonants /k/ or /g/, the allophone of /n/ was undoubtedly [ŋ], the velar nasal we now hear in *sing* [siŋ]. If the allophone of /n/ before /g/ or /k/ was always predictably [ŋ], then OE did

---

3 This is ordinarily represented by [j] in the International Phonetic Alphabet.

not have the three nasal phonemes we have: /m/, /n/, and /ŋ/. It had only two: /N/ and /m/, with the allophones of /N/ being [n] and [ŋ].

The combination written ⟨cg⟩ was pronounced [ǰ]: *ecg* [eǰ] /eǰ/ (edge), the result of another palatalization of [g]: Germanic **agjā* > OE /eǰ/, thereby creating another phoneme, /ǰ/.

The letter ⟨h⟩ represented in initial position the /h/ we use today: *hecg* [heǰ] /heǰ/ (hedge). But it also represented two sounds that we can hear today only in Scots and other northern British dialects: a **voiceless palatal spirant** after front vowels, symbolized [x̟]: *niht* [nix̟t] /niht/ (night), and a **voiceless velar spirant** after back vowels, symbolized [x]: *fuht* [fūxt] /fūht/ (moist). They can be approximated by very strongly stressing the /h/ in *huge* and *hoot*, respectively. Because [h], [x̟], and [x] do not occur in one another's environments, they constitute the three allophones of /h/.

PROBLEM 13.40: We have already seen that initial /v/ and /z/ sounds in English words almost invariably indicate foreign borrowings, good evidence that OE probably had no voiced /v/ and /z/ initially. We can conclude that it had no /ž/ phoneme at all, since evidence for the sound does not occur until Early ModE. It also had no initial /ǰ/ sound. Spirants that occurred finally in OE were also voiceless. But it is clear that many voiced spirants in native words now do occur in final position. Here are some with their OE sources: *love < lufu, bathe < baðian, live < lifian, dive < dyfan, lose < losian.* Comment.

The OE spirants thus appear to have had voiced and voiceless allophones depending on their environment. In other words, instead of the set of voiced and voiceless phonemes as in ModE:

ModE: /f/ /θ/ /s/ /š/
         /v/ /ð/ /z/ /ž/

OE had only one sequence of spirants with two allophones each (with the exception of /š/, which did not have a corresponding /š/ and /h/).

OE: /F/ /θ/ /S/ /š/ /h/

The voiceless allophones of the spirants occurred initially and finally and contiguous with voiceless consonants. Voiced allophones occurred when surrounded by voiced sounds. Thus the /F/ and /S/ phonemes in *ofer* (*over*) and *leosan* (*lose*) would have been pronounced [əver] and [lēəzan]; in *oft* (*often*) and *dust* (*dust*) as [əft] and [dūst].

Given this pattern of voiced and voiceless allophones, it is virtually certain that OE also had only one interdental spirant phoneme that we have arbitrarily represented as /θ/. It had two allophones, [ð] and [θ], distributed like the allophones of /F/ and /S/. No native ModE words have a single voiceless /θ/ medially; and the voiced /ð/ sound now at the end of ModE words like *bathe* resulted from the loss of voiced inflections or analogy. Those words which now have **initial** voiced /ð/ are all roughly the same kind of words: *the, this, that, these, those, then, there, thus, though.* They are all lightly stressed words whose original initial [θ] in the context of a whole sentence probably became voiced [ð] in late ME. It is easier to keep the vocal cords vibrating in an environment of voicing than it is to stop voicing and then start again. It is the source of the difference between /θ/ and /ð/ in *withstand* and *withall.* (25, 28, 148, 152, 175, 209)

We can now contrast the overall system of consonants of OE with the overall system of ModE consonants. There are really three stages of OE consonant evolution:

1. The development of /š/.
2. The split of /k/ into /k/ and /č/.
3. The split of the spirants into voiced and voiceless pairs.

Between Late OE and ModE, three more significant changes were yet to occur:

4. The velar and palatal spirants represented by ⟨h⟩ and ⟨g⟩ would be lost.
5. /ž/ would be acquired as a phoneme.
6. /N/ would split into /n/ and /ŋ/.

PROBLEM 13.41: Using a chart like Table 13.1, sort early and late OE consonants phonemes into points of articulation and manners of articulation.

One last significant difference between OE and ModE consonants is that OE had not only long and short vowels but long and short consonants. Long consonants were signalled by double letters: *cyssan, moððe,* and they seem to have been always voiceless. They were probably pronounced as we pronounce the sequence of two identical consonants at the juncture of compound words. Compare these ModE pronunciations of phonetic doubled consonants with the pronunciation of words which have doubled letters only to mark the vowel quality of the preceding syllable.

⟨pp⟩ in *hoppian* like the ⟨pp⟩ in *toppost.* Compare ⟨pp⟩ in ModE *apple.*
⟨bb⟩ in *ebba* like the ⟨bb⟩ in *ribback.* Compare ⟨bb⟩ in ModE *rubber.*
⟨tt⟩ in *cnyttan* like the ⟨tt⟩ in *flattop.* Compare ⟨tt⟩ in ModE *butter.*
⟨dd⟩ in *hlæddre* like the ⟨dd⟩ in *birddog.* Compare ⟨dd⟩ in ModE *ladder.*
⟨gg⟩ in *frogga* like the ⟨gg⟩ in *doggun.* Compare ⟨gg⟩ in ModE *digging.*
⟨ff⟩ in *offrian* like the ⟨ff⟩ in *lifefood.* Compare ⟨ff⟩ in ModE *offer.*
⟨ss⟩ in *mæsse* like the ⟨ss⟩ in *busstop.* Compare ⟨ss⟩ in ModE *lesson.*

⟨nn⟩ in *dynnan* like the ⟨nn⟩ in *penknife*. Compare ⟨nn⟩ in ModE *spinner*.
⟨mm⟩ in *swimman* like the ⟨mm⟩ in *homemaker*. Compare ⟨mm⟩ in ModE *plummet*.
⟨ðð⟩ in *moððe* like the ⟨thth⟩ in *wreaththorn*. Compare ⟨th⟩ in ModE *ether*.

For a variety of reasons, long consonants in Late OE or Early ME merged with single consonants. This meant that a sequence of two voiceless allophones like [ff] in a word like *offrian* [ɔffrian] became in Early ME a single voiceless [f], [ɔfriən]. But because [f] was now in a position that contrasted with a single voiced [v], medially between voiced segments as in *ofer* [ɔver], it meant that a new phonemic contrast resulted between [f] and [v]. In fact, this probably occurred before we borrowed foreign words with initial /v/ and /z/ sounds and before we lost final inflections at the ends of words that left voiced and voiceless spirants in contrast there. (113)

Chapter 14

PHONOLOGICAL CHANGE: FROM OLD ENGLISH TO MODERN ENGLISH

THE NATURE OF SOUND CHANGE

We have now described the two extremes in the history of English sound patterns: Modern English and Old English. The problem now is to recreate how the one changed to the other, when the changes occurred, and that most difficult of all questions, why they occurred. When we talk about how sounds change, though, we have to recognize the different ways in which they **can** change. In some cases, the changes are minor: Some words add or lose a sound without affecting the system of **oppositions** in the language as a whole: *heafod* > *head*, *spinl* > *spindle*, *dragan* > *draw*, *thimmle* > *thimble*.

In other cases, we change the ways we systematically **combine** sounds. In OE, for example, /kn-/, /gn-/, /hn-/, /hl-/, and /hr-/ were acceptable sequences of consonants: *cniht* (knight), *cnyttan* (knit), *gnæt* (gnat), *gnagan* (gnaw), *hnutu* (nut), *hnitu* (nit), *hlaford* (lord), *hleapon* (leap), *hrim* (rime), *hring* (ring). Since then, /k/, /g/, and /h/ have been dropped from those positions, but not from the inventory of sounds. A few new combinations of phonemes have entered the language through a handful of borrowed words: /pw-/ in *pueblo*, /sv-/ in *svelte*, /sf-/ in *sphere*, /skl-/ in *sclerotic*. But the minute number of words with these combinations has not affected the **system** of combinations in English. At the end of words, on the other hand, some new combinations resulted when vowels between some consonants disappeared: *glimpsed*, once pronounced /glímpsəd/, became /glimpst/ when the vowel was **syncopated**, or dropped in an unstressed syllable.

More basic changes create new sounds. When /š/ developed from /sk/, for example, the new spirant phoneme was a new sound that contrasted with other spirants. In other cases, sounds can change considerably without creating any new systematic contrasts. This occurred with OE /k/ before umlauted front vowels unrounded. The [č] allophone of /k/ developed before front vowels but did not systematically contrast with the [k] allophone of /k/ until /ö/ unrounded to /e/.

And some sound classes can be lost from the inventory. This reduces the number of contrasts, as when the rounded long and short front vowels unrounded to /e/ and /i/. This reduced the number of contrasting vowels from sixteen to twelve. But specific sounds can disappear without reducing the number of contrasting phonemes. This happened when some of the spirant allophones of /g/ disappeared. /g/ still contrasted with the other consonants, but in a more limited set of environments.

Perhaps the most basic kind of change is when the system of **features** on which contrasts are based changes. Rounding is no longer a way to contrast vowels. Nor do we any longer use length to distinguish consonants. On the other hand, we have lost length in vowels, but the system of contrasts remains the same because we have substituted diphthongization. (14, 85, 91, 115, 128, 188, 209)

Before we begin tracing any of these changes from OE to ModE, however, a warning is in order. Because we phrase a change in the form X > Y and because we have claimed that sounds change regularly, we might too easily assume that the history of sound changes is neatly linear, each discretely set off from the next, accomplished, as it were, almost overnight in all similar words, in a language with a single dialect in a classless society that speaks in only one style for all social contexts. Such is never the case.

Sound changes are more like ripples in a pond, beginning in one place, spreading, merging with other ripples, interrupted here and there by irregularities in the bank. But in addition to geographical dialects, there are the ripples that spread through social classes, with pronunciations popular among one class spreading to another. And complicating this whole set of relationships is the fact that speakers from particular social classes within specific geographical dialects vary their pronunciation according to the social context they happen to find themselves in. In formal contexts they will speak differently than they do in casual contexts.

Thus it is misleading to say that sound X changed to sound Y in 1400 just because the first respelling of a particular vowel in a written text was found at that date. Sounds change first for someone in some words in some contexts in some social class in some geographical dialect. The change may spread through social classes and styles until it becomes the form used in the "standard" formal style in that dialect, or it may remain in the shadows of an isolated social or geographical dialect or style. Other dialects might remain unaffected by the change or borrow it. It might or might not finally affect the core of the language.

We happen to be describing one social-geographical dialect: American English spoken in relatively formal contexts by educated upper-middle class speakers around the Great Lakes. There are other geographical and social dialects that we could have examined. In some of these, certain of the changes we will describe below never occurred.

So when we talk about sound changes, we have to specify four coordinates: **location, social class, style,** and **period.** Unfortunately, stylistic variations are difficult, indeed for the most part impossible to reconstruct. Differences among social classes are only a bit less difficult to account for. And it is not always clear how to determine the precise boundaries of geographical subdialects. Specifying time, too, must be indefinite. We have to operate within a span of years: From the date of the first citation which we might take as evidence that a sound has changed minus? number of years, to the date when the change seems to have permeated the formal style of the dialect being investigated. For example, the first indication that the palatal spirant [x] in words like *niht* was lost after front vowels seems to have appeared in mid-fifteenth century reverse spellings such as *wright* for *write.* Yet otherwise reliable seventeenth-century orthoepists, dictionary-makers and so on could write a century and a half later that a word like *light* was still pronounced by some conservative speakers with the spirant sound. Writing in 1632, Robert Sherwood commented that while he preferred the older pronunciation with the spirant, there was a more modern one used among Londoners, a pronunciation he seems to describe as /əy/. By 1650, the velar spirant seems to have disappeared entirely—in standard London English. But it is still heard today in parts of Scotland and elsewhere. So if we were writing a history of Scots English, this discussion about [x] would be beside the point. Describing a sound change is no simple matter if we are to be honest to our ignorance. With this in mind, we can explore some early changes.

OLD ENGLISH TO MIDDLE ENGLISH

Vowels

PROBLEM 14.1: In Early ME, in the twelfth century, words spelled with ⟨a⟩ began to turn up in some non-Northern dialects spelled ⟨o⟩ or ⟨oo⟩. We now pronounce these words with /ō/ as in *boat* and *whole.* By the thirteenth century, many more ⟨a⟩ words had changed to ⟨o⟩, but not all. Here are some data. What principle can you find to predict which vowels rounded and moved back and which did not?

OE bat > ModE boat–boot (Dut.)	OE ban > ModE bone–been (Dan).
OE cat > ModE cat–katt (Swed.)	OE ham > ModE home–heim (Germ.)
OE hamm > ModE ham–ham (Dut.)	OE mann > ModE man–man (Swed.)
OE swan > ModE swan–svanr (Ice.)	OE lam > ModE loam–leem (Dut.)
OE hal > ModE whole–hails (Gothic)	OE gat > ModE goat–geit (Dut.)
OE salt > ModE salt–salt (Swed.)	OE hlaf > ModE loaf–laib (Ger.)
OE calf > ModE calf–kalv (Dan.)	OE ar > ModE oar–aare (Dan.)

Dating this change of /ā/ to /ɔ̄/ is not difficult because both spelling and borrowed words can help. Since the ⟨o⟩ spellings begin to appear in the twelfth century, the change preceded 1100. Spelling always lags behind pronunciation. Moreover, certain French words with /ā/ which were very likely borrowed in the twelfth century did not change: *blame, fame, dame,* for example. Had /ā/ changed after these words were borrowed, the /ā/ of French words and the /ā/ of OE words would have changed together, giving us along with *boat, goat,* and *home,* the forms *bloam, foam,* and *doam.*

Lengthening and Shortening of Vowels

In Problem 13.30, we suggested that OE long vowels became ModE diphthongs and that OE short vowels remained short to become ModE monophthongs. This is too strong a generalization. It is clear from the comparative evidence that many OE short vowels have become ModE diphthongs and that many OE long vowels have become ModE short monophthongs.

For example, before certain consonant clusters, some short vowels in Late OE changed: *wămb > womb, clĭmban > climb, fĭndan > find, fĕld > field, cămb > comb, cĭld > child, scĕld > shield, cȳnd > kind.* In ME, *land, hand, word, earth* also became long, but later shortened. Before /-mb/, /-nd/, /-ld/, /-rd/, and /-rθ/, OE short vowels lengthened. But it was a permanent lengthening only for /i/ and /o/ before /-mb/: *climb* and *comb*; for /i/ and /u/ before /-nd/: *find–bound*; and for all vowels before /-ld/: *child, shield, bound, old.*

On the other hand, long vowels shortened before consonant clusters other than the above, or before a stressed syllable: All the vowels marked long in these words shortened: *sōfte, kēpte, mētte* (dream), *fīftene, wīfman, wīsdōm, āscian, bōsm, dūst.* So did unaccented long vowels in the second half of compounds or in unstressed prefixes and suffixes: *ārīsan, wīsdōm, cynedōm* (kingdom), *wurðlīche.*

PROBLEM 14.2: Here are some data regarding some other words. All of these were short in OE. Comment.

OE	ModE	OE	ModE	OE	ModE
glædlice	gladly	blædre	bladder	swingan	swing
nama	name	wudu	wood	þus	thus
appel	apple	cræft	craft	baðian	bathe
spere	spear	bæð	bath	ende	end
steppan	step	stelan	steal	bitela	beetle
wicu	week	sittan	sit	open	open
skinn	skin	broð	broth	duru	door
losian	lose	cuppe	cup	glæs	glass
god	god	caru	care	assa	ass
mete	meat	wifol	weavel	ofer	over
sunne	sun	rose	rose	tellan	tell
sacc	sack	med	mead	meltan	melt
smoca	smoke	stæf	staff	willa	will

Since many of the OE short vowels in these words have become ModE diphthongs, those short vowels apparently lengthened. The environment in which short vowels lengthen is in a **stressed open syllable** optionally followed by only one more unstressed syllable. An open syllable is one which ends in a vowel: *ri-dan* (ride) as opposed to *mel-tan*. But as they lengthened, OE /i/, /e/, /u/, and /o/ also apparently dropped to the next lower sound:

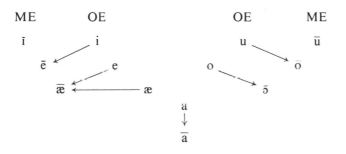

Had they not dropped, we would have expected the lengthened /i/ and /u/ of *wiku* and *duru* to have become /ī/ and /ū/. And we know that long /ī/ and /ū/ eventually became /ai/ and /au/ sounds *tid* (/tīd/) > *tide* (/taid/), *hus* (/hūs/) > *house* (/haus/). But *wiku* becomes *week*, and *duru* gives *door* (originally /dūr/), the normal development of /ē/ and /ō/.

PROBLEM 14.3: So far, we have seen three important vowel changes before the end of ME: (1) Lengthening before /-ld/, /-mb/, and so on; (2) lengthening in open syllables; (3) /ā/ shifting back to a rounded vowel, /ō/. Demonstrate the order in which these changes **must** have occurred. Use these two words in your explanations: OE *cald* /kăld/ (cold) and *nama* /nămă/ (name).

The System of Contrasts

When /ā/ changed to /ɔ̄/, it did not upset the system of ME vowel contrasts, however. It left the language without a phonetic long [ā], but the total number of contrasts remained the same: In Late OE and Early ME, we still find three long and three short low back vowels. But when short vowels lengthened before /-ld/, /-mb/, and so on, and in open syllables, ME regained an /ā/ from the short /a/ in words like *nama*, thereby creating one new contrast. There were then **four** long and three short low back vowels:

OE: u/ū >   Early ME: u/ū >   ME: u/ū
 o/ō   after   o/ō   after   o/ō
 a/ā   /ā/ > /ɔ̄/   /ɔ̄/   /ă/ > /ā/   /ɔ̄/
                a/ʊ̃   a/ā

Unfortunately for the modern student, the /ɔ̄/ and /ŏ/ words were often spelled alike in ME texts, both with ⟨o⟩ or ⟨oo⟩: *goose* (f. OE *gōs*), *goot* (f. OE *gāt*), *sooth* (f. OE *sōð*)–*hoom* (f. OE *hām*). To know how to pronounce these words, one must know (1) whether the word goes back to an /ā/ or an /ō/ in OE, or (2) how the word is spelled in ModE. If the word is now spelled with ⟨o⟩ or ⟨oo⟩ and pronounced /u/ as in foot, /ū/ as in food, or /ə/ as in *one*, then the ME pronunciation was probably /ō/. If the ModE spelling is ⟨oa⟩ or ⟨o–e⟩ and pronounced /ō/ as in *bone* or *boat*, then the word usually goes back to a ME /ɔ̄/, from OE /ā/. There are some exceptions, but the rule is a useful one for most cases.

A similar problem faces the student in regard to the front vowels. Just as there was (and is) no separate letter in our orthography to distinguish /ɔ̄/ from /ā/ or /ō/, so by Late ME there was no letter to distinguish /ǣ/ from /ā/ either. The short /æ/ apparently began to disappear in Late OE, merging with /a/ in some dialects and with /e/ in others. Evidence that /æ/ was beginning to merge with /a/ is in the ⟨a⟩ spellings of certain ⟨æ⟩ words in Late OE and Early ME when the ligature ⟨æ⟩ was still being used. Instead of using ⟨æ⟩ in all words that originally had /æ/, some scribes began spelling these words with ⟨a⟩, presumably to reflect the new pronunciation of /a/. When short /æ/ merged with a short /a/ and ⟨æ⟩ as a symbol was dropped, words with /ǣ/ from OE were left with no distinctive letter to distinguish them from OE words that originally had /ē/ or /ā/. In the dialects we are concerned with, Norman scribes consistently chose ⟨e⟩ or ⟨ee⟩ to represent words with an original /ǣ/, a fact which suggests that unlike short /æ/, which had moved toward /a/, long /ǣ/ may have moved closer to /ē/.

As a consequence, words spelled ⟨e⟩ or ⟨ee⟩ in ME were pronounced in two ways: /ē/ if they derived from original /ē/ words or from lengthened /i/

words: OE *spēd* /spēd/ > ME *spede* /spēd/ > ModE *speed*; OE *bitel* /bitel/ > ME *betel* /bētəl/ > ModE *beetle*. Or if they came from original /æ/ words or lengthened /e/ words, they had a vowel that was by this time probably higher than /æ/ but still lower than /e/: OE *sæ* [sæˆ] > ModE *sea*; OE *mete* [mēte] > ME *mete* [mæˆt] ModE *meat*.

Graphically, the sound spelling relationship resembled this:

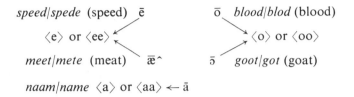

The phonetic symbols usually used for the two higher front vowels are called **open-e** for the lower vowel that was originally /æ/ and **close-e** for the higher vowel open-e: [ẹ], close-e [ẹ]. (To distinguish them more clearly in this text, the more /æ/-like sound, the open-e, will be represented with a large /Ē/ to suggest the wider jaw opening for lower sounds. The close-e will be represented with a small /ē/ to suggest its smaller jaw opening.)

Given these changes, the monophthongal long and short vowels of ME looked like this:

ī/i   u/ū
  ē/e   o/ō
    Ē
      ā/a
n.b. /o/ may have been closer to [ɔ].

PROBLEM 14.4: Transcribe these ME words: *boc* (book), *mild* (mild), *bac* (back), *bedde* (bed), *clene* (clean), *dele* (deal), *do* (do), *dwell* (dwell), *fede* (feed), *feld* (field), *flod* (flood), *fote* (foot), *gold* (gold), *gras* (grass), *gost* (ghost), *hasppe* (hasp), *hyde* (hide), *his* (his), *hog* (hog), *kynne* (kin), *klyffe* (cliff), *lokke* (lock), *mylc* (milk), *name* (name), *plate* (plate), *rise* (rise), *saaf* (safe), *slepe* (sleep), *sinke* (sink).

PROBLEM 14.5: What textual evidence would you look for to prove that two words spelled ⟨oo⟩ or ⟨o⟩, or two words spelled ⟨e⟩ or ⟨ee⟩ were not pronounced alike?

PROBLEM 14.6: How might you determine whether /æ/ merged with /a/ before or after vowels lengthened in open syllables?

In some ME dialects, West Midland and in the Southwest, the long and short rounded front vowels from mutated back vowels, that is /ǖ/, spelled ⟨y⟩ in OE, had not unrounded, as we can tell from some spellings: *kun* rather than *kin* from OE *cynn* (kin), *fur* rather than *fir* from OE *fyr* (fire), *mus* rather than *mis* from OE *mys* (mice). As we might expect of a city that attracted Englishmen from all dialect areas, Londoners vacillated in how they spelled and presumably pronounced some original /ü/ words. In **The Canterbury Tales** we can find *myrie, murye, merie* from OE *myrige*. In some cases we have a ⟨u⟩ spelling but an /i/ pronunciation: *build, busy, business*.

Diphthongs

Between OE and ME, diphthongs underwent some important changes, so great that we cannot detail them all. Both OE diphthongs, long and short /ǽ/ and /éɔ/ disappeared, merging with long and short /æ/ and /ě/. But a multitude of new diphthongs entered the language, many as the result of a sound change involving velar and palatal voiced and voiceless spirants, allophones of OE /g/ and /h/. As we saw in Problem 13.38, the spirants spelled ⟨g⟩ and ⟨h⟩ eventually disappeared. We can date this loss by noticing new spellings in ME and OE words that had these segments: ME *dai* for *dæg*, ME *owen* (owe) for OE *agan*.

PROBLEM 14.7: Before or after stressed back vowels, the spirants were velar. Before or after stressed front vowels, they were palatal. Their loss resulted in this sequence of changes (represented phonemically):

1. Palatal voiced: OE *dæg* /dæy/ > ME *dai* /dæi/ > ModE *day* /dei/
2. Palatal voiceless: OE *neah* /neəh/ > ME *neigh* /neih/ > ModE *nigh* /nai/
3. Velar voiced: OE *agan* /agan/ > ME *owen* /ouən/ > ModE *owe* /ou/
4. Velar voiceless: OE *ploh* /ploh/ > ME *plou* /pluh/ > ModE *plow* /plau/

The voiced spirants, (1) and (3) disappeared first, leaving offglides in their places. Before the voiceless spirants, (2) and (4), ME vowels first developed an offglide, then much later the spirants disappeared. The offglide that developed in (1) and (2) was /i/ and in (3) and (4), /u/. Why did these particular offglides develop?

In addition to these diphthongs, Norman French words borrowed into English contributed a few more, though most of these quickly merged with similar native diphthongs. The outstanding exception is found in *chois, noise, joie,* and *joyn*. The /ɔi/ pronunciation apparently changed to /ai/ later, since we find rimes like *join–fine* in the eighteenth century. Our /ɔi/ pronunciation is probably a result of the schoolmaster's insistence on spelling pronunciation. (25, 28, 98, 148, 150, 164, 209, 213)

Consonants

In describing some of the new diphthongs in ME, we necessarily had to describe one of the major consonant changes—the loss of the voiced velar and palatal spirant allophones of /g/. Because Norman scribes consistently respelled OE words with the voiceless /h/ as ⟨gh⟩ or ⟨h⟩ while often dropping the ⟨g⟩ that represented the spirant allophones of /g/, we can conclude that the spirant allophones of /h/ were still present in ME, a conclusion reinforced by sixteenth century orthoepists who describe them.

So far as can be determined, /ž/ did not appear in ME. We find no ME spellings of ⟨sh⟩ or ⟨zh⟩ for ⟨s⟩ in a word like *vision.* So words which we now pronounce with /ž/, as in *pleasure, confusion, invasion,* and so on were in ME probably pronounced /z/: [vizión], [pleziúr], and so on. And merely from spelling evidence, it is still impossible to determine whether the ⟨-ing⟩ in words like *thing* and *sing* represented [siŋg] or [siŋ]. As early as the fourteenth century, there are spellings of ⟨-in⟩ for ⟨-ing⟩ in words taking the past participle ending: *haukin* for *hauking* (hawking), but this has nothing to do with the problem of /-iŋ(g)/ in non-participial endings.

PROBLEM 14.8: If ME /N/ had not yet split into /n/ and /ŋ/, and /ž/ was not in the language, what did the **phonemic** consonant system at the end of ME look like? (Use the kind of chart illustrated in Table 13.1.)

PROBLEM 14.9: Here is a body of data that will suggest some of the common kinds of changes in the way individual consonants changed in particular words to the end of the ME period. Comment.

OE	ME	ModE		OE	ME	ModE
leofman	> lemman	—		beorht	> briht	> bright
spinl	> spindle	> spindle		byrðen	> burdin	> burden
þridda	> thirde	> third		wifman	> wimman	> woman
emtig	> empti	> empty		bridde	> bird	> bird
hafoc	> hauk	> hawk		gærs	> grass	> grass
heafod	> hed	> head		swa	> so	> so
þymel	> thimbel	> thimble		two	> to	> two

PROBLEM 14.10: As we have pointed out, long vowels shortened and short vowels did not lengthen if they were followed by two consecutive consonants, or if they were followed by a stressed syllable. This has obscured the historical sources of some common ModE words. Had the vowels not changed, we would have had combinations like those below. To derive the ModE word (1) shorten the vowel and return it to its original OE value and (2) unstress

the second syllable. *sheep + herd*; *moon + day*; *holy + day*; *bone + fire*; *dear + -ling*; *goose + -ling*; *break + fast*; *old(er) + man*; *roam + -ble*; *wise + -ard*; *Christ + mass*; *house + bonda* (*bonda* meant a freeholder, someone who owned his own house and land); *house + thing* (In the Danelaw, the *þing* was a council of elders. The descendant ModE word refers to political campaigning.); *good + spell* (*spell* means story); *nose + thyrl* (*thyrl* means hole); *wind* (as in *wind up*) *+ -l- + ass* (*ass* means pole.); *throat + -le* (*-le* is an ending that shortens the preceding vowel.); *wild + -er- + -ness*; *toad + poll* (*poll* here means head; it is respelled *pole* in this word.); *wife + man*. (There is a secondary change in the first word. The initial /w/ causes the underlying shortened vowel to become rounded to /u/, and the ⟨f⟩ disappears.)

MIDDLE ENGLISH TO MODERN ENGLISH

We usually pick 1500 as the end of ME and the beginning of Early ModE because we are past the major grammatical changes: In nouns, the inflections have leveled to a plural and genitive; in verbs, generally to a third person singular *-s*, a past, a perfect, and a progressive participle; and in adjectives, to a comparative and a superlative. Word order has settled into a S–V–(C) order, and prepositions have assumed their very large syntactic load. The auxiliary verbs continued to expand, particularly in combinations with the progressive. The verb endings *-th* and *-est* were still active. And questions and negatives allowing either *do-* or non-*do* forms were possible: *Came he | He came not. Did he come? | He didn't come.*

But except for those and a few other patterns, and except for vocabulary and style, the English of 1500 is very similar to twentieth-century English. If we modernize spelling and translate a few obscure words, only the style gives us pause in this passage dating from 1529. The original words are in brackets, the translations in boldface.

> The King, perceiving that she was thus gone, and considering well on the words she had there spoken, said to the audience thus in effect: "**Since** [forasmuch as] the queen is now gone, I will in her absence declare **to** [unto] you all that she **has** [hath] been to me as true, as obedient, and as **compliant** [conformable] a wife as I could wish or desire; she **has** [hath] all the virtuous qualities that ought to be in a woman of her high **position** [dignity], or any other, **yes** [yea] though she were of baser state. She is also a noble woman born, as her noble conditions will well declare, and the special cause that moved me in this matter was a certain scruple that pricked my conscience."
>
> From **The Life of Fisher**, ed. Ronald Bayne.
> Early English Text Society ES 97, 1921, p. 60.

Vowels

But in 1500, English phonology was close to the middle of a very major change in the quality of vowels, a change called **The Great Vowel Shift**. In Problem 13.30, we saw that certain ME long vowels correspond with ModE diphthongs:

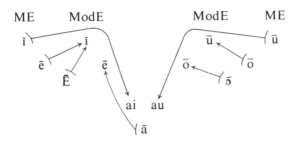

The earliest respellings that indicate when long vowels began to change date perhaps from the thirteenth century in some dialects, so the change may have begun as early as the 1200's.

/ī/ > /ai/ *and* /ū/ > /au/

Around the middle of the fifteenth century, there began to appear respellings like ⟨ei⟩ and ⟨ey⟩ for earlier ⟨i⟩ representing /ī/, along with respellings of ⟨eu⟩ and ⟨au⟩ for early ⟨ou⟩ representing /ū/. This suggests that at least by then, /ū/ and /ī/ had begun to become diphthongs. *bleynd* for *blind*, *meyld* for *mild*, *feyr* for *fire*; *faunde* for *founde* and *sauth* for *south*. The change probably began when an unstressed onglide was somehow introduced before the vowel. But then the stress shifted from the nucleus to the glide until the glide became the nucleus. The change probably went something like this:

$$
\begin{array}{cccc}
\textbf{1300} & \textbf{1400} & \textbf{1600} & \textbf{1700} \\
/\bar{\imath}/ \;>\; & /i\acute{\imath}/ \;>\; & /\acute{\mathturned{e}}i/ \;>\; & /\acute{a}i/ \\
/\bar{u}/ \;>\; & /u\acute{u}/ \;>\; & /\acute{\mathturned{e}}u/ \;>\; & /\acute{a}u/
\end{array}
$$

In 1540, William Lily claimed that the English pronounced the Latin /ī/ "too broad," which suggests that they were by then pronouncing it either /əi/ or /ai/. Since later orthoepists contrast some non-London pronunciations as being even broader than that in London, it is likely that in 1600, a word like *ride* was pronounced /raid/ in those dialects, /rəid/ in London.

/ē/ > /ī/ *and* /ō/ > /ū/

PROBLEM 14.11: Here are some spellings and dates. *spiche* for *speche* (*speech*) (c. 1200), *wyping* for *weping* (*weep*) (c. 1300), *spyde* for *spede* (*speed*) (c. 1350), *hy* for *he* (*he*) (c. 1350), *doun* for *done* (*done*) (c. 1300), *roude* for *rood* (*rood*) (c. 1320), *bloude* for *blod* (*blood*) (c. 1320), *bouc* for *boc* (*book*) (c. 1370), *goud* for *good* (*good*) (c. 1350). (Note: recall that ⟨ou⟩ was the standard spelling for /ū/, ⟨o⟩ the standard spelling for /ō/, ⟨y⟩ or ⟨i⟩ the standard spelling for /ī/.) What does this suggest about OE /ē/ and /ō/?

Such spellings as *wyping* for *weping* and *bloude* for *blod* indicate that as early as the thirteenth or fourteenth century in some dialects, /ē/ had already begun to move toward—perhaps become—/ī/, and /ō/, to move towards— perhaps become—/ū/.

PROBLEM 14.12: What does this have to do with the problem of dating when /ī/ and /ū/ began to diphthongize toward /ai/ and /au/?

PROBLEM 14.13: Here are some words that had long /ō/'s. Comment. *moon, blood, good, spoon, flood, soot, soon, glove, shook, brood, must, cook, tooth, done, rook, stool, month, food, mother, look, goose, brother.*

/ɔ̄/ > /ō/
The lower long vowels also raised during late ME and Early ModE, but describing their development is more complicated. Recall that ME /ɔ̄/ had two sources: (1) The /ā/ > /ɔ̄/ change between OE and ME, and (2) the lengthening of /o/ in open syllables:

1.   From /ā/ > /ɔ̄/: *stone, bone, boat, home, goat, rope.* All these had an earlier /ā/: *stān, bān, bāt, hām, gāt, rāp.*
2.   From lengthened /o/: *smoke, hope, float, robe, yoke.*

In London English, this /ɔ̄/ eventually moved up to replace the older /ō/, which, as we have just seen, had fairly early raised to /ū/. But in ME, recall that the original /ō/ and /ɔ̄/ were both spelled ⟨oo⟩ and ⟨o⟩. All the words in (1) and (2) just above had ⟨o⟩ or ⟨oo⟩ spellings: *blod* and *hoom*. So spelling cannot help us determine exactly when /ɔ̄/ raised to /ō/. By the sixteenth century, however, the lower /ɔ̄/ had in many cases been consistently respelled ⟨oa⟩ as in *road* (from OE *rad*) to distinguish it from the /ō/ that had moved up toward /ū/. For the most part, this /ū/ from earlier /ō/ was still spelled

⟨oo⟩ or ⟨o⟩, as in *food*/*fode* (from *foda*). From the descriptions of seventeenth century orthoepists, both pronunciations, /ō/ and /ɔ/ for original /ɔ/, seem to have been current, with the final selection of /ō/ in Standard English coming sometime in the seventeenth century.

/ā/ > /ē/ *and* /ǣ/ > /ī/

The most complicated problems of the Great Vowel Shift involve the raising of /ā/ to /ē/, whose main source was lengthened /ă/ in open syllables; and the raising of /Ē/ to /ī/, whose main source was OE /ǣ/ and lengthened ME /ĕ/. At first glance, the change seems perfectly straightforward:

1. /ā/ > /ē/: /nămă/ > /nāmə/ > /næm/ > /nĒm/ > /nēm/ (*name*). Also included in this change were *blame, same, flame, dame, lame, make, rake, take, tale*, some of which were original OE lengthened /ă/, others from French /ā/.
2. /Ē/ > /ī/: /sǣ/ > /sĒ/ > /sī/ (*sea*). Also included in this change were words like *speak, meal, meat, deal, heat, leap, read, seat, steal, weak.*

The dates of the /ā/ > /ē/ shift are difficult to pinpoint. Spellings of *credyll* for OE *cradol* (cradle) in the fourteenth century and *mede(n)* for *made* in the thirteenth century suggest an early movement in some dialects. But as late as 1631, Alexander Gill condemned the pronunciation of /ē/ for words with ⟨a⟩ as being faddishly uncouth. *Name*, according to him, should have been pronounced something like /nĒm/. By the second half of the eighteenth century at the latest, however, the /Ē/ had raised to /ē/ among educated Londoners: /nĒm/ > /nēm/.

/Ē/ > /ī/

The ME /Ē/ words have been left until last because their history is very confusing. As we have seen, /Ē/ is between /ē/ and /æ/ phonetically, but probably closer to /ē/ since ME words with this approximate sound were spelled ⟨ee⟩ or ⟨e⟩. Around the sixteenth century, though, these /Ē/ words were fairly consistently respelled ⟨ea⟩, as in *sea, meat, clean*, and so on. This would have orthographically distinguished them from the ⟨ee⟩ words, which had long since been raised to /ī/: *see* /sī/, *flee* /flī/.

At about this time, however, we find lists of rhyming words and poetic rhymes that indicate London speakers were pronouncing these words with /Ē/ from OE /ǣ/ (and from other sources) identical to words with original /ā/ and /e/. That is, we find in Shakespeare, for example, rhymes and puns based on pairs such as *created–defeated, speak–break, great–defeat, nature–defeature, great–seat, jest–beast, sweat–heat, entreats–frets, east–west, lease–excess, confess–decrease, appear–where, tears–hairs, ear–hair, years–forbears, spear–there, fear–bear, were–appear.*

From data such as these, it appears that at least by the late sixteenth century, /ā/ words had merged with /Ē/ words, probably in a pronunciation very close to /ē/. But then by the middle of the eighteenth century, this kind of rhyming and punning ceased. Instead, rhymes and puns began to link original /Ē/ words: *sea, meat, weak, beat, dear*, with original /ē/ words: *see, meet, week, beet, deer*. Since this /ē/ had long since risen to /ī/, the rhymes indicate that by 1750 those words spelled ⟨ea⟩ must also have risen past /ē/ to reach something very close to /ī/ as well. Graphically the change in rhymes looked like this:

$$
\text{1700 rhymes} \left.
\begin{array}{l}
seem \;/ī/ \text{ from ME } /ē/ \\
\left\{
\begin{array}{l}
seam \;/ē/ \text{ from ME } /Ē/ \\
same \;/ē/ \text{ from ME } /ā/
\end{array}
\right\}
\end{array}
\right.
\qquad
\begin{array}{l}
\left\{
\begin{array}{l}
seem \;/ī/ \text{ from ME } /ē/ \\
seam \;/ī/ \text{ from ME } /Ē/
\end{array}
\right\} \begin{array}{l} 1800 \\ \text{rhymes} \end{array} \\
same \;/ē/ \text{ from ME } /ā/
\end{array}
$$

This would not have been unusual were it not for the fact that those other words also pronounced /ē/—those original /ā/ words and some others—did not change to /ī/ along with the /Ē/ words. That is, when *seam* /sēm/ changed to /sīm/, the apparently homonymous *same* /sēm/ did not change. Nor did *blame, dame, fame, came, lame, tame, late, fade, shade, cake*, and so on.

Large scale sound changes occur independently of etymology. The Englishman who at one time seems to have pronounced *seam* and *name* as rhymes in /ē/ certainly had no idea they derived from different etymological sources and almost certainly never thought about their spelling as he pronounced them. But when he began pronouncing a word like *seam* not as /sēm/ but as /sīm/, he must have had some way to distinguish it from *same* the apparently identical /sēm/. Otherwise, he would have changed *same* to /sīm/ along with the originally homonymous *seam*.

One theory is that Londoners were influenced by a non-London dialect in which /Ē/ had changed to /ī/ much earlier than 1700, perhaps long before Londoners were even pronouncing /Ē/ as /ē/. Schematically, it would have looked like this:

	1250	1350	1450	1550	1650	1750	1850
London:	/æ/ >	/Ē/		> /ē/	>|	⟶ /ī/	
Dialect X:	/æ/ >	/Ē/ >	/ē/ >	/ī/ ———————			

Only *steak, break, yea*, and *great* (along with several /ē/ sounds before /r/: *bear, pear, tear*, and so on) seem to survive from that earlier London dialect.

The problem, though, is to imagine how hundreds of thousands of Londoners, entirely on the basis of haphazard contact with some nonlocal dialect, could change to /ī/ only those words with /ē/ that derived from OE /æ/ or lengthened /e/, and yet did not do what speakers almost inevitably do under such circumstances—overgeneralize. No words with etymological /ā/, which in 1700 were rhymed with etymological /Ē/ words, were mistakenly raised from /ē/ to /ī/. That is, we would expect that if *reap* and *rape* were homonyms, both pronounced close to /rēp/, then some few words like *rape*, *tape*, and *take*, might have mistakenly, by overgeneralization, been raised to /ī/, giving us *reap*, *teap*, *teak*, and so on. But apparently, this did not happen.

We can perhaps explain this if we rephrase the dialect theory in terms of social classes and styles. As we have seen, in each social dialect, speakers vary their pronunciation according to style. Pronunciation in formal styles differs from that in casual styles. When asked to read pairs of words, for example, upper-middle class New Yorkers will tend to pronounce a word like *bad* with a low front [æ] much more often than with the sound that characterizes lower-middle class speakers, a higher, fronter sound closer to [E] or even [e], making *bed* and *bad* almost homonyms. But in more casual conversational styles, even upper-middle class speakers tend to use the higher vowels toward [E] in words like *bad* more often.

This argues that no geographical dialect is a pure, monolithic dialect with no predictable variations across classes or their styles of speaking. We have no reason to assume that the verbal behavior of upper-middle class Londoners in 1700 was any different. In their most casual moments, they may very likely have distinguished *reap* from *rape* words, pronouncing *reap* as **either** /rēp/ or closer to /rīp/, while pronouncing *rape* only /rēp/. When the orthoepists, themselves educated but not always upper-middle class speakers, made their lists of homonyms, they were undoubtedly describing their most careful pronunciations, their most formal and prestigious forms: only /rēp/ for *reap*. Since they could list only one form of a word, they could not thereby reveal the statistical probability that they would occasionally, even in formal moments perhaps, also use the non-prestigious form.

Thus in c. 1700 London English, Londoners may have been able to raise only certain /ē/ words to /ī/ while leaving behind other /ē/ words: While they pronounced two different sets of words alike in a formal style, they pronounced them differently in a more casual style. As lower middle-class speakers moved into the middle classes, bringing their pronunciation with them, they tended to use their natural /ī/ forms. Since upper-middle class speakers may have had the same distinctions, though on a statistically smaller spread, they were able to distinguish the stigmatized form too. Thus when /Ē/ moved past /ē/ to /ī/ in the eighteenth century, it was not so much a sound change in process as a casual form statistically expanding in upper-middle class speech, until it became the only acceptable pronunciation, even in the most formal contexts. The change itself must have occurred in casual speech much earlier, before OE /ā/ and /æ/ rose to merge in Early ModE /ē/.

Perhaps the moral of this development is first, that pronunciations change —inevitably, and second that a new pronunciation will often be stigmatized. It certainly happened with the /ā/ > /ē/ change and with the /ī/ > /ai/ change.

And third, regardless of the stigmatization, the new sound may eventually be accepted by upper-middle class educated speakers.

We should not take this as license to accept or encourage **any** pronunciation that differs from the one considered "correct" by those who make their living telling other people how to speak. There are inevitable social penalties to pay for using stigmatized pronunciations in certain contexts. But the history of stigmatized sounds should caution us not to become outraged at what some seem to feel is moral turpitude in "vulgar" pronunciations. The fact is that, not always, but often enough, the once "vulgar" pronunciation has become the standard, to be as staunchly defended as it was once condemned.

Short Vowels

Among the short vowels since 1500, only the letters ⟨i⟩ and ⟨e⟩ have more or less consistently represented their vowels. In fact, these two segments have been relatively stable since OE. A few changes have occurred in individual words: Among many speakers, /i/ dropped to /e/; *since* is often pronounced *sence*, *till* as *tell*. Dryden rhymed *sense* and *prince*, for example. But any word spelled with an ⟨i⟩ or ⟨e⟩ in ME and Early ModE that we know is short was pronounced /i/ or /e/, and if it did not lengthen, it is very likely pronounced that way today.

The most confused and various relationships exist among the short lower vowels represented by ⟨a⟩ and ⟨o⟩. As we saw, the letter ⟨æ⟩ disappeared in Early ME when short /æ/ merged with short /a/, giving only two low or low back vowels: /a/ and /ɔ/.

But a number of further changes upset this relationship. First, since we do have words today with /æ/: *cat*, *sag*, *laugh*, and so on, sometime between ME and the present, English acquired a short /æ/ again. And in the dialect area around the Great Lakes, at any rate, most words spelled with ⟨o⟩, suggesting an earlier /ɔ/ or /o/ pronunciation, are now pronounced /a/: *hot* /hat/, *knock* /nak/, *top* /tap/. Sometime after ME, then, /ɔ/ or /o/ unrounded to /a/.

Dating the change from /a/ to /æ/ is extremely difficult because the spelling of /a/ and /æ/ is in both cases ⟨a⟩. Moreover, early orthoepists and phoneticians had a difficult time describing the difference between /æ/ and /a/. Not until the late seventeenth century do we find descriptions that clearly suggest an /æ/ in words spelled ⟨a⟩. It is at least likely that the /a/ > /æ/ shift occurred considerably earlier, probably during the sixteenth century.

PROBLEM 14.14: Comment on your pronunciation of these words with ⟨a⟩ Assume that at one time, all words with ⟨a⟩ were pronounced /a/. *wart, waddle, swamp, swan, wax, quack, was, swag, quart, warn, dwarf, swam, wharf, wasp, squalid, wander, watch, swagger, wad, hat, sand, fall, qualm, craft, harm, farm, tall, war, falter, quad, alley, valley, cart, squat, falter, pad, path, has, warp, talk, walk, palm.*

A note of contemporary relevance here is that sometime in the seventeenth century, perhaps earlier, one dialect of British English lengthened [æ] to [ǣ] and retracted it to [a], as in *father*. It is the vowel that we hear in British Received Pronunciation in words like *path, glass, calf, dance, command*, and so on—in general (though not invariably) before voiceless spirants and /n/. We can often identify an American speaker trying to sound like an Englishman when he self-consciously but incorrectly pronounces [a] in words where the [a] doesn't belong, in words like *hat, pack, cram*, and so on, the typical behavior of a speaker emulating an unnatural pattern of speech.

In Eastern New England, [a] in all the right places is the natural pronunciation, because the earliest colonialists probably came from the dialect area where this change had already occurred. They brought it with them and established it in, among other places, Boston, where because of the social prestige of that city, the broad-a became the mark of education and politeness. Boston's close contacts with British pronunciation helped maintain the vowel. (114)

PROBLEM 14.15: A change roughly similar to /ă/ > /ǣ/ is illustrated by the spelling and pronunciation of words like *hot, hog, rock, moth, nod, song, mom, toss, rob, scoff, sop, soft*, and *doll*. Assume an earlier pronunciation of the letter ⟨o⟩ in all these words was approximately /ɔ/. Comment.

PROBLEM 14.16: Did /a/ > /æ/ occur before or after /ɔ/ > /a/? What does the spelling of *stap* for *stop* by Queen Elizabeth I suggest?

Between ME and ModE, then, the Great Vowel Shift and some changes in the short vowels resulted in a somewhat different set of vowel phonemes, different enough, perhaps, to say that Chaucer's pronunciation of English words was closer to that of King Alfred's than Queen Elizabeth's. Yet on a deeper level, the changes are less radical than they might appear. Disregarding the multitude of ME diphthongs, the number of contrasts in the basic vowel system since ME has decreased by only two. East Midland had six short vowels; ModE as it is spoken in most (but not all) parts of this country, has seven.

$$ \text{ME:} \quad /i/, /e/, \quad /a/, \quad /o/, /u/, \text{ and } /ə/. $$

$$ \text{ModE:} \quad /i/, /e/, /æ/, /a/, /ɔ/, \quad /u/, \text{ and } /ə/. $$

East Midland ME had seven long vowels. ModE has four diphthongs closely corresponding to them, six if we count /ai/ and /au/ from ME /i/ and /u/:

$$ \text{ME:} \quad /ī/, /ē/, /Ē/, /ā/, /ɔ̄/, /ō/, \text{ and } /ū/. $$

$$ \text{ModE:} \quad /ai/, /ī/, \quad /ē/, /ō/, /ū/, \text{ and } /au/. $$

Thus even though the pronunciation of particular words has changed, the **system** of contrasts has changed much less. (43, 107, 108, 109, 209, 213, 239, 244)

Consonants

Between the end of ME and the present, several changes have occurred in the distribution of consonants, but most involve individual sounds in individual words.

PROBLEM 14.17: Here are some data. Are there any generalizations to be made? What information about the data would you like, in addition to the dates already provided?

1. laffe (laugh) 1563
2. alf (half) 1389
3. behaf (behalf) 1442
4. wosted (worsted) 1450
5. wusshuppe (worship) 1480
6. morgage (mortgage) 1448
7. offen (often) 1590
8. wich (which) 1494
9. whent (went) 1550
10. lameskynnes (lambskines) 1450
11. clyme (climb) 1580
12. troff (trough) 1553
13. conschens (conscience) 1469
14. sawgears (soldiers) 1550
15. owsold (household) 1451
16. sepukyr (sepulcher) 1450
17. Fakonbrige (Falkonbridge) 1465
18. passell (parcel) 1480
19. marster (master) 1480
20. Chrismas (Christmas) 1639
21. wyped (whipped) 1550
22. whear (wear) 1577
23. Lamhyth (Lambeth) 1418
24. dafter (daughter) 1634
25. thorf (through) 1465
26. sesschyonys (sessions) 1450
27. teges (tedious) 1647
28. drynkyn (drinking) 1389
29. pleshar (pleasure) 1642
30. eraftyr (hereafter) 1460
31. shudd (should) 1531
32. (A lack of /t/ sound noted in these words (1701)): gristle, costly, bristle, ghastly, whistle, ghostly, glisten, fasten, lastly.
33. blyn (blind) 1389
34. husbon (husband) 1450
35. col (cold) 1550
36. baptis (baptist) 1389
37. nex (next) 1450
38. prompe (prompt) 1545
39. corrup (corrupt) 1701
40. stric (strict) 1701

The last significant changes in the consonant system involve the loss of the velar and palatal spirant allophones of /h/, the split of /N/ into /n/ and /ŋ/, and the development of /ž/. Some orthoepists in the 1600's were still claiming that the spirants in words like *right, night, fight, daughter*, and so on could still be heard as very light aspiration. But rhymes, puns, and quibbles contradict their statements in some dialects. In Shakespeare's **Venus and Adonis** (1593), for example, we find these rhymes: *white–downright, nigh–eye*, *night–despite, light–delight* (an incorrect reverse spelling for *delite*), *spite–light*. The voiceless spirant was very likely lost to Standard London English at least by the end of the sixteenth century, in some dialects almost certainly during the fifteenth century.

The split of /N/ into /n/ and /ŋ/ through the loss of /g/ after the [ŋ] allophone of /N/ ([siŋg] > [siŋ]) probably occurred sometime in the seventeenth century. At least it was not until then that the lack of a /g/ was specifically noted.

The completely new phoneme /ž/ was acquired in a few borrowed French words with /ž/: *rouge, genre*, and so on. But in these words it has always been a foreign sound that almost inevitably was merged with /ǰ/, as *garage* has become /gəraǰ/ from /gəraž/. /ž/ has developed as a thoroughly assimilated native sound in borrowings like *vision, pleasure, osier*, and so on in quite another way.

When we rapidly pronounce combinations of words like *did you, hit you, press you*, or *raise you*, the sequences /-d + -y/, /-t + y-/, /-s + y-/, and /-z + y-/ coalesce to become new sounds:

/-t + y-/ /č/ as in /hiču/ (*hit you*)
/-d + y-/ /ǰ/ as in /diǰu/ (*did you*)
/-s + y-/ /š/ as in /prešu/ (*press you*)
/-z + y-/ /ž/ as in /rēžu/ (*raise you*)

The alveolar consonants /t/, /d/, /s/, and /z/ are pulled back by the following /y/ to become palatals. The spirants remain spirants but the stops become affricates.

Regardless of what those who prescribe "correct" pronunciation have to say about these patterns, they occur in the informal speech of even the most educated. In fact, they have resulted in the /č/, /ǰ/, /š/, and /ž/ phonemes in the middle of many words. Such words as *picture, soldier, issue*, and *vision* were all originally pronounced /piktyūr/, /soldyər/, /isyū/ and /vizyən/. The evidence for these pronunciations comes from contemporary French pronunciations of such words, from rhymes, and from metrical patterns. A word like *condicioun* (condition) in ME was certainly a four-syllable word if lines like these from Chaucer's **Canterbury Tales** are to scan correctly with ten syllables each: *Me thýnketh ĭt accórdaŭnt tŏ resoún | Tŏ télle yŏw all the condicioún | Of ech of hem. . . .* By the time of Shakespeare, poets often intended spellings of *-tion* or *-cioun* to represent one or two syllables as the meter required. Spellings like *picchure, sojer, isshu* and so on began to appear in the fifteenth century, evidence that the phonetic change had probably occurred in the casual speech of some dialects considerably earlier. Spellings like *vishion* for *vision*, however, did not occur until the seventeenth century. Perhaps the change lagged so long after the others because the /ž/ sound was so completely foreign to English. The phonemes /č/, /ǰ/, and /š/, on the other hand, were native sounds that occurred in other contexts: *ship*, *chip*, *edge*.

A sound change that has had very extensive social consequences is the loss of /r/ in a variety of phonological contexts. The earliest evidence for the loss may date from the OE period, though it became a much more common change from the fourteenth through the sixteenth centuries. Indeed, the loss of /r/ both before consonants, as in /ban/ for /barn/, and finally, as in /ka/ for /kar/ almost certainly occurred before this country was colonized, allowing those first colonists to bring an r-less pronunciation with them from their Southern and East Midland dialect areas.

By the end of the seventeenth century, then, the inventory of phonemes and possible ways of combining them into sequences was settled in Standard English. A few new combinations have entered the language through borrowings, but words like *svelte*, *pueblo*, *sclerotic*, and *sphere* are not part of any overall pattern of word formation. Among the consonants, we have since early OE gained seven new phonemes, most by a redistribution of old allophones in new environments; two, /š/ and /ž/, because new sounds evolved out of old combinations. It is more difficult to compare the vowels because the shift from length to diphthongization means that we are dealing with two different systems. It is safe to say, however, that English has added a short /ə/ to the short OE vowels, and has lost three long vowels, /ǣ/, /ā/, and /ɔ̄/. (43)

Here are three passages, one from OE, one from ME, and one from early ModE transcribed phonetically. The first is from the **Battle of Brunnanburg** (translated on p. 60). It dates from about A.D. 937. Some of the inflections have been regularized.

<table>
<tr><td>Hettend crungon</td><td>hettend kruŋgɔn</td></tr>
<tr><td>Scotta leode / and scipflotan,</td><td>skɔtta lēɔde / ɔnd šipflɔtan</td></tr>
<tr><td>fæge feollon, / feld dennode</td><td>fæɣe fēɔllɔn / feld dennɔde</td></tr>
<tr><td>secga swate, / siþþan sunne upp</td><td>seǰa swāte / siθθan sunne ūp</td></tr>
<tr><td>on morgentid, / mære tungol,</td><td>ɔn mɔrɣentīd / mǣre tuŋgɔl</td></tr>
<tr><td>glad ofer grundas, / Godes candel
beorht,</td><td>glād ɔver grundas / gɔdes kandel
beɔrxt</td></tr>
<tr><td>eces Drihtnes, / oð sio æðele
gesceaft</td><td>ēčes drixtnes / ɔθ sīɔ æðele
yešæɔft</td></tr>
<tr><td>sah to setle.</td><td>sāx tɔ setle</td></tr>
</table>

The second consists of the first 12 lines of the General Prologue to Chaucer's **Canterbury Tales**, written in the late fourteenth century:

Whan that Aprille with his shoures soote
[hwan θat āpril wiθ his šūres sōtə

The droghte of March hath perced to the roote
θə drūxt ɔf marč haθ pērsəd tō θə rōtə

And bathed every veyne in swich licour
and bāðəd evri væin in swič likūr

Of which vertu engendred is the flour;
ɔf hwič vertiu enjendrəd is θə flūr

Whan Zephirus eek with his sweete breeth
hwan zefirus ēk wiθ his swētə brĒθ

Inspired hath in every holt and heeth
inspīrəd haθ in evri hɔlt and hĒθ

The tendre croppes, and the yonge sonne
θə tendrə krɔppes and θə yuŋgə sunnə

Hath in the Ram his halv[e] cours yronne,
haθ in θə ram his halvə kūrs irunnə

And smale foweles maken melodye,
and smalə fūləs mākən melədīə

That slepen al the nyght with open ye
θat slēpən al θə nix̣t wiθ ōpən īə

So priketh hem nature in hir corages
sə prikəθ hem natiur in hir kurājəs

Thanne longen folk to goon on pilgrimage[s] . . .
θan lɔŋgen fɔlk tō gōn ɔn pilgrimājəs . . .]

The third is Macbeth's well-known speech in V.v.:

Tomorrow, and tomorrow, and tomorrow,
[təmɔrō ænd təmɔrō ænd təmɔrō

Creepes in this petty pace from day to day
krīps in ðis peti pĒs frum dĒ tə dĒ

To the last syllable of recorded time,
tə ðə læst silɔbɔl əv rəkɔrdəd tɔim

And all our yesterdayes have lighted fooles
ænd al əur yestərdĒz həv lɔitəd fūlz

The way to dusty death. Out, out, breefe candle!
ðə wĒ tə dusti deθ əut əut brīf kændəl

Life's but a walking shadow, a poore player
lɔifs but ə wɔlkiŋ šædō ə pūr plĒər

That struts and frets his houre upon the stage
ðæt struts ænd frets his əur əpɔn θə stĒj

And then is heard no more: it is a tale
ænd ðen iz hĒrd nō mōr it iz ə tĒl

Told by an ideot, full of sound and fury,
tōld bɔi ən idīət ful əv səund ænd fyūri

Signifying nothing.
signifəiiŋ nəθiŋ]

SOME POSSIBLE CAUSES OF SOUND CHANGES

The question which most interests us, naturally, is **why** these sounds should have changed at all. A few decades ago linguists generally gave up searching for specific reasons in the external history of a language—reasons like climatic changes, massive incidences of speech defects, diet, and the like, and instead, concentrated on describing **how** they changed.

In one sense, of course, an accurate description of **how** they changed itself explains **why** they changed. Some phonemes split into two because their environments changed. This only pushes the question one step back to why the environment changed. We must look into the speaker for the cause of those changes.

Most recent attempts to explain phonological change approach the problem from one of two directions: physiologically or psychologically. The least specific kind of physiological explanation depends on the idea of "phonetic drift." When we pronounce a sound, we can think of ourselves as aiming at an ideal point of articulation. Statistically speaking, however, we hit that exact point only rarely. Rather, like someone aiming at a bullseye, we scatter hits around the mark. It is through sheer statistical chance that the center of the spread defines the phonetic ideal. But also through statistical chance, the center of the spread can drift until, for example, an /a/ drifts to /æ/, an /ī/ or /ū/ begins to drift toward diphthong, an /ā/ drifts toward /ɔ/.

Working against this change is the presumption that sounds bearing a heavy **functional load**, sounds that are used frequently like /i/ or /e/, must not merge, lest too many words become confusing homonyms. Apparently, however, the increase in homonyms when /æ/ merged with /a/ in ME did not confuse speakers enough to prevent their merger. For many speakers in seventeenth-century London English, the sounds that developed out of /æ/ and /ā/ coalesced in /ē/ (*name–reap*), while in other dialects they did not, an outcome that casts some doubt on whether functional load satisfactorily explains any of these changes.

The opposite of one sound perhaps "pushing" another is one sound "pulling" another. If, for example, /ī/ began to diphthongize as the **first** step of the Great Vowel Shift, to shift away from /ē/, then /ē/ had more articulatory "room" to vary in, and so drifted toward the "empty" spot in the articulatory pattern left by /ī/. When /ē/ began to drift up and forward toward /ī/, a speaker was thereby allowed to spread his /æ/ "hits" higher and more forward without confusing the resulting sounds with one that had moved on. And as /æ/ drifted up toward /Ē/, /ā/ had articulatory room to vary in. (106)

Thus we can talk about one sound pulling another or pushing another in a way not too different from the way we talked about one lexical item in a pattern pushing another or leaving a vacuum and thereby pulling another item to replace it. But again, none of this explains why any of these sounds began pulling or pushing in the first place.

One physiological way to explain **some** kinds of phonetic movement is to look back at the way sounds influence surrounding sounds. Over and over, we have seen how one sound **assimilates** to another. As we pronounce words, our tongue moves toward one point in the mouth, but our nervous system has already prepared itself to fire off another impulse for the next sound. In some cases, the impulses pile up and jumble the articulation, as when we try to repeat a tongue twister like *rubber baby buggy bumpers* or *she sells sea shells by the sea shore.* Umlauting is a case of anticipatory assimilation; so is [ŋ] before /g/ and /k/. The velar and palatal voiced spirants in *dæg* and *dragan* eventually assimilated completely to the vowels around them, giving us *day* and *draw.* Thus one powerful force for change in the language is to be found in the neurophysiology of articulating sequences of sounds.

In other cases, the sequence of sounds may be too similar and the opposite of assimilation occurs. Sounds **dissimilate.** This is less frequent than assimilation, but it happens fairly often: *library* becomes *libary,* *athletics* becomes *atheletics.*

In talking about communicative efficiency and impulses in the nervous system, we have already touched on the psychology of sound changes. But motor skills and perception are not as complex a capacity as learning ability and that abstraction peculiar to man—linguistic competence. And once we move into these areas, we are in very uncertain territory. We can X-ray the tongue and mouth, but we can't X-ray the mind.

One purely mentalistic way to explain sound changes requires us to understand the psychology of the child. When a child first learns a language, he usually overgeneralizes the rules. Instead of learning first once and for all that some past tense verbs change their forms: *go–went gone, run–ran–run,* and so on, he reaches a point where he generalizes that all past tenses take *-ed: goed, runned, eated,* and then often overgeneralizes further to *wented, ranned,* and *ated.*

It may be that some of the same overgeneralizations occur when they learn sound patterns. For example, all of us have implicitly learned that in English only certain initial sequences of consonants are possible, others impossible: No spirant except /s/ may occur before stops; stops may occur only before vocalic elements like /r/, /l/, /y/, and /w/; these vocalic segments may occur only before vowels. OE and ME, on the other hand, allowed these: /kn-/ as in *cniht,* /gn-/ as in *gnætt,* /hl-/ as in *hleapan,* /hn-/ as in *hnutu,* /hr-/ as in *hring.* By eliminating such combinations, the general rules for combining sounds become simpler. If rules are acquired for sounds as they are for grammar, children may tend to simplify phonological rules as they learn them. In other words, language can change slightly as it is imperfectly passed on from generation to generation, as each generation simplifies the rules of the language. (239)

Another psychological explanation of sound change also depends on exceptions to rules, but here we might examine the question more graphically. Once a pattern begins to develop among the phonemic oppositions in a language, it is possible for "holes" to develop in the pattern. If we look at the spirants of OE, for example, we have the one set:

$$/F/-/\theta/-/S/-/\check{s}/-/h/$$

that split into two:

$$/f/ \ /\theta/ \ /s/ \quad /\check{s}/ \quad /h/$$
$$/v/ \ /\eth/ \ /z/$$

When the velar and palatal allophones of /h/ disappeared, /h/ more properly became a semi-vowel. This left only /š/ without a voiced opposition. It may be that the pressure of this pattern to fill out the systematic oppositions between voiced and voiceless segments allowed /ž/ to enter the language more easily than it might have otherwise, thereby providing an opposition to /š/.

A quite different kind of psychological pressure toward linguistic change has just recently been investigated quite intensively—the pressure of social identity. Enough evidence has been gathered in recent years to suggest that a social group can adopt a new pronunciation that will linguistically identify itself in one of two ways: (1) If they want to isolate themselves from other groups, they can develop their own pattern among themselves, or (2) if they want to join another group, they can identify a pattern in that group and emulate it. Neither explanation, however, is entirely without its problems as a way to explain large scale sounds changes. The first may apply only to relatively cohesive groups, such as Black young people in the inner city or fishermen on Martha's Vineyard who have come to identify themselves as the last of the real live Yankees. Both have developed speech patterns significantly different from those groups they have isolated themselves from.

The second explains why lower-middle class speakers overcorrect themselves and in formal styles use features of speech characteristic of upper-middle class speakers more than those speakers do themselves. But it does not explain why so often in the past, a pronunciation stigmatized as lower class, faddish, uncouth, or dialectal, ultimately displaces the polite one: /æ/ for /a/, /a/ for /ɔ/, /ɪ/ for /ē/, /ē/ for /Ē/, /ai/ for /ɔi/ have all been criticized as improper or unfashionable. Yet at least for educated speakers around the Great Lakes each has become the standard pronunciation.

It may be that as lower class speakers rise into the middle class, they correctly identify and successfully imitate certain middle-class pronunciations. But they also bring with them other phonological patterns that they failed to recognize are not part of upper-middle class speech. Thus while they success-fully emulate upper-middle class speech patterns in some respects, they overlook other characteristics of their pronunciation not part of middle class speech. Only when enough ex-lower middle class speakers become part of the middle class to threaten an accepted pronunciation do the orthoepists and handbook writers concern themselves with an encroaching "vulgarism." Ordinarily, they do not bother to condemn characteristics of lower class speakers that pose no threat to "refined" English. Few, if any, of the ortho-epists of the sixteenth and seventeenth centuries, for example, condemned /f/ for /θ/, *mouf* for *mouth*, *oaf* for *oath*, and so on, even though it was current among some speakers, for it never threatened to become part of standard middle class verbal behavior. (118, 121, 239)

In the same way, few handbooks of pronunciation ever comment on /b/ for /v/ in *debil* for *devil*, *bery* for *very*, and so on, because it is a characteristic of only a few lower class Black speakers. Such speakers pose no linguistic threat to upper-middle class speech patterns, so hardly any pre-1960 speech-teaching or pronunciation manuals bothered to comment on it.

A NOTE ON AMERICAN PRONUNCIATION

Had sounds not changed, of course, many of the differences between dialect areas and social classes in this country would not exist. For many years, scholars believed that American dialects began to differentiate after the main colonial settlement of the east. They thought that in the eighteenth century, Eastern New Englanders and Tidewater Southerners began to change the way they pronounced words because they were so receptive to British English influences, while those further inland who were more isolated did not change. Thus when educated standard English in London lost its /r/ in words like *barn*, *car*, and so on, the prestige of everything English made the Bostonian and Charlestonian drop their /r/ too. When /ɔ/ remained as the prestigious form in *stop*, *cod*, and *lot*, the New Englander developed his distinctive /ɒ/ in those words. When the standard British pronunciation of words like *calf* changed from [æ] to [a], the Anglophilic New Englander and Tidewater Southerner properly assumed their "broad-ah." It is the reverse of Bede's conclusion in regard to OE dialects (Chapter Three).

Encouraging this mimicry of British pronunciation, scholars also believed, was the schoolmaster, whose influence throughout New England in particular was very strong. His usually lower-middle class background in combination with the general belief that teaching was a way to middle class respectability made him linguistically insecure enough to look to a more prestigious dialect than his own as a model. And as a schoolmaster, he was able to drill his charges in those broad-ah's and rounded-o's.

More recently, however, some scholars have come to believe that American dialects differ because the dialects of the original settlers differed, because they came from different parts of Great Britain with their own characteristic speech patterns.

In order to decide between these two views, we have to know from where in England the earliest American settlers came so that we can match dialect features that characterized those areas with dialect features of the settlement areas here. We must then reconstruct how the settlers migrated West, taking their speech patterns with them.

Eastern New England and the Virginia Tidewater were settled by East Midlanders and Southeasterners, the New Jersey and Delaware area by a mixture of English, but many from the North and West. They later migrated east into central and southern Pennsylvania, Ohio, Indiana, and Illinois, and south into the Piedmont. Scotch-Irish from Ulster settled western New England, upper New York State, and along the Great Lakes.

This gives us three large dialect areas: Northern, Midland, and Southern, each with many subdialect areas. We are most concerned with eastern New England and the rest of the North and the Tidewater and Piedmont areas in the South, areas which illustrate those dialect features that characterize various American dialect areas:

1. The loss of /r/ before consonants and finally in words like *car* and *barn*.
2. The so-called broad-ah in words like *half*, *path*, and *dance*.
3. The short /o/ of eastern New Englanders.
4. The /hw/–/w/ variation between whales–Wales.
5. The various pronunciations of words like *bad* and *cod*.

Those features which characterize eastern New England and the Tidewater areas, (1)—(2), also characterize East Midland and Southeastern British English dialect areas which correspond to the source of the earliest settlers who colonized New England and Virginia. The middle Atlantic states, on the other hand, which do not share characteristics with Eastern New England and the Tidewater, were settled by several groups, the most prestigious of whom, however, were probably the Quakers from northern England. If their social prestige influenced the speech of the area, then those Southern and East Midland English who did not have an /r/ would by imitation acquire one to imitate the /r/ dialect of Northerners. Northern British settlers in western New England and the Great Lakes would have brought with them post-vocalic /r/'s; /a/'s instead of /ə/'s in words like *hot*; /æ/'s in *half* and *dance*; /hw/ instead of /w/ in *white* and *whisper*. These are the features which characterize the English spoken around the Great Lakes and in the Piedmont (though Piedmont speakers are beginning to change because of the local social prestige of /r/-less dialects). We could compare other features, such as the tempo of speech, other vowel sounds, and certain grammatical forms that would suggest further connections between British dialect areas and the original dialect areas in this country.

In the last two centuries, American pronunciation has, of course, changed. New diphthongs have developed in the South and North alike. But certain of our modern American patterns of pronunciation can be traced back to the dialect areas of seventeenth and eighteenth century England, dialect areas which themselves grew out of those in the Middle English period which, in turn, correspond to the OE dialect areas of Mercia, East and West Saxony, Kent and Northumbria, areas that the Venerable Bede (673–735) thought reflected the continental origins of the Angles, Saxons and Jutes, whose dialects were allegedly scattered along the North Sea from the Rhine to Denmark—all of which is a continuity that testifies to the enduring nature of language as well as its constant tendency for change. (114)

Black English

One final note about the history of English in this country concerns Black English. In dialect stories, racist jokes, old time radio serials and movies, and so on, where dialect is supposed to be part of the humor or realism, we often read or hear Blacks allegedly speaking like this: *mouf* for *mouth*, *bruvver* for *brother*, *dey* for *they*, *tick* for *thick*, *debbil* for *devil*, *nuffin* for *nothing*, *fa'* for *far*, *ca'* for *call*, *ma* for *man*, *'cep* for *except*, *jis* for *just*, *sich* for *such*, *s'pose* for *suppose*, *fuss* for *first*, and so on.

Those individuals entirely ignorant of the history of language and how it changes have attributed these patterns to laziness, inherent stupidity, some even to the anatomical structure of Black speech organs. Others who believe themselves more charitable explain these patterns by claiming that many young Blacks never had the opportunity to learn "correct" pronunciation and that special programs of speech therapy can eliminate the more obvious "faults," at least while these groups are speaking with speakers of standard dialects.

It is worth noting first that virtually every one of these pronunciations characterizes various southern American dialects and that each pronunciation can be found in various dialects of British English. Moreover, the kinds of assimilations and deletions that have produced these patterns have operated in the language since Old English.

This speech pattern illustrates two kinds of changes: substitution and loss. Initially, speakers of these dialects often substitute a voiced or voiceless stop for the corresponding spirant: *they > dey, thing > ting,* or /f/ for /θ/:

thing > *fing*. Medially, they substitute the corresponding labio-dental spirant: *nothing* > *nuffin*, *brother* > *bruvver*. Finally, /f/ replaces /θ/: *mouth* > *mouf*, *oath* > *oaf*. Medially, /b/ stereotypically replaces /v/: *devil* > *debbil*.

Because with one exception, each change has sporadically occurred in many dialects of English, it is difficult to argue that any of these patterns are peculiar to Black English. The /d/ in *Bedlam*, for example, derives from the /θ/ in *Bethlehem* (the name of an insane asylum in London). More currently, the stop-for-spirant characterizes the lower-middle class pronunciation of New York and Chicago, black and white alike: *Dese tings* is more often heard from older Chicago city officials than *these things*. English authors have frequently used these speech patterns to represent British class dialects: Charles Dickens wrote *nuffin* for *nothing*; William Thackeray wrote *oafs* and *mouf* for *oaths* and *mouth*; in one of his plays, G. B. Shaw wrote *wiv* for *with*. The substitution of /n/ for /ŋ/ in progressive participle endings, *goin' fishin'*, is attested to so often through the recent history of British and American English at all social levels that it is certain that at one time among some educated groups, it was the preferred pronunciation. Only the assiduous efforts of school teachers have changed the formal pronunciation of *singin'* back to *singing*, an accomplishment of debatable value.

The loss of the second of two consonants in words like *test* — *tes*, *cold* — *col* are potentially more interesting because some have claimed that these are distinctively Black characteristics. Yet even the most superficial examination of seventeenth and eighteenth century spellings turns up literally hundreds of such spellings among educated writers. Other patterns reflect the speech of the Tidewater English that has strongly influenced much Southern speech: The loss of pre-consonantal or final /r/: /ka/ for *car*, /ban/ for *barn*, and so on. But this is a British characteristic that was very likely brought here by the earliest settlers after the beginning of the loss of /r/.

The only phonological pattern that can be plausibly attributed to the influence of a Black linguistic heritage might be the substitution of the stereotype /b/ for /v/ in words like *debbil* (devil) and *bery* (very). This change is not attested to in the phonological history of English in Great Britain, so it is not likely that it was brought here and passed on to slaves. It **is** a change found in Neo-Melanesian and Chinese pidgins, but these are Pacific, not Atlantic pidgins. On the other hand, pidgins and creoles based on Portuguese and French used in the Atlantic area do have /v/ sounds. *Voodoo*, for example, is a Haitian creole word (probably inherited from Ewe, a West African language, meaning demon or titulary god). So we cannot attribute the /v/ > /b/ substitution to any of these creoles.

But when we push back beyond creole and pidgin languages to the West African languages, we find that /v/ is not a common phoneme. Though it is found in Ewe and Bini, it is not found in Yoruba, Hausa, Efik, Twi, and for the most part, Ibo. If we assume that the English pidgins learned by slaves reflected the phonological structure of their own native languages, much as a German speaker substitutes /v/ for /w/ because he has no native /w/ and substitutes the closest sound, so the majority of slaves perhaps had to substitute the sound they had closest to /v/. Most of their language did have a /b/ or /b/-like sound.

The substitution of /t/ or /f/ for /θ/, and the substitution of /d/ for /ð/ are frequently attested to in the history of British English, as noted above. But it is likely that the same change occurred in English pidgins and early creoles, since neither /θ/ nor /ð/ are found in West African languages. Thus even though these changes can be found in British dialects, it is likely that they too can be attributed to the phonological structure of African languages interfering with the acquisition of English phonological patterns. (42, 54)

Of course, none of this supports the claim that speakers of dialects other than what we have been calling standard English should be left uninformed of the differences between their pronunciations and the standard in their dialect area and of the social implications of using either pattern. Those speakers who as a rule drop final consonants in words like *passed* and *jumped* drop the past tense inflection: /pæs/ and /jəmp/ instead of /pæst/ and /jəmpt/. When this pronunciation is transferred to writing and a student writes *He jump down from the roof* instead of *He jumped down from the roof*, the consequences can be serious, because our written standard usage emphasizes very strongly not only correct spelling, but even more, correct verb forms. Unless a student can handle past tenses correctly (not to mention missing /l/'s as in *He'll be there* > *He be there*), he will be branded illiterate by educated middle class speakers and writers.

"Illiterate" in this sense, of course, means only "unable to use the dialect patterns of those who have the power to influence how others will spend their lives." The problem of education in this and future decades is to decide whether the social forces that stigmatize certain pronunciations are so strong that it would be irresponsible not to force students to learn the standard pronunciation of their dialect area. (This assumes that in fact we can give them a chance, whether they want one or not, to succeed later in a society that they might, at that moment, want nothing to do with.) The alternative, for the sake of supporting social identity and self-respect, is that the educational system should tacitly encourage the use of a speech pattern that later might contribute to social and occupational failure.

Whatever reasons are used to support either decision, however, historical reasons are utterly irrelevant, either to support a pattern of speech that has its historical roots in earlier forms, or to reject a pattern that has never had the support of history. The decision is ultimately a political one that will have consequences on society, but more particularly, on the minds of millions of school children.

SPELLING REFORM

Considering the apparently confused relationships between sound and spelling it is not surprising that many have argued we should bring our spelling and pronunciation more closely together. English speaking children must spend large amounts of time learning to spell. Spelling has become a major social indicator of literacy (and hence potential social value), probably because it is so difficult and requires so much formal education. If we can devise rational alphabets for preliterate societies, we should be able to devise one for a society that has become more dependent on reading and writing than any other in mankind's history.

Those with the least sense of how language works have argued that we should pronounce a word as we spell it. This usually takes the form of coercing school children to "sound every vowel," of pronouncing a sentence like *He always rejects her attempts to find the answer* like (1) rather than like the more normal (2):

1. hī ɔlwēz rījekts hər ætempts tū faind ðī ænsər /
2. /hī ɔlwiz rəjeks er ətemps tə fain ðə ænsər/

In other cases, it means pronouncing consonants that haven't been heard in standard spoken English for hundreds of years: The /t/ in *Christmas* or *often*, the /l/ in *balm*, *palm*, and *balk*; the /d/ in *graduate*, the /z/ in *vision*. Needless to say, this kind of advice is worthless both because it is based on ignorance and because, fortunately, it usually has little or no effect on the way children speak once the final bell rings.

With the exception of someone like Noah Webster, whose spelling book has sold millions of copies, no one person's advice about pronunciation makes much difference. The unfortunate consequences come when children grow up with a sense of guilt or inferiority over their "bad" English, usually over a pronunciation that is in fact entirely correct. And worst of all, some of them remember well enough what such teachers had to say for them in turn to become linguistic martinets.

Much more common but with equally little positive effect have been those who have tried to make spelling better reflect the way we speak. In recent years, spelling reformers have excited about the same degree of serious intellectual respect as vegetarians, Esperantists, and nudists. The beginnings of spelling reform go back to the Old English monks in their scriptoria silently changing an ⟨a⟩ to an ⟨e⟩ to reflect a vowel change. But all these respellings were unsystematic, idiosyncratic, and probably unconscious. The first change based on new **principles** of spelling was that of the late twelfth-century monk, Orm. In his **Ormulum**, a versified version of the Gospels, he consistently doubled a following consonant to indicate a preceding short vowel:

> annd all þuss (this) ennglisshe boc (book)
>   iss orrmulum ʒehatenn (called)
> . . .
> ʒet wile (will) ic shæwenn (show) ʒuw, forrwhi (why)
>   goddspell (gospel) is goddspell nemmnedd (named).

Unfortunately, this reform did not influence general scribal practice. Our habit of doubling consonants after a short vowel in two-syllable words: *bitter* as opposed to *biter*, is much more inconsistent than his.

The earliest Renaissance attempt at spelling reform was Sir John Cheke's translations of Matthew and Mark (c. 1550). It was a modest reform, at best, consisting only of doubling long vowels plus one or two other minor changes. The earliest serious treatise on spelling reform was that of Thomas Smith (1568), the first of several reformers who have taken the more radical step toward reform: He added new letters to represent consonants and accent marks to indicate long and short vowels. A year later, 1569, John Hart followed with a new orthography of the same type. In 1580, William Bullokar and in 1582, Richard Mulcaster proposed to reform spelling too, but with about the same effect as their predecessors. In the seventeenth century, a parade of names appeared to propose new orthographies: Alexander Gill (1619), Charles Butler (1634), Simon Daines (1640), Richard Hodges (1643), John Wilkins (1668).

The eighteenth century was less actively reformist, partly because of the immense prestige of Samuel Johnson, who damped enthusiasm when he rhetorically wondered whether there was even any point in trying to make an entire nation change its orthography if it would make its old books useless and create extensive confusion among its current writers.

But if Johnson's prestige may have effectively halted any serious attempts at reform in England until the middle of the next century, two Americans did propose vast reforms. As we might expect, Benjamin Franklin was one. In 1768, he published "A Scheme for a New Alphabet and Reformed Mode of Spelling." It consisted of a new phonetic alphabet that would fit pronunciation, and like all such attempts, it came to naught.

Much more influential, indeed so influential that many American dictionary makers invoke his name from the public domain, was Noah Webster (1758–1843). His fanciful theories on etymology and the genetic relationships of languages were without any foundation or subsequent influence. But his spelling books and dictionaries set new standards for American spelling and, some claim, pronunciation. Webster's early attempts at spelling reform were much more radical than those that survive. After a very conservative approach to spelling in 1783, he recommended in 1789 such spellings as *bred, bilt, giv, laf, arkitecture,* and *obliik.* He also recommended using various diacritics for both vowels and consonants. Most of these appeared in his first dictionary in 1806, **A Compendious Dictionary of the English Language**. But they began to disappear only a year later in his **A Dictionary of the English Language Compiled for the Use of Common Schools in the United States.** By 1841, when he last revised his **An American Dictionary of the English Language**, such spellings were very infrequent.

It was his conservative approach to spelling reform in his immensely influential **American Spelling Book** that has resulted in many of the modest differences between American and British spelling, differences that for some reason buried in the recesses of their souls have driven some British pedagogues to flights of indignation usually reserved for those who abuse horses or slander the Queen.

There are a few random differences: *mask–masque, check–cheque, jail–gaol, draft–draught, curb–kerb, plow–plough, story–storey, net–nett, gram–gramme, wagon–waggon, jewelery–jewellery, woolen–woollen, pajamas–pyjamas, gray–grey, tire–tyre.* The major systematic differences, most of which can be traced to Webster's influence, are these:

1. American ⟨-or⟩ vs. British ⟨-our⟩: *hono(u)r, labo(u)r, colo(u)r.*
2. American ⟨-ll-⟩ vs. British ⟨-l-⟩: *travel(l)ed, level(l)ed, enrol(l)ed.*
3. American ⟨-dg-⟩ vs. British ⟨-dge-⟩: *judg(e)ment, acknowledg(e)ment.*
4. American ⟨-se⟩ vs. British ⟨-ce⟩: *defense–defence, pretense–pretence, license–licence, practice–practise* (vb.).
5. American ⟨-ection⟩ vs. British ⟨-exion⟩: *connection–connexion, inflection–inflexion.*
6. American ⟨-er⟩ vs. British ⟨-re⟩: *center–centre, meager–meagre.* (225, 234)

If one has no better way to pass his time, he can debate the logic, efficiency, consistency, simplicity, or even the esthetics of these spellings. But finally, for either spelling, social context will determine social consequences. Given two (admittedly artificial) sentences, we can predict how readers will respond.

1. The meagre grey colour of the gaol scenery at the centre of the theatre's stage is a reflexion of the bad judgement, of the licence given to fledgeling designers who may labour hard at their craft but bring themselves little honour.
2. The meager gray color of the jail scenery at the center of the theater's stage is a reflection of the bad judgment, of the license given to fledgling designers who may labor hard at their craft but bring themselves little honor.

It is highly probable that most educated Americans would consider the first to be rather affected if written by another American, but if written by a Britisher, perfectly normal and therefore little if at all remarked. On the other hand, many, perhaps most educated Britishers would consider the second to be hopelessly illiterate if written by another Britisher and, if written by an American, proof of his irredeemably bumpkinesque background. While one might have personal reasons of orthographic integrity and so on for insisting on one spelling over another, the only valid reasons for preferring *theater* over *theatre* (or vice versa) are social consequences. Beyond some spurious appeal to history, neither spelling has any sanction except custom.

After a century lag, spelling reform became a popular issue again in Britain when in the middle of the nineteenth century, Isaac Pitman devised a shorthand system based on phonetic principles. Since that time, the reformer ranks have swelled with the names of such respected scholars and writers as Walter Skeat, Gilbert Murray, Daniel Jones, Harold Orton, Robert Bridges, and most prominently, perhaps, George Bernard Shaw, who left a substantial endowment to evangelize spelling reform.

In the United States, W. D. Whitney, one of the foremost American philologists of the nineteenth century, encouraged spelling reform. In 1875, the American Philological Association created a committee to investigate the project. From 1906 to 1919, Andrew Carnegie financially supported the Simplified Spelling Board. President Theodore Roosevelt supported its efforts to the extent of ordering public documents to use new spellings in certain words. Congress reacted predictably and there has been no official interest in spelling reform since. In the early thirties the **Chicago Tribune** began to champion reformed spelling in earnest, announcing several new spellings like *agast* for *aghast, iland* for *island, tho* for *though, crum* for *crumb, lether* for *leather*. By 1973, the list had shrunk to *tho* and *thru* (and their combinations) and some others as innocuous as *catalog* for *catalogue* and *cigaret* for *cigarette*.

In recent years, most of the scholarly effort has been devoted to creating alphabets for languages that do not have writing systems and to the teaching of reading to young children. The latter endeavor is based on the assumption that if children can learn to read quickly and easily with a simplified alphabet, they can then be gradually weaned to conventional orthography. In this way, they need not endure the *Oh, Oh, See, See* stage any longer than necessary. Since all experiments of this kind are judged successes by those who devise them, we will have to wait until the method is used by many teachers with no vested interest in the project before we can call it a success.

The objections to spelling reform are legion, though most of them are trivial. The desire to retain the etymologies signalled through traditional spelling hardly equals the pain children endure when they try to learn to read. The claim that phonetic spelling would eliminate one way to distinguish homophones is without merit since it is virtually impossible to think of any likely stretch of continuous discourse in which we could confuse *knot* and *not*, *bow* and *bough*, *sea* and *see*, *night* and *knight*, *son* and *sun*, *bare* and *bear*, *two*, *too*, or *to*, and so on.

The objection that spellings like *cawf*, *nife*, *skweez*, and *blud*, are unfamiliar, distracting or ugly is beyond rational discourse. Many of us are unable to repress a shudder at signs advertising the *Kreemi-krunch Kandi Kawnter*. But we must ask whether our eyes are so sensitive that shielding them from such orthographic horrors justifies the weekly spelling test or the occupational problems that dog the poor speller. In the eighteenth century, after all, *critic* probably offended the eyes of as many Englishmen as *honor* and *center* do today. (63, 92, 178, 182, 225, 245)

There are some objections to spelling reform that are more persuasive, however, particularly in a polydialectal society like our own. For example, a sentence like *I found a car in the creek* could be represented as either:

1. /a fæun ə ka in ðə krik/
2. /ay faund ə kar in ðə krīk/

We could simply say that the dialect with the greatest number of speakers would be the one on which to base a new spelling. But it would still be a minority dialect since no one dialect is uniformly spoken by a majority of speakers in this country.

Indeed, the fact that our spelling is so loosely tied to pronunciation allows speakers from all English dialect areas from England to the United States to Australia to use the same symbol for somewhat different pronunciations. This does not argue **for** alternative spellings of /ai/ such as *cite*, *sight*, *buy*, *by*, *lie*, *neither*, and so on. But it does point up the problems in trying to select one unambiguous symbol for one sound, and the value of having one symbol for different dialectal pronunciations of the same word. The alternative to excluding large numbers of speakers from the spelling system would be to have multiple spelling systems for different areas, a condition infinitely less desirable than an inefficient spelling system.

One other kind of systematic relationship between our spelling and pronunciation should also be noted, both because it reflects on the history of our language and because it is another case that testifies to how efficient a nonphonetic spelling can be. As we have abundantly seen, English spelling is not perfectly phonemic. But we could argue that given the variable pronunciation of many Romance words, the system should under any circumstances **not** be phonemic. If it were, then the vowels in boldface in these pairs of words would have to be spelled differently:

abd**o**men–abd**o**minal, acc**e**de–acc**e**ssion, adj**e**ctive–adj**e**ctival, **a**ngel–**a**ngelic, b**i**le–b**i**lious, ch**a**ste–ch**a**stity, c**o**ne–c**o**nic, el**a**stic–el**a**sticity, **i**nfant–**i**nfanti-

cide, please–pleasant, civil–civility, punish–punitive, remedy–remedial, sign–significant, title–titular.

How we spell these sets of words relates to how we pronounce them in three ways. (1) Under light stress, all vowels become a kind of obscured mid-central vowel, /ə/, or a high-central vowel, symbolized /ɨ/, the vowel of unstressed *just* in *just a minute* or in the inflection of *fitted.* Thus for this vowel, spelling is irrelevant, once we learn various kinds of stress rules that reduce any full vowel to an obscured vowel. If the two words, *cone* and *conicity,* were spelled *kon* and *kənisity,* then given only *kənisity,* we would not know from spelling alone the vowel of the root word. It could be an ⟨i⟩ as in the first unstressed vowel in *civility,* or an ⟨e⟩ as in the first unstressed vowel in *remedial,* or it could be an ⟨a⟩ as in the unstressed vowel in *alacrity.*

(2) The second kind of relationship pairs stressed and lax vowels. If we match the stressed and lax vowels /ō/–/ə/ and /ū/–/ə/, then certain sets of words regularly vary between them, depending on the suffix: *assume–assumption, verbose–verbosity.*

(3) A second kind of tense-lax relationship partially mirrors the Great Vowel Shift:

/ai/–/i/:	*bile–bilious*
/ī/–/ɛ/:	*acceed–accession*
/ē/–/æ/:	*chaste–chastity*
/au/–/ə/:	*profound–profundity*
/ō/–/a/:	*cone–conic*

In some cases, one (or two) letters represent three different segments:

/ai/–/i/–/ə/:	analyze–analytical–analysis
/ī/–/ɛ/–/ə/:	repeat–repetitive–repetition
/ē/–/æ/–/ə/:	explain–explanatory–explanation
/ō/–/a/–/ə/:	cone–conic–conicity
/ū/–/ə/–/ə/:	produce–productive–productivity

In each of these three sets of words, we would need different letters if we followed a strictly phonemic spelling system.

What English has in such words is not a **phonemic** spelling system but a **morphographemic** or **morphophonemic** spelling system. That is, given certain stress patterns and classes of suffixes, the letter or letters represent an underlying form that is realized in varying but predictable ways. Given the nonce-word *conclete,* we know we can generate *concletition* /kaŋklətišən/ and *concletitive* /kankletətiv/, just as we can, given, *Everyone knew that he left,* generate *that he left was known by everyone.* The letter actually represents an abstract phonetic deep structure that can be manifested in various kinds of surface structures.

The rules which we have to learn in order to manifest these deep structures as sound have been proposed at length by generative phonologists. But since the most profound generative analysis of English sound patterns is over 400 pages long, it is impossible to do justice here to the powerful insights these linguists have had into English phonology. (33)

The same kinds of underlying morphographemic or morphophonemic entities are relevant to consonant changes. Compare these:

/k/–/s/ : *electric–electricity*
/k/–/š/ : *logic–logician*
/t/–/ž/ : *divert–diversion*
/t/–/š/ : *insert–insertion*
/z/–/s/ : *analyze–analysis*
/t/–/č/ : *right–righteous*
/ǰ/–/g/ : *allege–allegation*
/s/–/š/ : *impress–impression*

In the same way, the first word in pairs like *bomb–bombard, resign–resignation, damn–damnation* spell an underlying segment, ⟨b⟩ in *bomb*, ⟨g⟩ in *resign*, and ⟨n⟩ in *damn*, that is phonetically manifested only in certain patterns. (33)

Precisely the same kind of morphophonological alternation characterizes certain dialects of non-standard English, including Black English. Although in Black English and in other dialects, final consonants in two-consonant clusters are often deleted: *tes* for *test*, *mas* for *mask*, *col* for *cold*, the dropped consonant is usually realized in inflected and affixed words: /testər/, /mæskiŋ/, /koldəst/. This precisely parallels *strong–stronger, long–longer, damn–damnation, resign–resignation* in standard English. All such speakers construct a highly abstract "image" of the word that manifests itself in different ways under different circumstances, circumstances that parallel word formation in standard English.

If we reformed English spelling so that it represented every different sound with a different symbol, we would, at least in regard to many words derived from Romance sources, represent only surface structures, not the more basic deep structures of words. So even if spelling reform were economically and socially feasible, it would not be an unmixed blessing. But the overriding objection still remains the economic and educational problems. Dr. Johnson's observation still holds: Would it be worth the trouble? All of which leaves the fifth grader about where he started.

REFERENCES

1. **Allen, Virginia F.** "Teaching Standard English as a Second Language," *The Teachers College Record*, 68:355–70 (1967).

2. **Anderson, George K.** *The Literature of the Anglo-Saxons*. Princeton, N.J., 1949.

3. **Anttila, Raimo.** *An Introduction to Historical and Comparative Linguistics.* New York, 1972.

4. **Atwood, E. Bagby.** *A Survey of Verb Forms in the Eastern United States.* Ann Arbor, Mich., 1953.

5. **Bambas, Rudolph C.** "Verb Forms in -s and -th in Early Modern English," *Journal of English and Germanic Philology*, 46:183–87 (1947).

6. **Barber, Charles.** *Linguistic Change in Present-Day English.* London, 1966.

7. **Baugh, Albert C.** *A History of the English Language.* 2nd ed. New York, 1957.

8. **Bender, Harold H.** *The Home of the Indo-Europeans.* Princeton, N.J., 1922.

9. **Berlin, Brent and Paul Kay.** *Basic Color Terms, Their Universality and Evolution.* Los Angeles and Berkeley, 1969.

10. **Berndt, Rolf.** "The Linguistic Situation in England from the Norman Conquest to the Loss of Normandy (1066–1204)," *Philologica Pragensia*, 8:145–63 (1965).

11. **Björkman, E.** *Scandinavian Loan-Words in Middle English.* Halle, 1900–2.

12. **Blair, Peter H.** *An Introduction to Anglo-Saxon England.* Cambridge, 1956.

13. ———. *Roman Britain and Early England, 55 B.C.–A.D. 871.* Edinburgh, 1963.

14. **Bloomfield, Leonard.** *Language.* New York, 1933.

15. **Bloomfield, Morton W. and Leonard Newmark.** *A Linguistic Introduction to the History of English.* New York, 1963.

16. **Bolinger, Dwight.** "Rime, Assonance, and Morpheme Analysis," *Word,* 6:117–36 (1950).

17. **Bréal, Michel.** *Semantics, Studies in the Science of Meaning* (trans. Nina Cust). New York, 1964, (originally pub. 1900).

18. **Brook, G. L.** *English Dialects.* London, 1963.

19. **Brown, Roger, Abraham Black, and Arnold Horowitz.** "Phonetic Symbolism in Natural Languages," *Journal of Abnormal and Social Psychology,* 50:388–93 (1955).

20. ——— **and Marguerite Ford.** "Address in American English," *Journal of Abnormal and Social Psychology,* 62:375–85 (1961).

21. ——— **and Albert Gilman.** "Pronouns of Power and Solidarity," in *Style in Language.* Thomas A. Sebeok, ed. Cambridge, Mass., 1966.

22. **Brunner, Karl.** "Expanded Verbal Forms in Early Modern English." *English Studies,* 36:215–21 (1955).

23. **Buck, Carl D.** *A Dictionary of Selected Synonyms in the Principal Indo-European Languages.* Chicago, 1949.

24. **Byrne, Sister St. Geraldine.** *Shakespeare's Use of the Pronoun of Address, Its Significance in Characterization and Motivation.* Washington, D.C., Catholic University of America. PhD Dissertation 36, 1936.

25. **Campbell, A.** *Old English Grammar.* Oxford, 1959.

26. **Carr, C. T.** *Nominal Compounds in Germanic.* London, 1939.

27. **Carr, E. H.** *What Is History?* New York, 1967.

28. **Cassidy, Frederic G. and Richard N. Ringer,** eds. *Bright's Old English Grammar and Reader.* 3rd ed. New York, 1971.

29. **Chafe, Wallace.** *Meaning and the Structure of Language.* Chicago, 1970.

30. **Chambers, R. W. and Marjorie Daunt.** *A Book of London English, 1384–1425.* London, 1931.

31. **Chomsky, Noam.** *Aspects of the Theory of Syntax.* Cambridge, Mass., 1965.

32. ———. *Syntactic Structures.* The Hague, 1957.

33. ——— **and Morris Halle.** *The Sound Pattern of English.* New York, 1968.

34. **Collingwood, R. G.** *Roman Britain.* New York, 1932.

35. **Curme, George O.** *English Grammar.* New York, 1966.

36. ———. "A History of English Relative Constructions," *Journal of English and Germanic Philology,* 11:10–29, 180–204, 355–80 (1912).

37. **DeCamp, David.** "The Genesis of the Old English Dialects: A New Hypothesis," *Language,* 34:232–44 (1958).

38. **Deese, James.** *The Structure of Associations in Language and Thought.* Baltimore, 1965.

39. **Dillard, J. L.** *Black English.* New York, 1972.

40. ———. "On the Beginnings of Black English in the New World," *Orbis*, 21:523–36 (1972).

41. **Diringer, D.** *The Alphabet.* 2 vols. New York, 1968.

42. **Dobson, E. J.** "Early Modern Standard English," *Transactions of the Philological Society*, 1955:25–54.

43. ———. *English Pronunciation, 1500–1700.* 2 vols. Oxford, 1957.

44. **Dyen, Isidore.** "Lexicostatistics in Comparative Linguistics," *Lingua*, 13: 230–39 (1965).

45. **Dykema, Karl W.** "Where Our Grammar Came From," *College English*, 22:455–65 (1961).

46. **Ekwall, Eilert.** *Studies on the Genitive of Groups in English.* Lund, 1943.

47. **Ellegård, Alvar.** *The Auxiliary " Do," The Establishment and Regulation of Its Use in English.* Stockholm, 1953.

48. **Emerson, O. F.** "English or French in the Time of Edward III," *Romanic Review*, 7:127–43 (1916).

49. **Engblom, Victor.** "On the Origin and Early Development of the Auxiliary 'Do'," *Lund Studies in English*, 6 (1938).

50. **Estrich, Robert M. and Hans Sperber.** *Three Keys to Language.* New York, 1952.

51. **Evans, W. W.** "The Dramatic Use of the Second Person Singular Pronoun in *Sir Gawain and the Green Knight*," *Studia Neophilologica*, 39:38–45 (1967).

52. **Farmer, John S. and William Ernest Henley.** *Slang and Its Analogues.* 7 vols. London, 1890–1904. (Republished in one volume, New York, 1970.)

53. **Fasold, Ralph.** "Tense and the Form BE in Black English," *Language*, 45: 763–76 (1969).

54. ——— **and Walter Wolfram.** "Some Linguistic Features of Negro Dialect," in *Teaching Standard English in the Inner City*, Ralph W. Fasold and Roger W. Shuy, eds. Washington, D.C., 1970.

55. **Fillmore, Charles J.** "The Case for Case," in *Universals in Linguistic Theory*, Emmon Bach and Robert T. Harms, eds. New York, 1968.

56. **Fischer, John L.** "Social Influences in the Choice of a Linguistic Variant," *Word*, 14:47–56 (1958).

57. **Förster, Max.** *Keltisches Wortgut im Englischen.* Halle, 1921.

58. **Foster, Brian.** *The Changing English Language.* New York, 1968.

59. **Francis, W. Nelson.** *The Structure of American English*, with a chapter on American English dialects by Raven I. McDavid, Jr., New York, 1958.

60. **Frazier, James George, Sir.** *The Golden Bough.* London, 1911–15.

61. **Freeman, E. A.** *History of the Norman Conquest.* 6 vols. Oxford, 1867–79.

62. **Friedrich, Paul.** *Proto-Indo-European Trees.* Chicago, 1970.

63. **Friend, Joseph H.** *The Development of American Lexicography, 1798–1864.* The Hague, 1967.

64. **Fries, Charles C.** "Linguistics, The Study of Language," Chapter 2 in *Linguistics and Reading*. New York, 1964.

65. ———. "On the Development of the Structural Use of Word-Order in Modern English," *Language*, 16:199–208 (1940).

66. ———. *The Structure of English, An Introduction to the Construction of English Sentences*. New York, 1952.

67. **Gaaf, W. van der.** *The Transition from the Impersonal to the Personal Construction in Middle English*. Heidelberg, 1904.

68. **Gardner, R. Allen and Beatrice T. Gardner,** "Teaching Sign Language to a Chimpanzee," *Science*, 165:664–72 (1969).

69. **Gelb, I. J.** *A Study of Writing*. 2nd ed. Chicago, 1969.

70. **Gleason, Henry A.** *Introduction to Descriptive Linguistics*. revised ed., New York, 1961.

71. **Goodall, Jane.** "Chimpanzees of the Gombe Stream Reserve," in *Primate Behavior, Field Studies of Monkeys and Apes*, I. DeVore, ed. New York, 1965.

72. **Goodenough, Ward H.** "Componential Analysis and the Study of Meaning," *Language*, 32:195–216 (1956).

73. **Greenberg, Joseph H.,** ed. *Universals of Language*. 2nd ed. Cambridge, Mass., 1966.

74. **Greenough, James B. and George L. Kittredge.** *Words and Their Ways in English Speech*. New York, 1901.

75. **Grose, Francis.** *1811 Dictionary of the Vulgar Tongue*. London, 1811. (Reprinted Chicago, 1971).

76. **Hall, John R. C.** *A Concise Anglo-Saxon Dictionary, with a Supplement by Herbert D. Meritt*. 4th ed. Cambridge, 1960.

77. **Hall, Robert A.** *Pidgin and Creole Languages*. Ithaca, N.Y., 1966.

78. **Harris, Zellig S.** *Methods in Structural Linguistics*. Chicago, 1951.

79. **Hartung, Charles V.** "The Persistence of Tradition in Grammar," *Quarterly Journal of Speech*, 48:174–86 (1962).

80. **Haugen, Einar.** "The Analysis of Linguistic Borrowing," *Language*, 26:210–31 (1950).

81. **Heffner, Roe-Merill.** *General Phonetics*. Madison, Wisc., 1949.

82. **Hewes, Gordon W.** "Primate Communication and the Gestural Origin of Language," *Current Anthropology*, 14:5–24 (1973).

83. ———. *Language Origins, a Bibliography*. Boulder, Colo., 1971.

84. **Hill, Archibald A.** *Introduction to Linguistic Structures*. New York, 1958.

85. ———. "Phonetic and Phonemic Change," *Language*, 12:15–22 (1936).

86. **Hockett, Charles F.** *A Course in Modern Linguistics*. New York, 1958.

87. ———. "The Origin of Speech," *Scientific American*, September, 1960:3–11.

88. ———. "The Problem of Universals in Language," in Greenberg, 1–29.

89. ———. "The Stressed Syllabics of Old English," *Language*, 35:575–97 (1959).

90. ———— and Robert Ascher. "The Human Revolution," *Current Anthropology*, 5:135–68 (1964).

91. Hoenigswald, Henry M. *Language Change and Linguistic Reconstruction.* Chicago, 1960.

92. Hulbert, James R. *Dictionaries, British and American.* London, 1955.

93. Jackson, Kenneth. *Language and History in Early Britain.* Edinburgh, 1953.

94. Jacobs, Roderick A. and Peter S. Rosenbaum. *English Transformational Grammar.* Waltham, Mass., 1973.

95. Jespersen, Otto. *Growth and Structure of the English Language.* 9th ed., Oxford, 1954.

96. ————. *Language, Its Nature, Development and Origin.* New York, 1922.

97. ————. *A Modern English Grammar on Historical Principles.* 7 vols. Copenhagen, 1909–49.

98. Jones, Charles. *An Introduction to Middle English.* New York, 1972.

99. Jones, Richard. *The Triumph of the English Language.* Stanford, Cal., 1953.

100. Joos, Martin. "The Five Clocks," *International Journal of American Linguistics*, 28:2 (1962).

101. Katz, J. J. *Semantic Theory.* New York, 1972.

102. ———— and J. A. Fodor. "The Structure of a Semantic Theory," *Language*, 39:170–210 (1963).

103. Kendricks, T. D. *A History of the Vikings.* New York, 1930.

104. Kennedy, Arthur G. *A Bibliography of Writings on the English Language from the Beginning of Printing to the End of 1922.* Cambridge, Mass. and New Haven, Conn., 1927.

105. ————. *The Pronouns of Address in English Literature of the Thirteenth Century.* Stanford, Cal., 1915.

106. King, Robert D. *Historical Linguistics and Generative Grammar.* Englewood Cliffs, N.J., 1969.

107. Kökeritz, Helge. "Elizabethan Prosody and Historical Phonology," *Annales Acadamiae Regiae Scientiarum Upsaliensis*, 5:79–102 (1961).

108. ————. *A Guide to Chaucer's Pronunciation.* New York, 1962.

109. ————. *Shakespeare's Pronunciation.* New Haven, 1953.

110. Krapp, George P. *The English Language in America.* 2 vols. New York, 1925.

111. Kuhn, Sherman M. "On the Syllabic Phonemes of Old English," *Language*, 37:522–38 (1961).

112. Kuhn, Thomas. *The Structure of Scientific Revolutions.* 2nd ed. International Encyclopedia of Unified Science. Vol. 2.2. Chicago, 1970.

113. Kurath, Hans. "The Loss of Long Consonants and the Rise of Voiced Fricatives in Middle English," *Language*, 32:435–45 (1956).

114. ————. "The Origin of the Dialectal Differences in Spoken American English," *Modern Philology*, 25:385–95 (1928).

115. ————. "Phonemics and Phonics in Historical Phonology," *American Speech*, 36:93–100 (1961).

116. ——— and Sherman M. Kuhn, eds. *Middle English Dictionary.* Ann Arbor, Mich., 1954—.

117. ——— and Raven I. McDavid, Jr. *The Pronunciation of English in the Atlantic States.* Ann Arbor, Mich., 1961.

118. **Labov, William.** "The Social Motivation of a Sound Change," *Word,* 19: 273–309 (1963).

119. ———. "Contraction, Deletion, and Inherent Variability of the English Copula," *Language,* 45:715–62 (1969).

120. ———. "On the Mechanism of Linguistic Change," *Monograph Series on Languages and Linguistics,* 18:91–114 (1965).

121. ———. *The Social Stratification of English in New York City.* Washington, D.C., 1966.

122. ———. "The Study of Language in Its Social Setting." *Studium Generale,* 23:30–87 (1970).

123. **Lancaster, Jane.** "Primate Communication Systems and the Emergence of Human Language," in *Primates, Studies in Adaptation and Variation,* Phyllis Jay, ed. New York, 1968.

124. **Lass, Roger,** ed. *Approaches to English Historical Linguistics.* New York, 1969.

125. **Lee, Donald W.** *Functional Change in Early English.* Menasha, Wisc., 1948.

126. **Lees, Robert B.** *The Grammar of English Nominalizations.* International Journal of American Linguistics, Publication 12, Bloomington, Ind., 1960.

127. **Legge, M. Dominica.** "Anglo-Norman and the Historian," *History,* N.S. 26:163–75 (1941).

128. **Lehmann, Winfred P.** *Historical Linguistics, an Introduction.* 2nd ed., New York, 1973.

129. ——— and Yakov Malkiel, eds. *Directions for Historical Linguistics.* Austin, Texas, 1968.

130. **Lenneberg, Eric.** *Biological Foundations of Language.* New York, 1967.

131. **Leonard, Sterling.** *The Doctrine of Correctness in English Usage, 1700–1800.* Madison, Wisc., 1929.

132. **Lester, Mark.** *Introductory Transformational Grammar of English.* New York, 1971.

133. **Loflin, Marvin D.** "Negro Nonstandard and Standard English: Same or Different Deep Structure?" *Orbis,* 18:74–91 (1969).

134. **Long, Ralph B.** *The Sentence and Its Parts.* Chicago, 1961.

135. **Mackenzie, B. A.** *The Early London Dialect.* Oxford, 1928.

136. **Marchand, Hans.** *The Categories and Types of Present-Day English Word Formation, a Synchronic-Diachronic Approach.* Wiesbaden, 1960.

137. **Marckwardt, Albert H.** *American English.* New York, 1958.

138. **Mathews, Mitford M.** *The Beginnings of American English.* Chicago, 1931.

139. ———, ed. *A Dictionary of Americanisms on Historical Principles.* 2 vols. Chicago, 1951 (republished in one vol., 1956).

140. **Matthews, William.** *Cockney Past and Present, a Short History of the Dialect of London.* New York, 1938.

141. **McDavid, Raven I. Jr.** "Postvocalic /-r/ in South Carolina: A Social Analysis," *American Speech,* 23:194–203 (1948).

142. **McKnight, George H.** *English Words and Their Background.* New York, 1923.

143. **McLaughlin, John C.** *Aspects of the History of English.* New York, 1970.

144. **Meillet, Antoine.** *The Indo-European Dialects* (trans. Samuel N. Rosenberg). Alabama Linguistic and Philological Series 15. University, Ala., 1967.

145. **Mencken, H. L.** *The American Language.* 4th ed. and two supplements, abridged with annotations and new material by Raven I. McDavid, Jr., with the assistance of David W. Maurer. New York, 1963.

146. **Moore, Samuel.** "Earliest Morphological Changes in Middle English," *Language,* 4:238–66 (1928).

147. ———. "Loss of Final *n* in Inflectional Syllables of Middle English," *Language,* 3:232–59 (1927).

148. ———. *Historical Outlines of English Sounds and Inflections,* revised by Albert H. Marckwardt. Ann Arbor, Mich., 1951.

149. ———, **Sanford B. Meech, and Harold Whitehall.** "Middle English Dialect Characteristics and Dialect Boundaries." *Essays and Studies in English and Comparative Literature.* University of Michigan Publications, Language and Literature. 13:1–60 (1935).

150. **Mossé, Fernand.** *A Handbook of Middle English* (trans. James A. Walker). Baltimore, 1952.

151. ———. *Histoire de la forme périphrastique être ǀ participe en présent en Germanique.* 2 parts. Paris, 1938.

152. **Moulton, William G.** "The Stops and Spirants of Early Germanic," *Language,* 30:1–42 (1954).

153. **Murray, James, A. H., Sir.** *Evolution of English Lexicography.* Oxford, 1900.

154. **Mustanoja, Tauno F.** *A Middle English Syntax, Part 1: Parts of Speech* Helsinki, 1960.

155. **Norman, Nathan.** "Pronouns of Address in the Canterbury Tales," *Mediaeval Studies,* 21:193–201 (1959).

156. **Ogden, C. K. and I. A. Richards.** *The Meaning of Meaning.* New York, 1923.

157. **Osgood, C. E., G. J. Suci, and P. H. Tannenbaum.** *The Measurement of Meaning.* Urbana, Ill., 1957.

158. *The Oxford English Dictionary.* A. H. Murray, H. Bradley, W. A. Craigie, and C. T. Onions, eds. 13 vols. Oxford 1933. Originally published 1884–1928 as *A New English Dictionary on Historical Principles,* reissued with *Supplement* in 1933. *Supplement* vol. 1, A–G. R. W. Burchfield, ed. Oxford, 1972.

159. **Partridge, Eric,** ed. *A Dictionary of Slang and Unconventional English.* 5th ed. New York, 1967.

160. ———. *Name into Word.* New York, 1950.

161. ———, ed. *Origins, A Short Etymological Dictionary of Modern English.* 2nd ed. New York, 1959.

162. ———. *Slang Today and Yesterday.* 3rd ed. New York, 1950.

163. **Pedersen, H.** *The Discovery of Language* (trans. John W. Spargo). Blooming-ton, Ind., 1962. (Originally published as *Linguistic Science in the 19th Century, Methods and Results.* Cambridge, Mass., 1931.)

164. **Penzl, Herbert.** "The Evidence for Phonemic Changes," in *Studies Presented to Joshua Whatmough,* Ernst Pulgram, ed. The Hague, 1957.

165. **Pound, Louise.** *Blends, Their Relation to English Word Formation.* Heidelberg, 1914.

166. **Poutsma, H.** *A Grammar of Late Modern English.* 4 vols. Groningen, 1904–1926. (Part I, 2nd ed., in 2 sections, 1928, 1929).

167. **Praz, Mario.** "The Italian Element in English," *Essays and Studies,*15:20–66 (1929).

168. **Premack, David.** "Language in Chimpanzee?" *Science,* 172:808–22 (1971).

169. **Price, H. T.** *Foreign Influences on Middle English.* Ann Arbor, Mich., 1947.

170. ———. *A History of Ablaut in the Strong Verbs from Caxton to the End of the Elizabethan Period.* Bonn, 1910.

171. **Pulgram, Ernst.** "Family Tree, Wave Theory and Dialectology," *Orbis,* 2:67–72 (1953).

172. **Pyles, Thomas.** *The Origins and Development of the English Language.* 2nd ed. New York, 1971.

173. ———. *Words and Ways of American English.* New York, 1952.

174. **Quirk, Randolph and Sidney Greenbaum.** *A Concise Grammar of Con-temporary English.* New York, 1973.

175. ——— and **C. L. Wrenn.** *An Old English Grammar.* New York, 1957.

176. *The Random House Dictionary of the American Language.* New York, 1966.

177. **Rantavaara, Irma.** "On the Development of the Periphrastic Dative in Late Middle English Prose," *Neuephilologische Mitteilungen,* 63:175–203 (1962).

178. **Read, Allen Walker.** "American Projects for an Academy to Regulate Speech," *Publication of the Modern Language Association,* 51:1141–79 (1936).

179. ———. "The Speech of Negroes in Colonial America," *The Journal of Negro History,* 24:247–58 (1939).

180. **Reed, Carroll E.** *Dialects of American English.* Cleveland, 1967.

181. **Roberts, A. Hood.** *A Statistical Linguistic Analysis of American English.* The Hague, 1965.

182. **Robertson, Stuart.** *The Development of Modern English.* 2nd ed. Revised by Frederic G. Cassidy. Englewood Cliffs, N.J., 1954.

183. **Robins, R. H.** *A Short History of Linguistics.* Bloomington, 1968.

184. **Rorty, Richard.** *The Linguistic Turn.* Chicago, 1967.

185. **Ross, Alan S. C.** "The Origin of the s-endings of the Present Indicative in English," *Journal of English and Germanic Philology,* 33:68–73 (1934).

186. **Rumbaugh, Duane M., Timothy V. Gill, and E. C. von Glaserfeld.** "Reading and Sentence Completion by a Chimpanzee (Pam)," *Science,* 182:731–33 (1973).

187. **Russell, Josiah C.** *British Medieval Population*. Albuquerque, 1948.

188. **Samuels, M. L.** *Linguistic Evolution with Special Reference to English*. Cambridge, 1972.

189. **Schreuder, H.** *Pejorative Sense Development in English*. Groningen, 1929.

190. **Scott, Charles T. and Jon L. Erickson,** eds. *Readings for the History of the English Language*. Boston, 1968.

191. **Searle, John,** ed. *The Philosophy of Language*. Oxford, 1971.

192. **Sebeok, Thomas A.,** ed. *Current Trends in Linguistics*. Vol. III. The Hague, 1966.

193. ———, ed. *Style in Language*. Cambridge, Mass., 1966.

194. **Serjeantson, Mary S.** *A History of Foreign Words in English*. London, 1935.

195. **Shannon, Ann.** *A Descriptive Syntax of the Parker Manuscript of the Anglo-Saxon Chronicle from 734 to 897*. The Hague, 1964.

196. **Shelley, Percy.** *English and French in England, 1066–1100*. Philadelphia, 1921.

197. **Shuy, Roger.** *Discovering American Dialects*. Champaign, Ill, 1967.

198. **Skeat, Walter W.** *English Dialects from the Eighth Century to the Present Day*. Cambridge, 1911.

199. **Skinner, B. F.** *Verbal Behavior*. New York, 1957.

200. **Sledd, James.** "Bi-dialectalism: The *Linguistics* of White Supremacy," *English Journal*, 58:1307–29 (1969).

201. ——— **and Wilma R. Ebbit,** eds. *Dictionaries and THAT Dictionary*. Chicago, 1962.

202. ——— **and Gwin J. Kolb.** *Dr. Johnson's Dictionary: Essays in the Biography of a Book*. Chicago, 1955.

203. **Slobin, Dan.** *Psycholinguistics*. New York, 1971.

204. **Southworth, Franklin C.** "Family Tree Diagrams," *Language*, 40:557–65 (1964).

205. **Starnes, D. T. and Gertrude Noyes.** *The English Dictionary from Cawdrey to Johnson, 1604–1755*. Chapel Hill, N.C., 1946.

206. **Stenton, F. M.** *Anglo-Saxon England*. 2nd ed. Oxford, 1947.

207. **Steinberg, Danny D. and Leon Jakobovitz.** *Semantics, an Interdisciplinary Reader in Philosophy, Linguistics, and Psychology*. Cambridge, 1971.

208. **Stern, Gustaf.** *Meaning and Change of Meaning with Special Reference to the English Language*. Göteborg, Sweden, 1931.

209. **Stevick, Robert D.** *English and Its History, the Evolution of a Language*. Boston, 1968.

210. ———. "The Morphemic Evolution of Middle English *She*," *English Studies*, 45:381–88 (1964).

211. **Stewart, William.** "Continuity and Change in American Negro Dialects," *Florida Foreign Language Reporter*, 6.2:3–4, 14–16, 18 (1968).

212. ———. "Sociolinguistic Factors in the History of American Negro Dialects." *Florida Foreign Language Reporter*, 5.2:11, 22, 24, 26, 30 (1967).

213. **Stockwell, Robert P.** "The Middle English 'Long Close' and 'Long Open' Mid Vowels," *Texas Studies in Literature and Language*, 2:259–68 (1961).

214. ———. "Mirrors in the History of English Pronunciation," in Lass.

215. ——— **and Ronald S. K. Macaulay,** eds. *Linguistic Change and Generative Theory*. Bloomington, Ind., 1971.

216. **Suggett, Helen.** "The Use of French in England in the Later Middle Ages," *Transactions of the Royal Historical Society*, 4th series, 28:61–83 (1946).

217. **Swieczkowski, Wolerian.** *Word Order Patterning in Middle English, a Quantitative Study Based on Piers Plowman and Middle English Sermons*. The Hague, 1962.

218. **Thieme, Paul.** "The Indo-European Language," *Scientific American*, October, 1958:63–74.

219. **Trager, George L. and Henry Lee Smith, Jr.** *An Outline of English Structure*. Studies in Linguistics, Occasional Papers 3. Norman, Okla., 1951.

220. **Traugott, Elizabeth Closs.** "Diachronic Syntax and Generative Grammar," *Language*, 41:402–15 (1965).

221. ———. *A History of English Syntax*. New York, 1972.

222. ———. "Toward a Theory of Syntactic Change," *Lingua*, 23:1–27 (1969).

223. **Trevelyan, G. M.** *History of England, Volume One: From the Earliest Times to the Reformation*. New York, 1966.

224. **Turner, Lorenzo D.** *Africanisms in the Gullah Dialect*. Chicago, 1949.

225. **Vallins, G. H.** *Spelling*. London, 1954.

226. ———. *The Pattern of English*. London, 1956.

227. **Van Dongen, G. A.** *Amelioratives in English*. Rotterdam, 1933.

228. **Venezky, Richard L.** *The Structure of English Orthography*. The Hague, 1970.

229. **Vising, Johan.** *Anglo-Norman Language and Literature*. London, 1923.

230. **Visser, F. Th.** *An Historical Syntax of the English Language*. 3 vols. Leiden, 1963–69.

231. **Wagner, Karl.** *Generative Grammar Studies in the Old English Language*. Heidelberg, 1969.

232. **Walcutt, C. C.** "The Pronouns of Address in *Troilus and Criseyde*," *Philological Quarterly*, 14:282–87 (1935).

233. **Waldron, R. A.** *Sense and Sense Development*. New York, 1967.

234. **Warfel, Harry R.** *Noah Webster, Schoolmaster to America*. New York, 1936.

235. **Watson, J. B.** "Psychology as the Behaviorists View It," *Psychological Review*, 20:158–77 (1913).

236. *Webster's Third New International Dictionary*. Springfield, Mass., 1961.

237. **Weinreich, Uriel.** "Explorations in Semantic Theory, in *Current Trends in Linguistics*, Vol. III. Thomas A. Sebeok, ed. The Hague, 1966.

238. ———. *Languages in Contact, Findings and Problems*. The Hague, 1968.

239. ———, **William Labov and M. I. Herzog.** "Empirical Foundations for a Theory of Language Change," in Lehmann and Malkiel.

240. **Wentworth, Harold and Stuart Berg Flexner,** eds. *Dictionary of American Slang*. New York, 1960.

241. **Wilson, R. M.** "English and French in England, 1100–1300," *History*, N.S. 28:37–60 (1943).

242. **Woodbine, George.** "The Language of English Law," *Speculum*, 17:395–436 (1943).

243. **Wright, Joseph,** ed. *The English Dialect Dictionary*. 6 vols. London, 1898–1905.

244. **Wyld, H. C.** *A History of Modern Colloquial English*. 3rd ed. Oxford, 1936.

245. **Zachrisson, R. E.** "Four Hundred Years of English Spelling Reform," *Studia Neophilologica*, 4:1–69 (1931).

INDEX OF MODERN ENGLISH WORDS

SUBJECT INDEX